Humanscape

ENVIRONMENTS FOR PEOPLE

Humanscape

ENVIRONMENTS FOR PEOPLE

edited by **Stephen Kaplan**

and **Rachel Kaplan**

University of Michigan

D U X B U R Y   P R E S S   North Scituate,   Massachusetts

Library of Congress Cataloging in Publication Data
Main entry under title:
Humanscape.

   Includes bibliographical references and index.
   1. Environmental psychology. I. Kaplan,
Rachel. II. Kaplan, Stephen, 1936–
BF353.H86   150   77-27531
ISBN 0-87872-163-0

Duxbury Press
A Division of Wadsworth Publishing Company, Inc.

© 1978 by Wadsworth Publishing Company, Inc., Belmont, California 94002

Humanscape: Environments for People was edited and prepared for composition by Bowden Anderson. Interior design was provided by Dorothy Booth. The cover was designed by Joseph Landry.

L.C. Cat. Card No.:
ISBN 0-87872-163-0
Printed in the United States of America
1 2 3 4 5 6 7 8 9 — 82 81 80 79 78

to
Abram
and
his grandparents

Contents

PART TWO / THE EXPERIENCE OF THE ENVIRONMENT   143

6 PREFERRED
ENVIRONMENTS

147 *By applying our knowledge of human evolution and of what humans care about to the environment, it is possible to speculate on which settings are likely to be preferred. These preferences include both informational properties and particular contents — such as elements of natural environments.*

7 STRESS AND
THE FAILURE
OF PREFERENCE

194 *Preference is not an idle whim, but an indication of what is healthy for and supportive of people. This connection is perhaps easiest to see in the negative, in terms of the costs of living in nonpreferred environments.*

8

COPING
STRATEGIES:
CHOICE AND
CONTROL

263   *People actively seek preferable settings (choice); they also attempt to maintain and improve what they have (control). These coping strategies subsume two pervasive themes of environmental psychology: territory and privacy.*

Preface

In dealing with environmental issues we are repeatedly confronted by the paradox that the biggest obstacle to a more humane world for people is — people. Again and again designers, planners, citizen groups, policy makers, and managers set out to solve "real" problems and end up mired in "people" problems. This book attempts to apply the skills and insights of the behavioral sciences to this dilemma. The approach is untraditional, not only in its theoretical framework, but also in its focus. The emphasis is not on the environment itself, but on how people know and experience it, for we believe that the first priority is not specific answers to specific problems, but a greater understanding of the creature we are dealing with, a larger view of what people are like.

Much is known about humans and their behavior, but too often this knowledge has been of limited help to those struggling to improve the human condition. Sometimes the problem has been the narrowness of viewpoint — a particular bit of knowledge has been applied without any concern for the characteristics and the goals of the individuals involved. At other times the tendency to measure only what is easily measured has led to decisions that are easier to make than to live with. Other potential applications have been ruled out because they are "too expensive," but only because implementation is assumed to be something carried out by high-priced experts rather than ordinary people.

Humans are not passive organisms waiting and hoping for help. Rather they are busy, dynamic creatures, actively striving to cope with the world around them. Thus it often happens that even the best-intentioned efforts to help in fact interfere with what people are trying to do. People seem to prefer not to have things done to them or for them — even good things. They seem to want a piece of the action, to influence the course of things themselves. It must be recognized that people are, when effectively informed, amazing in their capacity for problem solving, for creativity, for cooperation. Under suitable conditions they are the natural ally of the environmental professional and the environmental protector.

This volume started out as a book of readings, but the interdisciplinary audience and the orientation toward practical application have transformed it. As it stands, it is a perspective, an argument in many voices, an introduction to a way of thinking. It is a gathering together of insights and observations that are to a great extent ordinary and familiar, but whose interrelatedness seems to have gone largely unnoticed. The approach we have taken provides a common ground for the various professional groups concerned with the way people know and experience their environment. We believe that the disparate material collected here constitutes (or at least implies) a larger whole, a bigger picture. And further, that this bigger picture has an unusual potential for providing both structure for understanding and guidance for practical problems.

As environmental psychologists we have been dismayed to find so many psychologists unaware of the powerful relationship between their areas of expertise and the social/environmental problems surrounding us. Although the material in this volume has not (to our knowledge) been organized in this way before, much of it will be familiar to the behavioral scientist. It is our fond hope that many of our colleagues will join in this effort. We have learned from innumerable collaborative ventures that environmental designers and planners are eager for a new view of the environment, a view with people in mind.

ACKNOWLEDGMENTS

This book grew out of a course in environmental psychology, and it is the students — from such disciplines as geography, psychology, urban and regional planning, landscape architecture, parks and recreation, architecture, and various other fields — who are responsible not only for the form of this volume, but for its very existence as well. They located much of the material, discussed and criticized it, learned from it, and finally, demanded that it be assembled in some coherent form. In addition to their interdisciplinary spirit, they brought a strong emphasis on practical application. They were looking for material they could take with them and use, material that helped in comprehending and dealing with the often perplexing problems at the interface between people and the environment.

Evolving as it did in a stimulating academic environment over a considerable period of time, this volume is indebted to many people. Jerry Weisman was particularly helpful in providing thoughtful suggestions and analyses of pertinent material. Among other students and former students whose contributions come immediately to mind are Robert Erskine, Lou McClelland, Roger Peters, Chris Smith, and Roger Ulrich, all of whom participated in and helped shape the very first version of the course. More recently, Ann Devlin, Gary Evans, Thomas Herzog, and Linda Whitlock have played central roles. We would also like to thank our contributors, not only for the selections we are including but also for the enthusiasm and support so many of them have shown for our project. We wrote to them describing our plans, our hopes, and our uncertainties. The response has been heartwarming and encouraging.

Throughout this book we emphasize that humans are visual animals and that words often are insufficient for communicating the whole of a concept. We are particularly grateful to two friends who lent their unique talents to the challenge of preparing suitable illustrations. Howard Deardorff is a landscape architect by profession and his work appears on pages 31, 35, 52, 69, 114, and 159. Douglas Kinsey is an artist on the faculty of Notre Dame University and his contributions are on pages 20, 57, 88, 185, 196, and 284. Working closely with them we learned many things, not the least of which was to make our concepts clearer.

For some years now we have wanted to satisfy our students' requests for a book of this kind. Seeing this work finally come to fruition is ample reward for our efforts; the royalties are being donated to the Environmental Defense Fund.

Stephen Kaplan

Rachel Kaplan

Introduction

Humans have not endured danger and difficulty for millions of years only to emerge unmarked by this experience. On the contrary, they are a product of these hardships; they are profoundly influenced by the conditions of their evolutionary history. Specifically, the way we perceive and think, the way we take in and process information from the environment, are a consequence of this past. The kinds of places and objects we find intriguing and the activities we gravitate towards are equally rooted in this history.

The human animal has a niche that is neither localized, nor restricted by climate, nor dependent on a particular plant or other species. At the time our ancestors came down from the trees to the relatively open African savanna, the ground was hardly a safe place. The organism in question was not well endowed with the traditional defenses of exceptional size (either very large or very small), of fang and claw, or of great speed. Strategic use of tools must have required considerable information-handling sophistication. Survival probably also depended on taking advantage of a well-developed visual capacity (a consequence of having been a tree-dweller) to keep close tabs on what was going on. Taking in information, knowing what it means, and anticipating possible events would seem essential for achieving even a modicum of safety. So it seems that the unique factor in human evolution is living by one's wits.

Humans have been around for some time now. The setting has changed. Why continue to tell prehistoric tales of danger and uncertainty? Are not things much different in the contemporary world? Perhaps not. Uncertainty is still with us, and it taunts us, intrigues, frightens, cajoles, haunts, fascinates. . . . Information is still basic to human functioning, but a paradox of the current situation is that despite "information explosions" and the joys of "instant replays," it is in many ways increasingly difficult to know, to act, and to make a difference.

This book attempts to place the human environment in perspective. It deals with the uncertain environment in which humans find themselves and views this uncertainty as both a problem and a challenge. On the one hand, uncertainty brings with it the ever present threat of confusion; on the other hand, uncertainty provides the opportunity to test one's skills, to venture, to explore. Thus, we are viewing the environment in terms of people, in terms of the informational qualities that make human functioning possible. And when such functioning is stymied, one must examine the informational patterns that block people's capacity to comprehend and that undermine their effectiveness.

As we have increased our capacity to influence the environment, we have also increased our capacity to make it inhuman. Well-intentioned plans have many times led to unintended consequences, recognized too late to prevent their repetition. Many are the examples of promised "progress" gone awry. This book is concerned with the problems of environmental designers, planners, and decision makers, and with the skills of behavioral scientists. It attempts to bring together these elements through theory and analysis, through examples and data.

On one level the organizing theme of the book is simple and familiar. The first part deals with basic processes of information gathering, and the second examines the operation of these processes in increasingly complex situations. These may seem to be distinguishable in terms of going from abstract to concrete or from theoretical to applied. We have not chosen to differentiate the two parts along these lines. The material in the first part of the book is not isolated and out of context; it too deals with real people and real environments. But we have tried to select material that makes the operation of basic processes easier to observe. With the processes then well in hand, the reader is prepared to plunge into the second part, where the complexity of the forces operating makes recognizing these same processes a bit more challenging.

At another level, the organizational pattern is guided by an interplay of questions, where the answer to one question leads to the asking of the next. Thus, we begin with the question of what sort of animal are we dealing with. Since this turns out to be a creature deeply concerned with perceiving and knowing, our attention is directed (chapters 2 and 3) to how these processes work, to how humans embrace information so that it is available and accessible for continuous use. From there the question arises as to what an animal so strongly inclined to the use of knowledge as a means of survival cares about. Chapter 4 examines what kinds of things humans want to know about and whether it is meaningful to examine human needs from an informational point of view.

Part One concludes with a different sort of question. To the extent that the material up to that point tends to hang together, to make sense, to seem rather reasonable, there is a great temptation to assume that it is nothing new, that it is essentially what everyone realized all along. Thus, chapter 5 examines the question of what is the predominant way of looking at humans and at human nature in the modern world — particularly, at the predominant view among the planners and decision makers who play an important role in shaping our lives and our environment.

The second part emphasizes environments and begins (chapter 6) with the question of what sort of environments humans, as the peculiar animals that they are, would tend to prefer. From there it is but a small step to wonder what would happen to people when they found themselves in environments that fail to meet these requirements (chapter 7). Since the optimal or idyllic setting is rare rather than usual, humans must spend much of their time managing under circumstances that fall short of ideal. The next two chapters examine various strategies of coping with such situations. By examining examples of failures and successes we can hope to clarify priorities and possibilities. The final chapter develops the theme of participation as an integration of the various coping strategies. Here is a way to harness people's energy and creativity and at the same time foster a more reasonable relationship with the environment.

Throughout the book then we are concerned with such simple and direct questions as "What do people experience" and "What do people care about." The environment viewed in human terms includes all that surrounds us and the various settings and circumstances that we experience. It turns out that people are concerned to make sense of that environment, to comprehend it, and that at the same time they want to be able to learn more — but at their own pace. These reactions apply not only to the physical environment. They are also true of humans in their relations with institutions, in their reactions to schools, hospitals, and perhaps even the IRS. Thus, the environment includes not only the physical but the conceptual as well. There are in fact many contexts in which the environment extends beyond the physically present objects to those that are potentially present. It can include memories of past experiences, images of distant lands and of not-yet-present futures. After all, we can talk of palaces and castles, not to mention even heaven and hell, without firsthand experience.

PART 1

HUMANS AS PROCESSORS OF INFORMATION

FOR reasons not yet entirely clear, our ancestors came down from the trees a few million years ago. They were presumably well adapted to life in the trees; the ground, by contrast, presented rather grim challenges. First, it was dangerous. It was inhabited by numerous species that would have considered out ancestors tasty morsels. This danger was compounded by another awkward circumstance. The ground was well populated by the time our ancestors arrived, and all the convenient niches were taken. To survive, early humans had to range over large territories, but as home-based animals, they had to find their way back.

To meet these dual challenges required two apparently contra-dictory abilities. It was necessary to know a great deal — about the terrain, about potential predators, about how to get home from many directions. At the same time it was necessary to be quick, to decide and act with a minimum of delay. In other words, there was a premium on knowledge without contemplation.

There were a number of adaptations to these difficult circumstances. First, humans by and large can only think about things one at a time. In the technical literature concerning information processing, this is called "limited capacity." The limitation is not on how much one knows, but on how much of what one knows one can comtemplate at any given moment. Since humans by and large can only *do* one thing at a time, *thinking* only one thing at a time favors prompt action.

In a very general way, two human characteristics seem necessary to the operation of this high knowledge–low contemplation system. One is an ability, the other a motivation. They are both highly pervasive in human functioning, although perhaps so common as to go unnoticed most of the time.

First is the human capacity and tendency to build models. A "model" here does not refer to a physical object that is a miniature version of something else, although humans do indeed enjoy representing things in this way. Rather, it refers to a *mental model,* a simplified but coherent conception of some aspect of reality. The "simplified" part is, of course, what makes it a model. The "coherent" part is what makes it work. In other words, it hangs together; it is connected, it has a relatedness that enables one to play with it. A simplified but workable conception of the environment is a great help in handling a large amount of information in a hurry.

Since much of this first part is devoted to a discussion of these mental models — how they are acquired, how they are stored, and how they are used — it is probably unnecessary to describe them further here. However, one issue should perhaps be raised to show how directly this solution to an evolutionary problem is expressed in human/environment relationships. If indeed humans build such mental models and use them to facilitate and speed their commerce with a complicated world, then it follows that their experience of the world is heavily influenced by their previously constructed model of it. Thus, the effect of an environment on people cannot be studied without knowing the model people have of it in their heads. Those properties of environments that aid or hinder the construction of mental models are vital if humans are to cope effectively.

The second human characteristic necessary for a high knowledge–low contemplation system involves the desire or motivation to know much and to act quickly. To be more precise, the organism must be motivated not merely to know, but to know in a fashion that is simple and cogent, and that facilitates action. The organism must enjoy prompt decisions and be uneasy when decision making is drawn out. This pattern of concerns might be called the desire for clarity. It constitutes a thread running through much of the material in the "Caring" chapter and is a central issue in the second part of the volume, where human/environment difficulties are considered.

1 Evolution

When our ancestors came down from the trees to face the rigors of the African savanna, they were not some random, undifferentiated mammal. They came with a distinctive pattern of adaptations that reflected the requirements of the particular environment from which they emerged. The patterns of thought and behavior that are characteristically human have their roots in a sequence of evolutionary experiences probably not paralleled by any other species. Humans combine the adaptations to life in the trees characteristic of primates with the group hunting pattern characteristic of certain terrestrial mammals. The result of this unique combination is an adaptation that depends upon information — in quantity, in variety, in flexibility — to a degree never seen on earth before.

Although the study of evolution and the study of human behavior have gone their separate ways for many years, such was not always the case. Towards the end of the last century, William James and some colleagues began approaching behavior from what was called a "functionalist" point of view. This involved trying to understand different behaviors in terms of the *functions* they served; in other words, in terms of the way they aided the organism's successful adaptation to the environment. Such a perspective, of course, reflects the influence of Darwin's theory of evolution quite explicitly. As with other properties of an organism, a tendency to behave in a certain way must have been important to survival, or it would not have persisted. The functionalist perspective has a peculiar advantage for anyone studying human behavior. It demands reasons for what the organism does, insists that it make sense in terms of some larger picture. Since what makes sense is easier to remember, and only what is remembered can be used, that is already a substantial asset. In addition, there is a striking parallel between the functionalist's mode of analysis and the central focus of environmental psychology. The functionalist asks how a given behav-

The African savanna, sometimes referred to by anthropologists as parkland.
by Lynette T. Dobbs

ior contributes to the struggle for survival, to effective functioning. The environmental psychologist asks how a person makes his way through the environment, how one makes sense, how one copes, how one gets along. Indeed, environmental psychology might well turn out to be functionalism revived (Kaplan, 1972).

Many people, however, think that evolution is completely irrelevant to an understanding of human behavior. There are undoubtedly many reasons for this; perhaps one of the most important is that it is difficult at first glance to see how behavior could be inherited. In other words, for some people, accepting a role for evolution in the makeup of modern humans necessitates a link that makes no sense. As Hebb (1951) has pointed out, what makes no sense is likely to be rejected, no matter how strong the evidence.

However, what is inherited is not behavior, but structure. And structure, in turn, is responsible for behavior. The structure referred to here, of course, is the structure of the brain. Ultimately, it is the pattern of connections between neurons in the head that underlies a person's capacity to think, to feel, and to act. The structure of the brain constitutes the basis by which the environment is interpreted and behavior is generated. Admittedly we do not know in any detail how inheritance influences the brain patterns that control behavior. But our situation with respect to the learning process is not that different. We certainly believe that experience can affect behavior — even an experience that happened some time ago. But since that experience is now passed, it cannot currently be influencing behavior. Rather, it must have left some trace, some residue. In other words, prior experience could not influence current behavior unless it had some effect upon the structure of the brain. We know that the structure of the brain is in some measure inherited, just as we know that it must in some measure be influenced by experience. Despite our lack of detailed information in both cases, there is no more reason to reject the influence of inheritance on behavior than there is to deny the influence of learning on the same grounds.

The readings in this chapter help to show the lasting effects of the environmental demands faced by our various ancestors. (An excellent survey of the subject can be found in J. E. Pfeiffer's engaging *The Emergence of Man*.) The material on evolution here introduces several central themes of this book:

1   Humans emerged under conditions of danger and uncertainty. Under these difficult circumstances, the capacity to anticipate events, with all that entails, was probably central to their survival.

2   Humans are closely tied to the physical environment. Their concerns, their capacities, their hostilities, and their ways of identifying themselves all reflect this bond.

3   Given the requirements of their evolutionary backgrounds, humans are inherently difficult — and potentially dangerous — animals. They are not lamblike; nor should we expect them to be, in even an optimal human environment. If our hopes for the human future are overly pastoral, we shall surely be disappointed and probably disillusioned as well.

Norman J. Berrill
Life in the Trees*

The link between evolution and behavior necessarily involves the structure each individual inherits, most important, the fine structure of the brain. But Berrill's perceptive analysis points to many ways in which fairly gross, obvious aspects of structure also play a profound role in shaping behavior, in defining capacities, in making certain behavioral patterns far more likely to succeed than others. Berrill explores what it means to have vision as one's dominant sensory mode, what it means to possess a grasping hand, complete with opposed thumb. The opportunities our ancestors found on the African savanna were opportunities only for an animal possessing special talents not previously found in that particular environment.

■   Life amidst the crowns of trees in tropical forests must have been, as it still must be, a pleasant contrast to the life most mammals lead on the ground below. Color came back again, which must have enriched the mental world whatever meaning it may have possessed; while to a great extent fear has gone. Predators no longer lie in wait as they do for most of the earth-bound creatures whose dominant emotion is a nervous apprehension. In the trees all is changed except for the presence of certain snakes and the greatest danger lies in a faulty balance or a misplaced jump. Even at this distance nothing terrifies a child or a man as much as the sensation of falling into space. Trees tend to keep their folk in trim just as definitely as the air dictates the shape of an air-borne bird. Size, form and skill must be maintained.

Security, a wide variety of food, and a lively colorful environment comprised an arboreal Eden, and if the fall of man has any evolutionary meaning, this is the place we fell from.

I do not believe we can possibly overestimate the importance of arboreal life in our evolutionary upbringing. I cannot conceive how anything remotely like a human could have evolved in any other way, for the ground holds its creatures in mental and physical chains, shackling the senses and demanding that feet be used for running. We are not so free ourselves but we are at least partly emancipated, and such freedom as we have traces directly back to a tree-top life.

Consider what it means! It is more than the fact that vision increases in value and that feet convert into a kind designed for grasping boughs and branches. It is the combination and interaction of these, together with some other tree-born changes. And any monkey will serve as illustration. The tarsiers merely led the way.

To begin with there is increase in size, a change that is always significant no matter what sort of animal we are contemplating; for it is impossible to grow larger and remain exactly the same in other ways, whatever appearances may seem to show. Increased weight puts greater demands upon the climbing mechanism and both the fore and hind feet of monkeys and apes have responded by becoming grasping organs, with opposable thumbs or big toes according to how you wish to look on them. Pairs of grasping hands and feet are as definitely an outcome of climbing trees as is the degeneration of the sense of smell. First and foremost they are adaptations for the peculiar kind of locomotion required for running along branches of various thicknesses. This mode of life, especially in association with the increased body weight, places a heavy survival value upon balance and upon accuracy in judging distances to be jumped between one branch and another, much more than for the timid and lighter tarsiers.

Senses and brain have developed accordingly. The sensations for balance streaming both from the labyrinth of the inner ear and from all the muscles and tendons of the body are cleared in a correspondingly enlarged region of the brain. While sight is infinitely enhanced; eyes are more accurately aligned to the front, are movable, and their movements exactly coordinated; binocular vision has become more stereoscopic, with the visual cortex of the brain enormously increased. You can almost see how it has come about. For generation after untold generation those individuals who lost their balance or misjudged a distance, particularly when very young, fell fatally or were injured and played no part in reproducing the race. Propagation was left to those with better eyes and better balance, and the inexorable selection of such as these year in and year out for ten million years or so made the monkey what it is. And inasmuch as propagating in the tree tops is a precarious procedure for relatively heavy creatures, births become limited to a single one in place of litters, even at the tarsier stage. One offspring at a time is the rule when the mother runs and jumps among the branches and the baby has to hang on to her for its life.

Such are the fundamentals, the basic conditions for survival. Where do they lead? For one thing they lead to hands. It is easier and probably safer, when resting in a tree, to sit rather than lie down. It is safer and more proficient to reach out for an insect with a grasping appendage than to stretch your neck and use your jaws. When sitting or when moving but slowly about in search of food, two or three holdfasts are enough, leaving one or two free for other purposes. Sitting upright upon a branch not only gave rise to hands but started the trend toward an upright body. To be able to pick up and clutch a locust was simply an extension of the ability to hold on to a slender branch with four fingers and an opposable thumb. Almost inadvertently the primitive mammalian foot became transformed into a multipurpose tool-like hand, although its use depended greatly on changes in the eyes.

The improvements which the monkey eye developed are exactly those that we make the most use of, though we take them much too much for granted. For when we consider that our most remote mammalian ancestors were with little doubt both weak-sighted and color blind, it seems to me almost miraculous that we should be able to see in certain ways better than any other kind of mammal with the exception of our poor relations. The improvements are threefold and we owe them to our predecessors who lived out their lives in the colorful and blazing light in the uppermost layer of tropical forests. Flowers, buds, insects, birds' eggs and the birds themselves all contributed to a riot of color unknown on the ground below, and most of them were good to eat. And it was only natural to hold in front of your eyes for a moment what you were about to eat, to record its image for future reference. Yet somehow out of such a practice color vision has become resurrected in an eye which had lost it. Convergent eye movements which were necessary to bring into combined focus a close-up object conveyed an impression of depth and solidity. And the small central area of the retina of each eye became infinitely complex for registering the greatest detail. Three-dimensional color vision of marvelous acuity came from feeding on everything in sight in a colorful immediate world. Sight became dominant above all else and left us with windows opening on the universe.

The eye and the hand. They make most of a monkey and much of a man, for they work together. Large areas develop in the brain not merely for the sensations of light and touch but for the memories of past sensations also. The brain evolved great storage places for the past, of solid things with color and texture. Eyes do more than look at an object. With imperceptible movements they caress the outlines in three dimension and make a record of solid shapes. In a more obvious manner the fingers do the same — and for a creature's own body as well as things external to it. Between the two there comes a physical awareness of self and an ardent curiosity, from exploring with fingers and exploring with eyes. This also is our heritage, but it also goes back to our simian past in the early Oligocene. And so does the first great expansion of the frontal part of the brain, those lobes concerned with planning and the future in contrast to the sensory and memory regions that represent the present and the past. Our brains have expanded and improved since that distant time, but the kind of brain we have is essentially still the same — a brain that glories in sight; is avid for touch; appreciates sound; and knows hardly any smell. It is a special kind of brain with potentials and limitations that were set some forty or fifty million years ago. The more we know of it the better, for it shapes our destiny. ∎

Bernard G. Campbell
Adaptation to the Forest Environment*

■ We ourselves are primates, and the origin of our nature may be traced quite precisely to the adaptations of the primates that evolved in response to the forest environment. The special problems associated with that environment demand sensory awareness, precise mobility, and a brain able to make accurate and immediate prediction. We owe our nature primarily to the challenge of that environment. . . . Each aspect of man's physiology and behavior evolved in response to the challenge either of the forest or of the totally different open environment of the plains, in which he later achieved his manhood. The majority of mammals have evolved for tens of millions of years in one environment alone, antelopes on the grasslands, whales in the sea, primates in the forests; man's move from the forest to more open country made us finally into what we are and is the story of our own evolution.   ■

John Napier
Man's Dual Heritage†

■ When the behavior of arboreal primates is as well known as that of ground-dwellers, it is quite certain that the ethologists, social scientists, and psychologists will be amazed to discover what some anthropologists have been aware of all along — that the root of man's genetic inheritance is bifid, derived in equal parts from his phylogenetically older, arboreal "infancy" and his recent ground-living "adolescence." Man comprises a fascinating mixture of the timid and the aggressive, of the "flight" responses of forest animals and the "fight" responses of

---

*Reprinted by permission from Bernard Campbell *Human Evolution* (Chicago: Aldine Publishing Company); copyright © 1966, 1974 by Bernard G. Campbell. Page 113.
†From John Napier *The roots of mankind*. Washington, D.C.: The Smithsonian Institution Press. 1970. Pages 70–71. Reprinted by permission.

the savanna forms; the family allegiances of the gibbon and the mar-
moset and the community consciousness of the baboon; the arms and
trunk of an arboreal ape and the legs and hands of a ground-living
monkey; and a mind that is uniquely his own but derived, nevertheless, from a composite of psychological and neurological adaptations to
the demands of both forest and savanna life. Man reveals his distant
arboreal ancestry in times of chronic stress. Drop-outs from society for
whatever cause "take to the woods" because here is the security, the
anonymity, the natural food supply that promises survival. The little
cabin in the woods is every man's romantic idea of escapism. Man's
mythology contains countless references to woods and forests; we both
love and fear them — as exemplified by the immortal drawings of
Arthur Rackham which perfectly express this duality. The tales of
Snow White, Robin Hood, and of the Swiss Family Robinson, of
Winnie-the-Pooh and of the legendary wild man of modern times — the
Yeti, the Bigfoot, and the seemingly endless stream of hairy woodsmen
— living so it seems to urbanized man in an enviable and bucolic
dream world. Man, stripped down by circumstances to a psychological
base-line, returns to his remoter phylogenetic past where security from
predators, multiple escape routes, an abundant supply of natural food,
and a solitary existence meet his needs. The savanna is for the fighter,
the woods for the recluse. We can recognize both these conflicting pressures in our own way of life. We work in the city but commute at night
to our houses in the suburbs, the nearest most of us can get to the
forest. We relish the contact but we don't always recognize the biological roots of our satisfaction.   ■

Sherwood L. Washburn
Brain Evolution and Human Survival*

While some clues to seeing human nature in perspective come
from examining the similarities to other species, the differences are
also instructive. This is especially the case in tracing the pervasive
influence of an informational way of adaptation. Here Washburn discusses some particularly striking contrasts between humans and other
primates.

*From S. L. Washburn "Aggressive behavior and human evolution" in G. V. Coelho and
E. A. Rubinstein (Eds.) *Social change and human behavior*. Washington, D.C.: NIMH.
1972. Pages 21–22, 24–27. Reprinted by permission.

■   To understand the nature of man and his ability to cope with many problems of modern life — problems largely of his own creation — it is not enough to study his performance and development in recorded history, for man evolved to something very close to his present morphological state prior to the world as we know it — before the appearance of agriculture (Rubinstein and Coelho, 1970). Yet man's evolution to this state was comparatively late when viewed against the span of years going back to his separation from the apes, which occurred at least 5 million years ago (Washburn and Hamburg, 1968; Washburn and Jay, 1968). For approximately nine-tenths of that period, the human ancestor had a brain no larger than that of the apes. It was only with the evolution from the small-brained (but tool-using) *Australopithecus* to *Homo erectus,* about 1 million years ago, that the human brain began to increase in size; apparently it evolved in response to the success of the human way of life. The brain, then, and the way of life evolved together and evolved exceedingly late in our evolutionary history.

But although *Homo erectus* represented a big step forward in the size of his brain, his use of fire, and his mastery of relatively complex tools, what might be called his culture evolved at a very slow rate compared with that of his successor, *Homo sapiens sapiens,* who appeared on the scene approximately 40,000 years ago.[1] *Homo erectus* was a hunter, living in small groups and making only very gradual changes in the tool types used. With *Homo sapiens sapiens,* however, the rate of change suddenly accelerated: tools changed at a tremendous rate, and agriculture, complex social systems, and languages similar to the ones now spoken appeared. (A prominent linguist, the late Dr. Morris Swadesh, has suggested on the basis of linguistic evidence that the languages of *Homo sapiens sapiens* — our languages — have an antiquity of about 40,000 years).

So we are dealing with a highly successful, highly adaptable, very special kind of creature which developed its basic biological system hundreds of thousands of years ago in response to conditions which — because of the very rapid rate of change in human culture in the last 50,000 years or so — have ceased to exist. Consequently, certain peculiarities of human nature which were highly adaptive in times past are not at all adaptive today. Moreover, it will be no easy task for man to transform himself in response to changed conditions. Because the rate of biological evolution is so much slower than the rate of change now common in man's social systems, the natural feedback process between what he is and what kind of world he lives in has been disrupted.

This is not just an interesting bit of information about human evolution; it is a very serious matter, because a bitter rule of evolution is that creatures must adapt to the problems of their time or they will become extinct. The argument here is simply this: In the present technical age — with modern medicine, with molecular biology, with computers, all under the shadow of the atom bomb — the issues are new and different. If societies do not adapt to these new issues, they will become extinct as did certain animals of the past.

HUMAN UNIQUENESS: BEHAVIORAL CHARACTERISTICS

We might first look at some of those kinds of behavior which distinguish man from the other primates. Man is remarkable among the primates in that he requires a homesite, a location where he can go back and be helped, a place that will be there every night. In the nonhuman primates, the animals move around and the troop does not go back to the same place at night. This means that should an animal contract a disease, that disease has to be severe enough to separate an individual from the troop. Since an animal will not be helped by the other members of the group, it must either be able to help itself or it will almost surely die. The development of a home base of cooperation and of food sharing have been major events in human history; and we believe from the archeological records that these have taken place roughly about 500,000 years ago — perhaps earlier, but certainly about that period of time.

MANAGEMENT OF SPACE

Another way in which we are radically different from the nonhuman primates is in the matter of the amount of land used. Even the most primitive human beings, hunters and gatherers, without domestic animals and without cultivation of crops, used hundreds of square miles of land. By contrast, the largest area used by any nonhuman primate is about fifteen square miles, and most of the nonhuman primates use areas far smaller than that. Here then are intelligent animals who climb into trees, can see distances far beyond the areas to which they go, can see food and water, but will not move out of the relatively restricted area which they know. This can be tested. With baboons, for example, when the investigator thinks he knows what the troop's territory is, and he is no longer worried about disturbing the troop, he can try to drive the animals. It turns out that the troop can be easily driven until it gets to the end of what it regards as its universe, and at this point it turns back to the area it knows. Man is remarkable, even at the hunting and gathering stage, in that he knows hundreds of square miles rather than only a mile or two.

Despite the fact that man has always ranged over a larger area than the other primates, he has in the past easily learned to resent territorial intrusion. In the large human space occupied by the hunters and gatherers, some hundreds of square miles, the tribes concerned know their area, and normally resent other people's coming into it. The area has immediate emotional importance to the people who are living there. Even in industrial societies of recent times, human space has been conceived of in highly emotional terms. "Breathes there the man with soul so dead, who never to himself has said, 'This is my own, my native land.' " However, these kinds of attitudes and behaviors are not appropriate to life in the modern world, for human space has totally changed. Mankind is now moving all over the world. In flying across the country, we do not have a knowledge of the area passed across; we do not have the same emotional attachment to an area.

ADAPTIVE SIGNIFICANCE OF PLAY

Another way in which man differs from the other primates is in the greater length of time he spends engaging in play behavior. We find from observing juvenile nonhuman primates, that an enormous amount of effort goes into their play, as it does in juvenile man: both practice their future adult roles in play, and role-appropriate play behavior is reinforced with rewards of social approval by the group in which the juvenile grows up. (In nonhuman primates the play behavior of males differs from that of females from the very beginning, and the differences appear to be in part the result of hormonal differences. Probably such differences occur among human beings, but they are emphasized or de-emphasized according to the values of the culture.) Taking the average of the different species, monkeys play for only about the first four years. Chimpanzees play longer on the average — about eight years. The comparable period in man would be about fifteen or sixteen years. So, in man there is an enormous increase in this play period over that of the nonhuman primates, and this is probably part of the basis for the greater plasticity in man and part of the reason that the larger and more complex brain has a chance to learn quite different behavior patterns. The play events in a baboon's life, which take place while the brain is still very immature, take place in a period of less than a year. The comparable play events in the human being take place over a period of six or seven years, because that is the comparable time for maturation of the human nervous system.

TOOL-USING BEHAVIOR: COMPARATIVE HYPOTHESES

Patterns of tool use also differentiate man from the other primates. Fossil evidence indicates that tool use existed even before the human hand had developed into its present form, with the large opposable thumb. Thus, the hand probably evolved in response to the new selection pressures that came with the success of a tool-making way of life. The hand, then, is the result of a couple of million years of tool use. Living nonhuman primates, too, are capable of tool use. Primate tool users in general probably owe this ability to the fact that their ancestors were knuckle-walkers. Animals that walk with their hands spread flat on the ground cannot become tool users in the same way, because every time they put their hands down they build a psychological block, so to speak, against tool use. The animal that knuckle-walks, in contrast, can carry the tool even if he is walking quadrupedally.

Of the living nonhuman primates, the chimpanzee is the most skillful tool user. Chimpanzees throw stones, pull branches off trees and wave them about like clubs, and put sticks into bees' nests to get honey. Yet there is a vital difference between this and the typical pattern of human tool use. Consider the stone throwing for a moment. The chimp picks up any stone that happens to be handy and throws it; but field observations indicate the stones usually do not hit the objects at which the chimps appear to be aiming. In fact, this use of an object, randomly picked up and thrown or waved about with apparently no clear goal, often seems to be little more than agonistic display which contrasts markedly with the skillful utilitarian tool use of human beings. Human tool use involves changes in the brain; it involves the fact that man can easily learn to use tools and can easily learn to be skillful in a way that the ape cannot. It is not that an instinct for tool use is built into the brain but rather that there is a structure in the brain which makes learning to use objects almost inevitable for man. To be skillful in object use in this sense, we need to be human, we need to have a large brain, we need to play with the objects when young so that skills are developed, and we must have this play rewarded by society. We cannot, then, view efficient tool use simply as a matter of picking up an isolated stone and throwing it. Constant practice is a characteristic of human play, and it is not a characteristic of the play of nonhuman primates. So in thinking of the origin of tool use, we are concerned with play, with practice, and with social reward as well as just the types of tools that are found. ■

NOTE
1. The term *Homo sapiens sapiens* refers to humankind of the last 30,000 or 40,000 years: humankind of this period used to be referred to as *Homo sapiens,* but recently this latter term has been used to include some of the earlier men as well.

William S. Laughlin
Stalking*

It is generally believed that tools, more specifically weapons, accounted for the effectiveness of early humans as hunters of big game. But Laughlin points out that because of the extremely limited range of these primitive weapons, it was necessary to get close to the potential prey before they were effective. And this in turn required obtaining and interpreting a large amount of information. Thus, Laughlin shows that making a go of it as a primitive hunter put a high premium on information processing.

■   Stalking and pursuit of game ordinarily begins once the animal has been sighted. Attention then shifts to getting as close to the animal as necessary for an effective shot. In much of hunting, however, there is no sharp line of demarcation between these two portions of the sequence pattern. The hunter may commit himself to a particular animal or herd without having actually seen it. There may be ample evidence that a particular animal is being followed, and the animal may be aware of the pursuit without an actual visual sighting. The hunter and the hunted may smell each other, they may hear each other, they may see each other's tracks, and the animal may actually be attracted to its human pursuer by his urine. Following a polar bear for one or two days, running down a horse over a three-day period, and certainly some of the desert hunting in Australia and in the Kalahari involves a long pursuit and relatively short period for killing.

The hunter is concerned with the freshness of the track and the direction in which he is moving. He wants all possible information on his quarry's condition; its age, sex, size, rate of travel, and a working estimate of the distance by which the animal leads him. In the final stages, when he is closing with the animal, the hunter employs his knowledge of animal behavior and situational factors relevant to that behavior in a crucial fashion. For all birds, animals, and fish the hunter must estimate flight distance, the point at which they will take flight or run away. Conversely, with animals that are aggressive, he

*Excerpted from W. S. Laughlin "An integrating biobehavior system and its evolutionary importance." Reprinted by permission from Richard B. Lee and Irven DeVore, editors, *Man the Hunter* (Chicago: Aldine Publishing Company); copyright © 1968 by the Wenner-Gren Foundation for Anthropological Research. Pages 308–309.

Cave paintings provide a glimpse of the hopes and fears of early humans. This illustration, incorporating elements from several cave paintings, suggests the vast disproportion in size and strength between hunter and hunted.
by Douglas Kinsey

needs to interpret any signs, raising or lowering of tail, flexing of muscles, blowing, or salivation, etc., that indicate an attack rather than a flight. In many cases the animal is intentionally provoked to attack. The variations are innumerable.

One useful generalization of the problem faced by the hunter is that he wants to get as close as possible for the best possible shot but he would rather have a poor shot than none at all. The enormous labor and skill that is expended in approaching the animal, often hours of lying on the ground waiting for a change in direction of wind or in the position of the animal, testifies to the crucial importance of stalking.

The technological equipment of most primitive hunters is such that their quarry is usually shot at relatively short distances, usually less than thirty feet for harpoons, bows and arrows, and spears. Even the one generalization about the minimum distance for the best shot must be qualified because the hunter may want the maximum distance compatible with his weapon, in order to provide time for a second shot. Some animals tend to continue in the direction they were traveling after they are shot. Other animals have a tendency to simply stand and bleed, if not frightened by sight or smell of the hunter. The point here is simply that the enormous range and complexities of animal behavior; the influence of situational factors depending upon time of day, sex, age, nutritional state, degree of excitation, being in the company of a mate, with or without young, etc., these factors must all be read into the decision-making machinery of the hunter.

Hunting with high-powered rifles and telescopic sights, and to a lesser extent with modern archery equipment, is substantially different from the hunting of primitive man. In a general fashion, the better the technological equipment, the less intimate knowledge of animal behavior is required. Getting close to an animal represents the major investment of the primitive hunter and explains the extensive attention given to childhood programming and to the location of game.   ■

2 Perceiving

Thus humans evolved as far-ranging animals, attempting to cope with a not always friendly environment. To the extent that they lived by their wits, by anticipating events and acting accordingly, the first essential step was to perceive, to recognize objects, and to comprehend the space in which the objects existed.

While we tend to assume that the world is made of objects, and that all animals share our perspective, object recognition is more difficult and less universal then we realize. Simple response to an overall pattern of stimulation is quite distinct from comprehending an object. The awesome computer recognizes objects rather badly, despite considerable effort by computer scientists for more than twenty years. Two problems in particular plague would-be creators of artificial object recognition. Objects generally appear in the midst of backgrounds that are just as information-rich as the objects are. Separating the one from the other is an achievement. Beyond that, the particular pattern of stimulation arriving from an object is highly variable. The definition of what will and what will not be a feature of a given object is highly uncertain.

The evolutionary material in this chapter suggests that the experiencing of objects as distinct from the rest of the environment may be a special ability of primates. Other evidence indicates that not even all primates have this capacity. The integration of information received from the different senses is essential in separating a concrete "thing" from a sea of stimulation. An object must be experienced as the same object, for example, whether it is seen or touched. Trotter (1976) describes research by Davenport that examines this integrative capacity. The apparatus used has a window through which an object can be viewed and a slot through which two different objects can be touched. The task involves reaching into the slot and selecting the object similar to the one seen through the window. Chimps can solve such problems; monkeys cannot.

Recognizing objects, then, is far more demanding than it might appear. Considering the uncertainties in the pattern of light falling on the eye, the popular analogy of "the eye as camera" is totally unsatisfactory as a model for how people experience their environment. Object recognition is a highly active, interpretive process far beyond the simple sensation of a pattern of light on the retina.

The interpretive process relies heavily on the past, upon information gathered at previous times. Small wonder that humans are so curious — they are continuously collecting the basis of later perceptions. We experience the environment not as a series of snapshots of what is going on immediately in front of us, but rather as a construction. This construction is made up of a good deal of prior knowledge and only a sampling of current information. Despite the incompleteness of the information, this construction tends to feel both clear and definite. Experience, then, is both more and less than what is objectively present. It is more since it is deeply grounded in prior knowledge. It is less since it is based on only a small sample of the information potentially available in the environment at any particular moment.

Bernard G. Campbell
Evolution and Information*

Here Campbell explores a variety of ways in which informational considerations entered into the evolution of humans. His emphasis on the perception of space and on spatial knowledge is echoed many times throughout this book. Although he does not label it explicitly, another of his themes involves the issue of time. As memory is a critical component in perception, this process entails the past as well as the present. By generalizing or abstracting from experience we anticipate the future — we "escape from the present," as Campbell says. Thus, the human world is a world of expanded space and expanded time.

*Reprinted by permission from Bernard Campbell *Human Evolution* (Chicago: Aldine Publishing Company); copyright © 1966, 1974 by Bernard G. Campbell. Pages 88, 90, 196–197; 332–337.

■   We are visual animals. Three-dimensional vision gives a wide range of precise information about the environment that cannot be obtained by any other means. Because light travels in straight lines and because the nature of reflected light is determined by the chemical and physical structure of objects, very precise data about the nature of objects can be obtained at a distance. Stereoscopic vision and competent motor investigation (in particular, manipulation) make the world view of the higher primates unique both in quality and in kind. Primates alone have come to know the structure of the environment in terms of both pattern and composition. They see the environment as a collection of objects rather than merely as a pattern, and the recognition of objects is the beginning of conceptual thought. With the coming of stereoscopic vision, the primate can begin to perceive nonspatial abstractions, and this advanced perception finds its foundation in combining the analytic functions of the two sides of the brain. The evolution of vision is one essential basis for the evolution of an animal that came to understand its environment so well that it could control it for its direct benefit.

THE EVOLUTION OF THE HUMAN HAND

Monkeys use their hands for a wide variety of purposes, and one of the most important, which we must now consider, is their contribution to the satisfaction of the exploratory drive: the hands make possible a detailed examination of parts of the environment that can be manipulated. Monkeys, apes, and man are almost the only animals that fiddle about with things, that turn them over and examine their form and texture. This manipulation of objects is not necessarily directly related to the procurement of food but is simply a process of investigation, equivalent to the olfactory investigation of the environment so characteristic of a dog. But in manipulation a monkey is investigating not the whole environment but only one particular part of it — and frequently a part that can be separated physically from the rest. This ability of higher primates to extract an object from its setting and examine it visually and three-dimensionally from all sides is a development of the utmost importance in human evolution. A carnivore will examine the olfactory nature of objects but cannot at the same time see them as part of the visual pattern of the environment, because during examination by the nose the objects are more or less out of sight. Admittedly, a ball or bone can be manipulated with the paws and tossed with the mouth, but the range of objects examined is limited, and compared with the primate hand, the paws and mouth give only a rough indication of shape and texture.

The detachment of objects from the environment appears to be a most important prerequisite for the evolution of primate perception. This examination of things as objects we owe to the evolution of the primate hand and the opposable thumb. The recognition of different kinds of objects we owe to primate visual and tactile examination. Only a primate can, as it were, extract an object from the environment, examine it by smell, touch, and sight, and then return it to its place in its surroundings. In this way the higher primates came to see the environment not as a continuum of events in a world of pattern but as an encounter with objects that proved to make up these events and this pattern.

PERCEPTS AND CONCEPTS

In our consideration of the evolution of man and his culture, it is necessary to refer to what has been described as man's unique mental[1] characteristics: conceptual thought. Treatment of this subject is difficult because it involves the discussion of perception, and neither the formation of percept nor that of concept is yet well understood. What follows, therefore, is a personal and immensely simplified account of a very difficult subject, but one that cannot be omitted in any treatment of human evolution.

A *percept* may be considered to be the mental image of the external environment. Just how this mental image comes into existence is not yet known, but it is clear that it is based on two kinds of information; one is the input from the senses, and the other is the memory of previous experience. It can be shown with ease that a given percept is not necessarily a true if limited interpretation of the present environment but that it is strongly influenced by previous experience. It seems clear that in the growth and development of each individual mammal, motor investigation of the environment plays an essential part in building up its appropriate perceptual interpretation. There is no doubt that the content of perception varies beyond our understanding among the different kinds of animals, and we cannot conceive the world of a dog, for example, or of a nocturnal prosimian. Our own perception of the outside world has evolved with the primates, to which the motor component is of fundamental importance in understanding the environment. Spatial relationships must be first experienced to be later perceived, and we inherit from our primate ancestors a very spatial — a very three-dimensional — perception of our environment.

From these considerations follow two conclusions:

1 If primate perception depends so much on motor investigation, the quality of perception will depend on the extent and refinement of the motor investigation. Primates, more than all other mammals (except bats), live in a three-dimensional world; their eyes are stereoscopic, and their movements are in all three planes of space. They must have very precise ideas of spatial relationships, for arboreal locomotion involves a knowledge of space far greater than that which may be necessary to ground-living forms. The prosimians as well as the higher primates have no doubt come to perceive the environment as a three-dimensional rather than a two-dimensional pattern. The integration of spatial data from the senses to form a composite perception of the environment has clearly gone further among primates than among other groups of animals. Visual, somatic sensory, and auditory inputs will be analyzed and integrated with the motor and proprioceptive patterns. Such integration appears to take place, at least in part, among the association areas of these different sensory inputs on the parietal lobe of the brain.

2 Our second conclusion is that the memory component of perceptions is of fundamental importance and must almost inevitably come to include not merely an experiential record of events but some generalizations about spatial relationships. These generalizations are immeasurably expanded and deepened by the information obtained about the environment as a result of the manipulation of objects. By manipulation, the higher primate can extract an object from the environment, free it, as it were, from spatial implication, and build up a perception of it as a discrete object, not merely as part of a pattern. In time, the primate will come to perceive the environment not only as a three-dimensional pattern but also as an assemblage of objects.

Man, though a primate, is no longer an arboreal herbivore, a fact that has played an important part in the evolution of his perception. Kortlandt (1965) records that if food or any other familiar object is given to zoo chimpanzees at a place where they are not accustomed to receive it, the apes are inclined to react to it as though it were something entirely strange, and they may even refuse to consume their meal. For apes, things tend to lose their identity when they are displaced. Among carnivores, on the other hand, a displaced food tray or other object usually causes no problem, as every dog or cat owner knows. As Kortlandt puts it, the perception of apes carries a certain quality of "thereness," that is, its position in relation to other things, for among these primarily visual creatures the patterning of the environment is still the basis of their perception. Carnivores, on the other hand, identify food primarily by scent, and no strong visual pattern contributes to their perception of it. Visual perception in primate functions to identify static objects that comprise their food; in carnivores olfactory perception functions to identify mobile objects that comprise their prey.

When man began to hunt, his perception evolved accordingly. Using his prime sense, vision, man evolved the ability to identify objects on the move without reference to their relationship to the fixed

The view from the trees that was a factor in the course of human evolution continues to fascinate us even today. Many favored human places are associated with such vistas; among them are rotating restaurants, towers, mountain tops, and sometimes even trees.

Reprinted by permission, U.S. Department of Navy.

part of the environment; he saw them as totally separate from their environment. Here was a fundamental improvement in perception and something novel among land animals: a carnivore that hunted by sight.

It is clear that, first, manipulation and, later, hunting came to make man's perceptual world different from that of other primates; indeed, different from that of all other animals. Man's analytic perception, more than any other factor, opened the door to the development of conceptual thought and eventually to his remarkable culture.

Let us now turn to concepts. A *concept,* as generally defined, is an abstraction from the particular to the class. The concept "bird," for example, must be abstracted from the perception of, first, "this flying object" and, later, "that flying object." The concept "bird" does not apply to "many birds" or "all the birds I have seen" but to all birds possible in space and time. Similarly, the concept "food" applies not to "this food" but to all possible and potential food — fruit not yet plucked, animals not yet hunted. Consideration of the evolution of perception, such as we have attempted, seems to imply some degree of abstraction from experience, from the particular to the class. The abstraction may not have gone far, and it may not be complete as a concept, for intermediate stages of abstraction can exist. Nor is such abstraction conscious, for perception is not a conscious activity. But it does seem likely that conceptual thought may perhaps have had its origin in the classification of experience that was necessary for the sophisticated interpretation of the environment involved in perception.

It seems likely, then, that concepts form part of the mental activity of animals, but there may still be an important distinction in the mental activity of man, for thinking is a conscious process, and so, it follows, is conceptual thought. Apes can deal intelligently with objects here and now — objects they can see and the function of which is clear. They can be trained to carry out activities that appear to show foresight, and they can learn appropriate behavior for future needs. For example, chimpanzees will select straws and prepare vines (by stripping off side shoots), even when they are out of sight of any termite hills, and then set out to visit a known but distant group of hills to obtain termites. Apes in zoos will use sticks to reach bananas too high above them to be plucked by hand and will pile up boxes to get closer to them; yet they have limited creative and imaginative ability. An experiment was performed by Köhler (1925) to demonstrate the limitations of ape mentality. He constructed a box loosely out of sticks, so that they looked like boards. When the chimpanzees were presented with bananas out of reach, they were unable to see, within the structure of the box, the sticks they needed to get the fruit. Thus, an ape is unable to make a tool out of a natural object; he is able only to use a natural object as a tool with, perhaps, slight modification. An ape cannot conceive the tool without seeing it. He cannot see the stick in the plank or a hand-axe within a piece of rock. This man alone can do.

Freedman and Roe (1958) have suggested that frustration may well be one prerequisite in the development of conceptual thought; it is certainly a component of it. If a biological need arises and is not quickly satisfied, the requirement for such satisfaction will appear in the mind, not as a particular object, perhaps, but as a generalized one.

Thus frustration may bring with it imagination, and imagination is the consciousness of sets of concepts, which are the classification of experience. Man, having in his possession the concept of a small cutting stone, can look for it in a rock. He can see the possibility of its manufacture in future time, even though he may not have it at present. Abstraction means escape from the present, escape for man's mind from the immediacy of life. It has been said that what distinguishes man from animals is the length of time through which his consciousness extends. In animals, this dimension is small, stretching a little way into past and future; in man, it grows both qualitatively and quantitatively. The evolution of conceptual thought gives man greater power to live in the past and in the future by abstraction from the past.

To summarize, we find in mammals evidence for a classification of experience, which might be called unconscious conceptualization. This sort of classification, at even a very low level, seems to be necessary for the development of perception. As perception improves and incorporates more data from sensory investigation, especially in the higher primates, we find the probability that certain associational patterns of such data are crystallizing as concepts that might be equated with "things" and perhaps with relationships. Human conceptual thought appears to be characterized particularly by its conscious nature, but it is no doubt the result of a steady process of evolution from less conscious and indeed unconscious concepts in primates. Man's achievement was the fully conscious concept of things he does not possess but needs; the recognition of game, weapons, women, or children as classes brought with it the classification of more and more of man's environment and the possibility of foresight of future needs. Man, leaving behind the narrow limits of present time experienced, entered the broad expanse of past memory and future concepts. His foresight depends upon abstraction from the past in a manner that is termed intelligent. ■

NOTE
1. *Mental* is the adjective of *mind,* the functional and subjective aspect of the living brain.

Stephen Kaplan
Perception of an Uncertain Environment*

This selection looks at the demands that human evolution placed on perception. Ideally perception would be both fast and accurate, but under conditions of uncertainty speed and accuracy trade off — one can only be had at the expense of the other. To resolve this difficulty, the *representation* is introduced. This concept is both central to the analysis of perception and serves as the basic building block for the treatment of "knowing" developed in the next chapter. For some readers, the concluding discussion of how the representation might work may be somewhat technical, but it provides a bit more imagery for those who find description without mechanism unsatisfying.

■ Making a go of it requires, first of all, comprehending what is going on. This in turn requires the capacity to recognize things, that is, to react to patterns of stimulation as instances of categories that one has experienced previously. Such recognition is more difficult the more uncertain the environment is. In fact, the mechanism humans have evolved for achieving this feat is so powerful that it provides a foundation not only for recognizing things, but for the process of thought as well.

Although the environment is uncertain, it by no means is random. Regularities abound, and the organism must identify them. A lion, for example, presents many regularities. A lion has teeth (unless it is a very old lion), a mane (unless it is a female lion), impressive stature (unless it is a cub), and a tail (unless, of course, something happened to it). Lions also roar. Sometimes. But quite apart from the variability of lions, there is the variability in the way one happens to observe them. A side view provides certain information, a back view looks different, and an eyeball-to-eyeball view looks very different indeed. Yet to a potential lion prey, the appropriate action may be the same.

The variability in stimulation from the same objects has still other sources: the background or setting in which it appears can vary; the foliage may obscure portions of the animal; and so on. (Those who think these many sources of environmental uncertainty insignificant

*This is the first publication of this article. All rights reserved. Permission to reprint must be obtained from the author and publisher.

by Howard L. Deardorff

should study the literature on computer recognition of patterns. These problems are so thorny that, despite a very substantial investment of time and talent, computer pattern recognition is still relatively primitive.)

SPEED AND ACCURACY

Much of the problem in perception seems to arise from the inadequacy of any one particular glimpse of an object. Presumably, a close inspection of the lion will reveal many properties not noticed at first glance. Unless the lion is stuffed or caged, however, this procedure is not recommended. Here is one of the basic dilemmas in the struggle to make sense out of the environment: It is vital to come to a conclusion speedily, but one's judgements should also be accurate — and this unfortunately takes time. Speed and accuracy are opposing goals; increasing one will in general decrease the other.

In an environment where the slowest tend to get eaten, the resolution of this dilemma is fairly obvious: It pays to be fast. To aid the organism in its struggle for survival, perception must lead to prompt action.

With the emphasis on speed, accuracy necessarily suffers. This is not in itself disastrous, since accuracy — in the sense of information obtained through close, detailed inspection — hardly seems necessary. What is required is a reasonably close contact with reality, with the environment. The organism must know in a general way what objects are in the vicinity, where they are in relation to it, and which way they are going. Adaptive perception thus requires both the capacity to facilitate speedy response and the maintenance of reasonable contact with reality.

SOME PROPERTIES OF PERCEPTION

Perhaps one of the most useful and durable descriptions of the perceptual process is William James's: "Perception is of probable and definite things."[1] By "probable" he meant that we tend to perceive what is likely, what is familiar, even when the stimulus is in fact not familiar. By "definite" he meant that we tend to perceive clearly, even when the stimulus is vague, blurred, or otherwise ambiguous.

The parallel between the functional or adaptive requirements for perception and the properties identified by James are remarkable. Consider the necessity for a reasonable contact with reality. James's concept of the perception of probable things points to an efficient means of meeting this requirement. Since the vital importance of speed precludes a detailed inspection of the environment, some other way must be found to insure that what the organism perceives reasonably approximates what is there. Clearly, knowing what is *usually* found in a given environment reduces the need for close inspection. Past experience can enhance the value of a limited glimpse of the environment. In other words, the organism would be influenced in its perception of what is going on at the moment by information it already has as to what the likely possibilities are in such a setting. Or — to return to James's terminology — perception is of probable things.

The need for a speedy response provides an equally compelling parallel to James's observations. A "speedy response" depends on a clear reading of what is going on in the environment. No matter how swiftly features of the environment are detected, if the result is ambiguous, a quick response cannot follow. Thus, in an uncertain environment, speed of response depends upon a clear interpretation of the environment. This is precisely the property of perception that James called "definiteness." It can be illustrated, following our previous example, by a percept of a "splotch of yellow and maybe something fuzzy and some sort of whiskers and really big feet." Such a perception is considerably less likely to lead to decisive action than the percept "lion," with all it entails. The difference between the two is similar to what the Gestaltists have called "closure"; given a reasonable amount of information, the percept will be of the completed whole, not of the parts.

Thus, the need for accuracy and speed is dealt with in the Jamesean terms of the probable and the definite. A percept that is definite is a necessary condition for speedy response. And being probable makes the percept reasonable; it reduces the need for accuracy, even if it is not a direct substitute for it. Essentially what the organism is doing, in classical functionalist terms, is making a "best guess" (Bruner, 1957a; Brunswik, 1956; Ittelson, 1962). It is far from a random guess, since it is influenced both by features extracted from the environment and by prior experience. Yet it is clearly a guess in the sense that it is made promptly rather than delayed until all the information is in. It is also a guess in the sense that it is definite or concrete despite whatever ambiguity characterizes the stimulus information.

ON MECHANISM   Being probable and definite is thus central to the adaptive character of perception. But a nagging doubt remains. What precisely is it that is probable and definite? It is certainly not the stimulation arising from the environment, which, as we have seen, is fraught with ambiguity. Nor is it the set of features extracted by the organism, since that brief glimpse constitutes only a sample of the larger uncertainty in the environment. What must be probable and definite is the "guess" the organism makes, the tentative conclusion about what is going on out there. Clearly, the organism must have many possible guesses, many potential percepts, already stored in its head when it faces a given environmental circumstance. If these are probable (based on past experience) and definite (organized around particular objects and events) then with the help of a little input the most appropriate one can be selected. Such a selection would require far less time than starting from scratch, as it were, each time one looked out over the environment.

While thinking of this mental entity as a "best guess" or a "potential percept" will be satisfactory enough for many purposes, a slightly more technical treatment has the dual advantages of making the concept more general and placing it in a clearer relationship to other central concepts.

According to this framework, to recognize a particular object one would require a "potential percept" for that object. Further, one would expect it to "turn on" in some sense when that object was present, and generally not to turn on when it was not. Such a mental entity can be said to *correspond* to the object in question. Further, since its "turning on" signals to the organism the presence of the object in its environment, it is said to "represent" that object and is frequently referred to as an "internal representation" (S. Kaplan, 1973a, 1976; Neisser, 1968; Shepard, 1968).

Possibly such a representation could be an internal copy of an object, a little template to hold up against whatever is going on in the environment at the moment. One would then decide whether or not it was a good match. This was, in fact, a popular theory at one time, but it has turned out to be unsatisfactory (Neisser, 1968). The trouble with the notion of an exact copy is that (1) one would need too many of them to cover all versions of an object one had previously experienced, and (2) the next meeting with an object is likely to be different yet — which means one would fail to recognize it.

Thus, a representation must be far more generalized, more schematic, than a copy; instead it must stand for a *class* of objects. This is a crucial issue for the approach to perception proposed here. Such generalized or schematic representations would be expected to arise given varied experience and traditional rules of learning (Hebb, 1949;

1972). Essentially the process involves learning whatever the varied instances have in common. This results in a considerable loss of detail. What is left is a rather generalized prototype that summarizes the individual's experience with the pattern or object in question. Research on the recognition of unfamiliar patterns indicates that such schematic prototypes do in fact arise in the course of learning (Posner, 1973; Posner and Keele, 1968).

The internal representation is thus something of a paradox; it is at the same time concrete and abstract. It is built out of perceptual experience and stands for some object or class of objects — for example, "chair" — rather than standing for an idea. It has, in other words, a certain concreteness. On the other hand, it is a distillate of many experiences. Rather than a copy of one encounter, it is a sort of essence extracted out of many, a collection of properties that tend to characterize that kind of object. Much information is discarded in the process. In other words, it is an abstraction.

It may seem surprising that an individual has a head full of representations without having noticed them. Yet representations are not as unfamiliar as all that. When they are turned on by the presence of the appropriate object in the environment, our experience is, of course, of that object. It does not "feel like" a representation. But consider the experience created by a large gray object passing the door, an object with tusks and a tail and wrinkled skin. In general this much information will suffice to yield the experience of having seen an elephant. The elephant as experienced will be complete with eyes, ears, and a trunk. Thus, partial information yields a probable and definite percept.

The role of the representation in the perceptual process is perhaps more readily apprehended in instances where the object is absent. A representation may be weakly turned on even when the object it stands for is not present. In such a case it is called an "image." Images, conveniently enough, have many of the properties one would expect of a representation. They tend to be of objects. They are probable and definite. At the same time they are abstract; upon close inspection an image turns out not to have the detail it seemed to have.

While contemplating one's images is an instructive experience (especially if one has sufficiently durable imagery to contemplate — there is wide variation from one person to the next), it has its limitations. Much of the perceptual process is not accessible to introspection. While the operation of representations in perception can be described figuratively as a "best guess," one should not expect to notice oneself guessing except in the most unusual of circumstances. The process is very rapid and occurs at a molecular level. What one experiences is the outcome of a competition among alternative possible representations,

Note how little the distortions and omissions interfere with the recognition of these familiar objects.
by Howard L. Deardorff

a competition that involves many very small internal events and usually is over in a matter of milliseconds. Things are further complicated by the fact that such small rapid processes are occurring all the time. It is undoubtedly a great advantage not to be aware of them. We are built to be concerned with what is going on in the world, not with how we are figuring out what is going on.

The limited nature of consciousness applies to the environment as well as to our own process. Much of the information we take in is discarded without our even being cognizant of it. And even information that has some impact will at times elude consciousness. Consciousness, in other words, is a matter of degree. The greater the impact of information from the environment, the greater the likelihood of being aware of it. This is hardly surprising from an adaptive point of view, from the perspective of an organism's making its way in a dangerous and uncertain environment. But it is surprising to some whose exposure to popular psychology has led them to regard anything that people are not conscious of as dark, mysterious, and insidiously powerful. When it comes to perception, what escapes consciousness does so more often because of the capacity to focus on the important than because of insidious internal forces. ■

NOTE
1. The discussion that follows is deeply indebted to the chapter on perception in Williams James's *Psychology: The Briefer Course* (1892; Collier edition, 1962). It is heartily recommended for those interested in a fuller picture of the issues considered here. For that matter, the entire book is packed with insight and delight. Although some people are put off by the slightly archaic language, the book is brilliantly written, with a fine sense for concrete example and penetrating abstraction. Probably no other book has as much to say about psychology in so little space, and certainly none is so engagingly written.

Ernest R. Hilgard
The Goals of Perception*

This discussion of perception, written quite a few years ago, provides a particularly good example of a functional perspective. Hilgard examines the key psychological goals of perception: stability of environment and definiteness of information. While his detailed examples have a solid empirical foundation, they also reflect the common experiences of us all.

■   Perception is not a passive process of registration, but an active process of interaction between organism and environment. Perception is an achievement. As in the case of other achievements, it is regulated and given direction by what the organism is trying to do. Let us now turn our attention to two of the goals of perception and then consider how these goals are determined and how perceptual dilemmas are resolved according to these goals.

ACHIEVEMENT OF ENVIRONMENTAL STABILITY

The organism seeks a perceptually stable environment in somewhat parallel fashion to the way in which it seeks an internally stable environment. There is a kind of environmental homeostasis parallel to physiological homeostasis. In both cases the stability is one of dynamic equilibrium, not of static equilibrium. An environment that has some stable reference points in it can still be a changing one. The organism tolerates perceptual differences between night and day as it does physiological differences between sleep and waking. But the organism does not like an environment that distorts too rapidly. If a man's environment distorts too rapidly, he gets upset or seasick.

In normal perception, the goal of stability accounts for many of our perceptual achievements. For example, were it not for this achieved stability, the visual world would move as you move your head from side to side. That stability is an achievement is easily demonstrated by seeing what happens when you view the world through reversing lenses. When the visual world is unfamiliar, as it is through reversing lenses, the line of regard is the anchoring point, so that when you move your head the world races by in the direction opposite to the movement of your line of regard. The anchorage thus involves a choice

*From Ernest R. Hilgard "The role of learning in perception" in Robert R. Blake and Glenn V. Ramsey (Eds.) *Perception: an approach to personality.* New York: copyright 1951, The Ronald Press Company. Pages 103–108, 110. Reprinted by permission.

between the line of regard (used in inverted vision) and a stable world (used in normal vision). Confronted by a familiar visual world, you prefer to have the world stay put as you look about.

This stability of the world has two features to it. One is the stability of objects, the other the stability of the world in which these objects have position. We have all sorts of object constancies. Our goal is to have both objects and the environment remain constant. But in a choice between a reference frame and an object, we will sacrifice the object to the framework. . . .

DEFINITENESS

Definiteness and stability have much in common, but they are not alike. In reversible geometrical figures, definiteness is achieved at the price of stability. Stability might be better achieved if a geometrical figure were seen as only so many lines. But we prefer to see it as something, even though it is ambiguous, and so the "somethings" it represents tend to alternate.

Woodworth (1947) is convinced that there is a fundamental motive to perceive clearly. As he puts it: "To see, to hear — to see clearly, to hear distinctly — to make out what it is one is seeing or hearing — moment by moment, such concrete, immediate motives dominate the life of relation with the environment" (p. 123).

He goes on to show how the clarity that comes as the goal of search is satisfying and hence, in terms of learning principles, reinforcing. There may, of course, be further reinforcement through the needs that the perceived objects satisfy.

The tendency to structure into figure and ground is one indication of the strain toward definiteness and thing-quality. The tendency is to construct concrete things out of the patterns we perceive, for concrete things have definiteness. The present writer is not too sure which is the cart and which the horse. It may be that the figure-ground relation is learned as an abstract residue from our experience with objects. The real figures of our experience are those manipulable things that we see and touch, that slide over their backgrounds, that cast shadows. Because our ends are served by these real things, we tend to see ambiguous patterns as thinglike.[1]

Edna Heidbreder's work on concepts (1945), according to the present writer's interpretation, fits what is said above. When shown figures and asked to assign the appropriate nonsense concept name, her subjects always found it easier to name objects rather than to name the abstract relations of space or number. We want to see things clearly, and what we prefer to perceive is a concrete thing.

These two goals of perception, first, to have our perceptions keep the world about us a stable one and, second, to achieve definiteness in what we perceive, may be accepted as valid without committing ourselves as to their origin. Perhaps a little speculation is in order.

The present writer's conjecture is that perceptual goals are intimately related to the other goals of the learner. The basic reason for achieving a stable world is that such a world is the most convenient one in which to satisfy our needs. Only in such a world can we use maps and libraries and filing cabinets. We want to know where we are, where we are going, where we have put things. It is difficult even to see a problem here. Imagine, if you can, a pulsating world in which everything was as mobile as man. The cabbages you planted in rows might move across the street, your house would turn around to face the sun, you would not know whether you lived on a hill or in a valley. So accustomed are we to a predictable and orderly world that such notions are fantastic. Fortunately, the world is the kind of world in which a measure of stability can be achieved. It serves our purposes to have our perceptions correspond to such a stable world. There are, in fact, many mobile features to our world. Lights and shadows change the colors of objects; many objects, both animate and inanimate, are mobile. To keep our world of objects stable, we have to learn to take distance and motion into account, as well as light and shadow. We achieve more constancy, in fact, than is present to our senses. Were this not the case, we would not have to think of stability as an achievement. What this means is that the goal of environmental stability arises out of our need for a stable world in which to satisfy other motives. The stability of the world is not an end in itself.

The second goal, the achievement of definiteness, is likewise in the interest of other motives. The objects recognized while they are not yet too clear may be dangerous ones to be avoided or desirable ones to be pursued. It helps us to be ready for them before they are clear. Therefore, it helps us to identify things from partial cues. This is enough to encourage object perception as an aid to need satisfaction.

There is another motive that supports our desire for clarity. This is related to the tendency for strange objects to invoke fear. Spitz (1946) observed that infants during the first year of life show increasing responsiveness to strangeness. They smile at all faces during the first few months, but by six months they are frightened by strange faces. In another study by Bayley (1932) infants in the test situation were observed to cry more frequently in response to strangeness than to other features of the test situation as they grow older. Hebb (1946) reports that chimpanzees reared in captivity show marked fear of strange things and of strange people. The clinical experience of depersonalization, when everything is strange, is terrifying. It may be that the desire to find something clear and familiar in what is presented to the senses is part of feeling secure in the world, of being protected against the anxiety that strangeness engenders. It is no fun to be lost in a homogeneous environment, like a fog, the open sea, a dense forest, or even a dark corridor. We seek something familiar and identifiable, something that gives us anchorage. Possibly curiosity, a motive sufficiently important for McDougall (1921) to have called it an instinct, is a defense against the anxiety that strangeness and lack of clarity produce.

These conjectures about the origin of the desire for a stable world and for definiteness of perception may or may not be correct. Whether they are or not does not prevent our accepting stability and clarity as goals of perception.

HARMONIZING THE CONTRIBUTIONS OF THE SEVERAL SENSES

In order for the world to provide a firm and stable environment in which we may carry on our enterprises, it must be the same world that we see and hear and smell and touch. This sameness is an achievement, for our sensory givens are not in harmony except in the grossest of fashions. A hole in a tooth is not the same size to the tongue as it is to the eye; so far as our ears tell us, a cricket might be almost anywhere in the room, not only where our eyes find it.

The most plausible basis for making the world of objects one world is that of manipulation. In meeting our own needs, we have commerce with many objects. We go where they are, we carry them about, we dodge them if they are thrown at us, we place them in our pockets, and in countless other ways handle them according to their sizes, shapes, distances, and movements. We are not fooled by sizes, shapes, distances, or movements if our locomotion and manipulation are appropriate. Most of us are realists according to the way we find the world of things to exist outside ourselves and to be manageable according to stubborn and substantial characteristics.

In fact, the real world seems so real that we are persuaded, so long as we are not being fooled by recognized illusions, that our perceptions are accurate. They are, indeed, reasonably accurate, but they are not copies of real objects. Our perceptions achieve *for us* a world that is relatively stable by excluding so far as possible contradictory evidence. If a pail is to be filled with water, we soon learn its size relative to other vessels and relative to our own bodies. Its true perceived size fits with other size perceptions of things we handle. We never have to gather in the moon, so we have no way of knowing whether it is the size of a cheese or a dishpan or a silver dollar. Consequently, we see it as of some convenient size and at some convenient distance, without concern over its true size or its true distance. There is nothing to conflict with it, so the dimensions of size and distance need not conform in any precise manner to the sizes and distances of other objects.

Perceptual harmony is an achievement. It is not a given. Von Hornbostel (1927) once wrote a lyrical paper on the "Unity of the Senses" in which he showed the great extent to which we do use analogies from one sense in dealing with the data from another. We can give fairly consistent answers to questions that appear silly. Students, when asked to tell how much a minute weighs, may think the question is insane, but nobody ever thinks it weighs as much as 100 pounds, and scarcely anyone thinks it weighs as much as 10 pounds. The present writer agrees that Von Hornbostel is right in postulating a kind of unity or interrelatedness to which the various senses contribute but is inclined to believe that we achieve this unity largely through experience.

The senses, when acting alone, provide different phenomenal worlds from the one yielded when they act together. The blind man gets around all right and recognizes objects by touch. His phenomenal world corresponds to reality and is satisfactory, so far as it goes. But if by removal of cataracts he is made able to see, the phenomenal world that comes to him by sight must be harmonized with the phenomenal world that comes to him through touch. Many observations show that the two worlds have to be harmonized by learning. Senden (1932) reports, for example, that with restored vision the man once blind may distinguish between a ball and a block as visual objects, but he does not know which is the ball and which the block until he handles them. We are able to parallel these experiences to some extent in the laboratory. For example, a subject who has learned a maze blindfolded tends, if asked to draw the pattern that he has learned, to draw it too large.

The Stratton (1896, 1897) experiments with inverted lenses are appropriate in this connection. The distorted world that Stratton saw when he wore the lenses had to be harmonized with the world in which he moved about. Soon there was no problem of locating objects in the new visual space. Sounds seemed to come from the places where objects were seen. That is, after an observer had worn the glasses for a while, he heard the fire sputter audibly where the fire was seen to be. The visual scene did not swing with head movements as much as it did at first. The return to normal vision was at first bewildering; the world would again swing when the head was turned. The old habits were, of course, quickly restored.

The experiments of P. T. Young (1928) with the pseudophone gave results similar to those of Stratton. With the ears reversed, the subject presently learned to see and hear things as though coming from a common source. It appears, however, that the reorganization was accomplished largely through accommodating the auditory experience to vision for, with the eyes closed, auditory localization took place as before the reversal. After the pseudophone was removed, there was no residual effect from wearing it. Had Young attempted to regulate his behavior largely by audition (say by blindfolding himself while wearing the pseudophone) his reorganization of auditory localization might have been more complete.

We coordinate the data from the various senses by manipulating objects in the environment. We can know that our sense data are "true" and "accurate" only if they lead to objects that serve our purposes. If the paper fits the envelope, if the car gets through the garage door, if the pen fits the penholder, then all the perceptions involved have been realistic. Our world is in order; whether or not it is a real world may be difficult to answer philosophically, but by pragmatic tests we know that the real and the perceived are alike, for the environment meets our expectations and suits our purposes.

ACHIEVING CLARITY FROM AMBIGUOUS CUES

When cues are ambiguous, we can accept them as such and postpone judgment pending their clarification. But perceptual mechanisms do not work that way. Instead, we are impatient, and we struggle to achieve clarity and definiteness even when the cues are insufficient to provide an objective basis.

If we do not know, then we guess. That is what we do when we recognize someone at a distance too great, when we try to anticipate who would be sending us a telegram from St. Louis, or when we infer that the noise is coming from an airplane rather than a motorcycle. There is a strong tendency to jump ahead, to take a short cut, to act in accordance with a few indicators, even though more information might be forthcoming if we but waited. This is a general characteristic of behavior, based on a need to be prepared for what may be coming. Perhaps the person coming down the street is someone we would rather not meet, or someone from whom we wish to ask a favor in an auspicious manner; maybe the telegram will bring bad news, and we must guard against an undue display of emotion; possibly our son has threatened to buy himself a motorcycle, and so we are apprehensive about noises that might confirm our fears. We not only respond to the stimuli that confront us but respond in preparatory ways to expected stimuli. Such preparatory or anticipatory response is an achievement of learning and intelligence in which perception shares. ■

NOTE
1. Hebb (1949, pp. 19–35) distinguishes three conceptions: (1) a primitive, sensorily determined unity, as that of a splash of black ink on a white card; (2) a nonsensory unity, affected by experience, as in the perception of familiar geometrical figures like squares and circles; and (3) the identity of a perceived figure, also affected by experience. A figure may be seen as unified without being identified for what it is. The paragraph to which this footnote is appended was written before Hebb's book appeared. The discussions do not appear to be in conflict, but Hebb's analysis would have permitted a more pointed interpretation.

3 Knowing

When geographers, designers, and others interested in the human/environment interface refer to "environmental perception," the issues they raise often turn out to involve knowing the environment at least as much as perceiving it. Humans take in only a small portion of the stimulation impinging on them at any one time; nonetheless, they experience the environment as full and complete rather than partial and fragmentary. They are thus relying rather heavily on the prior experience with the environment that is stored in the mind. Information from the environment is used to call up stored information that is in some way appropriate to the situation at hand. In this sense, the experience of the environment is a mental construction based on memories of prior encounters.

But storing information from each of the many encounters one has with the environment could have its drawbacks. If the storage were not well organized, the more experience one had, the longer it would take to bring it into play. Knowing an environment involves more than knowing what the important things and places are. It requires that we also know how they connect — where they stand in relation to each other. Thus, to constitute knowledge of an environment we need not only the representation; the representations must also be connected to each other. Such a collection of connected representations constitutes an internal model or cognitive map of the environment.

The cognitive map idea, although proposed by Tolman back in 1948, has sparked little interest until relatively recently. But planners, geographers, environmental psychologists, and other kindred spirits have revived the concept with considerable enthusiasm (Lynch,

1960; Downs and Stea, 1973; Moore and Golledge, 1976). This enthusiasm is easy to understand. The cognitive map provides a link between the human thought process and the physical environment. The way an individual experiences and reacts to a given environment begins to be understandable in the context of an experience-based internal structure that corresponds, at least in certain respects, to the environment in question. A cognitive map so generated provides the basis for hopes, expectancies, and plans. Gaps in the map might account for ignorance, apparent irrationality, and misguided despair.

There are cognitive maps of many kinds. Some concern temporal relationships, others logical connections, and still others, affective bonds. But as the word *map* implies, the origin of the concept and its major applications remain in the spatial domain.

The selections in this chapter examine various issues related to the cognitive map idea. What kinds of environmental qualities are important in the development of mental representations of external events and places? Are there differential effects of different ways of experiencing the environment? The Appleyard and Lee articles also address the thorny problem of measuring environmental knowledge. While asking people to "draw their cognitive map" is appealing and seemingly direct, it generates data that are strikingly difficult to analyze and understand. But the information these studies seek is by definition subjective; to understand what is stored in the mind of humans, one cannot look at an objective "truth." These studies ask questions such as how far away things *seem* or *feel,* or about the relative juxtaposition of places in the mind — not in the world.

It is, in fact, the very juxtaposition of places, the places that are subjectively "connected," that forms the basic structure of a cognitive map. The pattern of connections between representations is assumed to reflect the pattern of connections one has experienced in the world. These connections in turn constitute the paths in the map. They provide the relational structure that makes the stored information more than a mere collection of places. In other words, they impose an orderly arrangement that makes the term *map* appropriate.

David Stea
Environmental Perception and Cognition: Toward a Model for "Mental" Maps[*]

In this thoughtful analysis of what people must know about their spatial environment, Stea explores two important issues. First, he examines some reasons for assuming that people act on the basis of information that they cannot directly perceive at the time they are using it. They behave, in other words, as if they have stored the results of their prior perceptions in a reasonably orderly and useful manner. Second, Stea develops what might be considered a set of criteria that any theory of cognitive maps would have to meet.

■   The subject matter of, and the issues within, what is usually called "the psychology of perception" are among the oldest within the field of scientific psychology. In most of the traditional work in perception within psychology, the subject is told what to perceive — or at least, he is told where to look for what he is supposed to see. A majority of the studies in perception using human subjects have been done in the visual-sense modality. This is reasonable, since most of our intelligence concerning the outside world comes through this modality; in other words, to abuse a reasonably common cliché, "we are visual animals." Such experiments present subjects with stimuli that can be perceived instantaneously, or over a very short interval of time.

Experiments dealing only with this form of perception treat intervals of time much smaller than the intervals usually involved in gaining "useful" information, such as learning how to get around in a city, or even learning, or "appreciating," a single building. However, in this era of interdisciplinary endeavor, some architects have become enamored of the word "perception" and what it connotes. They are often convinced that what they have been trying to do in the past is, through manipulation of certain hypothesized visual characteristics of architectural products, to "tell" people what to perceive. Sometimes they have been successful, many times for reasons they do not know; more often they have failed. Urban designers have also tried, with somewhat less success.

[*] From David Stea "Environmental perception and cognition: toward a model for 'mental' maps" in G. J. Coates and K. M. Moffett (Eds.) *Response to environment.* 1969. Student Publications, School of Design, North Carolina State University. Reprinted by permission.

The suggestion here, and it is by no means a new one, is that the majority of our actions, thoughts, etc., *vis-à-vis* the physical environment, are by no means based upon a *perception* in the strict sense in which the term is used by experimental psychologists, nor upon any simple combination of such perceptions, memories, and learned modes of organizing these. Except in very simple, but not always trivial cases, we know very little about these modes of organization, complex combinations that could be and have been called "images," "cognitive maps," "mental maps," "conceptual spaces," "schemata," etc. — the name often depends upon the discipline to which one subscribes. Before the First World War, the then-dean of psychology, John B. Watson, had dismissed the "image" from psychology.[1] The concept briefly reappeared again in the work of Sir Frederick Bartlett and Kurt Lewin in the 1930s and 1940s, but remained relatively dormant until George Miller, Eugene Galanter, and Karl Pribram revived it in their now nearly classic little book, *Plans and the Structure of Behavior*. Perhaps it will again become respectable.

To clarify the distinction between a "perception" and an "image" or "mental map." We can get around the Watsonian objection, which was largely that there exists no direct way for the scientist to "see" this image, by stating very simply that what we are interested in is not necessarily the map itself, but its manifestations. That is, we shall define the image "operationally" in terms of resulting behavior. Or, in other words, "images" may not exist at all, but some representation of certain real-world characteristics, no matter how far divorced from veridicality, must exist. It might be no more than an unordered list of place names. But once we have gotten some idea of what *is* there (and to do so we shall have to construct a theoretical framework and formulate hypotheses), we can put together a model — with all the shortcomings that models usually have — which may tell us something about the ways in which people orient themselves in, and form conceptions of their surroundings.

First, we are speaking only about spaces so large that they cannot be perceived at once, not of those perceivable in a brief series of glances; problems of the latter kind already have been treated adequately. Larger spaces, which must be cognitively organized, we hypothesize to have the following "conceptual" characteristics (in terms of the possibly fictitious "mental representation" of which we have spoken earlier):

1 The space consists of a series of "points" (not points in the mathematical sense, because our points may have dimension) arranged in some one-, two-, or three-dimensional way.

2 There may be several possible hierarchical arrangements among these: in terms of size, importance, etc. In fact, several

hierarchical arrangements may coexist, or may exist at different times within the life of an individual. In a child's drawing of a visit to a zoo, the largest animal drawn is usually the most important to him — often a monkey; similarly, in drawing his home, mother is often drawn much larger than father.

3   The space is somehow "bounded." The boundaries may be clear or indistinct; they may be in the form of lines or other imaged areas. A neighborhood may be bounded by a street or another neighborhood, for example. Further, there may be boundaries within the boundaries; as an individual "images" a city, he may image neighborhoods within the city as bounded entities.

4   If it is possible to get from one given point in the imaged space to another by *any* means of transportation, we say that they are "connected." If it is possible to get from one point to another by *some* means of transportation, they are "semiconnected." In either case, there exists a "path" between the points. If the two points are semiconnected or nonconnected, there exists a "barrier" between them. However, the converse is not necessarily true; the existence of a barrier does not necessarily imply that there exists some means of transportation by which it is impossible to get from one point to another. The barrier may simply make certain forms of transportation more difficult.

5   Barriers differ in their *permanence,* their *permeability,* and their *quality* ("natural" or "artificial"). A construction project in the middle of a superhighway decreases permeability and is impermanent; a flood, also impermanent, reduces permeability to zero. The frontier between Mexico and the United States is temporarily quite impermeable when rumors are received that a shipment of marijuana is expected; all travellers attempting to cross the border then experience difficulty.

6   Barriers may be symmetrical (the same when approached from one member of a pair of points as from the other) or nonsymmetrical. The city of Providence, Rhode Island, for example, was for most travellers between Boston and New York prior to the completion of the turnpikes, a nonsymmetrical barrier; that is, the north-south and south-north routes through the city were different and it was considerably more difficult to traverse the city in one direction than in the other.

In summary, the space of which we are speaking is bounded; one-, two-, or three-dimensional; and consists in a probably finite (given the limitations of the human organism) collection of points [of anywhere from zero through three dimensions]; of paths between them; and of interposed barriers. We need be no more mathematically rigorous than this in our specification. Further, we need not postulate an entity which might arouse the wrath of the late Dr. Watson. The "mental maps" of which we are speaking need not necessarily be "geography in the head"; indeed, they may be an utter fiction — that is, there may be no reportable imagery at all — without loss of heuristic value. It matters not a whit that we cannot observe a "mental map," that we cannot know for sure that it is actually "there"; if a subject behaves *as if* such a map existed, it is sufficient justification for the model.

What we are proposing is no more than that the large and complex real world must be handled by people with limited capacity for information storage, manipulation, and retrieval. Hence, certain simplifications and distortions take place, in accordance with the needs and experience of the individual in the conceptualization of these large and complex spaces. These alterations are distortions only in the sense that they do not correspond with maps objectively prepared by objective geographers. The distortions may be expected to vary from individual to individual, but where certain kinds of distortions are consistent across a given class of persons, they are interesting in and of themselves. The measures to be used may be behavioral, in the sense that we observe the individual's actions vis-à-vis a real or artificially created environment and infer the "image" that yielded the observed behavior, or "introspectively descriptive" in that we ask him to describe an *imagined* interaction with the environment.[2]

We may also speak of "static" and "dynamic" maps. To form a "static" map, the subject need only imagine himself within a space, either standing or moving, and describe its "points," either in the form of free or directed recall, or by sketching a map from memory. We may then evaluate the verbal description in terms of the relative salience of various points when a number of subjects have been interviewed, or in terms of the physical placement of the points on a sketch map (both the relative positions of these points and their deviation from "reality" — what might otherwise be termed "accuracy" of memory).[3]

The "dynamic" map differs from the static in that not only are the points of the map important, but the individual's *interaction* with these points — how he imagines himself to be moving among them. We hypothesize that it is imagined or actual movement that ties the elements of the image together — they may define the *nature,* if not the *details* of the image. They may also answer some questions regarding human orientation in a civilized world consisting largely of designed environments. Assuming that there may exist several modes of orientation, we may ask whether there is such a thing as a *generally* well-oriented person, what orientations are best for what kinds of urban areas, and what is the role of one's previous interactions with physical environments ("Where'd you grow up, sonny?"), etc.

We will not address ourselves here to the chicken-and-the-egg problem of the extent to which "cognitive maps" generate movements versus the extent to which movements generate "cognitive maps." We may assume that both occur. As merely an outline of a viewpoint, this paper will concentrate upon certain easily definable interactions of an individual (in real or imagined motion) with an environment that he cannot immediately perceive in its entirety. From a highly simplified view, certain testable hypotheses will be generated. In all, we can present herein only a "theory in the rough" and, at that, only a portion of what really should be a much more complete theoretical development.

We begin by asking the most general question: "What does a person do?" First, he is or imagines himself in a location, that is, at a "point" (origin) in space. Second, he moves, or imagines movement to another "point" (goal), probably passing through intermediate "points" (which may be termed subgoals) on the way. These various points bear a certain relation to each other, the weakest of which (in correspondence with the real world) is the preservation of order — which point comes first, which second, etc. in the direction of travel. Third, the origin and goal are separated — there exists some *distance* between them. Fourth, movement is initiated in a certain direction (bearing — which is presumably related to the imaged location of the goal vis-à-vis the origin). Fifth, this bearing is generally not maintained throughout the entire journey or "virtual trip"; changes in direction which we call *turns* periodically occur. Finally, the person usually operates on the basis of some system of coordinates.

Let us examine each of these and the experiments they suggest.

Topological Correspondence

It is hypothesized that when maps are drawn or descriptions given, the product is not an exact description of the "real world," but that under specifiable conditions, the order in which these objects appear and such other ordinal characteristics as relative size, relative path length, etc. are conserved. The depiction of the "mental map" will thus be an *order-preserving transform* when the following conditions hold:

1 the difference in magnitude between the length of two paths, the sizes of two subspaces, etc., is demonstrably recognized (demonstrable in the sense that we have some other, independent measure); and

2 the elements involved (paths, points, spaces, etc.) are equal in importance, cogency, and valence (attractiveness of goal value), and are equally well known to the subject; or

3 differences in importance, valence, or cogency are in the direction of objective differences in magnitude.

It is further hypothesized that when "mirror reversals" occur in the order of things, from the subject's point of view, left-right reversals will be more common than front-back reversals. That is, it would seem to be easier to err across the body's line of symmetry than otherwise. People giving directions on the street in terms of their own position seem more likely to commit errors of left-right confusion than others. This problem will be further treated in the section on coordinate systems.

Distance

The conceptualization of what "distance" may be in spatial imagery may be aided by phrasing the issue in quasi-mathematical terms. The "real world" is, mathematically speaking, a metric space; that is, if we take any nontrivial portion of it and call it "X" ("X" may be a [nonmathematical] neighborhood, a region, or a nation), we may consider a function defined on the nonempty set "X." This function will be called "d" (distance), and the pair (X,d) is then a metric space if the following three conditions are satisfied for any pair of points (a and b) in "X" [for d (a,b) read "the distance between "a" and "b"]:

1   $d(a,b) \geqslant 0$; $d(a,b) = 0$ if and only if $a = b$.

2   $d(a,b) = d(b,a)$.

3   $d(a,c) \leqslant d(a,b) + d(b,c)$; this is the familiar "triangle inequality."

Distance can be thought of loosely as a line of communication or transportation. It is obvious that the real world is metric in the above sense; the interesting question is whether the image world is too. There is at least some evidence from a recent study of "virtual trips" among cities in New England (Buckman, 1966) (in which a person imagines that he is travelling by a specified means of transportation between two points known to him) that condition (2) does not necessarily hold in imagery; it makes a difference whether the question asked is: "What is the distance between Providence and Boston?" or "What is the distance between Boston and Providence?" That is, distance estimates are "noncommutative." When familiarity with the end points and the routes of such "virtual trips" are equated, a number of factors may account for the discrepancy in estimation; two potentially powerful ones are the desirability ("valence") of the goal relative to the origin, and the nature of the barriers between the two.

There is apparently no available evidence on (1) and (3). Failure of condition (1) to hold seems absurd; such failure would imply the statement "I am not where I am." But if we shift the emphasis from simple distance estimation to communication, the statement is not so absurd at all. With the increase in size and number of "megalopoli," especially within the United States, it is becoming increasingly common for people to give the major population center nearest to their homes as their actual location. Thus, the statement "I am from San Francisco," might imply, "I am from that area of which San Francisco is the center" (Palo Alto, for example). What is conveyed to the receiver of this message is equivocal; if the image generated is that of San Francisco itself, then for that pair of communicating individuals, "a" and "a" are not coincident.

Failure of (3) means simply that a less direct route may be conceptually shorter than a more direct one between two points. Students trained in geography classrooms in which the Mercator projection of the world was the major teaching aid are presently suffering difficulties in studying air routes, which seem, in terms of the maps with which they are familiar, to be most indirect indeed (the "great circle route" problem). And, especially with reference to air travel, it must be noted that *distance* (yards and miles) is not the only measure of "distance." *Time* is for many people the most common, useful, and meaningful measure. "It is five hours from San Francisco to New York," for example (but "longer" in the reverse direction).

Bearings

In addition to impressions of distance, the image must include the initial direction taken from the point of origin to the goal. The question of bearing cannot be divorced from the issue of orientation systems, of which there appear to be two basic classes:

1 body or "ego-centered" orientation — directions given in terms of the individual's position, i.e., left-right, back-front, etc.;

2 "objective" orientation, which can be further divided into

a "universal" compass coordinates,

b "local" compass coordinates.

These are especially interesting, since what is considered to be "north" often varies with locality. Indeed, each town in New England seems to have its own system. Orientation on the San Francisco peninsula is complicated by the fact that its inhabitants "consider" it to run north-south (in fact it is oriented northwest-southeast). Freeway signs in this area are based upon universal rather than local coordinates. The resulting confusion is prodigious.

Turns

A turn is simply a change in bearing and may be described with reference to a previous bearing or direction of travel (e.g. "turn right") or with regard to compass coordinates. But the most interesting characteristic of an "imaged" turn is its magnitude. With an infinity of possible variations, people tend to simplify these imaged turns, the most common simplification among dwellers in gridiron cities being a right angle. A psychologist once jokingly remarked, "There is no such thing as an obtuse angle — only a poor right angle." For dwellers in those cities in which a radial pattern is superimposed upon a grid (or vice versa), as is the case with Washington, D.C., simplifications of 45° and of 90° may be made. The point to be made here is that turns may well be remembered as other than what they are, and that the nature of the simplification is likely to be a result of one's accustomed interaction with the environment. Thus, we hypothesize that people whose experience has been largely with "irregular" lines of communication — cities such as Guanajuato in the Republic of Mexico — are likely to have received the last reinforcement for "simplifying assumptions" and, while they may experience some difficulty in adjusting to gridiron urban environments, will probably experience much less difficulty than others when lines of communication depart slightly from rectilinearity (as is the case in Mexico City, which is a complex radial pattern superimposed upon a complex grid). The experimental question here is: For a given individual, how large does a departure from strict rectangularity have to be before it is perceived (treated as) a departure?

In this connection, a consideration of what has come to be called "The Boston Common Problem" may be instructive. The Boston Common is an irregular five-sided figure. The cues surrounding it are well-known to Bostonians (although partly occluded by foliage in the spring and summer), but are generally not known to the stranger walking around the Common, who tends to rely upon the turns for his cues. Since the figure is five-sided, these turns are not right angles, but they may be "perceived as" or "simplified to" right angles, leaving the befuddled traveler 90° out of phase with the environment when he has traversed the five sides. We would hypothesize that this problem would be greatest among recent arrivals from highly regular midwestern cities, and least among those Americans whose home, while not necessarily Boston, has always been some "irregular" New England town.[4]

Bearings and Turns Combined — the Formulation of Orienting Schemata

Finding one's way about a city is essentially a problem in the utilization of paths, junctions, and cues (the paths and junctions themselves providing some of the cues). In the present terminology a person continues along a certain bearing, then changes bearing by making a turn, and so on. This constitutes a *route* from an origin to a goal; a complex of such routes for a given area constitutes a *schema*. We contend that two fundamentally different types of *schemata* may be formed, that they depend upon the coordinate system and mode of imagery utilized, and that the two are not equally well suited to all areas.

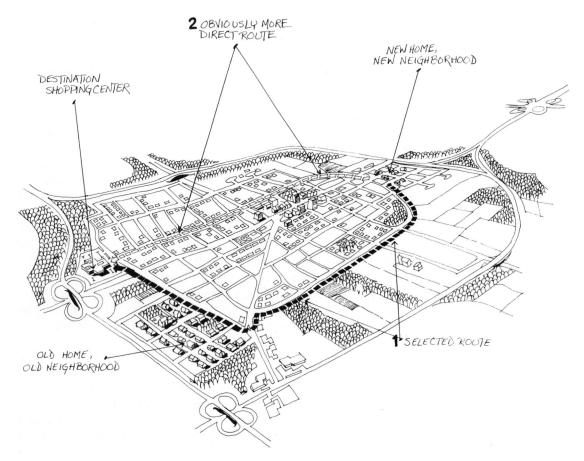

Wayfinding in the urban environment
by Howard L. Deardorff

The distinction should be clear to anyone who has ever taken directions (or given them) over the telephone. One way to give directions is
to specify an origin, an initial direction (street name or number), a
"cue" at which one turns "right" or "left," a succeeding cue at which
one does something else, etc., to the goal. This can be mapped or "imaged" but it can just as well simply be listed; not even the vaguest
graphic image is really necessary. The second way of giving directions
is to minimize the emphasis upon specific cues and to give information
in terms of compass coordinates and general characteristics, generating what the psychologist E. C. Tolman referred to figuratively, and
what we shall refer to literally, as a "cognitive map." Image-wise, it
allows for alternative routes within a general framework; the former
method does not, in the sense that "if you miss a cue (choice-point),
you're lost." On the other hand, where the channels of communication

and transportation are exceedingly irregular, the former system may be easier to learn and may "work better." If images in their most generic sense are built up, however, those based upon one of the above systems of "route-following" will be very different from the other. One will be a conglomeration of independent routes, the other a "cognitive map."

A TENTATIVE CONCLUSION

We have assumed that people "operate" (make plans and execute them) in accordance with their *representations* of the "real world"; hence, it would appear important for geographers and planners (and even, perhaps, for political scientists) to know and to understand these representations, and the nature and magnitude of their distortions. Such things as the relative attractiveness of cities and the barriers restricting communication among (and even within) them are of interest to planners and urban geographers. Research on noncommutativity of distance estimates may yield some information on this. Similarly, it may be supposed that "getting lost" is often a matter of making a wrong assumption about the nature of a turn that must be made.

There are possibilities for supplementing the body of knowledge within the psychology of perception too, if interest in this heretofore uninvestigated form of "imagery" is revived. It might be possible to develop a crude "psychophysics" of conceptual spaces — for example, what are just noticeable deviations from rectangularity perceived through other than the visual mode, how do these vary depending upon how they are experienced, etc. If results from early studies support our initial hypotheses, we might "probe" the cognitive map — insert unreal or misleading "cues" to see how much additional distortion can be introduced. Alternatively, assuming that the "virtual trip" represents the most impoverished stimulus field, we might "enrich" the field by inserting features that are progressively more veridical (or simply inserting more features) to see how much additional information is required to get genuinely veridical estimates.[5]

The possibilities are myriad. It remains only to revive interest in an area of research long neglected, but of undeniable interest to researchers in many fields. ∎

NOTES

1. Prior to this time, interest in imagery had centered about the relative "clarity" of images — such issues as identifying characteristics of "eidetic imagers" were then central. The distortions which occurred in imagery, particularly in successive reproductions, later occupied the interest of some. The emphasis here is upon what might be called the "metric characteristics" of specifically spatial or geographical imagery, a subject heretofore largely neglected.

2. We shall call this the "virtual trip."

3. This is the nature of the work reported by Kevin Lynch in his book *The Image of the City.*

4. It would be ideal if we had some form of control over the previous environments of our human subjects. Such, of course, is impossible; we cannot dictate where they shall

live (or shall have lived); even if we could, the period of environmental learning is much too long to yield an experiment which could be realized within any reasonable period of time. What we can do, however, is to *simulate* the experiences of humans developing in environments of various forms by using animal subjects whose period of maturation is much shorter — hooded rats, for example (an organism with which the author has had considerable experience). One colony of rats could be raised in an environment in which all changes of direction were constrained to right angles (very much like the mazes presently used in many studies in psychology); another colony could be raised in an essentially "circular" environment where corners simply did not exist. These, of course, represent the extremes. At maturation these animals could then be tested in mazes with "variable-angle" turns; the degree of "confusion" experienced by these animals, defined in terms of difficulty experienced in solving the problem posed by this "variable" maze, would then be the datum of interest.

5. Borrowing the "sequential notation" devised by the architect Philip Thiel or utilizing slide sequences described by Gary Winkel and Serge Bouterline, which simulated visitor experiences at the Seattle World's Fair.

Stephen Kaplan
On Knowing the Environment*

This selection raises a number of issues. It attempts to describe the links between the perceptual mechanism and the cognitive mechanism. It suggests how the cognitive map could serve as an efficient means for storing predictive information. And finally, it points to some difficulties in the common philosophical view that equates knowledge with "truth."

■   "Knowing" is difficult to define. Some philosophers speak of knowledge in terms of "true propositions," but truth is an elusive quality. Most of what we know falls short of the "truth" in many respects. It is selective and hence incomplete; people disagree on matters of emphasis, thus denying the possibility of truth in any ultimate sense. Further, some convenient simplifications would surely be considered oversimplifications from someone else's perspective. And, as we shall see shortly, certain links or connections in what we know exist either only indirectly or not at all in the world.

*This is the first publication of this article. All rights reserved. Permission to reprint must be obtained from the author and publisher.

But to say, then, that people in fact know little or nothing is hardly helpful. The long-time resident of a given city "knows" a great deal that the first-time visitor does not, even though this "knowing" is necessarily flawed. This limited kind of knowledge is crucial to human functioning.

While it is difficult to define, or even to describe in a few words, a rough characterization of "knowing" might go something like this:

> Knowing is being able to see it in your head, to think about it a lot, to imagine it, to wonder about it, to feel it. Sometimes knowing something is being able to say it, but what one can say is often only a fraction of what one knows, and often what one says is far from what one really feels. Knowing is being able to figure out what it is when you have seen only a little bit. Knowing is being comfortable and familiar and being able to guess what might happen next and what you would do about it if you had to. Knowing is having lots of choices about how to get somewhere and, if you go part way wrong, finding your way without starting over again. Knowing is not getting lost, and not even having to worry about that.

COGNITIVE MAPS

The human environment is highly diverse, rich, and uncertain; the amount of potential information is overwhelming. At the same time, the human is faced with limited time to decide and limited capacity for holding information. The cognitive map is the structure that holds the information a person has about the environment.

Humans tend to store in memory primarily those events and objects they encounter frequently. These are grouped into classes or categories (Bruner, 1957a) or schemata (Attneave, 1957). Such a strategy for handling the richness of the environment might sound a bit familiar — as well it should. This is essentially the same scheme proposed in the previous chapter as a possible basis for perception. The internal representations of recurring objects and events constitute a basis for knowledge as well as a means of coping with the thorny problem of recognizing objects.

Having a collection of representations in one's head is a great help in identifying objects, but little help as a model of the environment. What one wants of a model (or map) is the capacity to see where one is going, not merely where one is. One would like, in other words, to be able to predict from the knowledge of present objects or events what the likely future objects or events might be. A way that takes advantage of the collection of representations already available is through patterns of association between them. Let us assume that each is associated with representations of objects and events that are likely to come next. Going from one representation to its associated "next" representations may not seem very impressive, since it involves only a single predictive step. But from any next representation one can make still further predictions, since these representations have their associations in turn. This step-by-step pattern of associations thus defines a quite complex structure and permits predictive sequences that can be indefinitely long. And the resulting *network of representations* constitutes a cognitive map of the environment (S. Kaplan, 1973a; 1976).

In order to test whether this proposal is consistent with an intuitive notion of a mental map, consider an individual making his way through a large room cluttered with furniture without bumping into anything. Under ordinary conditions, one would hardly consider that this demonstrated an internalized map of the environment. But if the individual in question accomplished this feat with his eyes closed, the performance would be considerably more impressive. Clearly, when we refer to a cognitive map we mean that the individual has information about the environment that extends beyond what is perceived at the moment. The theoretical proposal made here satisfies this criterion in that the perception of the environmental circumstances leads (by association) to possible next alternatives, and from them to possibilities still farther down the road.

While this conception may be equated in a very rough way with the idea that a person has a "picture of the environment" in his head, the information is far more schematic and incomplete than "picture" implies, to say nothing of the fact that this "picture" will in general never have been seen all at once. A cognitive map is rather an abstraction. While an ordinary map is based on a continuous space, a cognitive map is based on familiar objects and events, connected by discrete paths. Such a structure is an approximation to the continuous environment. In areas of great experience, that approximation will be very close; otherwise, it may be extremely gross. Thus, for many young Americans, the United States is made up of the East Coast, the West Coast, and Denver. One can get from one to the other — the points are not disconnected — but the map is a rather crude approximation to continuity.

Thus, if the concept of "true propositions" is held as an ideal, then human knowledge is imperfect indeed. But the incompleteness, the abstractness, the sometimes gross "connectedness" are, from a functional perspective, strengths rather than weaknesses. They are, after all, characteristic of any model, of any viable attempt to comprehend enormous complexity.

Perhaps a story will provide a helpful illustration. Many years ago, so the story goes, a king requested that his advisors make him a model of his entire kingdom. This was done, and it was a fine model indeed, and the king was pleased. But the king was concerned that some important things had been left out, so the advisors built a model twice as big as the first. It too was very nice, but there were *still* impor-

"Knowing is being able to figure out what it is when you have seen only a little bit." Here a landscape is obscured by mist and light condition.

by Douglas Kinsey

tant things left out, so the king requested yet a bigger, more detailed model. It too was very nice, but . . . and at last the advisors offered the king a "model" that contained every detail in the kingdom — for it was the kingdom itself.

A model, then, must be an abstraction. It necessarily leaves out information. And since there are choices of what to leave out and what to emphasize, there are many possible models. But given a finite brain in a world of potentially overwhelming diversity and richness, models are characteristic of the ways humans know their world. While this accounts for some of the limitations of human thought, it also accounts for much of the power as well.

While the physical model (like a model railroad) is an engaging concretization of the idea of models, it should be emphasized that "models" as used here refers to any simplification of reality, any "as if" structure — whether in the head or on paper or embodied in epic tales — that is used to stand for, and to help comprehend, some aspect of reality. Physicists devise models to help them understand the structure of matter. Humans for eons have created and shared models that help explain why the seasons come as they do, why the stars are arranged as they are, and why some humans behave peculiarly. From the perspective of cognitive map theory, human knowledge itself is made up of internal models of various aspects of the environment. Indeed, having a model inside one's head is a great help in coping with the environment. It is doubtful that anyone has said this better than Kenneth J. W. Craik, the British psychologist and cyberneticist, did quite a few years ago:

> If the organism carries a "small-scale model" of external reality and of its own possible actions within its head, it is able to try out various alternatives, conclude which is the best of them, react to future situations before they arise, utilize the knowledge of past events in dealing with the present and future, and in every way to react in a much fuller, safer, and more competent manner to the emergencies which face it.*   ■

Terence R. Lee
A Theory of Socio-Spatial Schemata†

Lee, a British environmental psychologist, has provided an analysis that is far-reaching and striking in several respects. The theoretical content closely parallels the ideas developed previously in this book. A particularly valuable addition is the idea of "whereness," the spatial component that is a part of so much of our knowledge. (The student who knows exactly "where on the page" the answer is but — alas — not what it is will have no problem recognizing this concept. In a similar way, people with large bookcases often relate books on a particular subject to a particular spatial locus.) Lee's extension of the cognitive mapping idea to the concept of neighborhood is another important contribution. The empirical work on this topic impressively demonstrates both the ease with which people identify their neighborhood and the variability that exists from person to person.

*From K. J. W. Craik *The nature of explanation.* New York: Cambridge University Press. 1943. P. 61. Reprinted by permission.
†Reprinted by permission from T. R. Lee "Do we need a theory?" in D. V. Canter (Ed.) *Architectural psychology.* 1969. RIBA Publications, London. Pages 20–25.

■   We must begin with the assumption that man is an organism that survives only if it interacts appropriately with the environment. In fact, this interaction is what human behavior is about. The form it takes seems to rely only to a very small extent on programs that are built into the equipment at the time of birth. This is in marked contrast to more primitive organisms (with which environmental psychologists, beguiled by ethologists, are nonetheless reckless in drawing analogies) that rely on instincts that are triggered by environmental signals.

The human being has to learn two principal things about the environment. He has to learn the value to himself of different objects that he encounters and the location of these objects. The information comes to him through receptors tuned to the physical energy emissions of the objects, but he is saved the inefficiency of constant exploration and discovery by having a huge capacity for storing the residue of past sensations. This storage mechanism of learning and remembering about the environment does not, however, take the simple form of a static accumulation of bits of knowledge heaped up in order of arrival. On the contrary, we seem to be equipped with a continuous sorting process in which fresh information is allocated to existing material of the same kind. It is dispatched to relevant departments and if necessary duplicated many times and sent to a variety of places. We thus each have unique bundles of information about different aspects of the environment, and these are slowly and laboriously constructed in our central nervous system during the course of repeated actions and probably after the actions are terminated.

As children develop, these inner representations become more and more accessible to examination by the child in the absence of the external "real" objects themselves. In other words, they form images or "schemata" which are open to inspection at any time. They also serve the function of endowing meaning to fresh input which cannot be experienced in isolation from what is there already. In a true sense, then, the environment — both natural, social, and built — becomes a unique representation in the nervous system of people who experience it. Once the process has begun, every new perception is an act of construction following referral and it always modifies the organism to some extent either then or later.

However, what we have been describing so far is familiar enough; it is an attempt to account for the ways in which human beings learn to distinguish between objects in the environment — to know about their value or "whatness." Environmental psychologists need to concern themselves also, it seeems to me, with the hitherto neglected aspect of "whereness."

The necessary or desired objects are scattered about in the environment and separated by something we call space. Space is a nonobject; it cannot be touched, poured, seen, heard, broken, bent, or holed. It can only be experienced indirectly as an interval between objects, just as time can only be experienced as an interval between events. The size of the interval must depend on our experiences of journeying between objects. These phenomena are so basic to existence in the environment that in addition to coding information about the "whatness" of objects, we simultaneously code and store information about their "whereness." It is virtually impossible to conceive of an object that does not have a correlated spatial tag.

Even objects such as grass which appear at first to be everywhere are coded as somewhere, and we would be surprised to find it sprouting out of our breakfast table or growing on the roof of the car. We would be equally disturbed to find the moon sitting on the grass, or a plate of sausage and mash caught in the branches of a tree. This is because although the "whatness" of these objects is entirely familiar, they also have a "whereness" which has been thoroughly embedded in our brain and which governs our behavior. Without this knowledge we could not locate objects, and a large part of behavior consists in making journeys within a range from arm's length to the space separating the earth from the moon. It is man's extraordinary capacity for navigation and mobility and the factors that determine it which should, in my opinion, form the basis for a theory of environmental psychology.

Every journey which he undertakes must involve a more or less conscious deliberation similar to a profit-and-loss accounting. He has to consider the rewards of arriving at a goal (for which he refers to his whatness schema) and the costs of traveling. The latter will include the regrettable consideration that if we navigate towards one object we cannot be simultaneously enjoying another if this is situated elsewhere. More obviously, however, we have to refer to our spatial schemata to be apprised of the whereabouts of the object and how much energy will need to be expended in reaching it. It is this subjective or phenomenal calculation, based on a unique and personal perception of the world, that determines whether we move towards a goal.

Our next requirement is a plan. We have the capacity to evoke and examine long sequences of images. This is experienced (presumably because we have learned early on to make the real world stand still while we travel through it) as an impression of the self moving through a static image — although, of course, it must be that we are running a sequence past a window in consciousness and running it much faster than in direct behavior. A simple test of this mechanism can be readily experienced by asking oneself how many road intersections there are between any two familiar points in a city. Sometimes the plan is very patchy and we begin to run off the behavior itself in the confident hope that as we advance into the environment fresh input will revive more spatial schemata which will help us to complete the plan. The schemata, which can be consulted or ignored, sorted, ordered, and conjoined are the raw material of imagination, thought, dreams, and plans. Spatial schemata, like all others, are structures that become organized for particular purposes. We first develop a body schema, then establish succeeding layers, each inclusive of the preceding one and concerned, for example, with rooms, houses, streets, neighborhoods, cities, counties, countries, the world, universe, etc. Put together, they are the space we inhabit and the images we select from in order to form a plan.

For the large majority of navigations, we merely refer to these schemata. Their very uniqueness does lead to difficulty, however, as soon as we need to coordinate our behavior in space with other people who undoubtedly have somewhat different systems. This awkwardness is overcome by the development of large numbers of techniques designed not only to extend the range of accurate navigation but also to proceed by commonly shared standards. Thus we develop rules, compasses, maps, plans, diagrams, and so on which require us to take the further step in mental operation of converting images into symbols. We can specify a location by a map reference or a compass bearing and describe a journey with a chain of words.

This "error" is removed in modern maps by the adoption of standardized measuring techniques for distance and direction. Even then, however, the external symbolization can only be used to create, revive, or reinforce the internal schema — or to communicate it from one person to another. It cannot itself program an action sequence, only a schema can do that. Moreover, the existence and indeed the use of an accurate map does not preclude a person from behaving in accordance with a subjective "inaccurate" schema.

Probably the greatest advantages of symbolization are in storing a greater quantity of spatial information than can be carried by a single individual, in storing it more durably than the central nervous system, and in providing a means of conjoining the schemata of more than one person.

It is interesting to note that the many forms of map, plan, and itinerary are no more than externalized representations or symbols of the internal schemata. They do not exist until they are made by man, and there are two stages, the perceptual and the executive, at which distortion can occur.

If every individual develops through learning in the environment a repertoire of schemata which govern his mobility, these can be used as mediating variables in a theory. There must be lawful relationships between the physical environment and the types of schemata and a further set which link the schemata to behavior. Since we are dealing with correlated bundles of stored perceptions, the number of connections need be much smaller than if we were dealing with piecemeal units. It is the discovery of such relationships which should concern us and this becomes quite feasible if we ask people to externalize their schemata by converting them into a drawing or a verbal description. These can then be compared with the physical environment in which they developed and the behavior which they give rise to.

The remainder of this paper will be devoted to a brief description of some applications of this approach.

SOME APPLICATIONS OF THE THEORY

The urban neighborhood: Perhaps the most contentious problem in postwar planning has been that of the urban neighborhood unit. This is a concept which emerged as a reaction to the drab and anonymous uniformity of uncontrolled housing development in the thirties. The notion is not rigidly defined, but characteristically it is recommended that a "socioeconomically balanced" residential population of about 10,000 people be given a distinct identity by emphasizing the boundaries of an area with flanking main roads, green belts, etc. A school, a community center, and a shopping precinct should be at the focus of a radial network of residential roads. Many of the houses will be of the Radburn, or path-access, variety. Industry is to be sited at the edges of units. The aims are aesthetic, economic and, most important, social; i.e., to create a "sense of community."

The neighborhood unit has a long history with a strong flavor of social idealism. It has been supported by many of the most eminent architects and planners and officially adopted for much postwar development, including most of the early New Towns. There has, however, been a pervading air of doubt about the principle on the grounds that it is an outmoded "village green" form of planning, more nostalgic than real, and wholly inappropriate for the supposedly highly mobile city dweller of the twentieth century.

The investigation (Lee, 1957a; Michelson, 1969; Peterson et al, 1969; Sanoff, 1969) was a limited attempt to evaluate the principle. The theoretical approach tried to circumvent a problem that has been troubling sociologists for some years, that is, whether the urban neighborhood is a social group of mutually interdependent residents or a piece of urban territory. It did this by measuring neighborhood in the place where it appears to be most salient, that is, in the minds of people. It was found that far from being a defunct phenomenon, its boundaries could be drawn on a map by a high proportion of the housewives who were interviewed, so strongly conscious were they of a section of their locality which was distinctive both in people and place.

When the maps were superimposed, however, there was almost

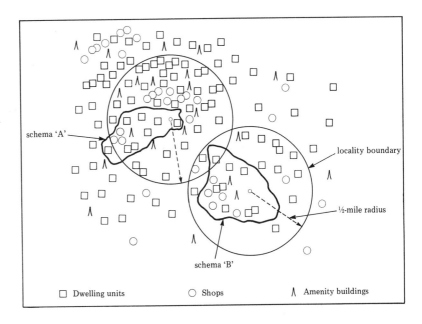

FIGURE 1

Examples of two neighborhood schemata. The average area of neighborhood remains constant across wide variations in housing density. By expressing the content of neighborhoods (in terms of the number of houses, shops, amenity buildings) as a ratio of the content of a standard half-mile radius locality, it is possible to compare their physical and social composition.

no coincidence of boundaries, even for residents living close to one another. It appears that neighborhood, though highly salient, is personally unique.

The next step was to analyse the causes of individual differences in a sample representative of the city. This was done by making a complete count of the houses, shops, and amenity buildings in each neighborhood and comparing this with a similar count for a standard physical environment, the half-mile radius drawn about the subject's house (figure 1).

The area of neighborhoods, though varying widely, is not related to density of population. People do not delineate an optimal number of local residents but a piece of individual territory (average size about 75–100 acres, i.e., about 30–40 hectares) and the number of residents follows from the prevailing density. The social and physical aspects of an individual schema are, however, inseparable. Certain people are included in neighborly awareness (not necessarily overt interaction) because they live within the selected territory, but the territory is extended or contracted to include or exclude selected people.

By expressing the size and complexity of the neighborhood in quantitative terms, corrected for differences in the locality wherein it occurs, it was shown that there is a dimension of neighborhood involvement which is related to other variables such as age, social class, length of residence, and the location of husband's work.

Brennan's Law: Another area that may be used to illustrate this general approach begins with shopping behavior. Brennan postulated from a planning survey in Wolverhampton (Lee, 1962) that housewives prefer to use shops in a downtown direction even when these are not the nearest. "This observation of the deflection from the true geographical pole of the magnetic pole attracting people's custom is so important to town planners that one may perhaps be permitted to speak of Brennan's Law" (Smith and Sargent Florence, 1948; Van der Ryn and Boie, 1963).

The empirical finding was amply confirmed by some data I collected in Cambridge, which is shown in figure 2. It will be seen that if housewives are divided into those whose nearest shopping subcenter lies in a downtown direction and those whose subcenter lies the other way, there is a substantial difference in shopping pattern. Usage is very high when proximity and direction are both positive, but when the two variables are put in opposition, direction appears to be more influential than proximity.

Brennan's explanation was that people's behavior is not really violating the "principle of least effort" — it is merely that the local shopping subcenter is the place that they pass on their way to and from the town center. However, I found that local and town center journeys are only rarely combined, and although this does not exclude a perceptual explanation, it does imply that the subjective view of the city is not based on the frequency of overt behavior. It is also unlikely to be due to the increasing scale and attractiveness of the subcenter as one proceeds downtown, for in the present example the city had grown by the adsorption of large villages on the periphery and these provide subcenters of at least equal attractiveness.

It seems necessary to have recourse to a theory such as the sociospatial schema with a subjective metric that is partially governed by the value attached to the objects within it. Thus, the satisfactions provided by the center will impose a focal orientation on the city schema and a general foreshortening of all distances in a downtown direction. This deduction takes us well beyond shopping behavior, which would appear as a special case of a general principle.

It was tested by presenting a sample of students with twenty-two assorted distance estimations to be made within the city of Dundee. They recorded each judgment separately on a linear scale marked off in one-mile intervals and, of course, in random order. However, the desti-

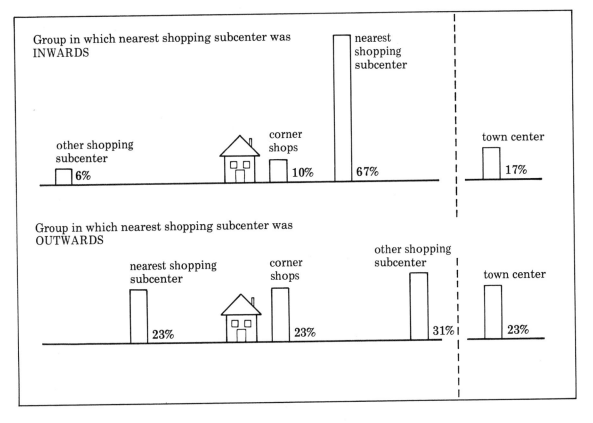

FIGURE 2

Data from "Brennan's Law" of shopping behavior. Percentage of people using different shopping locations for daily food shopping.

nations were selected in eleven pairs of roughly equal distance, but with one of each pair being an inwards journey and the other an outward journey.

The results are shown in figure 3. It appears that there is a general tendency operative. In almost all cases the outward journey is overestimated more than the inward and the effect is highly significant statistically.

A plausible alternative explanation was that the downtown journeys may be more complex, containing a greater variety of valued objects and hence interesting experiences and that this (to draw an analogy from findings in the related area of time-perception) may make the journeys subjectively shorter.

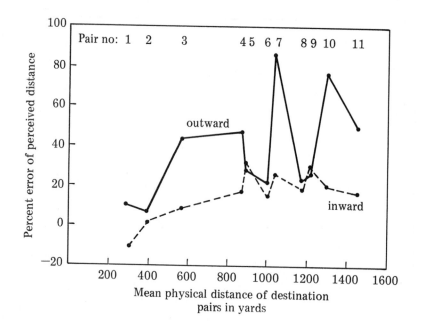

FIGURE 3

Rank order of destination pairs by distance

This was tested by comparing the estimations made within an experimental design that considered three variables — inward/outward; complex/simple; and towards/away from a single base. In this study, the inward/outward distinction was again shown to be significant. The other variables showed no effect on estimations, but the number of journeys involved was small and the results must be considered tentative.

There is one further variable of the physical environment that apparently has some influence on the formation of spatial schemata of the city. This is the linearity of journeys. It is not yet possible to say whether this factor could be related to Brennan's Law, but it certainly has applications to the design of both the inside and outside of buildings.

The hypothesis is that straight-line journeys appear shorter than multicornered ones and that the size of the effect is a function of the number of corners. It has not yet proved possible to test this in the field, but a simulation using lines has given positive results. The subjects were asked to manipulate an extensible line apparatus and to adjust it to equality with a series of presented diagrams. Lines of three lengths and with 0; 3; 5; 7 corners were used and the distance between starting point and destination was kept constant for each line length.

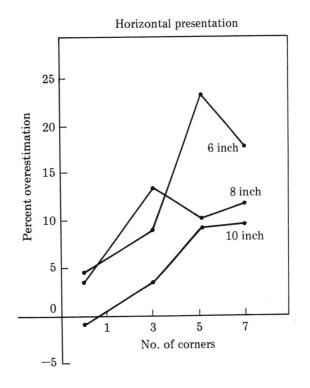

Horizontal presentation

FIGURE 4

Visual estimation of length as a function of number of corners (unpublished data)

The results, which are shown in figure 4, indicate an overestimation of length which increases with number of corners.

THE SOCIO-SPATIAL SCHEMATA OF RURAL INFANT CHILDREN

My final example is drawn from an educational problem. For some years now rural education authorities have followed an administrative policy that involves the closure of small one- and two-teacher schools and the transportation of the displaced children to larger schools by bus or by an extended walking journey. There has been some misgiving expressed about the effects of this policy on rural communities and on the children themselves. In the latter case, with which we are concerned, anxiety has centered on the possibility that children undertaking long journeys may be fatigued and possibly fractious on arriving at school.

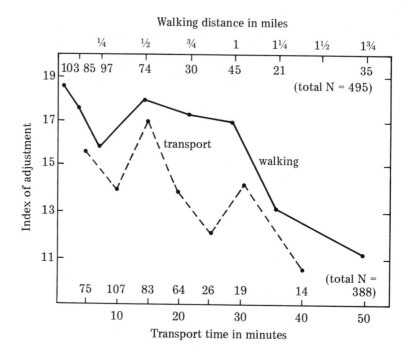

FIGURE 5

Index of assessed social-emotional adjustment (high score = "good" adjustment) as a function of school journey

The investigation (Lee, 1957b) was conducted in fifty-seven rural schools in Devonshire and involved 883 children aged between six and eight years. Measures were taken of the children's classroom adjustment in a series of assessments made by their teachers. These included such dimensions as "ability to concentrate," "aggressiveness," "response to affection," etc., and when it was shown that eleven from a total of thirteen such traits indicated the same pattern, they were combined into a single, "index of adjustment." This was then related to the length and type of journey undertaken by the children, and it was found that for both bus and walking journeys the adjustment of the sample progressively deteriorates with duration. The most revealing finding, however, was that children who travel by bus are more affected, time for time, than those who walk (figure 5). This, together with supporting evidence, effectively ruled out a fatigue explanation. The hypothesis that provides a better fit to the results is that children who walk to school have two familiar sociospatial schemata, the home and the school, which are well connected with a causeway of well-known, articulated territory which they perceive themselves as capable of crossing at any time and on their own volition. Bus children, on the other hand, have two quite separate schemata divided by a "no-man's-land" which they cannot traverse at all from the time the bus discharges them until about six hours later.

Enough has been said, I hope, to persuade you that a profitable way to advance knowledge and to facilitate predictions from the built environment towards human behavior is to include as mediating variables the organized inner representations of physical and social relationships which I have labelled sociospatial schemata. These are relatively easily available for observation either directly or by inference, and they do seem to reduce disorder in data and to add organization to our theoretical ideas. ∎

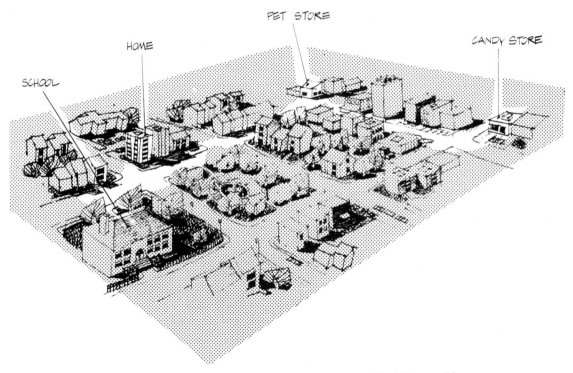

Landmarks in a small child's world
by Howard L. Deardorff

Donald Appleyard
Styles and Methods of Structuring a City*

This paper describes a study that was part of a planning project for a new South American city. The setting was ideal for an empirical study of cognitive maps. The city was not only new, but built over a highly complex terrain. The variety of cognitive solutions to the problem of comprehending the city is certainly striking. Also noteworthy is the fact that a planning effort included sophisticated behavioral research of this kind. For a more extensive treatment of the project, see Appleyard's *Planning a Pluralistic City: Conflicting Realities in Ciudad Guayana* (1976).

■   How do people relate different parts of the city to each other, how do they "place" themselves within the urban environment; in other words, how do they mentally structure the city? Kevin Lynch (1960) found that his subjects structured different cities by different elements. The inhabitants of Boston usually organized it as a set of loosely related districts, Los Angelenos tended to organize their downtown by its gridiron street system, while the people of Jersey City used the main roads and the view of Manhattan. Lynch also found that elements were related in varying degrees of accuracy, from those which were loose and free to those which were firmly interconnected or rigid.

In Ciudad Guayana, the new city in eastern Venezuela, we carried out a study of the inhabitants' maps of their local areas and the whole city, to explore further the several ways in which people structured cities and to see whether different groups in the population would structure the same city in different ways. The city at the time of the interviews possessed certain unique features that distinguished it from other cities (figure 1). Thirty thousand people were living in a number of settlements located along a main road that meandered from the west to the east by the steel mill, past an airport, through a middle- and high-income new community, Puerto Ordaz, through a squatter settlement, Castillito, across a ferry, alongside and through the scattered ranchos of El Roble, to the old colonial-type rectilinear village of San Felix. The city therefore was generally linear with no dominant

*"Styles and Methods of Structuring a City" by Donald Appleyard is reprinted from *Environment & Behavior* Vol. 2, No. 1 (June 1970), pp. 100–116 by permission of the Publisher, Sage Publications, Inc. (Somewhat abridged)

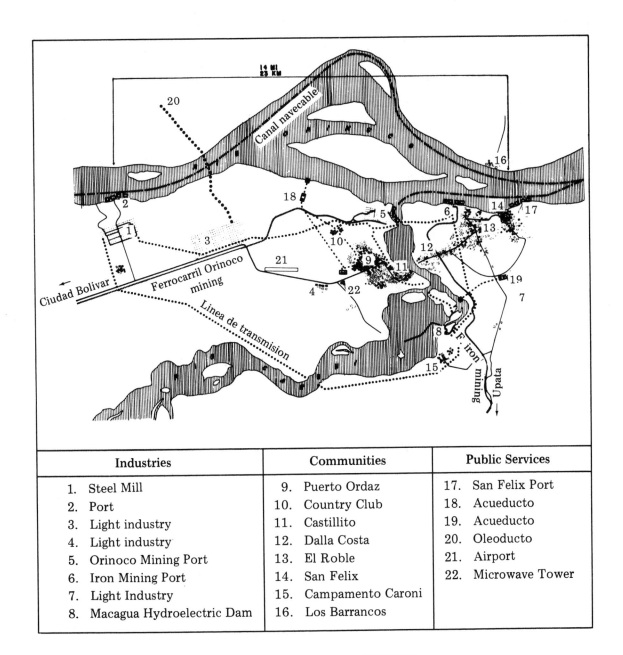

Industries	Communities	Public Services
1. Steel Mill	9. Puerto Ordaz	17. San Felix Port
2. Port	10. Country Club	18. Acueducto
3. Light industry	11. Castillito	19. Acueducto
4. Light industry	12. Dalla Costa	20. Oleoducto
5. Orinoco Mining Port	13. El Roble	21. Airport
6. Iron Mining Port	14. San Felix	22. Microwave Tower
7. Light Industry	15. Campamento Caroni	
8. Macagua Hydroelectric Dam	16. Los Barrancos	

FIGURE 1

Existing urban development. The map describes the existing settlements and infrastructure in 1964.

center. It was disrupted in its structure by the River Caroni and was flanked by the River Orinoco to the north and the Caroni Falls to the south. Each part possessed a somewhat different internal street system. Puerto Ordaz was made up of neighborhood units; Castillito had a ladder-like system; El Roble was amorphously spread around an acutely angled main road; and San Felix was a rectangular grid.

The city was also unique in that there was available no public map to assist (or contaminate) public perception of the city's structure.

DESCRIPTION OF RESPONDENTS

As described in the earlier article (Appleyard, 1969b), seventy-five respondents were drawn from Puerto Ordaz, Castillito, El Roble, and San Felix. In each area seventy-five units were selected and a quota system to ensure sufficient number in each age, sex, and education cell was established. The total sample (Appleyard, 1969b) contained a broad cross-section of the population. Respondents were distributed about evenly among those under twenty, those between twenty and thirty, and those over thirty years of age. Approximately one-half had received only a partial or complete primary education. One-sixth had been in the city under one year, and one-half lived there for less than five years. Over one-half traveled predominantly by bus, and about one-quarter each traveled by car or *por puesto* (collective taxi running along a set route). Two-thirds were male and one-third were female. Although only about one-half responded particularly to the map question, the cross-sectional proportions remained approximately similar to those of the general sample with slightly more losses from the aged, the uneducated, the unfamiliar, the female, and the bus-traveler groups.

METHOD OF INVESTIGATION

Among many other questions, respondents were asked to draw a map of the whole city between the steel mill and San Felix. They were also asked to draw a map of their local area. The questions follow:

Free Map Recall (General Map) Suppose now that here is San Felix and here is the Steel Mill, please draw a map indicating the points and places in the city you have just mentioned (places they could remember verbally). After that add any other important features that come to mind.

Free Map Recall (Local Maps) Please make a map of (___) and (___), including schools, the police stations, hospitals, markets, shopping areas, churches, places where people meet, the Concejo Municipal, CVG offices, political party offices and any other things which you think important to mention.

Each question naturally biased the responses slightly. The first, by stipulating the extremes in the city may have emphasized its linearity, the second by asking for facility locations probably emphasized landmarks, but the variety of the results suggests that the effects were slight.

TYPES OF MAPS

We analyzed the inhabitants' maps in two ways, first simply by scanning all the maps and grouping those that appeared to have similarities, second by looking at collections of maps produced by contrasting subject groups. The maps appeared to group along two dimensions, according to the *type of element* predominantly used, and according to their *level of accuracy,* that is their congruence with the objective plan of the city.

The maps predominantly used *sequential elements* (roads) or *spatial elements* (individual buildings, landmarks, or districts). The most accomplished maps employed combinations of both elements. In the sequential maps the parts were more obviously connected, and the connections were dominant. In the spatial element maps, parts were quite often scattered over the map and connections were apparently incidental.

Within each of these map types, four subtypes were identified. Within the sequential type there was a fairly clear gradation from the most primitive-looking, which contained *fragments* of sequences, through *chains, branch,* and *loop* maps to more complex and usually more accurate *network* maps. The spatial maps were more difficult to place neatly on any gradient. A number were *scatter and cluster* maps of dots, points, or names, and these appeared to be the most primitive. Another set were *mosaic* in form; still others were *linked.* The final group, the more accurately *patterned,* was the only spatial group that stood out definitely as more sophisticated and assured. Figure 2 diagrammatically illustrates the dominant types, and figure 3 reproduces one example of each type either from a local or a citywide subject map. Approximately 75 percent of the maps drawn concentrated primarily on the circulation system and were coded as sequentially dominant maps. Approximately 25 percent were spatially dominant maps.

Sequentially Dominant Maps

Fragment   The most primitive kind of sequential element maps consisted of fragments of paths or lists of elements unconnected to each other and frequently out of serial order. About 8 percent of all maps were of this type.

Chain   An equally simple but more schematic type of map treated the major east-west road with all its intersections, right-angle turns, and other bends as a straight line. Some of these maps were no more than lists of places encountered on this route, others swept the line around in a curve, a small concession to the complex curves and bends of the actual road system. About 13 percent belonged to this category. Another 20 percent were more accurate chain-type maps attempting to show all major bends, but they were undeveloped laterally. Some of these showed impressionistic bends, merely to indicate that the road contained them somewhere.

Topological

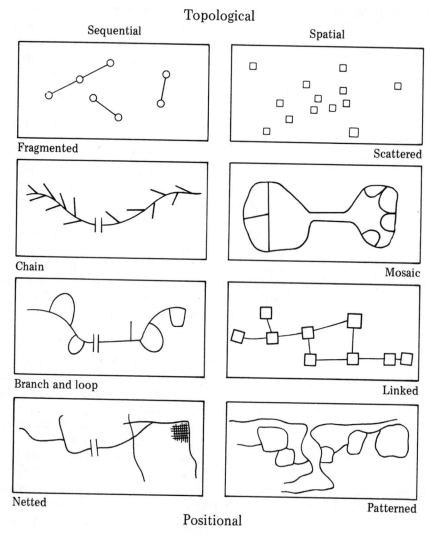

Positional

FIGURE 2

Map types[a]

[a]*Reprinted with permission from Planning Urban Growth and Regional Development (1969), by Lloyd Rodwin and Associates, p. 437. © 1969 by MIT Press, Cambridge, Mass.*

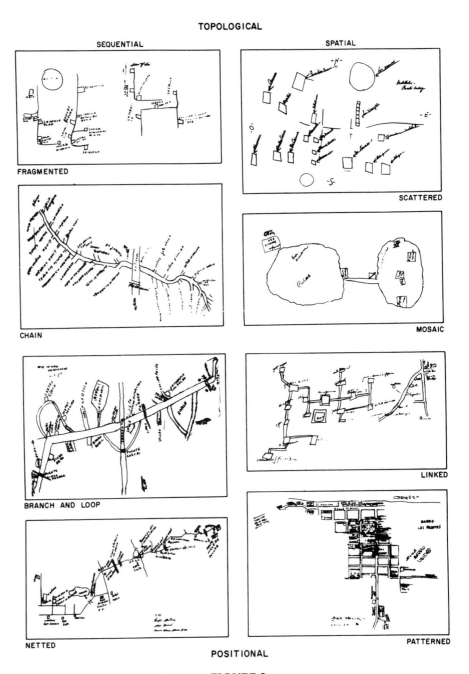

FIGURE 3

Examples of map types[a]

[a]*Reprinted with permission from Planning Urban Growth and Regional Development (1969), by Lloyd Rodwin and Associates, pp. 438–9. © 1969 by MIT Press, Cambridge, Mass.*

Branch and Loop   More laterally developed maps contained loops and branches as common outcrops from the basic linear system. The loops were often drastically simplified versions of circuitous routes, as in the case of the route up to the Centro Civico in Puerto Ordaz. Twenty-one percent of the maps belonged to this type.

Network   More complete road systems, often incrementally and laboriously constructed, and in many cases accurate representations of the true city, were produced by only about 15 percent of our sample. A few of these maps were schematically laid out, with the rivers outlined and the roads correctly located. These may have been drawn by the few subjects familiar with a map of the city.

Scatter and Cluster   The most primitive spatial maps contained elements like individual buildings or establishments which would be grouped together freely without any drawn connections. Frequently just the names were distributed over the sheet. Not all of these maps were inaccurate. Some distributed the elements more or less in their correct spatial positions. This technique was used more in local areas where the direction and distance of each point appeared to be positioned in relation to the home that was the place of interview. As many as 11 percent of the respondents constructed scatter maps; 6 percent clustered the elements.

Mosaic   The enclosure of districts by schematic boundaries and their division into subdistricts, whether shopping centers or residential neighborhoods, created maps that were less specific or accurate than the scatter maps, yet plotted out major zonal relationships. These looked more like planners' zoning or neighborhood-unit maps. Only 4 percent belonged to this group.

Link   Places or districts were connected with schematic linkages, which occasionally stood for parts of the road system. The spatial units were, in any case, dominant. In maps of the whole city, only 1 percent were found to employ this method, but in their local maps 5 percent used this method.

Pattern   These were the more complete and the most accurate spatial maps, with the outlines of areas and rivers as dominant features. Like the network maps, they demonstrated a subject's ability to handle and draw maps, but comprised a mere 1 percent of our sample.

To summarize, the most common maps were the *chain type,* the *branch and loop,* and the *network,* followed by the spatial-type *scatter* map. The dominance of sequential maps confirms the importance of the path system as a structural organizer of the city.

But it must be emphasized that we do not gain a complete understanding of city structuring purely through examination of subject maps. The task of drawing a map can tell us a great deal about some structuring methods, but tells us little about structuring through visual imagery, association, or symbolism. More on this later.

What these different map types do emphasize is the extraordinary variety of methods that people use to conceptualize cities. The meaning of these results and their implication for planners and urban designers will be difficult to assess.

Group Differences in Structuring

Education   . . . The less educated employed no common method of structuring, although it was dominantly sequential. . . . Their maps tended also to be noninferential, predicting very little beyond direct experience. Several subjects drew zig-zag paths through San Felix without extending them to form the gridiron system. The river edges too would only be drawn where they were actually seen from the road.

The maps of the less educated conveyed a strong sense of subjective experience. Most of them were flow-dominant, describing their own journeys rather than the physical form of the transportation system. Even the people who distributed points in a scatter pattern seemed to be placing them in relation to their position at the time of the interview.

The more educated groups were able to draw the city more objectively, fitting their maps together more coherently, inferring more about the city, even from limited experience (Bruner, 1957b). They would sketch out the rivers and lay out the rectangular street pattern of San Felix as schematic concepts, and the maps would be well fitted to the sheet. They seemed better able to fit perceptual experience to plan concepts. Even so, only about 20 percent could produce network maps.

Inference did not always lead to accuracy. After three months in the city, a newly arrived European engineer drew in three railroad lines instead of the actual two. His previous experience told him to expect a railroad linkage between the steel mill and the Orinoco mining port, a connection that did not yet exist. Abstraction and inference enable an inhabitant to cope with larger areas and more complex environments more rapidly and with greater mastery, but he may miss the detail in his skimming of the information given.

Temporal Familiarity   The newcomers were a widely diversified group, so we expected very different degrees of structuring in their first year. Mobility would affect the rate at which they came into contact with the city; conceptual abilities would affect their speed of acquiring knowledge; travel mode would influence their methods of acquiring knowledge.

Nevertheless, there were some consistent variations along the dimension of familiarity. With increasing familiarity, the use of spatial elements became slightly more common. Newcomers produced overwhelmingly sequential maps (80 percent). Older residents did the same to a lesser extent (60 percent). First-year subjects produced more restricted maps. Fifty percent could draw only their own side of the Caroni River. On the other hand, newcomers of six months to one year made less errors per zone in the parts of the city that they could draw than longer-time inhabitants, indicating that their level of interest and concern was probably high.

Age   There were no striking differences between age groups except for a tendency of the under-twenties to emphasize sequential elements.

Spatial Familiarity   Spatial elements were more predominant in maps of inhabitants' local areas than those of other parts of the city. Even so, both were drawn in predominantly sequential style. There were more spatial element local maps in the old town of San Felix (46 percent) and the new community of Puerto Ordaz (32 percent) than in the other parts. This was probably due to the gridiron plan of San Felix and to the confusing street system of Puerto Ordaz.

We postulated that the classic type of urban schema would be spatially well developed in the home area, with strands of sequential knowledge stretching out into other areas of the city. The local area would be accurately positioned and well fitted together, the distant, unfamiliar world becoming progressively more amorphous, topological, and less accurately related, with locations imprecise and distances vague. While this was true to a degree in Ciudad Guayana, well-structured islands of knowledge in parts of the city other than local areas were common, particularly for those who lived outside the main centers.

Travel Mode   Variations in travel mode seem profoundly to influence structuring style. About one-half of our sample used buses as their dominant form of transportation, while one-quarter used cars or *por puestos*. There were, however, problems in distinguishing the influence of travel mode because most people used more than one mode. For the purposes of more precise analysis, we sorted out those that traveled solely by bus and solely by car.

Of the subjects who traveled only by bus, 80 percent were unable to draw a coherent map of the urban road system. All the maps found in this group were either scattered or fragmented. Although these subjects were low in education, they differed from an equivalently educated set who used *por puestos* or traveled by car.

There were several bus services in the city. In 1964 the buses traveled from the eastern terminal south of San Felix along an indirect route through several barrios before reaching the plaza in San Felix. They continued westward along an old route in El Roble rather than along the new shortcut, then directly across the river and through Castillito following another circuitous path through the camps of Puerto Ordaz. The sign "Circumvalacion" on the front of the buses aptly described the journey. Add to this the difficulty of seeing through the front window of a crowded bus, the agonizing slowness of bus travel in Ciudad Guayana, the absence of announcements at each stop, and the form of the bus riders' maps can easily be understood. This kind of experience seemed inevitably to lead to fragmentation and the creation of islands of knowledge with only schematic, vague, or unknown links in between.

All the maps drawn by the selected group of car-only travelers presented a coherent and continuous system. In the total sample of those who drew maps, however, distinctions between the travel groups were not as sharp, probably because each group was to some degree mixed. For both bus and automobile groups, sequential maps were more common, but among the citywide maps, 16 percent more auto-dominant travelers than bus travelers drew spatial element maps, and 30 percent more bus-dominant travelers than auto travelers drew sequential element maps. Automobile-dominant travelers developed their citywide maps more broadly, relying less on the individual routes, while bus travelers kept very much to repeated sequential journeys. Those traveling by collective taxi produced maps slightly more similar to the auto-dominant travelers, but less accurate than those of the other groups.

Occupation   The more accurate maps were drawn by business executives and skilled workers, the least accurate by housewives and professionals. The elements used by business executives, however, were dominantly spatial, while those of the skilled workers were overwhelmingly sequential, an interesting contrast in styles between maps that were equally accurate. The better-educated business executives were perhaps able to place elements positionally through acquaintance with maps of the city, while the skilled workers learned through regular daily travel. The poor showing of professionals has no obvious explanation.

CONCLUSIONS   There appear to be several important dimensions to the structuring of cities. Some are confirmed by the findings; others I shall only hypothesize here.

1   We know already from Lynch's work that cities can be understood and structured by different elements, either sequential or spatial. In the classification presented here, Lynch's paths and modes are considered sequential elements, and landmarks, districts, and edges group more or less under spatial elements. In Ciudad Guayana the sequential mode was dominant.

2   By comparing field surveys of *form, visibility, use,* and *significance* patterns (Appleyard, 1969a) with the inhabitants' maps, it was apparent that they were using each of these attributes to structure the city. Areas of similar physical character were frequently grouped together. At points on the road system where visibility was low, directional clarity on the maps was frequently lost. The influence of personal use on structuring was clearly evident in the chain maps which straightened out all physical kinks to create a continuous personal linkage between parts of the city. As for the influence of social and functional significance, one of our interviewers can serve as an illustration. She insisted on associating her neighborhood with the more prestigious but distant Puerto Ordaz, than with the physically adjacent but less prestigious rancho settlement of Castillito. Perceptual distance from a similar social area is apparently less than actual distance, while perceptual distance from a lower social group is greater than actual distance.

In addition, the power of names and naming systems over the mental structuring of cities should not be underestimated. Several maps were no more than distributions of names.

3   Three fundamental methods of relating parts of the city emerge from the map interpretations and the field surveys: the *associational* method, which depends on the differentiation, association, and patterning of functional, social, or physical character; the *topological* method, which depends on continuity and juncture of movement and character; and the *positional* method, emphasizing spatial placement, direction, and distance.

4   People appear to structure the city in *varyingly schematic* ways. Many subjects strove to fit their urban knowledge into a coherent schema. However, given the disjointed nature of the street system, extreme simplification was necessary. The meandering rivers and even the main east-west road connection with its acute-angled bends and intersections were frequently drawn as straight lines. Other subjects worked more incrementally, seemingly unable to grasp the larger structure of the city, adding sections of road or area together, or simply setting down disjointed fragments with little regard to overall placement. Schematic maps that attempted to grasp the pattern of the city in some simplified and systematic way were found both at the lowest levels of competence, where they suffered from oversimplicity, and at the highest levels, where maps were laid out in close congruence with the actual urban pattern. The better maps appeared to use a combination of deductive and inductive methods.

5 There was also evidence of *inferential structuring*. The European engineer who predicted, wrongly, the three railroad lines epitomized this influence. Those who drew a gridiron street system for San Felix were inferring also, probably from much more limited experience. Inferential structuring depends on a person's previous experience of cities, and the unconscious personal rules about environmental relationships that develop from that experience. As long as a city structure conforms to that of other cities, the inhabitant knows it will be relatively easy to structure. It is the unique aspects that confound the newcomer.

The influence of inferential structuring makes it very difficult to disentangle images derived from direct experience from those based on *interpretations* of given experience. It will be necessary to learn more about our generalized mental models of cities before the mental structures of a particular city can be properly assessed.

6 The differences in the structuring of population groups appear to be due more to *cognitive differences, travel mode,* and *familiarity* than to other personal variables.

The subjective map was found to provide a rich souce of information about urban perception, particularly when correlated with field surveys of the visible, functional, and social character of the city. Maps picture spatial relationships that are very difficult to verbalize. That they do not usually indicate visual imagery, however, makes it important to devise other survey methods to fill out exactly how people structure their cities. In more recent work on U.S. cities, we have used photo-sorting, film recognition, and actual travel through the city as part of the interview task, together with questions on route planning, route choice, and route imaging. We have also found it helpful to trace the personal histories of how people learned to travel around a city.

Here is not the place to draw the implications of such structuring methods for planners and other environmental designers. Suffice it to say that when planning, transportation, and design professionals plan new towns and cities, they usually structure them so that they read well at an altitude of 30,000 feet. The methods used by ordinary people on the ground are perhaps more relevant and, apparently, more interesting. ■

4 Caring

From the functional perspective developed so far, it would seem reasonable to say that if humans depended upon information for survival, then they would necessarily have to care deeply about it. Efficient perception and the capacity to store extensive information in a useful form are of little value if one is indifferent to whether they are ever used or not. The individual must, in fact, be strongly motivated not only to use them but also to seek circumstances that favor their use. At the same time, humans must also favor situations where they can extend their cognitive maps and dislike circumstances where they cannot.

Many human motives are in fact very closely tied to knowing and to finding out. People crave new information and at the same time are repelled by information too far from what they can comprehend and deal with. But these apparently contradictory themes are quite reasonable in the light of the evolutionary context introduced previously. That humans seek information is not suprising — they need it for survival. But that they avoid circumstances where the information is beyond their comprehension is reasonable also, since they would be helpless in such situations, lacking their most powerful tool.

One can thus view much of human motivation, and of emotion as well, as information-based. The need to comprehend, to make sense of one's environment, is pervasive and vital. At the same time, a cut-and-dried world with everything "under control" does not content us either. There is a lack of excitement and adventure in such a situation. Thus, a tension exists between understanding and finding things yet to be understood, between comfort in certainty and thrill in uncertainty. Boredom is no more desirable than chaos. We seek opportunities to be involved, to be "where the action is."

Each of the selections in this chapter bears on the centrality of these information-based concerns, though they were by no means all written from such a perspective. The first three pieces, by Coles, Cantril, and Hebb, pertain to the powerful and deep-rooted drive to *make sense,* to have a larger picture of things both in the momentary sense and in the long run. The remaining selections speak to the strength of the *desire for involvement,* even where it is clearly stress-increasing. But these two themes are frequently intertwined; many of the selections necessarily bear on both issues at the same time. These ideas are further developed in the short paper on attention and fascination that begins the chapter.

In the area of human/environment relations as a whole there is a striking lack of concern with the issue of human needs. One might think that what humans care about, what their psychological needs are, would be central to this growing area of study. Yet probably no topic is so systematically ignored. In some respects it is understandable that human needs have a near taboo status in environmental psychology. There may well be the concern that an attempt to identify such needs would generate an almost endless, perhaps random list. Further, there is the justifiable suspicion that diametric opposites might be involved: people might seek both excitement and tranquility; they might both be curious about new things and fear the strange.

There is some reason to believe, however, that the decision to ignore human needs is exceedingly costly. Back when things "just growed," when architecture without architects was the rule, the culture guided the design and structuring of space in ways that had satisfied a wide range of human needs at least reasonably well over the years.

But now we plan. We make explicit, (more or less) rational decisions, weighing in various factors of importance. But those factors that we cannot name, that we cannot identify, do not enter into the equation. And given our tendency to make the most of all identified factors, the unidentified ones are consistently slighted.

There have been, to be sure, some efforts to incorporate need-related factors. But many of these have been from an economic perspective, with an emphasis on scarcity or on market values or on some other variable more convenient than pertinent. (The inappropriateness of this type of approach is the focus of the next chapter.)

Another approach has been to apply the lists of needs that originally arose in the context of personality research and were popular in motivational psychology some years ago. These date from a time when the major human "environment" considered by many psychologists consisted of other people. Serious consideration of the role of the physical environment in human experience requires a fresh look.

Stephen Kaplan
Attention and Fascination: The Search for Cognitive Clarity*

This paper explores some possible relationships between human needs or motives and the patterns of stimulation provided by the environment. The central concept here is cognitive clarity, a state of mind characterized by a strong focus and the suppression of distraction. This state of mind is of vital importance to an information-based animal. Further, there are reasons for believing that it is in fact experienced as pleasurable, and conversely, that its absence is painful. Clarity can be thought of as an outcome of rapt attention, and attention, in turn, works best when something in the environment has the capacity to fascinate. Both content and process can contribute to fascination. Special contents that have this effect include things of great value, things of great danger, and other items of evolutionary significance like snakes, fire, water, etc. The processes that compel attention are those that both demand involvement and make sense. The greatest fascination tends to occur when content and process factors operate together.

■ The search for cognitive clarity is a pervasive human concern. The need is so strong that people will turn their backs on comforts and on traditional rewards to achieve it. For some, a move toward a simpler, more tranquil existence is an expression of this search. Others seek fulfillment through a group or movement that demands a strong commitment to a (sometimes bizarre) set of beliefs.

The importance of cognitive clarity is not solely, or even usually, at such a cosmic level. People have a great dislike for being confused, for having an unclear state of mind, in all sorts of situations. It does not take very many experiences of not understanding what's going on for a youngster to develop an enduring aversion to, say, mathematics. A graduate student demonstrated the same phenomenon when he became lost on his first venture into the university's graduate library. "I am never going in there again!" he announced.

Perhaps one of the most vivid examples of the failure of clarity in the experimental literature was reported by Bruner and Postman (1949). Participants were given brief glimpses of playing cards and simply had to identify the suit and number. Admittedly, some of the

*This is the first publication of this article. All rights reserved. Permission to reprint must be obtained from the author and publisher.

cards were printed in the opposite color from the way one is accustomed to seeing them, but on the other hand, the consequence of *not* recognizing them was hardly severe. In fact, a failure meant another chance with a somewhat longer duration. One participant, who continued to fail to recognize the cards even at a full-second duration, exclaimed: "I can't make the suit out, whatever it is. It didn't even look like a card that time. I don't know what color it is now or whether it's a spade or heart. I'm not even sure now what a spade looks like! My God!"* This was a relatively trivial situation and yet his statement shows that failure of clarity was responsible for a rather distressing experience.

Nonlaboratory examples of the intense reactions to simple failures of cognitive clarity are easily observed where modern art is on display. The often-heard reaction "What the hell is *that*?" vividly expresses the intensity of emotion. At the other extreme is the identity crisis. Even well-fed, well-liked, and well-reinforced people have been known to become intensely uncomfortable because of a state of confusion about themselves. Not knowing who one is or where one is going or what it is all about can lead to depression and even suicide. Cognitive states can have profound motivational consequences.

Confusion might well have disastrous consequences for an organism that evolved under intense pressure to handle information adroitly. Without a clear state of mind an individual is in no shape to recognize subtle patterns, to anticipate the future, and, most important, to take prompt, decisive action. From an evolutionary perspective, liking clarity and disliking confusion would be essential.

TWO KINDS OF ATTENTION

While little research in psychology bears directly on cognitive clarity, the concept of attention, which is closely related, has been studied extensively. Traditionally, attention has been thought of in the context of stimulus selection rather than of clarity. But when attention is successful, all the stimulation has a common focus. Clarity, then, is the outcome of successful attention.

The concept of attention received some of its most thoughtful analysis quite a few years ago. In 1892, William James put forward several basic distinctions that form the basis of this paper. *Voluntary attention,* in James's terminology, is attention that requires effort. When one is tempted by distractions, but pays attention, as it were, by an effort of the will, that attention is voluntary. By contrast, some attention occurs in spite of ourselves. It not only requires no effort, it would take an effort not to attend. Something very beautiful might call forth attention of this kind, but so might something strikingly ugly, or potentially dangerous. James calls this kind of attention *involuntary.*

*From Bruner, J. S. and Postman, L. "On the perception of incongruity: a paradigm." *Journal of Personality,* 1949, 18, p. 218. Copyright 1949 by Duke University Press.

Voluntary attention is all too familiar. We fall back on it constantly as we make our way through the dull but necessary requirements of everyday existence. So much of what we do has little intrinsic fascination and demands an effort to keep our minds on the task. Indeed, it might be argued that in the modern world, the interesting is no longer important, and the important, no longer interesting.

The effect of this effort to stay with the task is the suppression of all potential distractions. Some mechanism, presumably inhibitory, must play this role. The more stimuli that must be attended to, even though not particularly gripping in themselves, the more this mechanism must be brought into play. Likewise, the more distractions there are, the more stimuli that must be ignored, then the greater is the need for this mechanism. As Milgram (1970) has pointed out, the city is an environment of overwhelming stimulation, a source of stress to which people respond by growing more insensitive. One can readily see how the stresses of modern life could lead to the fatigue of the mechanism that suppresses distraction. Recovery presumably requires resting this overworked capacity. This could be achieved by avoiding circumstances that require an effort to pay attention. Thus, recovery of voluntary attention could ultimately hinge on the availability of environments that were involuntarily interesting. If nature could be shown to have this property, then the popularity of natural settings for recovery from overload and stress would make considerable sense.

James distinguishes two kinds of involuntary attention, which he calls the immediate and the derived. The derived is based on experience, as (in James's example) the reaction to a faint tap on the window pane when it is a prearranged signal between lovers.

The immediate form of involuntary attention has a strikingly primitive flavor, as is clear from James's list of examples: "strange things, moving things, wild animals, bright things, pretty things, metallic things, words, blows, blood, etc. etc. etc." (p. 231). This colorful list is rich in implications. First, it suggests that "immediate involuntary attention" involves the property of fascination. At the same time, James's list shows the close linkage to evolution; survival may well have depended upon paying immediate attention to stimuli of this kind. Another striking aspect of this listing is its very unsystematic character. Its disorder and incompleteness, even to James's exuberant use of "etc.," fairly cries out for a more orderly, more coherent framework.

SOURCES OF FASCINATION

Such a framework follows readily from the evolutionary significance of this process. An individual's likelihood of survival would be enhanced if certain kinds of patterns or events were innately fascinating, if attention required no effort. These might include circumstances where it was likely that useful new information could be acquired (as in watching a highly skilled individual carry out some task). It would also be adaptive for potentially dangerous situations to be fascinating. If such situations were simply perceived as bad or painful, the reaction might be headlong flight without calculation or strategy. But fascination with potential danger would lead to the close scrutiny of the situation called for in a creature whose survival was far more dependent upon wits than speed (S. Kaplan, 1976). Such fascination would also make possible the group cooperation and group defense that is characteristic of many primate groups. Headlong flight is rarely conducive to cooperative efforts.

Thus, a variety of circumstances — the potentially educational, the potentially dangerous, the potentially important in one way or another — would appropriately be fascinating to humans. To identify these circumstances would require a research program of major proportions. One might, for example, present visual patterns on a screen and observe people's behavior. Any stimuli that failed to hold people's rapt attention would be discarded and replaced by others until one had a vast collection of material, all of which had proven fascination value.

Fortunately for our purposes this research has already been carried out, and on a large scale. It is called "television," and it provides an excellent overview of what people in fact find fascinating. For those who decry modern trends of this kind, and long for a simpler time gone by, the circus constitutes a similar experiment — and leads to similar conclusions.

Based on these and other circumstances that elicit rapt attention in humans (e.g. zoos, auto racing, theater), the various aspects of fascination emerge. A central distinction appears to be between content and process.

Content

The contents that people find fascinating presumably are related to coping with the environment, just as the basic processes are. Thus, it is hardly surprising that people have strong reactions to wild animals. In fact, wild animals are so fascinating that compounds where such creatures can be viewed by the public are available in most of our major cities.

Snakes are legendary in this respect. While their powerful hold on attention might be argued to have cultural roots, it could also be that so many cultures deal with snakes in their mythology precisely because they hold the attention so powerfully. (Chimpanzees too show a strong reaction to snakes — even if they are reared in captivity and have never seen one before.)

Snakes are not the only animals to hold attention. Wolves and bears elicit particular interest, as do any animals that are particularly large. There are also strong reactions to the young of many species.

by Douglas Kinsey

Needless to say, among the most fascinating of animals to the human are fellow humans. This is true not only in the sense of "people watching" as "sport," but in the content of much that the television "research program" exemplifies.

Green things too have their special claim on human attention. Gardens (R. Kaplan, 1973; Lewis, 1977), parks, wilderness, even house plants (Iltis et al., 1970) reflect this area of fascination. While television seems not to specialize in this domain, efforts to evoke a feeling of tranquility (e.g. cigarette commercials) tend to rely heavily on patterns of natural vegetation.

The preference for green things blends into the related issue of landscape preference. Here water must be added as a powerful (and evolutionarily appropriate) factor. A host of other factors are involved at this scale; while there is not the space to discuss them here, they are quite consistent with the overall emphasis on attention and survival (S. Kaplan, 1975).

This variety of fascinating living things readily merges into various survival-related physical phenomena. Here we might include fires, caves, the weather (especially bad weather), and miscellaneous natural hazards. We might also include certain transformed portions of the environment that humans have altered, adapted, or constructed for their own use. Shelters, tools, and food would be good examples.

This collection of fascinations may sound more like the preoccupations of a myopic caveman than like things that concern modern people. But urban children still are fascinated by fires (Ladd, 1977); an occasion that involves free food (or drink) is still very attractive even to people who could well afford to buy their own; and even today people with little else in common talk about the weather.

Process

The process that people find fascinating is, in the largest sense, the process of coping with uncertainty (S. Kaplan, 1973a). There are two critical facets of this process. They complement each other and together encourage the acquisition and utilization of information likely to foster survival in an information-oriented organism.

Making sense is the first of these; recognizing (e.g. bird watching) and predicting (e.g. gambling) are frequently fascinating and are the basics of the making sense process. People are strongly motivated to comprehend, to understand. Insight is fun, confusion is painful, and being lost, as Lynch (1960) has convincingly argued, is frequently adequate grounds for panic.

Involvement is the other key facet of the process. Curiosity and exploration are familiar examples. The fascination of these activities is so well known that it hardly needs discussion. Involvement is also the underlying issue in circumstances that are difficult or even dangerous but where strong positive feelings exist nonetheless. Challenge, which involves an effort undertaken, at least in part, because of the uncertainty or risk involved, provides a familiar example of this.

Purpose, too, fits a similar pattern. However, in the case of purpose there tends to be a long lookahead, that is, a focus on a more distant goal. The focus on a desired outcome that characterizes purpose contrasts with the overcoming of danger and uncertainty that is, after all, what makes a challenge challenging.

Making sense and involvement are complementary facets of a person's experience with the environment. They are neither mutually exclusive nor opposite ends of a continuum where some "optimal value" is desired. They are both necessary if fascination is to occur. Making sense without involvement characterizes the boredom with the familiar; involvement without making sense is the essence of being lost.

Some of the most frequently encountered areas of human fascination appear to be a tightly knit fabric of content and process. Two of these are of particularly great concern to humans, despite their rather intangible quality. While in one sense at opposite poles, they are nonetheless strikingly similar. People are fascinated with issues that pertain to the self on the one hand, and the cosmos on the other. The attention and interest an individual has available for personal matters, for information that provides perspective on one's own person, is widely recognized. But at the other extreme there is great concern for that larger framework within which one's daily experiences either do or do not make sense, either do or do not offer involvement. This larger framework is variously seen as one's values or the meaning of the universe or the operation of a higher power. Such a framework has the special property of not only making sense and offering involvement in itself, but also of attaching sense and involvement to many other activities and events as well.

The importance of these rather intangible areas of fascination is perhaps particularly acute when other problems are solved. Coping with danger, struggling to obtain shelter, foraging for food are activities with a great deal of built-in fascination. Solving these problems, while obviously highly desirable in most respects, also has the effect of eliminating the very activities that provided challenge and purpose for our ancestors and for many people today. It is ironic that the affluence and ease that are so attractive at a distance are capable of undermining clarity and even creating considerable pain. There is no doubt that people can be tough and resilient under conditions of hardship and difficulty. Whether they are comparably well equipped to thrive under conditions of leisure and plenty is still an open question. ∎

NOTE

This article is adapted from S. Kaplan's "Tranquility and challenge in the natural environment," a part of the Children, Nature, and the Urban Environment Symposium. Northeastern Forest Experiment Station, Upper Darby, Pa., 1977. This research was supported, in part, by the Forest Service, USDA (North Central Forest Experiment Station, St. Paul, Minnesota).

Robert Coles
A Domain of Sorts*

This selection begins the portion of the chapter that looks at the need for making sense as a possible component of human motivation. One might wonder how one would know if making sense was so important to people. If knowing where one was and what was going on was such a vital consideration, how might this need be expressed? Here Coles provides imagery in the context of rural America, in this case among the Appalachian hollows.

■   They live up alongside the hills, in hollow after hollow. They live in eastern Kentucky and eastern Tennessee and in the western part of North Carolina and the western part of Virginia and in just about the whole state of West Virginia. They live close to the land; they farm it and some of them go down into it to extract its coal. Their ancestors, a century or two ago, fought their way westward from the Atlantic seaboard, came up on the mountains, penetrated the valleys, and moved stubbornly up the creeks for room, for privacy, for a view, for a domain of sorts. They are Appalachian people, mountain people, hill people. They are white yeomen, or miners, or hollow folk, or subsistence farmers.

From the first months of childhood to later years, the land and the woods and the hills figure prominently in the lives of mountain children, not to mention their parents. As a result, the tasks and struggles that confront all children take on a particular and characteristic quality among Appalachian children, a quality that has to do with learning about one's roots, one's territory, as a central fact, perhaps the central fact of existence.

In Wolfe County, Kentucky, I became rather friendly with a whole hollow of Workmans and Taylors, all related to one another.† The Workmans had followed a stream up a hill well over a century ago, and Kenneth and Laura Workman are there today, in a cabin in Deep Hollow, so named because it is one of the steepest hollows around. Kenneth Workman is forty as I write this. He is now a small farmer.

*From Robert Coles "A domain of sorts." *Harper's* (November 1971). Pages 116–117. Copyright 1971 by *Harper's Magazine*. Reprinted by permission. Other portions of this article appear in chapters 8 and 9. Article based on Vol. 2 of *Children of Crisis: A Study of Courage and Fear*.

† At the request of the people mentioned in this essay I have changed their names and some place-names.

He used to dig for coal in the mines down in Harlan County, Kentucky, but he was lucky enough to lose his job in 1954. Many of the older men he worked with also lost their jobs around that time, when the mines were becoming increasingly automated, but they came back to Wolfe County sick, injured, often near death.

"If we're going to be good parents," Kenneth told me, "we've got to teach our kids a lot about Deep Hollow, so they can find their way around and know everything they've got to know. It's their home, the hollow is. People who come here from outside are not likely to figure out that we've got a lot of teaching to do for our kids outside of school, and it's not the kind they'll get in books. My boy Danny has got to master the hollow; that's what my dad used to say to me; all the time he would tell me and tell me and then I'd be in good shape for the rest of my life."

How does Danny get to master the hollow? For one thing, he was born there, and his very survival augurs well for his future mastery. Laura received no medical care while she carried Danny; the boy was delivered by his two aunts, who also live in Deep Hollow. Danny's first encounter with the Appalachian land took place minutes after he was taken, breathing and screaming, from his mother. Laura describes what happened: "Well, as I can recall, my sister Dorothy came over and showed him to me, and then he was making so much noise we knew he was all right. His birthday is July tenth, you see, and it was a real nice day. She brought me a pail of blackberries that she'd picked and she said they were for later. When Danny was born Dorothy took him over and showed him the blackberries and said it won't be long before he'll be eating them, but first he'll have to learn to pick them, and that will be real soon. Then he was still crying, and she asked me if I didn't think he ought to go outside and see his daddy's corn growing up there, good and tall, and the chickens we have, and Spot and Tan, because they're going to be his dogs, just like everyone else's. I said to go ahead, and my sister Anne held me up a little so I could see, and the next thing I knew the baby was out there near Ken's corn, crying as loud as he could.

"Ken held him high over his head and pointed him around like he was one of the guns being aimed. I heard him telling the baby that here was the corn, there was the beets, and there was cucumbers, and here was the lettuce, and there was the best laying chicken we've got. Next thing he told the baby to stop the crying — and he did, he just did. Ken has a way with kids, even as soon as they're born. He told him to shush up, and he did, and then he just took him and put him down over there, near the corn, and the other kids and my sisters all stood and looked. Dorothy was going to pick him up and bring him back to me, but Ken said he was fast asleep and quiet, and let him just lie there and we should all go and leave things be for a while. So they did; and Ken came in and told me I'd done real well, and he was glad to have a red-haired son, at last, what with two girls that have red hair but all the boys with brown hair. He said did I mind the little fellow lying out there near his daddy's farm getting to know Deep Hollow, and I said no, why should I."

Shortly after each child of hers is born the boy or girl is set down on the land, and within a few months he is peering out at it, moving on it, turning over on it, clutching at wild mountain flowers or a slingshot (a present from an older brother) or a spoon (a present from an older sister). Next comes crawling; and mountain children do indeed crawl. They take to crawling and turning over and rolling down the grass and weeds. They take to pushing their heads against bushes and picking up stones and rocks. They take to following sounds, moving toward a bird's call or a frog's. I have rarely seen mothers like Laura Workman lift up babies like Danny and try to make them walk by holding them and pulling them along.

"I never hurry a child. The Lord made them the way He did, and when they're going to do something they're going to, and that's what you have to know."

Certainly she does know that; and she also knows that the chances are her children will leave her very early to wander far over the hills — and in so doing stay close to what she considers "home." When her children grow up, however, she expects they will have little interest in going any farther away than they have already been — even as many other American children, kept relatively close to their parents' small front yard or backyard during early childhood, begin to leave home almost with a vengeance when older. At three, Danny had been all over his father's land, and up and down the hollow. He would roam about with his older brother or sister, tagging after them, trying to join in with their work or play. He had learned how to pick crops and throw a line into a stream and catch a fish. He knew his way down the creek and up the hill that leads to the meadow. He knew about spiders and butterflies and nuts and minnows and all sorts of bugs and beetles and lizards and worms and moles and mice — and those crickets making their noise. He went after caterpillars. He collected rocks of all sizes and shapes; they were in fact his toys. He knew which branches of which trees were hard or soft, unbending or wonderfully pliable. He knew how to cool himself off and wash himself off and fill himself up — all with the water of a high stream. At three, he had been learning all that for about a year. ∎

Hadley Cantril
The Human Design*

This paper was written in the context of a multinational survey of people's satisfactions and concerns. The book reporting the results of this huge undertaking deals with various comparisons between different groups of people — between wealthy and poor nations, between people living under different forms of government, and the like. The final chapter in Cantril's book, the one included here, is composed of leftovers, of those results that did not vary from one nation to the other. They are, if you will, universals. They are not particularly well organized, and they seem to overlap one another to varying degrees. In fact, the reader may find it instructive to see if they can be recast in a more systematic fashion. Nonetheless, the portrait they provide of the human condition is profound and moving. Here is an organism admirable and sad at the same time, an organism both heroic and pathetic, and an organism deeply concerned with recognition, with comprehension, with prediction — in short, with information.

Thus, this paper makes two contributions of particular significance. It provides fresh evidence for the importance of information to our species. And, looked at the other way, it shows how rich and varied are the human concerns that have direct links in one way or another to information. It is surprising how many of Cantril's points speak to the importance of the quest to make sense — to understand one's world, one's circumstance, and one's self.

■   In describing the differences found among people in any study of wide scope, it is all too easy to neglect basic uniformities which take diverse forms in different cultural settings. Differences between individuals or groups of individuals are often dramatic and easier to detect than the similarities they may obscure.

I conclude this study, therefore, with a statement of what seem to be the demands human beings everywhere impose on any society or political culture because of their very nature. For human beings have a genetically built-in design that sooner or later must be accommodated. I shall try here to orchestrate the diversities of mankind found in different societies into some systematic unity.

*From H. Cantril *The pattern of human concerns*. New Brunswick, N.J.: Rutgers University Press. 1966. Chapter 16: The human design. Reprinted by permission.

1 *The satisfaction of survival needs.* Any listing of the characteristics of any living organism must begin here. Neurophysiologists have located and described in a most general way two built-in appetitive systems found in higher animals: one system propelling them to seek satisfying and pleasurable experiences, the other protecting them from threatening or unpleasant experiences. These two systems together can be thought of as the basic forces contained within all human beings which not only keep them and the species alive as their simple survival needs for food and shelter are gratified, but which are involved in the desire for life itself.

These appetitive systems of course become enormously developed, refined, and conditioned, especially in man, as new ways are learned to achieve satisfactions and avoid dangers and discomforts. But it has been noted over and over again that unless the survival needs are satisfied, a person devotes himself almost exclusively to fulfilling them. Most people in the world today were found to be still concerned with living a type of life that constitutes well-being on a relatively simple level with what amenities their cultures can provide.

2 *Man needs a sense of both physical and psychological security to protect gains already made and to assure a beachhead from which further advances may be staged.* Man wants some assurance that one action can lead to another, some definite prehension which provides an orientation and integration through time. People invariably become embittered if they nurse a dream for a long time with no signs of it becoming a reality.

The story of evolution tells us that members of every species stake out some territory for themselves within which they can provide for their needs and carry on their living. The extent of this territory depends on what is required for the survival of the species and it is extended if it will contribute to such survival. In the present era the territories human beings stake out for themselves are largely bounded by the nation-state, a territorial unit rapidly replacing narrower geographical and psychological identifications but doing so just at the time when it is becoming more and more apparent that the concept of nation itself limits and threatens man's development in an age of increasing interdependence and highly developed weaponry.

3 *Man craves sufficient order and certainty in his life to enable him to judge with fair accuracy what will or will not occur if he does or does not act in certain ways.* People want sufficient form and pattern in life to be sure that satisfactions already enjoyed will be repeatable and will provide a secure springboard for take offs in new directions. The fears, worries, and apprehensions people express are by definition that their desires will not be attainable or that conditions beyond their own control will so upset the order of things that aspirations will not be realized.

The conflict of old loyalties with emerging new loyalties in the case of developing people is bound to create uncertainties, doubts, and hesitations. If these people become frustrated and anxious enough they will do almost anything in a desperate attempt to put some order into apparent chaos or rally around the symbols and abstractions of a new order that promises to alleviate the uncertainties experienced in the here and now.

In stressing process and change, the desire of people to preserve the status quo when it has proved satisfying and rewarding and to protect existing forms against alteration must never be overlooked. And the craving for certainty would include the satisfactions that come from the sense of stability provided by our habitual behavior, including much of our social and political behavior.

4 *Human beings continuously seek to enlarge the range and to enrich the quality of their satisfactions.* I have frequently emphasized the ceaseless quest impelling man to extend the range and quality of his satisfactions through the exercise of his creative and inventive capacities. This is, of course, a basic reason why order of any kind is constantly being upset. Alfred North Whitehead expressed the point eloquently in his statements that "the essence of life is to be found in the frustrations of established order" and that "the art of progress is to preserve order amid change, and to preserve change amid order" (Whitehead, 1938, p.119; 1929, p.515).

The distinguished British philosopher John Macmurray has used the phrase "the self as agent" as the title of his book analyzing the role of action in man's constant search for value satisfactions. And in a companion volume he has noted that "human behavior cannot be understood, but only caricatured, if it is represented as an adaptation to environment" (Macmurray, 1961, p.46). The search for an enlargement of satisfactions in the transactions of living can also be phrased as the desire for development in a direction, the desire to do something which will bring a sense of accomplishment as we experience the satisfaction of successfully handling new challenges. During a conversation in Beirut, a wise man once remarked to me that "people are hungry for new and good experiences."

It seems worthwhile to differentiate this search for value satisfactions into two varieties: (a) value satisfactions that are essentially new, different, more efficient, more reliable, more pleasurable, or more status-producing results of activity along familiar and tried dimensions, and (b) value satisfactions that are new in the sense of being emergent, new qualities people discover or create themselves for the first time, as does the child who tries out and relishes new experiences as his own developmental pattern unfolds. The former variety, like the growth on the limb of a tree, extends people's range, while the latter, like the new growth at the top of the tree, lets them attain new heights and see new vistas. The satisfactions sought by a newly developing people are at first most likely to be of the former type.

The particular value satisfactions man acquires are the result of learning. Some of the values learned will serve as the operative ideals of a people, others will be chiefly instrumental. People in rich countries were found to have learned to want and to expect many aspects of a good life that less-favored people had not yet learned were possibilities. From this point of view one might say that the competition between social and political systems is a competition in teaching people what to want, what is potentially available to them, and then proving to them in their own private experience that these wants are best attainable under the system described.

5 *Human beings are creatures of hope and are not genetically designed to resign themselves.* This characteristic of man so clearly brought out in the results reported here stems from the characteristic just described: that man is always likely to be dissatisfied and never fully "adapts" to his environment.

Man seems continually to hope that the world he encounters will correspond more and more to his vision of it as he acts within it to carry out his purposes while the vision itself continuously unfolds in an irreversible direction. The whole process is never-ending. It is characteristic of man in his ongoing experience to ask himself, "Where do I go from here?" Only in his more reflective moods does a person ask, "Where did I come from?" or "How did I get this way?" Most of the time, most people who are plugged into the changing world around them are future-oriented in their concerns. Throughout this study it was found that few people indeed — no matter how unfavorable or how favorable their circumstances — resigned themselves to staying put: all people without exception expected an improvement in the future both for themselves and for their country.

6 *Human beings have the capacity to make choices and the desire to exercise this capacity.* Any mechanical model of man constructed by a psychologist or by anyone else is bound to leave out the crucially important characteristic of man as an "appetitive-perceptive agency." Perceptions are learned and utilized by people to provide various prognoses to weigh alternative courses of action to achieve purposes. Consciously or unconsciously, people are trying to perceive the probable relation between their potential acts and the consequences of these acts to the intentions that constitute their goals.

The human brain and nervous system has the capacity to police its input, to determine what is and what is not significant for it, and to pay attention to and reinforce or otherwise modify its behavior as it transacts in the occasions of living. In this sense, the human being is a participant in and producer of his own value satisfactions. The data here further demonstrate that people perceive only what is relevant to their hopes and fears and make their choices accordingly.

7 *Human beings require freedom to exercise the choices they are capable of making.* This characteristic of man related to freedom is deliberately worded as it is rather than as a blanket statement that "human beings require freedom," since the freedom people want is so relative to their desires and the stage of development they have attained. Human beings, incidentally, apparently require more freedom than other species of animals because of their much greater capacity to move about and to engage in a much wider variety of behavior.

While it seems true that maximum freedom is a necessary condition if a highly developed individual is to obtain maximum value satisfaction, it is eqully true that too much freedom too soon can be an unbearable burden and a source of bondage if people, like children, are insufficiently developed to know what to do with it. For freedom clearly involves a learning of responsibility and an ability to take advantage of it wisely.

In these studies, few people indeed seemed to be self-consciously concerned with "freedom" as a category in the code. This is not because freedom is unimportant but because the coding had to follow the prevailing narrow, nonpsychological connotation of the concept, such as freedom of speech, of religion, and the like. But the concept of freedom is essentially a psychological and not a political concept. It describes the opportunity of an individual to make his own choices and to act accordingly. Psychologically, freedom refers to the freedom to experience more of what is potentially available, the freedom to move about and ahead, to be and to become. Freedom is thus less and less determined and more of a reality as man evolves and develops; it emerges and flowers as people learn what it can mean to them in terms of resolving their frustrations.

The authoritarian leadership sometimes required to bring about man's awakening and to start him on the road to his definition of progress appears to go against the grain of the human design once man is transformed into a self-conscious citizen who has the desire to exercise the capacity latent within him. The definition of freedom in the Soviet dictionary, *Ushakov,* as "the recognition of necessity" is limited to those periods in the life of an individual or a people when they are willing to let others define what is necessary and to submerge their own individuality.

8 *Human beings want to experience their own identity and integrity,* more popularly referred to as the need for *personal dignity.* Every human being craves a sense of his own self-constancy, an assurance of the repeatability of experience in which he is a determining participant. He obtains this from the transactions he has with other individuals.

People develop significances they share with others in their membership and reference groups. If the satisfaction and significance of participation with others ceases to confirm assumptions or to enrich values, then a person's sense of self-constancy becomes shaken or insecure, his loyalties become formalized and empty or are given up altogether. He becomes alienated or seeks new significances, new loyalties that are more operationally real.

9 *People want to experience a sense of their own worthwhileness.* A human being wants to know he is valued by others and that others will show that his own behavior and its consequences make some sort of difference to them in ways that give him a sense of satisfaction. When this occurs, not only is a person's sense of identity confirmed, but he also experiences a sense of personal worth and self-respect.

People acquire, maintain, and enrich their sense of worthwhileness only if they at least vaguely recognize the sources of what personal identity they have: from their family, their friends and neighbors, their associates or fellow workers, their group ties, or their nations. The social, religious, intellectual, regional, or national loyalties formed play the important role of making it possible for individuals to extend themselves backward into the past, forward into the future, and to identify themselves with others who live at more or less remote distances from them. Shared experiences are thus compounded into a bundle that can be conceptualized and felt in the here and now of daily living, thus making a person feel a functional part of a more enduring alliance. Man accomplishes such feats of self-extension largely through his capacity to create symbols, images, and myths which provide focal points for identification and self-expansion. After reviewing the lessons from history, historian Herbert Muller noted as one of the "forgotten simplicities" the fact "that men have always been willing to sacrifice themselves for some larger cause, fighting and dying for their family, tribe, or community, with or without hope of eternal reward" (Muller, 1954, p. 392).

The process of extending the sense of self both in space and in time appears also to involve the desire that one's "presence" shall not be limited merely to the here and now of existence but will extend into larger dimensions. The almost universal desire people had that their children should enjoy more opportunities would appear in part to reflect this extension of self into the future. The value satisfaction obtained by an individual in being part of a community we found demonstrated in high degree among the members of the Kibbutzim whose personal goals in life so completely overlapped community goals in their identification.

10 *Human beings seek some value or system of beliefs to which they can commit themselves.* In the midst of the probabilities and uncertainties that surround them, people want some anchoring points, some certainties, some faith that will serve either as a beacon light to guide them or a balm to assuage them during the inevitable frustrations and anxieties living engenders.

People who have long been frustrated and who have searched for means to alleviate their situations are, of course, particularly susceptible to a commitment to a new system of beliefs or an ideology that they feel holds promise of effective action. Hence the belief in the rewards of nationalism was found by and large most widespread and intense among people for whom nationalism was a new way out of their difficulties. And the most widespread fear that national unity would not be achieved turned up in areas such as India and Nigeria where ancient belief systems bounded by tribal and regional loyalties linger on.

Beliefs are confirmed insofar as action based on them brings satisfying consequences, and they are denied with growing skepticism if disastrous results consistently occur because they are followed. For example, West Germans have apparently given up the thought of achieving status as a world power or spreading their ideological influence as a result of their total defeat in World War II.

Commitment to a value or belief system becomes more difficult among well-informed and sophisticated people who self-consciously try to reconcile what they believe with what they know and what they know with what they believe. In such circumstances, beliefs become more secular and less important as personal identifications. While most Americans felt religion was important, this belief had little relationship to the way they perceived themselves in terms of their self-respect, their self-confidence, and their satisfaction with life in general; it was the least educated, the poorest Americans, who felt religion was most important.

11 *Human beings want a sense of surety and confidence that the society of which they are a part holds out a fair degree of hope that their aspirations will be fulfilled.* If social mechanisms deny people satisfactions they aspire to in achieving potential goals, then obviously their frustrations and anxieties mount, they search for new means to accomplish aims, or, on the other hand, they make any sacrifice required to protect a society they feel is fulfilling their needs but is seriously threatened.

It cannot be stressed too strongly that any people will become apathetic toward or anxious about ultimate goals they would like to

*"Don't you understand? The pipeline will bring you everything you ever wanted —
color TV, a split-level ranch-style home, a snappy sports car, a trip to Hawaii . . ."*
Reprinted by permission of Newspaper Enterprise Association.

achieve through social organizations if they continually sense a lack of
reliability in the means provided to accomplish these goals. Obviously
any viable society must satisfy basic survival needs, must provide security, must insure the repeatability of value satisfactions already attained, and must provide for new and emerging satisfactions. The effective society is one that enables the individual to develop personal
loyalties and aspirations which overlap with and are congenial to social values and loyalties, and which at the same time take full account
of the wide range of individual differences that exist.

Such a social organization must, too, become the repository of
values, must provide symbols for people's aspirations, must comprise
customs, institutions, laws, economic arrangements, and political
forms which enable an individual to give concrete reference to his values in his day-to-day behavior. If the gap between what society actually provides in terms of effective mechanisms for living and what it
purports to provide becomes too great, the vacuum created will sooner
or later engender the frustrations that impel people to seek new social
patterns and new symbols. Whitehead wrote that "the major advances
in civilization are processes which all but wreck the societies in which
they occur: — like unto an arrow in the hand of a child. The art of free

society consists first in the maintenance of the symbolic code; and secondly in fearlessness of revision, to secure that the code serves those purposes which satisfy an enlightened reason. Those societies which cannot combine reverence to their symbols with freedom of revision, must ultimately decay either from anarchy, or from the slow atrophy of a life stifled by useless shadows" (Whitehead, 1927, p.88).

Every social and political system can be regarded an an experiment in the broad perspective of time. The studies reported here have given us a few insights into different types of experiments in their different stages. Whatever the circumstances, the human design will in the long run force any institutional framework to accommodate it. This has been the case throughout human history. And few would deny that the varied pattern of experiments going on today hold out more promise of satisfying the human condition for a greater number of people than ever before.   ■

D.O. Hebb
The Causes of Fear*

In the previous selection, Cantril speaks to what people care about or desire; he describes their aspirations and hopes. Another view of the role of information in human motivation is in terms of the problems that arise when it is deficient. What is the effect of discrepant informational patterns? What is the reaction to things that do not make sense? The reaction to such strangeness is often, as Hebb so effectively argues, one of fear. The more highly developed the intellectual capacity of the organism, the more there is that can be comprehended and anticipated, and, therefore, the greater the susceptibility to fear of the unfamiliar. Note also Hebb's ingenious interpretation of culture as a means for preventing such upsetting strangeness.

It should be noted that Hebb's explanation extends to other primates as well. This is a powerful argument against those who would explain away each bit of evidence for an informational position in terms of a particular cultural norm or other idiosyncratic element of

*From D. O. Hebb *A textbook of psychology* (3rd edition). Philadelphia: W. B. Saunders Co. 1972. Pages 214–215; 203–208. Reprinted by permission.

experience. The parallels between the behavior of humans and that of laboratory monkeys, whose culture is presumably limited and whose experience is both limited and known, is too striking to be ignored.

■   The development of a large cortex in mammals presumably increased their capacity to learn and to solve problems, but it also increased their susceptibility to emotional disturbance and their capacity for altruistic behavior. Emotional susceptibility is correlated with intelligence in the growing animal also, so it is the older rather than the younger subject that is most easily disturbed.

Man's emotional sensitivities have led him to organize social patterns that reduce the frequency of emotional stimulation, allowing him to think of himself as unexcitable. But apparently trivial things can cause strong reactions, and the persistence of racial, religious, and national prejudice — because all people do not look alike, think alike, and talk alike — and the violence that goes with it, show how far man is from being the unemotional and peace-loving creature he thinks he is.

With fear we find an increasing variety of causes as we go from lower to higher mammals, and a parallel increase in duration and apparent severity of disturbance. Pain, sudden loud noise, and sudden loss of support cause fear in any mammal. For the rat, we need add only strange surroundings to have a complete list of the causes of fear as far as we know them. With the dog, the list becomes longer: strange persons, certain strange objects or situations (such as a balloon being blown up before the dog), a large statue of an animal, the dog's owner in different clothing, or a hat being moved across the floor by a thread that the dog does not see (Melzack, 1952). Not all dogs are equally affected — H. Mahut has shown, for example, that working dogs, bred for intelligence, are more susceptible to fear than bulldogs and terriers, bred for pugnacity (1958). Monkeys and apes are affected by a still greater variety of stimulating situations than dogs, and the degree and duration of disturbance is greater.

Causes of fear in the captive chimpanzee make up an almost endless list: a carrot of an unusual shape, a biscuit with a worm in it, a rope of a particular size, color, and texture (but not other ropes), a doll or a toy animal, a particular piece of apparatus or part of it, and so on. What one animal fears another may not, but as a species chimpanzees are much more susceptible than dogs to fears that do not arise from pain or threat of pain. [ED. NOTE: Note that this provides a definition for the informational in the context of fear — in other words, fear whose basis is informational in content.]

Figure 1 is a picture of two objects that are capable of producing a remarkable reaction in chimpanzees. The "death mask," left, in particular produced screaming, panic-stricken flight in a fifth of the adult

FIGURE 1

Objects that caused fear in adult chimpanzees: left, a plaster of paris cast from a death mask of an adult; right, a clay model of an infant's head, nearly life size.

animals who were simply shown the object, carried in the experimenter's hand as he walked up to the cage. The response of the remaining adults varied in strength, but most were very frightened and no animal failed to show erection of hair and avoidance of the test object. The same reaction was produced by a clay model of an adult chimpanzee head about half life-size (this was more frightening than the modeled infant head shown in figure 1); an actual chimpanzee's head that had been preserved in formalin; a life-like model of a human head, sawn from a display dummy; and various related objects, such as a detached human hand (from the same dummy). With repeated testing there was some habituation, but no animal got to the point of coming near any of these objects. A doll, representing a human infant, was placed in the cages of five adult chimpanzees, one after another, but despite the chimpanzee's well-known curiosity and destructiveness with things he can take to pieces, the doll remained intact and untouched.

These were the results with adults. The behavior of younger animals was quite different. One- and two-year-olds (corresponding roughly to human two- and three-year-olds) paid no attention at all to the test objects; as the experimenter approached carrying one of the objects the infants came toward him and apparently not noticing the object at all, tried to get the experimenter to pick them up. All their attention was focused on his face. Half-grown animals of five and six years (corresponding ages in man: eight to ten) were fascinated by the objects; as the experimenter neared an enclosure containing half a dozen of these youngsters they approached as close as they could (quite unlike the adults), forming a tight cluster clinging to the cage wire and poking their fingers through to prod the model head being shown them. The same things that terrified the adults — or horrified them — were exciting but not frightening to the half grown, and not even noticed by the infants.

There is a clear parallel in the different reactions of human children and adults to distorted and damaged human bodies. To the limited intelligence of the chimpanzee a model of a head may be in the same class as an actual head severed from the body for man. (In both cases there is a perceived identity with part of a living person, and at the same time a clear discrepancy.) It is not children but their elders who are most upset by scenes of violence and broken bodies on TV; a color movie of a major operation can produce nausea and fainting in adults, but not in children; we tolerate the extraordinary brutality of many of the classic fairy stories as adults, presumably, only because we were introduced to them at the more bloodthirsty age of five or six years.

An experiment by H.E. and M.C. Jones provides direct evidence of the increase of emotional susceptibility with age (1928). They recorded the reactions of children and adolescents to a snake, which was rather torpid and which was shown to be quite harmless. The subjects were city dwellers and had not had contact with snakes before. There was little fear in the youngest (about five years old), increased interest with only slight signs of caution in those of intermediate ages, and strong avoidance by most of the older subjects. "Fear" is not the right word to apply to the older subjects' reaction; "horror" is better, since they did not expect to be injured (they knew the snake could not hurt them), but in general it can be said that the reaction of most adults to a snake that they know is not capable of injuring them is hardly less vigorous than to a dangerous one. (It should be emphasized that the "fear" of snakes is not learned. Why it should be so strong is not understood, but it is a product of psychological maturation rather than learning. The year-old chimpanzee is not disturbed by contact with a snake, but the adult who sees one for the first time is disturbed, very much so, his reaction being about as strong as a man's).

EMOTION AND THE SOCIAL STRUCTURE

It was proposed in the preceding section that emotionality increases as mental age increases in the growing child. Now at first sight this seems false. It is true that temper tantrums and unreasoning fears increase in frequency and strength between the ages of one and four years, but in the study of a large number of children by A. T. Jersild and F. B. Holmes (1935) this trend reversed itself about the age of five, and though we know that some things such as the fear of snakes continue to increase in strength, are these things not exceptions to a more general tendency to become *less* excitable at maturity?

To ourselves as adults we seem civilized, urbane, not given to senseless fears and outbursts of rage like the young child or the explosive chimpanzee. The reason, however, may not be that we are less susceptible, but instead that we are sheltered by what we call a civilized environment, within which we are not much exposed to the causes of emotional disturbance. It offers actual physical protection from wild animals or freezing to death and, mostly, makes it possible to avoid starving to death, but it also offers psychological protection from emotional disturbance by reducing the causes to near zero. In a "civilized environment" one never has to be in strange places in darkness (thus many adults never discover that they are subject to fear in such circumstances). The adults in it have learned elaborate rules of courtesy, good manners, and how to behave in public, so their behavior is predictable and usually will not cause one embarrassment, shame, anger or disgust. All this is achieved by prolonged training in childhood and later enforced by legal penalties (e.g. for slander, indecent exposure, dumping garbage in the street) or by social ostracism. In this environment, in short, one can count most of the time on not being suddenly exposed to the causes of strong emotion without warning and without adequate opportunity to avoid them. All this of course implies also that we as adults have been trained to suppress strong emotion when it does occur, as far as we can. Emotional outbursts are thus rare in the civilized adult on his own ground, but there is no reason to conclude from this that he is less susceptible to attacks of emotion than his five-year-old son, who must live in an environment tailored to adult needs rather than those of a five-year-old.

The social problems of race and religious prejudice should show us what we are like as a species, if nothing else does. It is common to assume that social prejudice is wholly learned, and that if one never let the child hear bad things about other groups he would grow up to be without prejudice. We know, however, that more is involved. Such learning does occur and it is important to prevent it whenever possible, but prejudice can spring up where there has been no occasion for learning, and the learning, when prejudice is taught, occurs with extraordinary ease. An essential component in prejudice is the emotional reaction of human beings to the strange, to what is the same and yet different, to the thing that can cause a conflict of ideas.

At first it seems unreasonable to suppose that emotions as strong as those involved in social prejudice could be set off by such small things as a difference of skin color or the knowledge that the other person does not share some religious belief. Here the comparative evidence has great weight. The chimpanzee's outright panic at the sight of a model of a chimpanzee head shows how strong the effect of a perceptual discrepancy, as such, can be. Also, if a human being is excited and hostile on seeing a stranger, we might think that this is because he has been taught that strangers are dangerous, but the chimpanzee born in captivity and never before exposed to a stranger, chimpanzee or human, shows the same thing. Clearly the hostility is not something that needs to be learned.

Clearly, strong emotional reactions may be induced by apparently trivial things, in man as in chimpanzee: consider that healthy young men, known to be capable of withstanding very serious injury without crying out, are also known to be capable of fainting at the *idea* of hypodermic injection, before a needle has even touched them. Or, among trivial differences with large consequences, consider the social use of two words that mean precisely the same thing, one a Latin anatomical term, one coming from Anglo-Saxon and classed as obscene.[1] All that "obscene" can mean in this case is that one word is taboo and the other is not. Society is shot through with taboos, and failure to observe them involves considerable risk. These are taboos in the most primitive sense.[2] The whole structure of society contains a large irrational or emotional factor; failure to recognize it means failure to understand the social behavior of the human animal.

The attempt to explain race and religious prejudice as products of learning arises from the assumption that man, being a rational animal, makes his important decisions on the basis of reason. Once we see this is not so, and that the possession of intelligence may in fact, through imagination, *increase* the causes of emotional disturbance, we can see better the nature of our problem in dealing with prejudice, and how dangerous is the assumption that prejudice will disappear if the child is not taught bad things about others.

Left to itself, the child's emotional reaction to the other, to the one who differs, is likely to result in hostility. *But it need not do so.* Learning, which can have bad effects and increase hostility, can instead guide the emotional reaction in the direction of warmth and friendliness. Man's motivational characteristics are not all undesirable. The same comparative approach which shows us that unreasoning hostility can arise spontaneously, allows us also to see another and more favorable side of man's nature. To this we will turn in a moment.

To sum up the argument of this section: the comparative evidence indicates that the capacity for emotion increases with intelligence. It is the higher animal of whom fear of innocuous objects, or unfounded hostility, is characteristic. Also, it is the older rather than the younger chimpanzee that is more fearful and hostile. At first it may seem that these conclusions cannot be extended to man: adult civilized man is less emotional than the fearful wild animal, and less emotional than the young child? But looking at the environment in which the traits are manifested, we see that something has been left out of account. The structure of "civilization" is such as to cushion the adult's sensitivities, to protect him from the causes of fear, anger, and disgust. The extent and strength of social prejudice (in which reason is used only to reinforce one's unreasoning emotional responses) show how deeply rooted these sensitivities are. Thus, the lack of emotional outbursts in the civilized adult is evidence, not of a lack of susceptibility, but of the effectiveness of the social cocoon in which we live. It does not refute the proposition that emotional susceptibility rises with intellectual capacity.   ■

NOTES

1. The publisher advises that the student be allowed to think of his own examples. These are the words that in English are generally spelt with four letters but in Latin take five or more, showing the superiority of English to Latin.

2. Consider some of the sexual taboos, for example. A prison sentence for statutory rape or indecent exposure does not require evidence that the behavior has done anyone any harm, physically or mentally — all that must be shown is that the taboo has been broken. Or consider the taboos attaching to the dead body: there are severe legal penalties for "offering indignity" to a corpse, as for example stuffing one into the trunk of your car when taking it to be buried.

Seymour M. Farber
Quality of Living — Stress and Creativity*

This selection speaks to the second aspect of information-related human needs — involvement. Here Farber, a physician, touches on a variety of elements of a full and satisfying human existence that are threatened by the very success of security-oriented social programs.

■ Most of us need to aspire, to create, to give, and to belong. It is not necessary that all our yearnings be realized, only that they find some mode of expression.

In fact, it is always important to remember that coming too close to any ideal, however noble it may appear from a distance, is likely to be a disheartening experience. In contrast with other nations and other times, the social achievements of the United States, Switzerland, Sweden, Denmark, and parts of the British Commonwealth are truly wondrous. The dreams of the nineteenth-century reformers have been largely realized. Did any of the kindly Fabians ever suspect that their vision of efficient humanitarianism could lead straight to 1984?

Social planning is indispensable in a crowded world, but if our society is to remain viable, our planning must recognize our nonmaterial needs more than it has; and it must offer us worthwhile goals without exalting one at the expense of others. Security cannot make up for the loss of adventure; comfort for the lack of hard, creative work; nor togetherness for the lack of true companionship.

Even health, in the sense of freedom from any demonstrable disease, is not worth having if it means abstaining from all that makes life worthwhile. One might as well be dead. Indeed, we all have noticed that the individual preoccupied with the preservation of his body as anxiously as a medieval Christian with his soul often seems to be only technically alive.

As we have seen, conflict and stress are far from inimical to creativity; and every culture necessarily seeks to imprint its pattern on the growing mind. Yet we need the possibility of escaping this pattern from time to time. Even small children should be thrown on their own resources now and then. Just as we have set aside areas of wilderness

*Excerpted from S. M. Farber "Quality of living — stress and creativity" in F. F. Darling and J. P. Milton (Eds.) *Future environments of North America*. New York: Natural History Press. 1966. Pages 347–348; 354. Reprinted by permission.

as sacred, not to be used for any practical end, we need to set aside holidays in the original sense of the word, which will not be desecrated by the clamor, the trivia, and the "pathological togetherness" which make our leisure such a rat race.

The enthusiasm for wilderness trips and mountain climbing is, of course, one way of recovering some of the values we have lost: solitude, self-reliance, challenge, adventure, and genuine friendship, tested by adversity and danger.   ■

Charles S. Houston
The Last Blue Mountain*

Mountain climbing is for many people the very essence of adventure, of challenge, of what we have been calling involvement. Risk or uncertainty combine with an element of danger to create a degree of involvement that is hard to match. While Houston's writing is more poetic than analytic, it most effectively communicates how important the informational aspects are to the quality of the experience.

■   We must differentiate risk from danger. Experienced climbers understand, enjoy, and seek risk because it presents a difficulty to overcome and can be estimated and controlled. He equally abhors danger because it is beyond his control. Injury while crossing a slope swept by avalanche is unpredictable and dangerous, whereas the risk of an exposed climb up an overhanging face lies within his capability.

The existence of a challenge has always stimulated response from man. And when the challenge exceeds known limits, the response brings increased capacity. Does the death of a climber make a certain mountain or route more attractive to others? The answer is probably yes, at least where the severity of the climb has been the prime factor in the accident. It is not necessarily true, however, where a fortuitous avalanche or sudden storm has been the killer. The north face of the Eiger is often tried despite its formidable death toll, because the accidents have been due primarily to the climber's failure. By contrast, the

*From C. S. Houston "The last blue mountain" in S. Z. Klausner (Ed.) *Why man takes chances.* New York: Doubleday & Co., Inc. 1968. Pages 52; 57–58. Reprinted by permission.

Marinelli Gully, whose avalanches have killed many, does not have the same attraction. The manageable risks that make a route difficult do attract climbers, while the uncontrollable dangers do not.

There have been tragic accidents where one or more climbers have faced life-and-death decisions. Should a man save himself after an accident, but only at the price of abandoning his companion who cannot be saved? Such a stress tears at the moral fiber. It is a known stress which each must accept if he is to try the great endeavors, and it is not evaded.

I must end as I began, by reiterating my conviction that climbing is one of the few human activities where the stress is clear, apparent, and freely sought. The goal is sharp and visible. There is no doubt when one has succeeded or failed. Mountaineering is more a quest for self-fulfillment than a victory over others or over nature. The true mountaineer knows that he has not conquered a mountain by standing on its summit for a few fleeting moments. Only when the right men are in the right place at the right time are the big mountains climbed; never are they conquered.

Climbers court and control risk, seek stress, but avoid the uncontrollable dangers. By their repeated self-testing, capacity grows as it does in so many other and unrelated activities. By such expansion of capability, man finds that he has wider limits than we know.

William R. Catton, Jr.
The Quest for Uncertainty*

Once again mountain climbing serves as the vehicle for an analysis of involvement. Here the informational component is even more explicit. Perhaps too high a probability of success undermines involvement, while too low a probability undermines one's capacity to make sense, to conceive of actions that could reasonably lead to a successful outcome. Since the central issues here have nothing to do with mountains per se, but are informational in character, Catton quite appropriately generalizes to the broader domain of play, a topic that receives further attention in the final selection of the chapter.

■   Mountaineering has been studied as a way of gaining insight into human play motivation (Emerson, 1968). Why do rules emerge within play? What does the emergence of rules do to the character of play?

Mountain climbing, Emerson says, epitomizes the difficulty in accounting for any form of play in terms of the ordinary instrumental motivation that presumably characterizes the rational activities of the world of work. There are, as he points out, such obvious reasons for not climbing mountains, such as fatigue and danger, and yet people do it in increasing numbers.

Emerson was a member of the American Mount Everest Expedition in 1963 and made sociological studies of his fellow climbers. Over a three-month period he had each member of the expedition record his own impressions and his own reactions to each day's efforts in a research diary. The expedition was attempting to climb Everest from two different approaches — the Southeast Ridge which had been climbed before, and the West Ridge by which the summit had never before been reached. At the end of each day, Emerson had each member of the expedition write down in his diary a subjective estimate of the probability of success by each route. Each climber also wrote down each evening what activities he wanted to perform the next day. Emerson later coded these activity statements in such a way that he could derive from them a measure of task motivation strength.

*From W. R. Catton, Jr. "Motivations of wilderness users" *Pulp and Paper Magazine of Canada*. National Business Publications. Quebec. December 19, 1969. Pages 121–122. Reprinted by permission.

By comparison of day-to-day variations of an individual's responses, and by comparison of the responses of the West Ridge party and the responses of the conventional Southeast Ridge party, Emerson found that motivation varies directly with uncertainty of outcome. If success seemed highly probable, or if failure seemed highly probable, motivation was reduced; when there was genuine doubt as to whether the party would succeed or fail, then motivation was high.

Still more interesting, he found that the communications between climbers tended to fall into a pattern which had the effect of fostering uncertainty about end results. If success began to seem assured to one climber, others would begin to point out ominous signs. If failure began to seem inevitable, one began to hear his partners asserting grounds for optimism. The higher the motivation, the greater the tendency for conversations to be so patterned as to maintain uncertainty. In short, there is a self-regulating group process that operates in a mountaineering expedition: uncertainty of success generates motivation, and this leads to interpersonal communication processes which tend to maintain or maximize uncertainty.

The fun obtained from mountain climbing is not in reaching the summit but in carrying on the task in the face of doubt as to whether the summit will be reached or will prove unattainable. If the goal is known to be unattainable, the task ceases to be pleasurable. But if it is a foregone conclusion that the goal will be reached, then, too, the task loses its lustre. The summit of a mountain defines a problem, but the pleasure of climbing lies less in the achieved solution than in the problem-solving process. Emerson goes on to generalize this interpretation to other forms of play, ranging from athletic to intellectual, and argues that motivation toward a goal is highest if the goal outcome is uncertain. This explains, he feels, why first ascents are especially valued: a summit which has never been reached may not be reachable but is not known to be unreachable. A problem which has never yet been solved may not be soluble but it may not be known to be insoluble.

We hasten to add at this point that a mountain which has been climbed, even repeatedly, or a puzzle which has been solved many times, does not thereby lose all its value. It may remain uncertain for any given individual whether he can climb that mountain or solve that puzzle.

Games with clear-cut rules may emerge from unregulated play. At least some of the rules perform the function of preserving uncertainty. In mountaineering, for example, climbers shun equipment which makes the climb too easy.

Techniques which would make success a foregone conclusion would rob the activity of much of its pleasure. In competitive sports, the optimal matching of opponents maintains uncertainty. Elaborately

Mountain climbing is not the only example where fascinating content and fascinating process combine into a powerfully involving activity. Here again, risk or uncertainty constitutes the process aspect, but instead of danger, the fascinating content involves elements (one might even say "tokens") of high value or worth.

by Howard L. Deardorff

organized games are contrived sources of the sort of pleasure that derives from uncertainty of outcome. The fly fisherman is apparently less motivated by the trout he occasionally catches than by the uncertainty as to whether he can catch any fish with a line of less tensile strength than the fish's weight (LaPiere, 1954, p. 132).

Turning our attention from the rather extreme example studied by Emerson, we can suggest that one important type of motivation underlying the recreational use of wilderness by the average devotee may be the mystery it holds for him. He implicitly asks by entering the wilderness, "How well can I do with limited resources?" As I will try to show a bit later, on the basis of some other research, the challenge lies not merely in the question of coping physically with the uncertainties posed by the environment, but also in coping with intellectual problems it poses.   ■

D. O. Hebb
Altruism and the Need for Excitement*

The previous selection by Hebb dealt with the consequences of things that fail to make sense. This excerpt examines two aspects of involvement that are particularly interesting for the contrast they provide. Hebb argues in the previous selection that humans (and other animals) fear the strange — and, oftentimes, the stranger. Here he shows the other side of the coin: the interest in other members of the species that extends to helping them, and the interest in the strange in general — as long as it is not *too strange*. Thus emerges a thoughtful portrait of the tension and restlessness characteristic of human feelings about information, a portrait Hebb has entitled "man's ambivalent nature."

■   Two other motivational characteristics are major factors in our social structure. One is the capacity for altruism, which is fundamental to man's nature but for some reason has always been disregarded or denied by social scientists. The other is a need for excitement when the social cocoon becomes too effective and thus causes boredom. Man avoids strong fear but seeks mild fear; and so with frustration (in mental or physical work) and disgust (avoiding outright obscenity, but enjoying off-color jokes). The stability of society appears to require harmless sources of mild excitement. If they are not provided, worse ones may be found.

ALTRUISM IN THE HIGHER ANIMAL   Among the distinctive features of behavior in the human species is the frequency of *altruism,* defined as intrinsically motivated purposive behavior whose function is to help another person or animal. In

*From D. O. Hebb *A textbook of psychology* (3rd edition). Philadelphia: W. B. Saunders Co. 1972. Pages 215; 208–214. Reprinted by permission.

this definition, "intrinsically motivated" means that the behavior does not depend on primary or secondary reinforcement: that the helper receives no benefit except the knowledge that he has helped; and "purposive" implies that the behavior is under the control of mediating processes, thus excluding the reflexive cooperation of the social insects (ant, bee, termite).

Common experience tells us how frequent such behavior is. Giving money to a beggar, working in societies for the prevention of cruelty, helping a stranger start his car, contributing to disaster funds, helping with the dishes, lending a set of notes to another student or giving him a match — trivial or not, there are endless ways in which human beings do things for others with no expectation of a return. Often, of course, such things are also done with hope of later benefits, but this does not change the fact that truly unselfish acts, great and small, are frequent. Some of them are great indeed, considering the number of persons who die annually in the attempt to rescue someone from drowning or from a burning building.

The facts are clear. What do they mean? There is a long tradition of interpreting *all* of man's motivation as selfish; generosity is not in the child's nature but imposed by rewards and punishments and maintained at maturity by social pressure. It is assumed that the adult is generous — when he is generous — only because of habit or because he is rewarded by social approval and punished for selfishness by disapproval. It is difficult to refute this proposition directly, because of the multifarious learning of the growing child in society. But there is a disproof in animal behavior.

H. W. Nissen and M. P. Crawford have shown that begging, for example, is a very powerful stimulus for the chimpanzee (1936). Two animals are in adjoining cages and one is given food; if the two are friends, the second may get as much as half the food as a gift. If they are not friends, the importunate begging of the second animal may still be irresistible, but annoying, and the rich animal may end up by throwing the food violently at the beggar. There is no suggestion in this latter case that the "rich" animal gets any pleasure from giving to the poor. There is some deeper compulsion, and it quite clear from the history of the animals, reared in the laboratory, that the gift is not made because the giver was trained as an infant to be kind to beggars.

Chimpanzees and gorillas living free in the wild have been observed giving help to half-grow youngsters in trouble, sometimes when it meant that the helper himself had to venture into the dangerous neighborhood of the human observer. A similar kind of behavior has been observed experimentally.

Two adult female chimpanzees, Lia and Mimi, are caged together. A disguised human observer approaches, playing the part of the "bold man," one who is unafraid of chimpanzees. Thanks to the cage wire between him and them, and a stout pair of gloves, he can pretend to answer attacks in a most intimidating manner. Both Lia and Mimi, seeing a stranger approach without the caution usually shown by strangers, attack; Lia is frightened by the vigor of the stranger's responses and runs away, but Mimi is not. Mimi stays close to the wire trying to catch hold of him; then Lia, though clearly afraid, returns and repeatedly tries to pull the reckless Mimi out of the danger zone. This scene is repeated on subsequent testing.

The porpoise, or dolphin, a sea-going mammal, must be classed as a higher animal on the ground of its behavior as well as its large brain, a fifth larger than man's with a highly developed cortex. There is well-attested evidence of adults helping other adults in trouble. J. B. Siebenaler and D. K. Caldwell (1956) report two cases in which a stunned animal was supported at the surface till he could swim again (for porpoises of course must breathe). Other females besides the mother have been seen helping the newborn porpoise to the surface to breathe for the first time. Finally, W. N. Kellogg reports two separate instances in which a porpoise helped a human swimmer to reach safety (1961).

In short, the evidence from infrahuman mammals indicates that altruism is a product of evolution and not something that must be beaten into the growing human child because of the needs of society. Here, apparently, we have another motivational consequence of the development of complex mediating processes. It is clear in the chimpanzee and porpoise, at least on occasion, but it is most evident in man and obviously an important element in the structure of human society.

PLAY, BOREDOM, AND THE SEARCH FOR EXCITEMENT

Living things must be active, and this is as true of brain as of muscle. Ordinarily both are kept exercised as a result of environmental stimulation and in the satisfaction of biological needs. There are times, however, when an animal has no threat to escape, no need of food and no young to care for, no sexual motivation and no need of sleep. One need remains: to be active, physically and mentally.

The play of birds and the lower mammals seems largely muscular, though there is evidently a neural component also. The animal does not merely tense and relax his muscles alternately, but indulges in activities that require elaborate neural control, generally ones that depend on past learning. In monkey, ape and man, however, a kind of play occurs that is almost entirely mental, with a minimum of muscular activity.

H. F. Harlow (1953) has shown that monkeys will work for hours at solving simple mechanical puzzles, with no reward other than finding a solution. The chimpanzee will work for a food reward, but he works much better if the task interests him, and then he may work even if he does not want the food. One female solved a series of problems, getting a slice of banana for each solution, but not eating it; instead, she piled the slices in a neat row on top of the apparatus. Then she repeated the whole series of problems, putting one slice of banana back into the food dish after each trial, apparently for the experimenter.

Such behavior is *play,* when play is defined as work done for the sake of doing it. Obviously it is not primarily physical play, but must exercise the brain more than the muscles. Even the laboratory rat shows something of the same kind.

It is evident that "mental play," involving the brain as much as the muscles, is a characteristic of the mammal and one that becomes more prominent in the higher mammals. Much of man's mental play — in bridge, chess, and so on — is competitive, and we tend to think of it as motivated by the secondary reinforcement of the "prestige" or social approval that comes from being better than someone else. But there is also noncompetitive play such as knitting or singing or birdwatching, and the lower-animal data show that the need of mental exercise exists in its own right. *Boredom* is a state in which the subject seeks a higher level of excitement, usually in some form of play, and the avoidance of boredom is a most important factor in human behavior.

The extent to which we are dependent on our normally varied environment and the mental activity it gives rise to is seen in perceptual-isolation (Sometimes referred to as "sensory deprivation") experiments (W. H. Bexton, W. Heron, and T. H. Scott, 1954). College students were paid $20 a day to do nothing, lying on a comfortable bed with eyes covered by translucent plastic (permitting light to enter, but preventing pattern vision), hands enclosed in tubes (so that the hands could not be used for somesthetic perception, though they could be moved to prevent joint pains), and ears covered with earphones from which there was a constant buzzing except when the subject was being given a test. These conditions were relaxed only to allow the subject to eat or go to the toilet. Few could stand the monotony for more than two or three days, the upper limit being six. The subjects became willing to listen to childish or meaningless talk that otherwise they would have avoided contemptuously — anything to break the monotony. Eventually the need became overwhelming to see, to hear, to be in normal contact with the environment, to be *active.* Nothing like the same pressure develops when a subject is equally immobilized (with a broken leg, say) but has books, radio, and friends to keep him occupied mentally. The need thus is more for mental than for physical activity.

The experiment showed that man can be bored, which we knew, but it showed, too, that boredom is too mild a word for some of the effects. The need for the normal stimulation of a varied environment is fundamental. Without it mental function and personality deteriorate. The subjects in isolation complained of being unable to think coherently, they became less able to solve simple problems, and they began to have hallucinations. . . .

MAN'S AMBIVALENT NATURE

Man is a mammal and a product of evolution, and fundamental to his motivation is the satisfaction of basic biological needs; when these are not met — particularly if the lack is chronic — the attempt to satisfy them generally becomes a dominant motive. (Even here, however, the mediating processes of a large cerebrum have a powerful influence; the starving man may share his food, the man in danger may invite even greater risk to help another, and sexual need is characteristically subordinated to the rules and customs of society.)

But when the individual's biological needs are satisfied we see a very different picture. . . . We all know that man dislikes work, but if he has none he invents it — though then he calls it play. By definition, fear entails avoidance, and so do horror and disgust; yet man seeks situations that produce fear, in the guise of "thrill" or "adventure," he is fascinated by newspaper accounts of the mangled human bodies in Monday's report of the weekend highway toll, and he is notoriously charmed by risqué joke and bawdy song. . . .

One must see how extensively these tendencies penetrate into, and determine, the structure of society. It was suggested above that "civilization" is a protective cocoon, an ordering of the physical environment and of man's own social behavior of such sort as to insulate the adult member of society from most of the emotional provocations that he would otherwise be subject to. This is still its primary function. But the result in an economically successful society, such as that of Rome (because of its tributary provinces) or of the United States today, is that life may become dull and the need to find excitement pressing — at least for part of the time and for a majority of citizens. In this light we can recognize a source of motivation that underlies mountain climbing, skiing, and auto racing: activities all of which depend largely on thrill for their attraction, which means to say that they are ones in which some degree of fear is deliberately courted. We can recognize the *raison d'être* of golf, which might be an old ladies' game if it were not for its furious frustration and constant threat of frustration. It is a notoriously anger-provoking game, as bridge is also. But only relatively few people get a chance to climb mountains or play golf, and above-average intelligence is needed to be really frustrated by bridge. These occupations offer escape for only a minority of the population. Rome made the great discovery that the populace needs circuses as well as bread; our circuses are the organized sports. The brutalities of

Canadian hockey and American football are a pallid substitute for tossing Christians to the lions, perhaps, but they serve the same function. When we add soap opera, TV, movies, comics and paperback thrillers, it can be seen that we do fairly well in this respect, and the important thing for our present purposes is to realize that such things are not luxuries but necessities, at least at the present stage of development of social institutions.   ■

5 On Knowledge and Rationality

The informational position developed so far may have seemed so obvious as to be "simple common sense" and "what everyone believes." In this chapter we look at a widely held and widely used alternative position known as Rational, or Economic, Man. It assumes that decisions are made by considering all the alternatives and seeking the solution that leads to the greatest gain. This too may seem to involve "simple common sense," but the concept of Rational Man and the informational perspective hold sharply contrasting views of how people use information and make decisions.

Rational Man is a set of assumptions used by economists to make the human element in their models easier to handle. Since planners, policy makers, and managers tend to take courses in economics, it is perhaps not surprising that Rational Man is by far the most widely held and influential theory among environmental decision makers. It should be noted that the widespread influence of this theory is not the result of a sinister plot. Human behavior can be very confusing to contemplate, and a position that is readily grasped and widely sanctioned is understandably attractive. Unfortunately, these convenient and apparently innocent assumptions are in fact profoundly distorting; they are an efficient means of translating good intentions into poor policy. It is through guiding assumptions of this kind that we have moved people off the farm and into the cities — with unfortunate consequences for both farm and city. Other well-intended efforts thwarted by these assumptions include public housing and urban renewal. Aid to less developed countries also reflects the pervasive influence of this theory. The suffering and waste thus created is forcefully described by Schumacher in his engaging book *Small is Beautiful*.

The central assumption of the Rational Man position concerns what people care about. It states, simply enough, that people act to maximize their gain. This statement seems so obvious as to be almost innocuous. At the same time, two slightly sticky points should be noted. First "maximize" is a strong word, and it is intended quite literally. Second, "gain" might make one suspect that the theory gathers all the various things people care about into a single concept of "gain." This suspicion turns out to be correct.

Let us look at these points more closely. Within the context of the Rational Man position two major factors are of central interest. One is the magnitude of the gain under consideration. (In more modern revisions of the position, the magnitude is replaced by the perceived value, or utility, of the gain.) The other major factor is the probability of attaining the gain in question. (Again, modern revisions look to the perceived, or "subjective," probability.) The product of the magnitude of the gain and the probability of reaching it then provides a basis for comparing possible alternative decisions. The rational decision maker of course chooses the one with the highest product. If all possibilities have been considered, then this choice will result in the maximization of gain. (Dyckman, 1961; Edwards, 1954).

However, as Simon points out, maximizing can be an expensive luxury. While the best out of all possibilities can be a fine alternative indeed, considering all those possibilities can be time consuming. And if some of the possibilities must be sought or discovered or invented before they can be considered, a good deal of effort can be involved as well. Many times something less than the best is quite satisfactory. Indeed, when speed and effort are important considerations, maximization can be disastrous, however "rational" it might seem in principle.

The difficulties with the matter of "gain" are at least as severe as those concerning maximization. The advantage of placing all the various needs and desires of an individual on the same scale is obvious: they can be compared directly, using some sort of universal metric. It is hardly surprising that the Rational Man position is most comfortable dealing with considerations of economic gain or with other motives readily translated into the same coin. The more aspects of human motivation that are noneconomic in character, and not readily translatable into economic terms, the more distortions in the Rational Man view of human needs. Thus, such a translation of human concerns into a single concept often merely caricatures them.

While the motivational assumption of the Rational Man position is perhaps its most prominent characteristic, what it dismisses is as important as what it proposes. And what it dismisses is nothing less that the importance of information. The maximization of gain is assumed to occur in the minds of all-knowing beings. There is no room here for ignorance or incomplete information. As Kates points out, it is this assumption of perfect knowledge that separates the Rational Man conception most decisively from the experience and behavior of finite humans attempting to cope with a world that is potentially overwhelming in its uncertainty and complexity.

Another View of Information

Another approach, on the face of it every bit as rational as Rational Man, takes very nearly the opposite position with respect to the "perfect knowledge" issue. This position might be called "faith-in-education." Its guiding assumption is simple: inappropriate behavior can be remedied by the provision of corrective information. It assumes that once in possession of the facts, humans will alter their behavior accordingly.

This position is attractive enough to have been a guiding principle in the United States for many years and across many fields of endeavor. At the same time, it is sufficiently misleading to have generated considerable disappointment and wasted effort. Several factors probably operate here:

1 People indeed crave information, but what they want to learn and what the experts want to tell them are not necessarily the same. People are eager for new things and for the expansion of old knowledge. What they do not want is information that conflicts with what they already know.

2 People often think that where they already have information they don't need more. The definiteness of representations and the connectedness of cognitive maps in general inspires enough confidence to make it difficult to realize how incomplete and inaccurate one's knowledge might be.

3 People enjoy learning, discovering, finding out. They do not like to be told, and further, being told does not in general substitute for the collection of experiences usually involved in the development of new concepts.

4 People tend to learn most readily from concrete instances and from information strong in imagery. Information, however, is often provided in rather abstract form. It often stresses conclusions rather than steps leading to them. It often fails to provide an opportunity for active involvement. (These issues will receive fuller discussion in the last chapter.)

The failure of the "faith-in-education" position is convincing evidence of the problems of communicating with an information-processing animal. It does not prove that information is unimportant after all, but neither does it permit the comforting belief that the gap between what people want to know and what people need to know is small or easily bridged.

Robert W. Kates
The Underlying View of Man's Rationality*

Rational Man, like any other theory, is not a single idea but a set of notions that for some reason or another have come to be associated with each other. Kates here provides a helpful introduction to these associated ideas, and to some of the reactions they have provoked.

■ *Rationality* may be used to simply describe that ability to choose clearly and consistently those alternate courses of human behavior that are most appropriate towards attaining some end or goal. Among the difficulties in comparing inter-disciplinary research in decision making are the conflicting assumptions as to man's rationality. These have been sharply defined by Simon in the following manner:

> The social sciences suffer from an acute case of schizophrenia in their treatment of rationality. At one extreme we have the economists, who attribute to economic man a preposterously omniscient rationality. Economic man has a complete and consistent system of preferences that allows him always to choose among the alternatives open to him; he is always completely aware of what the alternatives are; there are no limits to the complexity of the computations he can perform in order to determine which alternatives are best; probability calculations are neither frightening or mysterious to him. Within the past decade, in its extension to competitive game situations, and to decision making under uncertainty, this body of theory has reached a state of Thomistic refinement that possesses considerable normative interest, but little discernible relation to the actual or possible behavior of flesh-and-blood human beings.
>
> At the other extreme, we have had tendencies in social psychology traceable to Freud that try to reduce all cognition to affect. Thus, we show that coins look larger to poor children than to rich (Bruner and Postman), that the pressure of a social group can persuade a man to see spots that aren't there (Asch), that the process of group problem solving involves the accumulation and discharge of tensions (Bales), and so on. The past generation of behavioral scientists have been busy, following Freud, showing that people aren't nearly as rational as they thought themselves to be. Perhaps the next generation is going to have to show that they are far more rational than we now describe them as being — but with a rationality less grandiose than that proclaimed by economics (Simon, 1957a, p.xxiii).

*From R. W. Kates *Hazard and choice perception in flood plain management.* University of Chicago: Department of Geography. Research Paper #78. 1962. Pages 13–16. Reprinted by permission.

Simon goes on to offer his own alternative:

> The alternative approach . . . is based on what I shall call the *principle of bounded rationality:*
>
> > The capacity of the human mind for formulating and solving complex problems is very small compared with the size of the problems whose solution is required for objectively rational behavior in the real world — or even for a reasonable approximation to such objective rationality.
>
> If the principle is correct, then the goal of classical economic theory — to predict the behavior of rational man without making an empirical investigation of his psychological properties — is unattainable. For the first consequence of the principle of bounded rationality is that the intended rationality of an actor requires him to construct a simplified model of the real situation in order to deal with it. He behaves rationally with respect to this model, and such behavior is not even approximately optimal with respect to the real world. To predict his behavior we must understand the way in which this simplified model is constructed, and its construction will certainly be related to his psychological properties as a perceiving, thinking, and learning animal (Simon, 1957b, p. 198).

Thus does Simon construct a trichotomy, fraught with perils of oversimplification. By utilizing the *extremes* of economic or psychological man, some scholars may insist, Simon has caricaturized the mainstreams of economic or psychological thought. Be this as it may, the writer in his review of the decision-making literature of the social sciences has found few exceptions to Simon's description of the prevalent underlying assumptions of rationality. If one acknowledges the descriptive aptness of Simon's trichotomy, what of its prescriptive value? Restated in another way: granted that decision-making analysts, consciously or unconsciously, formulate an underlying assumption as to man's rationality, is there one of these assumptions that is more useful for formulating decision-making schema?

To the writer, the stance, or assumptions as to man's rationality from which the decision-making analyst prepares to discuss the process of decision making has utility only in terms of the analyst's objectives and study matter.

One such objective is the intent of the analyst in terms of the normative-behavioral dichotomy or, as the writer prefers, those models of man that aspire to *describe and predict* his behavior as opposed to those that aspire to *prescribe* what his behavior ought to be. If the intention of the analyst is to describe correctly human behavior in decision-making situations and to predict future behavior, then it is clear to the writer that an assumption of omniscient rationality for economic man is at variance with both the potential and actual behavior of men.

It must be recognized that there are many who have wearied of the failure of behavioral theory to provide generalized descriptions of human action. Stimulated by computer technology, they are constructing a closer approximation of the rational economic man by prescribing rules and routines to help men become more nearly rational. These research workers appear ready to leap-frog the question: How does man perceive choice and act upon it? and replace it with the question: How can he make his choices and choice mechanisms better? For some the horizon is endless and their ultimate goal might well be the following:

> We assert that it is possible to describe analytically any human function which can be reasonably defined in objective terms — and we specifically include in such functions "thinking" insofar as the term is definable. If by "thinking" one means being able to do arithmetic, or play a good game of chess, or learn from experience, or make optimal decisions in exceedingly complex situations, then we assert that thinking can be described analytically, and there are two important corollaries: if it can be described analytically, it can be simulated; and if it can be simulated, it can be performed mechanically (Machol, 1960, pp. viii–ix).

Omniscient, rational economic man is a viable model for describing the behavior of a select group of human beings, though this group may be limited to the very proponents of the model. With an objective of prescribing rules for making better choices, surely one cannot argue that men ought not aspire to the very heights of rationality. What makes this view so vulnerable to Simon's attack is that its proponents do not restrict themselves to a prescriptive role, and often take the either/or position of Marschak:

> The theory of rational behavior is a set of propositions that can be regarded either as an idealized approximation of the actual behavior of men or as a recommendation to be followed (Marschak, 1950, p. iii).

The writer would suggest Marschak's set of propositions are indeed recommendations to be followed, but at best could be an idealized approximation of the actions of very few, if any, men.

If the intention of the analyst is to devise descriptive-predictive models of human behavior, his attention might be directed to either Simon's stance of bounded rationality or that of psychological man dominated by affect.[1] The choice between these two assumptions as to man's rationality is influenced by the subject matter under study. In the writer's view, bounded rationality appears most appropriate for those situations in which one can hypothesize substantial conscious choices and an underlying view of psychological man lends itself to areas of decision in which there is evidence that less conscious, or instinctive, choice processes are involved. ∎

NOTE

1. John Krutilla and Leslie Curry have pointed out, quite correctly, that many useful studies of a descriptive-predictive nature have been carried out within the framework of traditional economic man or, more commonly, a rational man subject to a variety of constraints including the costs of obtaining additional information, human fallibility and lack of clairvoyance, chance, and the like.

The more constraints placed on the omniscience of the rational man, the closer such a model moves to that of bounded rationality until such time as the difference might be more semantic than real.

Essentially a matter of focus, the espousal of bounded rationality found in this volume is not intended as a denial of the utility of other formulations but rather to assert the utility of focusing on the limitations in decision making rather than on an ideal from which men deviate.

Herbert A. Simon
Satisficing and the One Right Way*

Upon first exposure to the word *satisficing* many people assume that it must be a typographical error. But it stands for an important concept that deserves its own word. Satisficing not only serves as a contrast to the optimizing concept favored by the adherents of the Rational Man position; in Simon's ingenious analysis it also plays a central role in the possibility of choice. Optimizing, by attempting to find the "right" answer, severely limits the available options. Satisficing, by contrast, involves a more relaxed decision rule that encourages the consideration of alternative solutions.

■   There is a proverb to the effect that the best is enemy of the good. A little reflection shows that the proverb can be read in two diametrically opposed ways, and that it is not clear which reading is intended — or is the more defensible. By one interpretation, the proverb means that if we are willing to settle for the good enough — to satisfice — we will never attain the best. By the other interpretation, it means that our striving to reach an unattainable best may prevent us from reaching an achievable good-enough. It is this latter interpretation that describes the stern realities of the design process in the world we know — in any world, for that matter, that is even moderately complex.

Since I have made the satisficing argument at length elsewhere, I will review it only briefly here, and then apply it specifically to the

*From "Style in design," by H. A. Simon, in *EDRA 2* (Proc. 2nd Envt. Design Res. Assn. Conf.), edited by J. Archea and C. Eastman, 1970, pages 1–3 (slightly abridged). Copyright ©1970 by Charles Eastman and John Archea. Reprinted by permission of the publisher, Dowden, Hutchinson & Ross, Inc., Stroudsburg, Pa.

It is hard to assess the costs for many of the resources people value.
Reprinted by permission of Newspaper Enterprise Association.

problem of design.[1] Most problem solving can be represented as a search through a large space of possibilities. For real-world problems, the spaces are not merely large, but immense, and there is not the slightest chance for either man or computer to search them exhaustively for the solution that is absolutely best.

Best solutions are therefore only attainable in those situations where there exist some systematic procedures, or algorithms, for going more or less directly to the optimum with only a moderate amount of highly selective search, or, in favorable instances, with no search at all. . . .

In other kinds of problem spaces, the available algorithms are not powerful enough to eliminate entirely the need for search, but are sufficiently selective to reduce search to tolerable proportions. . . .

Where optimizing algorithms are unavailable, or are impractical for problems of the size we must solve, settling for a satisfactory solution instead of seeking the best one is generally an excellent way out. Techniques for satisficing are often called "heuristic programming techniques."

Satisficing is sometimes dismissed as obvious and not very interesting common sense: "If you can't do the best, do the best you can." Alternatively, economists sometimes argue that satisficing is simply optimizing under a constraint on the resources available for search. The optimizing rule, in this view, is: Continue searching until the expected improvement in the solution from investment of additional search effort is just worth that effort; then halt.

Because they overlook two important points, the arguments from common sense and economics underestimate the importance of taking a satisficing viewpoint. First of all, when no selective optimizing algorithm is available, the cost of a search to find the best tends to increase at least linearly with the size of the space searched. In contrast,

Photo by De Wys Inc.

the cost of a search to find a satisfactory solution depends only on the density of distribution of solutions of varying quality through the space, and is more or less independent of the size of the total space. The familiar needle-in-haystack problem illustrates the point. In a haystack throughout which needles of varying sharpness are distributed randomly, finding the sharpest needle requires a search of the entire stack. Finding a needle sharp enough to sew with requires a search of a pile of hay big enough to contain one such needle — a pile whose size does not depend at all on the size of the whole stack. For most practical purposes, the real world is an infinite haystack, hence a place where we are well advised to satisfice.

The second point often ignored by optimizers is that, if the general magnitude of the available search effort is known in advance, then following an optimizing procedure until the marginal cost of additional search exceeds the expected gain is *not* equivalent to employing the best satisficing procedure. *Given* a resource limit, there may exist many satisficing procedures that will, on average, find better solutions than a truncated optimizing procedure. This proposition can again, of course, be translated into optimizing terms, but as a practical matter, it has often been overlooked by optimizers, who have consequently invested too little of their effort in the search for powerful heuristic procedures. Some of us would argue that this has resulted, in the past two decades, in a serious imbalance between the amount of research devoted to improving the kit of optimizing tools and the amount devoted to improving the kit of satisficing tools; and a consequent imbalance in the kits themselves. But pursuing this point would take me away from my main topic, which is style. What has the distinction between satisficing and optimizing to do with style?

*"The way I look at it, there's a price tag on
everything. You want a high standard of
living, you settle for a low quality of life."*
© 1971 J. B. Handelsman

Optimizing techniques generally produce unique solutions or
small sets of similar solutions. Although one can construct all sorts of
more or less pathological counterexamples to this generalization, they
have little relevance to the real world. Hence, an optimizer faces no
question of style, but simply a question of finding the best solution. If
we insist on according the optimizer a style, we can only equate it with
an extreme functionalism, in which function determines form, utterly
and completely. Few designers who subscribe to the functionalist view
would feel comfortable with the doctrine that they exercise no choice
and that no questions of style enter their design. But that is certainly
where an attempt to combine functionalism with optimizing leads us.

For the satisficer, the unique solution is the exception rather then
the rule. Mushrooms can be found in many places in the forest, and the

time it takes us to fill a sack with them may not depend much on the direction we wander. We may feel free, then, to exercise some choice of path, and even to introduce additional choice criteria (for example, the pleasantness of the walk or the avoidance of wet places) over and above the pragmatic one of bringing back a full sack.

There are really two cases to be distinguished here. In the one case, two distinct search paths may be generated by two different heuristic procedures each of which is designed only to find mushrooms. In the other case, two distinct search paths may be generated by two different heuristic procedures because one of them incorporates criteria beyond the basic one of finding mushrooms — or both incorporate auxiliary criteria, but different ones. In the former case, the choice of one or the other of the heuristic procedures is a choice of style; in the latter case, the choice of auxiliary criteria is a choice of style. In both cases, it is the nonuniqueness of satisfactory solutions that permits us the choice. Hence, in a world where the best is the enemy of the good, there is almost unlimited room for the expression of preferences in style even for the functionalist. ■

NOTE

1. The reader wishing to pursue this point will find a fuller discussion in my *Models of Man* (Wiley, 1957), particularly the introduction to part IV, and chapters 14, "A Behavioral Model of Rational Choice," and 15, "Rational Choice and the Environment."

Uriel G. Foa
Interpersonal and Economic Resources*

In addition to the commitment to perfect knowledge and optimization, Rational Man involves the assumption of substitutability, that is, the notion that it is always possible to find acceptable substitutes for what an individual wants. It is this assumption that allows all motivational considerations to be translated into a common coin. The resources considered in Foa's paper — love, status, services, goods, information, and money — provide a useful tool for looking at exchange, at the degree to which any one resource can be traded for another. (It should perhaps be noted that these resources are not commensurate in a number of respects. Some are primarily needs, while others are primarily instrumentalities, or means, rather than ends. Also "information" is used in a limited sense in this selection relative to our usage of the term. Any of the other five resources may carry informational value in this larger sense.)

The paper not only demonstrates the lack of free substitutability across these six resources, but also identifies the dimensions along which the substitutability breaks down. In addition, a series of properties have been identified upon which the various resources can be seen to differ. Foa then uses these properties to analyze the effect of urbanization upon the availability of different resources. Interestingly, urbanization tends to favor the more economic (in his terms, the less particularistic) resources, with a resulting difficulty in satisfying certain needs. From the perspective of Rational Man, there should be no problem here — yet there clearly is. Indeed, this paper suggests that substitutability is the exception rather than the rule.

■

Man doth not live by bread only.

DEUTERONOMY 8:3

Human needs are seldom satisfied in solitude; because people depend on one another for the material and psychological resources necessary to their well-being, they associate to exchange these resources through interpersonal behavior. In the study of these ex-

*Excerpted and reprinted by permission from U. G. Foa "Interpersonal and economic resources." *Science,* 29 January 1971, 171, 345–351. Copyright 1971 by the American Association for the Advancement of Science. (See Uriel G. Foa and Edna B. Foa *Societal Structures of the Mind.* Springfield, Ill.: C. C. Thomas, 1974, for an extensive treatment of Resource Theory.)

changes there has been a traditional division of tasks. Economists have long been concerned with the exchange of money with goods, and more recently, with labor and with information, while psychologists and sociologists (Etzioni, 1968; Maslow, 1967) have investigated transactions that involve more subtle resources, such as attraction, devotion and affect, esteem, respect, and status. This professional specialization does not, however, obviate the fact that the same behavior is often influenced by both economic and noneconomic factors: one may, for example, prefer a less paid but prestigious job to another where salary is higher but status is lower; and a small shop may attract customers by giving them the individual attention they miss at the less expensive but more impersonal department store. In view of this interplay of economic and noneconomic resources in the conduct of human affairs, it appears unrealistic to expect that social problems will be solved by material means alone. "There are no 'economic' problems; there are simply problems and they are complex," observes Myrdal (1970; Herbers, 1970) in discussing international development. Closer to home one can see model housing projects built a few years ago turning into model slums, possibly because their dwellers were provided with houses, but not with self-pride and a sense of community.

Attempts to bridge the dichotomy between economic and noneconomic resources came mainly from sociologists and social psychologists who sought to interpret every interpersonal behavior as an exchange, characterized by profit and loss (Blau, 1967; Homans, 1961; Longabaugh, 1963; Thibaut and Kelley, 1959). Extension of the economic model to noneconomic resources, however, produced difficulties for the social exchange theory. The fact, for instance, that resources like information and love can be given to others without reducing the amount possessed by the giver has been considered contradictory to the very notion of exchange (Cartwright and Zander, 1968) since this effect does not occur in transactions of money and goods.[1] Likewise it makes little sense to consider economic transactions of a person with himself; one can, on the other hand, express self-esteem or give information to himself by exploratory behavior. If, as these examples suggest, different resources follow distinct rules of exchange, how can they be reconciled within the same conceptual framework? A way out of this dilemma is to develop a theory that will reveal order in this diversity. In this article I review part of the research recently directed toward this goal and discuss some of its applications to social problems.

CLASSIFICATION OF RESOURCES

A first step in the search for order among various exchange rules is to devise a classification system that will group and distinguish resources in a manner that reflects similarities and differences in the behaviors associated with them. In order to achieve this purpose the classification should be based on those resource attributes which account for behavioral variance so that similarity of attributes correspond to similarity of behavior. If such a classification system can be found, it will then be possible to predict which resources share more similar rules and to anticipate conditions under which certain resources will be valued and exchanged and what exchanges will not take place.

This article will propose a classification system based on two coordinates of resource characterization: concreteness versus symbolism and particularism versus universalism. By classifying resources on the basis of these two attributes it is suggested that the resulting spatial location will provide a parsimonious framework for the beginnings of a theory of resource exchange.

Observation of interpersonal behavior shows that it varies from concrete to symbolic. Some behaviors, like giving an object or performing an activity upon the body or the belongings of another individual, are quite concrete. Some others are more symbolic: language, posture of the body, a smile, gesture, or facial expression (Duncan, 1969). Another characteristic on which resources differ is the significance of the person who provides the resource. Changing the bank teller will not make much of a difference for the client wishing to cash a check. A change of doctor or lawyer is less likely to be accepted with indifference. One is even more particularistic with regard to a friend, a spouse, or a mother. Harlow (1970) showed that when the facial features of a surrogate mother are altered, the baby monkey reacts with fear, refusing to accept the change. In some animal species certain communications are more target specific than others. Mating calls are more particularistic than status signals and the latter are less general than distress or alarm signals (Johnsgard, 1967).

In order to facilitate plotting interpersonal resources on the two coordinates, I first grouped them into six types (Foa and Foa, 1972): love, status, information, money, goods, and services. "Love" is defined as an expression of affectionate regard, warmth, or comfort; "status" is an expression of evaluative judgment which conveys high or low prestige, regard, or esteem; "information" includes advice, opinions, instruction, or enlightenment, but excludes those behaviors which could be classed as love or status; "money" is any coin, currency, or token which has some standard unit of exchange value; "goods" are tangible products, objects, or materials; and "services" involve activities on the body or belongings of a person which often constitute labor for another.

Each of the six resource types can be classified on the basis of the two coordinates suggested: concrete-symbolic and particularistic-universal. On the first coordinate, concreteness, services and goods involve the exchange of some overtly tangible activity or product and are classed as concrete. Status and information, on the other hand, are typically conveyed by verbal or paralinguistic behaviors and are thus

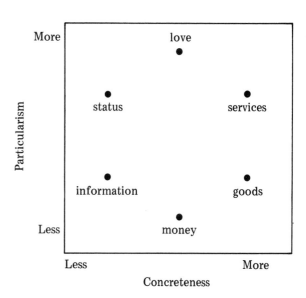

FIGURE 1

Position of the six resource classes plotted on the two coordinates of particularism and concreteness. The resources flow an approximate circular order so that each class has two neighbors, one on each side. The order shows the relative proximity of any two resources. Love, for example, is near to services and status and most distal from money. Information is a neighbor of status and money and is most distant from services.

more symbolic. Love and money are exchanged in both concrete and symbolic forms, and thus occupy intermediate positions on this coordinate.

The positions of love and money are extreme and opposite on the particularistic coordinate. It matters a great deal from whom we receive love since its reinforcing effectiveness is closely tied to the stimulus person. Money, on the other hand, is the least particularistic resource, since, of all resources, it is most likely to retain the same value regardless of the relation between, or characteristics of, the reinforcing agent and recipient. Services and status are less particularistic than love, but more particularistic than goods and information.

The position of the six resource classes plotted on the two coordinates is shown in figure 1. For simplicity's sake these six classes of resources have been represented by discrete points. It is more accurate to consider each class as occupying a range in the order, so that some of its elements will be nearer to one of the two neighboring classes than to the other. A verbal expression of love such as "I like you very much" is symbolic and thus is more similar to status than to services. Conversely, fondling and kissing are concrete ways of expressing affection, closer to services than to status. Services to the body are proximal to love, while services to one's belongings are nearer to goods. Likewise, consumption goods are closer to services than durable goods. A credit card can be considered a kind of money, but it is more particularistic than currency; not every merchant will honor a credit card, and the card is not issued to everybody. This form of payment is also more symbolic than currency; although nothing concrete is given in a credit card payment, currency actually changes hands. Thus a credit card will be nearer to information than currency. In fact, the card provides information on the solvency of its holder.

EMPIRICAL EVIDENCE

The value of the proposed theoretical structure depends on the possibility of deriving meaningful empirical predictions from it. It is hypothesized here that resources proximal to one another in the structure will be responded to more similarily than distal ones. In particular, it is predicted that resources proximal in the order will (1) be perceived as more similar, (2) be more substitutable for one another, and (3) elicit similar resources in social exchange. These hypotheses were tested in a number of studies (Turner, Foa, & Foa, 1971). . . .

ORDER-RELATED PROPERTIES OF RESOURCES

Six exchange properties have been identified and related to the position of the resources in their space. These properties may well provide an explanation for the value that each resource takes on the particularistic-universalistic dimension. Indeed, love and money, the two classes at opposite poles of this dimension, appear to differ most with regard to these properties; stating the values that love and money assume on each property will therefore be sufficient to provide an approximate idea of the values appropriate to other resources as well. Services and status will be more similar to love than to money, while the contrary will hold for information and goods. Differences, within each pair of classes, on the concreteness dimension will not be discussed here. The first two properties refer to exchange outcomes, while the others deal with environmental conditions which enhance or hinder particular exchanges.

Relationship between Self and Other   The relationship between giving the resource to the other and giving it to self is positive for love but decreases and becomes negative as one moves from love toward money, its opposite in the order. This prediction is related to the intuitive notion that the ability to love others requires self-acceptance and is supported by the repeated finding of a positive relationship between giving love to self and to others (Foa, 1966). Quite the opposite is true with regard to money, since one person's gain is another's loss. In consequence, an exchange of money can be a zero-sum game, while an exchange of love cannot.

Relationship between Giving and Taking   In love there is usually a certain degree of ambivalence even in normal individuals; giving love does not exclude the concurrent presence of some hostility, or the taking away of love (Foa, 1966). However, giving and taking away money are unlikely to occur in the same act.

Relationship between Interpersonal Situation and Exchange
Money does not require an interpersonal relationship in order to be transmitted or kept for future exchanges, and it can conveniently be sent through a third person. Love, on the other hand, can hardly be separated from the interpersonal situation, kept for a long time in the absence of actual exchange, or transmitted by an intermediary without incurring loss.

Time for Processing Input   Giving and receiving love cannot be done in a hurry; it requires time. Money, to the contrary, can change hands very rapidly.

Delay of Reward   Love is a relatively long-term investment, with rewards being reaped only after several encounters; a friendship needs to be "cultivated" so that trust (that is, expectation that the exchange will be completed) is a necessary condition. On the other hand, an exchange of money with another resource can be completed in a single encounter.

Optimum Group Size   It has been noted that in animal species living in groups, such as monkeys and apes, there is an optimum group size, presumably related to the input processing capacity of the species. When this size is exceeded, behavior disruptive to group life seems to increase (Calhoun, 1962; Carpenter, 1963). In the human species the optimum group size for an orderly exchange of resources may vary with the resource class, being smallest for love and largest for money. Indeed, Nye et al. (1970) reported a decrease in affective exchanges among members of nuclear families when the number of children increased beyond two. Similar findings regarding services, a neighbor of the love class, were described by Latané and Darley (1969). While investigating helping behavior in emergency situations, they found that the larger the number of bystanders, the less likely it is for any one of them to intervene and help. On the other hand, large groups meet for trade in a stock or commodities exchange and access to a large market is considered advantageous by businessmen.

The relationship between order and properties of resource classes may originate in the sequence of cognitive development of these classes during socialization; the characteristics of each resource indeed appear to reflect the conditions which existed when it became a distinct cognitive class (Foa and Foa, 1972). Love develops early, in the small and relatively permanent family group, before the "self-other" and "giving-taking" differentiations have become firmly established. Money, on the other hand, acquires its meaning much later, after one has learned that "self" is not "other" and "giving" is not "taking," and from the beginning it is used mostly for exchanges outside the family. Thus resources are best exchanged in conditions that resemble those under which they had been learned in the past.

After having presented an ordered classification of resources, which was empirically validated, and after discussing differential rules and environmental conditions for exchanging the various resources, I shall give some illustration as to how resource theory explains behavioral patterns, which are otherwise less understandable. In particular, I turn now to examine how urbanization results in deprivation of certain resources and to discuss its effects on social functioning.

INFLUENCE OF URBAN ENVIRONMENT ON EXCHANGE

The aspects of resource theory developed in this article may be useful in understanding the effects of urbanization upon human behavior. Three properties of resources — time required for processing inputs, delay of reward, and optimal group size — converge in making the urban environment more suitable to the exchange of universalistic resources than of particularistic ones. Milgram (Milgram, 1970) proposed that reducing the time allocated to each input is an adaptive response to the overload of interpersonal stimuli which characterizes an urban center. If the processing of input requires more time for love than for less particularistic resources, it follows that, in the city, love will be curtailed more than the latter resources. In an urban setting many interpersonal contacts occur only once, while love, unlike money, requires at least several encounters to be exchanged. Finally, if optimum group size is smaller for love than for money, the large metropolitan crowds will again favor universalistic exchanges over personalistic ones (Zimbardo, 1969).[2]

A consequence of the selective influence of urban society on exchange is the facilitation of antisocial or asocial behavior. Particularistic resources, especially status, are powerful instruments for social-control; a person who misbehaves is likely to lose status in the community long before he runs into conflict with the law and meets its less particularistic forms of punishment. The relative scarcity of particularistic exchanges in the city deprives society of informal means for social control so that individuals tend to behave less responsibly in the metropolis (Zimbardo, 1969). The difficulties posed by an urban environment to particularistic exchanges will also result in isolation and alienation since the feeling of belonging is provided by love, the resource with the highest positive relationship between self and other.

These difficulties are further compounded in modern American society by the tendency of its social institutions to specialize in a narrow range of resources, thus excluding the exchange of particularistic resources from several institutions, even when environmental conditions are favorable. Cultural norms are quite specific with regard to the resources which may be used in a given institution. These norms, as previously noted, are reflected in the institutional frequency distribution of resources. Institutional specialization is less pronounced in traditional cultures, so that the profiles of their institutions are more similar to one another than in American society. More precisely, exchange of particularistic resources tends, in our society, to be restricted to fewer institutions than in traditional cultures. Discussing personal problems with the boss, for example, is customary for a Thai worker, but not for an American one. It has been shown that these cross-cultural differences can be reduced by training American subjects to behave in a manner appropriate to a traditional culture by a more liberal use of love and status (Chemers et al., 1966; Foa, 1964; Foa, 1967; Foa and Chemers, 1967; Foa and Donnenwerth, 1971; Mitchell and Foa, 1969; Fielder et al., 1970). Increasing particularistic exchanges is also the goal of various forms of sensitivity training and encounter marathons, particularly those stressing nonverbal communication. Thus, while in traditional cultures opportunity for particularistic exchanges is offered by less institutional specialization, in our society, in line with its strong institutional differentiation, special institutions for these exchanges are set up.

The importance of adequate provision of resources for the social functioning of the individual has become painfully apparent only recently in America, as changes in the social environment have created conditions which are unfavorable to particularistic exchanges. In the same way as with physical environment, we have begun to recognize indispensable features of the social environment only after they had been altered in the wake of technological change.

CONCLUSION AND SUMMARY

High population density and increased institutional specialization, which are relatively novel features of human society, have provided conditions for a more efficient exchange of universalistic resources, while decreasing the opportunity for exchanging particularistic ones. The parallel with physical environment is striking: in both cases technology has created new problems in the process of solving old ones. Whether it is natural resources or interpersonal resources, physical ecology or social ecology, recognizing and defining the new problem is the first step toward its solution.

The importance of particularistic resources in solving problems of modern society has scarcely been recognized. Welfare institutions, for example, often require clients to lose status for the money they receive.

This form of exchange deprives the client of a resource which is already scarce for him, thus further reducing his chances of autonomous performance as a resource exchanger in society. By ignoring the significance of particularistic resources for social functioning, we tend to see the solution of social problems exclusively in terms of a better distribution of economic resources. Improvement of education, for instance, is considered almost equivalent to allocating more money for schools. Truly money is one of the neighbors of information in the order, but the other one is status. Evidence to suggest that higher status improves educational achievement has, indeed, been repeatedly reported (Coleman, 1966; Rosenthal and Jacobson, 1968).

The very mention of particularistic resources in social planning causes uneasiness and bafflement. The economist Levitan (1969), for example, in reviewing the activities of VISTA (a program of the Office of Economic Opportunity), wonders how to evaluate goals such as dedication, involvement, and good feeling. The reluctance to include particularistic resources in social engineering will hopefully decrease as we improve techniques for their observation and measurement and as we begin to understand their rules of exchange and their relationship to other resources. The work described here may constitute a step in such a direction.

The opportunity to progress more decisively toward a comprehensive picture of the state of resources in society is provided by the proposal to institute social indicators.[3] Properly constructed they could supply much needed information about resource deficiencies that affect the health of society and could suggest measures to overcome them.

The purpose of this article has been to summarize some of the knowledge we already possess about interpersonal resources and to outline its application to certain problems of modern society. It has been shown that when resources are classified into six categories and plotted on a two-coordinate space a definite structural pattern emerges. The position of each resource class in the structure appears related to certain properties which in turn affect differentially the exchange of resources in an urban environment. The structural characteristics of resources provide a theoretical basis for the understanding and solution of social problems in modern culture.[4]   ■

NOTES
1. The price asked for giving information was lower than for giving material goods in an experimental three-person game described by S. Rosen (1966).
2. Recent experimental results suggest that these environmental factors affect exchanges of giving but not exchanges of taking. Lack of previous contact and reduced feedback from the potential victim have been found to increase the probability of aggressive behavior (Turner, 1970).
3. A recent discussion and a selected bibliography on the social indicators pro-

posal is given in *Annals of the American Academy of Political and Social Sciences* (March 1970).

4. Supported in part by grant GS-2094 from the National Science Foundation. I thank B. J. Biddle, E. B. Foa, and J. L. Turner for suggestions.

■ Yes. In the narrowest material sense, large-scale organization is very efficient. But in *human* terms, it is inefficient to a degree that surpasses our ordinary powers of imagination.

The bigger our institutions become, the more lost and powerless and alienated most of us feel. The larger our assembly lines grow, the less satisfaction we take in our work. The more our farms are consolidated into agribiz conglomerates, the less taste and nutrition there is in our food.

The simplest things, which only fifty years ago could be done without difficulty, now — in the name of "efficiency" — cannot be done anymore. They "cost too much." They "take too much time." It seems that the richer we become, the less we can afford.

When you really stop to think about it, the most striking thing about modern society — which we constantly tell ourselves is supremely organized for "efficiency" — is that it requires so much and accomplishes so little that we really want to accomplish. It is safe to say that the human race has never known an economic system in which the relationship between the input of irreplaceable resources and output of human satisfaction has been so unfavorable as it is now.   ■

— E. F. Schumacher*

■ As a rough first definition we can start by recognizing that any valid concept of dignity and equality includes a number of nonmaterial "goods" — responsibility, security, and participation, the free exchange of thought and experience, a degree of human respect that is independent of monetary rewards or bureaucratic hierarchies, and a realization that this respect is lacking where rewards and hierarchies are too restrictive or too skewed. All these goods of culture, of man's mind and spirit, need not be costly in terms of material resources. Indeed, they belong to the sphere of life where growth is truly exponential — in knowledge, in beauty, in neighborliness and human concern.   ■

— Barbara Ward †

*Excerpted from a Plowboy Interview with E. F. Schumacher in *The Mother Earth News,* Issue No. 42. Copyright © 1976 by The Mother Earth News®, Inc., P.O. Box 70, Hendersonville, N.C., 28739. Excerpted by permission.

†From Barbara Ward *The Home of Man.* New York: W. W. Norton and Company, 1976. Page 6. Reprinted by permission.

PART 2

THE EXPERIENCE OF THE ENVIRONMENT

THE first part of the book concerned the beast. We have described an organism that builds maps and that seeks opportunities to use and extend them. People struggle to make sense of their environment, to comprehend their lives, their surroundings, their universe. In pursuit of this goal, they form representations of the recurring patterns that they experience. These representations make it possible to see clearly even when the available information is not at all clear. (This efficiency is, of course, not without its price. Errors occur, and misplaced confidence is not rare.) Representations in turn are assembled into larger networks, into cognitive maps that permit prediction, anticipation, and even planning. The development of such structures thus serves the desired goal of sense making. In time, however, they tend to be taken for granted, and the individual seeks involvement — and hence further map building — elsewhere.

We turn now to a more concrete consideration of some of the problems the environment creates for people and some of the ways that people attempt to deal with them. How well does the modern environment fit the needs and abilities of this model-building, information-processing organism? What are the costs of the many ways in which this fit has become increasingly unsatisfactory? This second part begins with the issue of "the preferred environment" and some of the manifestations of its absence. It concludes with a consideration of various ways humans have found for dealing with such nonpreferred settings, both in terms of modifying the environment where possible and adapting to it when not.

In certain crucial respects the modern environment is unlike the one in which humans evolved, and to which they are adapted. It is not that the environment is no longer uncertain. Adversity, too, has not vanished. But in evolution, humans were few, and now they are many. In evolution, humans were surrounded by natural stimuli, while now such surroundings may require considerable effort to achieve. In evolution, humans had limited technological capacity and limited impact on the appearance of the environment. Today, people are often surrounded by man-made structures and man-made arrangements.

Given a conception of human capacities and human needs, it becomes possible to sketch out some environmental properties that humans prefer. In chapter 6 we examine the applicability of the needs to make sense and to be involved to qualities of the environment. In other words, the issue is not "Where would it be fun to be?" so much as a consideration of the properties or characteristics of environments that are, relatively speaking, supportive.

Deviations from these preferred circumstances produce a variety of modern-day stresses. Such human costs of the failure of humane environmental conditions are considered in chapter 7. For the individual in an environment that is in many respects strange, noisy, and crowded, the threat of overload is probably far more immediate than it was when humans evolved. On the other hand, an individual who feels neither needed nor challenged by a bland and uncaring environment may feel uninvolved and alienated. Much of the current confusion and frustration on the human scene may be a symptom of these pervasive problems. Indeed, some of the most distressing human behavior may be the outcome of environments that go counter to human preferences in so many ways.

But powerful and adaptive organisms are not necessarily helpless in the face of such stresses. Humans have a profound stake in keeping the information generated by the environment manageable. They are flexible and inventive. And they are social animals. As such, they have developed a variety of strategies for coping, for controlling the stresses that confront them. These strategies are many and various, and occur in a variety of blends and combinations. R. W. White (1974), through his concrete imagery of coping in children, effectively develops the richness and power of the concept.

As an approximation to a framework for analyzing and understanding these patterns of strategies, chapters 8 and 9 are organized in terms of three different ways of coping. It should be remembered that these distinctions are a conceptual tool; in actual cases the boundaries tend to blur, and pure strategies are rarely adaptive.

Choice is essentially action based on preference. If a preferred environment can be found, an individual could migrate to it or perhaps visit it periodically. *Control* involves the creation and/or management of an environment in such a way as to enhance its preference value. The selections in chapter 8 incorporate both these strategies. Choice and control often go hand in hand, both because control is often necessary to defend what one has chosen, and control is often utilized to make an environment more like what one would have chosen had it been available.

Interpretation entails an essentially conceptual solution to the problem of a world that makes little sense and/or fails to be involving. While individuals can impose their own pattern of meaning and importance, the most striking use of this mode of coping is by groups holding shared understandings. As discussed in chapter 9, such cultural interpretations impose patterns on environment and experience; they provide a ready-made structure for identifying what matters and for making that portion of the world comprehensible.

Participation, the topic of the final chapter, involves taking an active role in what happens in the environment. In a sense it involves a synthesis of the various coping strategies. It can be viewed as a restoration of what once was a more common human/environment relationship. It is important not only in improving environmental design and planning, but also as a model of how humans can relate to decision making in an increasingly complicated and increasingly expert-dominated world. Nowhere are the requirements and tendencies of the knowledge-oriented human more clearly displayed than in the context of participation. So often the failure of participation is directly attributable to failure to provide a basis for achieving a shared view of the problem. Conversely, when the nature of the beast is recognized, participation can be the key to powerful and effective solutions, to small steps in the direction of creating a more humane environment.

6 Preferred Environments

We now recognize that "war is unhealthy for children and other living things," but beyond that, surprisingly little seems to be known about the requirements for a healthy human environment. Modern zoos reflect great advances in understanding of supportive habitats for many different forms of life, but similar progress in the human sphere has not been evident.

Given a basic understanding of what humans know and care about, it should be possible to form at least a tentative conception of an environment that would be supportive and satisfying for humans. What kind of environment would be suited to a knowledge-hungry organism, one concerned to comprehend and to explore, and yet quite limited in how much it can handle at any one time? What kinds of environments do humans prefer? What properties must environments possess to enhance people's well-being and effectiveness?

A problem in discussing preferred environments, and in identifying their properties, is the almost frivolous connotation of the term *preference*. It suggests the decorative rather than the essential, the favored as opposed to the necessary. But viewed within the larger evolutionary context, preference — even aesthetics for that matter — is closely tied to basic concerns. An organism must prefer those environments in which it is likely to thrive; likewise it must dislike environments in which it is likely to be ineffective or handicapped or harmed in any way. Preference in this context is to no small degree an expression of human needs. In other words, preferred environments will in general be ones in which human abilities are more likely to be effective and needs are more likely to be met (S. Kaplan, 1973b). This does not mean that people are necessarily aware of their needs, nor that preferences do not include idiosyncratic elements, as well as distortions caused by social influences, unrepresentative experiences, and the like. But it does imply that preferences cannot be taken lightly, that they are important indicators of environments in which humans can be constructive and effective.

One approach to preferred environments follows from William James's observation that "the best attention is effortless." Since the selection of information is a vital issue, surroundings where attention presents no problem are likely to be safer and more desirable for effective functioning. Such environments, where the management of information seems to take care of itself, where attention is, as it were, inherent in what one is experiencing, are likely to be preferred.

If this is the case, then, remembering the discussion of attention and fascination in chapter 4, one would expect certain contents and certain processes to contribute to preference. Contents that play a role here might be expected to have a connection to important properties of the environment in which humans evolved. And indeed, fire, water, and caves seem to have properties that hold people's attention. "Green" places, or settings that are at least partially "natural," seem to be preferred. Such content concerns are frequently expressed in what are considered desirable residential areas, vacation settings, and places to eat one's lunch on a warm day.

In terms of process, environments that are likely to be preferred are those that permit "involvement" and "making sense." These factors are complementary: a desirable environment presumably provides both. They are also rather broad categories, each subsuming a variety of properties that might or might not be present in a given environment.

For an environment to be "involving" it must have some complexity or diversity. Involvement can also come from features that are not actually present but are suggested or implied. The road turning around a bend and disappearing is the classic example of a promise of more information, of what we have called mystery (R. Kaplan, 1973a).

For an environment to "make sense" requires coherence; the parts need to hang together and in some sense "belong" there. Ground textures that provide continuity and the repetition of elements (windows on a building or a row of trees) play a role here. Lynch's concept of legibility, first introduced in the urban domain, is also an important component in making sense. One might view legibility as a promise that the environment will be comprehendible as one continues to make one's way through it. In the natural environment, legibility is enhanced by a sense of depth and by the smoothness of the texture, both of which facilitate seeing where one is headed.

One kind of environment that seems to offer both the capacity to make sense and the opportunity for involvement is the miniature. By providing "the bigger picture" (necessarily through the judicious loss of some detail), the miniature permits one to comprehend the situation and to explore at the same time. Japanese gardens exemplify the fragile balance among these various components that maximizes a pleasurable environment.

While the origin of these concepts is in the context of the physical environment, and of landscapes in particular, the concepts themselves are reasonable in terms of human information processing quite apart from a particular setting. Certain properties are common to any cognitive map, no matter what the environment. Likewise, there are certain properties common to any environment that is readily comprehended, i.e., that one readily builds a map of. Coherence is what makes it possible to organize the field, to divide it into units for which one already has appropriate representations. Complexity or diversity provide a sufficient number of representations to fill the mind and to insure that the focus will not be shared with other content. Mystery is an indication that there is the possibility of exploring, of extending one's cognitive map. And legibility is a kind of reassurance, an indication that the informational environment yet to come will be manageable. (For a fuller discussion of these issues, see S. Kaplan, 1975, and R. Kaplan, 1977c).

But a preferred environment is not completely a function of the environmental configuration. The organism's prior experiences necessarily play an important role here. "Making sense" depends, in part at least, on one's knowledge and expectations. But that is not to say that the relationship between preference and the familiar is straightforward. (See, for example, Herzog et al., 1976). One does not necessarily prefer that which one knows better. What is needed is not necessarily a familiarity with a particular setting, but a means of grasping the situation, a way to relate it to something else that is already well represented. (The last selection in the book provides an excellent example of this.)

It should be clear that we are concerned with identifying properties of the environment that enhance some sense of appropriateness or rightness or fit. If we recognize some characteristics of a supportive environment, we are more likely to incorporate them in planning and decision making. There is no thought here that all people share these preferences, any more than that they have identical cognitive maps of even the same setting. At the same time, the elements of preference described here, despite different weightings, presumably play some role in every individual's experience.

The selections in this chapter provide examples of preferred environments both in terms of a wide range of settings and in terms of a variety of informational properties. One relatively straightforward way to distinguish them is in terms of a "man-made" versus "natural" dimension. Certainly Lynch and Carr speak to the requirements of cityscapes and built environments, while Eliovson and Kaplan focus more on the natural settings. Jackson and Zube, by discussing the residential, fall somewhere in between. The selections can also be distinguished in terms of scale — from a whole city to a backyard or a miniature landscape in a garden.

Another dimension distinguishing these various selections is the degree to which process or content is the primary issue in preference. Jackson and Zube emphasize content, the feelings people have toward particular elements in the environment. Watt, and to a large degree Lynch and Carr, all emphasize process, that is, the informational properties that make any environment involving and sensible. Eliovson and Kaplan fall in between on this dimension. They deal with preferred contents, while at the same time identifying informational properties. To the extent that the environments they describe have both content and process going for them, their powerful hold on preference is hardly surprising.

Kevin Lynch
The Image of the Environment[*]

Lynch's discussion of legibility stands as a landmark in the literature relating the experience of the environment to the process of knowing. This is a perceptive statement both of the benefits of legibility and of the costs of its absence. From this perspective the importance of familiarity in preference is not hard to comprehend.

■   Looking at cities can give a special pleasure, however commonplace the sight may be. Like a piece of architecture, the city is a construction in space, but one of vast scale, a thing perceived only in the course of long spans of time. City design is therefore a temporal art, but it can rarely use the controlled and limited sequences of other temporal arts like music. On different occasions and for different people,

[*]From Kevin Lynch *The image of the city*. Cambridge, Mass.: MIT Press. 1960. Pages 1–8. Reprinted by permission.

the sequences are reversed, interrupted, abandoned, cut across. It is seen in all lights and all weathers.

At every instant, there is more than the eye can see, more than the ear can hear, a setting or a view waiting to be explored. Nothing is experienced by itself, but always in relation to its surroundings, the sequences of events leading up to it, the memory of past experiences. Washington Street set in a farmer's field might look like the shopping street in the heart of Boston, and yet it would seem utterly different. Every citizen has had long associations with some part of his city, and his image is soaked in memories and meanings.

Moving elements in a city, and in particular the people and their activities, are as important as the stationary physical parts. We are not simply observers of this spectacle, but are ourselves a part of it, on the stage with the other participants. Most often, our perception of the city is not sustained, but rather partial, fragmentary, mixed with other concerns. Nearly every sense is in operation, and the image is the composite of them all.

Not only is the city an object which is perceived (and perhaps enjoyed) by millions of people of widely diverse class and character, but it is the product of many builders who are constantly modifying the structure for reasons of their own. While it may be stable in general outlines for some time, it is ever changing in detail. Only partial control can be exercised over its growth and form. There is no final result, only a continuous succession of phases. No wonder, then, that the art of shaping cities for sensuous enjoyment is an art quite separate from architecture or music or literature. It may learn a great deal from these other arts, but it cannot imitate them.

A beautiful and delightful city environment is an oddity, some would say an impossibility. Not one American city larger than a village is of consistently fine quality, although a few towns have some pleasant fragments. It is hardly surprising, then, that most Americans have little idea of what it can mean to live in such an environment. They are clear enough about the ugliness of the world they live in, and they are quite vocal about the dirt, the smoke, the heat, and the congestion, the chaos and yet the monotony of it. But they are hardly aware of the potential value of harmonious surroundings, a world which they may have briefly glimpsed only as tourists or as escaped vacationers. They can have little sense of what a setting can mean in terms of daily delight, or as a continuous anchor for their lives, or as an extension of the meaningfulness and richness of the world.

LEGIBILITY

This book will consider the visual quality of the American city by studying the mental image of that city which is held by its citizens. It will concentrate especially on one particular visual quality: the apparent clarity or "legibility" of the cityscape. By this we mean the ease with which its parts can be recognized and can be organized into a coherent pattern. Just as this printed page, if it is legible, can be visually grasped as a related pattern of recognizable symbols, so a legible city would be one whose districts or landmarks or pathways are easily identifiable and are easily grouped into an overall pattern.

This book will assert that legibility is crucial in the city setting, will analyze it in some detail, and will try to show how this concept might be used today in rebuilding our cities. As will quickly become apparent to the reader, this study is a preliminary exploration, a first word not a last word, an attempt to capture ideas and to suggest how they might be developed and tested. Its tone will be speculative and perhaps a little irresponsible: at once tentative and presumptuous. . . .

Although clarity or legibility is by no means the only important property of a beautiful city, it is of special importance when considering environments at the urban scale of size, time, and complexity. To understand this, we must consider not just the city as a thing in itself, but the city being perceived by its inhabitants.

Structuring and identifying the environment is a vital ability among all mobile animals. Many kinds of cues are used: the visual sensations of color, shape, motion, or polarization of light, as well as other senses such as smell, sound, touch, kinesthesia, sense of gravity, and perhaps of electric or magnetic fields. These techniques of orientation, from the polar flight of a tern to the path-finding of a limpet over the micro-topography of a rock, are described and their importance underscored in an extensive literature. (Casamajor, 1927; Fischer, 1931; Griffin, 1953; Rabaud, 1927). Psychologists have also studied this ability in man, although rather sketchily or under limited laboratory conditions. (Angyal, 1930; Binet, 1894; Brown, 1932; Claparède, 1943; Jaccard, 1932; Ryan, 1940; Sandström, 1951; Trowbridge, 1913; Witkin, 1949). Despite a few remaining puzzles, it now seems unlikely that there is any mystic "instinct" of way-finding. Rather there is a consistent use and organization of definite sensory cues from the external environment. This organization is fundamental to the efficiency and to the very survival of free-moving life.

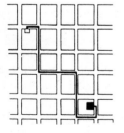

To become completely lost is perhaps a rather rare experience for most people in the modern city. We are supported by the presence of others and by special way-finding devices: maps, street numbers, route signs, bus placards. But let the mishap of disorientation once occur, and the sense of anxiety and even terror that accompanies it reveals to us how closely it is linked to our sense of balance and well-being. The very word "lost" in our language means much more than simple geographical uncertainty; it carries overtones of utter disaster.

In the process of way-finding, the strategic link is the environmental image, the generalized mental picture of the exterior physical world that is held by an individual. This image is the product both of immediate sensation and of the memory of past experience, and it is used to interpret information and to guide action. The need to recognize and pattern our surroundings is so crucial, and has such long roots in the past, that this image has wide practical and emotional importance to the individual.

Obviously a clear image enables one to move about easily and quickly: to find a friend's house or a policeman or a button store. But an ordered environment can do more than this; it may serve as a broad frame of reference, an organizer of activity or belief or knowledge. On the basis of a structural understanding of Manhattan, for example, one can order a substantial quantity of facts and fancies about the nature of the world we live in. Like any good framework, such a structure gives the individual a possibility of choice and a starting-point for the acquisition of further information. A clear image of the surroundings is thus a useful basis for individual growth.

A vivid and integrated physical setting, capable of producing a sharp image, plays a social role as well. It can furnish the raw material for the symbols and collective memories of group communication. A striking landscape is the skeleton upon which many primitive races erect their socially important myths. Common memories of the "home town" were often the first and easiest point of contact between lonely soldiers during the war.

A good environmental image gives its possessor an important sense of emotional security. He can establish an harmonious relationship between himself and the outside world. This is the obverse of the fear that comes with disorientation; it means that the sweet sense of home is strongest when home is not only familiar but distinctive as well.

Indeed, a distinctive and legible environment not only offers security but also heightens the potential depth and intensity of human experience. Although life is far from impossible in the visual chaos of the modern city, the same daily action could take on new meaning if carried out in a more vivid setting. Potentially, the city is in itself the powerful symbol of a complex society. If visually well set forth, it can also have strong expressive meaning.

It may be argued against the importance of physical legibility that the human brain is marvelously adaptable, that with some experience one can learn to pick one's way through the most disordered or featureless surroundings. There are abundant examples of precise navigation over the "trackless" wastes of sea, sand, or ice, or through a tangled maze of jungle.

Yet even the sea has the sun and stars, the winds, currents, birds, and sea-colors without which unaided navigation would be impossible.

The fact that only skilled professionals could navigate among the Polynesian Islands, and this only after extensive training, indicates the difficulties imposed by this particular environment. Strain and anxiety accompanied even the best-prepared expeditions.

In our own world, we might say that almost everyone can, if attentive, learn to navigate in Jersey City, but only at the cost of some effort and uncertainty. Moreover, the positive values of legible surroundings are missing: the emotional satisfaction, the framework for communication or conceptual organization, the new depths that it may bring to everyday experience. These are pleasures we lack, even if our present city environment is not as disordered as to impose an intolerable strain on those who are familiar with it.

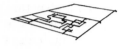

It must be granted that there is some value in mystification, labyrinth, or surprise in the environment. Many of us enjoy the House of Mirrors, and there is a certain charm in the crooked streets of Boston. This is so, however, only under two conditions. First, there must be no danger of losing basic form or orientation, of never coming out. The surprise must occur in an over-all framework; the confusions must be small regions in a visible whole. Furthermore, the labyrinth or mystery must in itself have some form that can be explored and in time be apprehended. Complete chaos without hint of connection is never pleasurable.

But these second thoughts point to an important qualification. The observer himself should play an active role in perceiving the world and have a creative part in developing his image. He should have the power to change that image to fit changing needs. An environment which is ordered in precise and final detail may inhibit new patterns of activity. A landscape whose every rock tells a story may make difficult the creation of fresh stories. Although this may not seem to be a critical issue in our present urban chaos, yet it indicates that what we seek is not a final but an open-ended order, capable of continuous further development.

BUILDING THE IMAGE

Environmental images are the result of a two-way process between the observer and his environment. The environment suggests distinctions and relations, and the observer — with great adaptability and in the light of his own purposes — selects, organizes, and endows with meaning what he sees. The image so developed now limits and emphasizes what is seen, while the image itself is being tested against the filtered perceptual input in a constant interacting process. Thus the image of a given reality may vary significantly between different observers.

The coherence of the image may arise in several ways. There may be little in the real object that is ordered or remarkable, and yet its mental picture has gained identity and organization through long familiarity. One man may find objects easily on what seems to anyone else to be a totally disordered work table. Alternatively, an object seen for the first time may be identified and related not because it is individually familiar but because it conforms to a stereotype already constructed by the observer. An American can always spot the corner drugstore, however indistinguishable it might be to a Bushman. Again, a new object may seem to have strong structure or identity because of striking physical features which suggest or impose their own pattern. Thus the sea or a great mountain can rivet the attention of one coming from the flat plains of the interior, even if he is so young or so parochial as to have no name for these great phenomena.

As manipulators of the physical environment, city planners are primarily interested in the external agent in the interaction which produces the environmental image. Different environments resist or facilitate the process of image-making. Any given form, a fine vase or a lump of clay, will have a high or a low probability of evoking a strong image among various observers. Presumably this probability can be stated with greater and greater precision as the observers are grouped in more and more homogeneous classes of age, sex, culture, occupation, temperament, or familiarity. Each individual creates and bears his own image, but there seems to be substantial agreement among members of the same group. It is these group images, exhibiting consensus among significant numbers, that interest city planners who aspire to model an environment that will be used by many people.

Therefore this study will tend to pass over individual differences, interesting as they might be to a psychologist. The first order of business will be what might be called the "public images," the common mental pictures carried by large numbers of a city's inhabitants: areas of agreement which might be expected to appear in the interaction of a single physical reality, a common culture, and a basic physiological nature.

The systems of orientation which have been used vary widely throughout the world, changing from culture to culture, and from landscape to landscape. Appendix A gives examples of many of them: the abstract and fixed directional systems, the moving systems, and those that are directed to the person, the home, or the sea. The world may be organized around a set of focal points, or be broken into named regions, or be linked by remembered routes. Varied as these methods are, and inexhaustible as seem to be the potential clues which a man may pick out to differentiate his world, they cast interesting sidelights on the means that we use today to locate ourselves in our own city world. For the most part these examples seem to echo, curiously enough, the formal types of image elements into which we can conveniently divide the city image: path, landmark, edge, node, and district. ∎

Stephen Carr
Some Criteria for Environmental Form*

Here Carr provides a variety of practical suggestions for improvement in city form. These help make more tangible and concrete Lynch's suggestions in the previous selection. A number of Carr's proposals also speak to the issue of making the city more responsive. (While responsiveness undoubtedly contributes to preference, it also plays a central role in encouraging participation, the topic of the final chapter. Thus, a selection by Carr and Lynch that offers some further thoughts on the issue of responsiveness can be found there.)

■   Given the current limited state of our knowledge about the relationship between the city of the mind and the city "out there," what criteria for environmental form can reasonably be deduced? In very general terms, we might conclude that a good environment should at the least support socially desirable planful behavior and facilitate man's effort after meaning. However, such statements are not much help to the hard-pressed city planner or designer. Much more research is needed of course, but even without it a number of still general but somewhat more operational criteria are suggested by what is known. Before stating these, I must stress that such criteria must be more in the nature of hypotheses than design tools at the moment. They are deductively derived and projected from present knowledge, testable but untested, capable of being made operational but not yet made so, and certainly incomplete. Further, since they are not applied to a specific case, they are unweighted, and no attempt has been made to eliminate possible conflicts between them. They are, in short, very much like the other criteria we use in city planning. While some speculation is unavoidable, I will list only those criteria which seem to me to be rather well supported by current knowledge:

1   *Increase the exposure of people to a variety of environmental settings and potential interactions.* This will of course provide choice and allow for individual differences, but it should also have important effects on increasing people's sense of the possible and level of aspiration. For this reason it may be especially important for children. It can be

accomplished by increasing the real variety of action settings, linked together in space and accessible within some limited time, or by increasing the mobility of people. When applied to the settings of daily activities or the routes of typical trips, increasing accessible variety means a reduction in the need for detailed planning of daily activities and increasing personal efficiency. What constitutes accessible variety depends in part on particular publics: a great variety of high-priced, upper-class stores nearby will offer few benefits to a population of poor Negroes. Finally, exposure to new or different environmental types can be accomplished by various special aids such as field trips or presentations by television or other media, with the implications for the quality of life made concrete.

2 *Stimulate and facilitate exploration of the environment.* While exposure may be helpful in this it does not by itself guarantee that seen environments will be explored. What is apparently required is the right level (not yet established) of novelty and complexity to stimulate curiosity plus sufficient openness and connectedness to allow easy access to new settings and experiences. Exploration can satisfy what may be a basic human need for new experience. By increasing individual interaction with novel and complex environments it leads to growth both by broadening the individual's categories and concepts about the world and by increasing his sense of competence and capacity to formulate and execute new plans. Increases in the rate and scope of interaction can also be accomplished by means of special enrichment programs and techniques, but these are clearly more artificial and may be less effective than if the environment itself facilitates exploration.

3 *Increase the perceptual accessibility of city form.* We can make environmental elements and settings easier to recognize, identify, and remember by making sure that those few form attributes which are critical in recognition are most visible, as well as by simplifying and clarifying visual shape. Simplification of shape is easiest to accomplish at the moment because more is known about it. We may have a good intuitive sense of which attributes are critical in identification, mainly by attending to tradition and stereotypes, but not much is objectively known as yet. And of course the identity of some settings, such as slums, should probably not be clarified as such. Further, by decreasing ambiguity and incongruity in city form we tend to increase conventionality and reduce novelty and complexity. Thus this criterion might best be stated as a constraint on the facilitation of exploration or vice versa. Either way, there is a delicate balance to be drawn in design.

4 *Structure city form to facilitate the various modes of structuring mental representations.* This would require attention to sequential, areal, and schematic structures. By facilitating various modes of structuring we can make city form comprehensible to more types of people. Clearly some parts of the city such as commercial centers should facilitate all three types of structuring. In general, however, sequential structuring is most appropriate for habitual trips and the extended spatial structuring of an area where there is a concentration of heavily frequented action settings. Simplified schematic structuring may be most appropriate over large sectors of the city to facilitate fitting together sequences and limited spatial images.

A further help in structuring and in comprehension would be to increase the number and variety of available information aids and their correlation with city form. This may seem trivial but could be very important in facilitating more effective planning. In some European cities telephone books contain maps which indicate both street names and how the numbers run, a great aid in locating places. Information boards could be placed at strategic points, preprogrammed to light up the quickest or the most scenic route to any destination. Much could also be done to aid more important, longer-range planning. For example, detailed and generally accessible information on the real estate market in various parts of the city would greatly aid in house hunting.

5 *Enhance the unique qualities of environmental settings.* By emphasizing the special character of places we can encourage the formation of individual or small-group attachments and meanings. It is also a way of increasing variety and novelty. It may act as a further constraint on the conventional aspects of perceptual accessibility or it may in many cases be more highly valued than ease of recognition.

6 *Increase the relative exposure of city elements and settings of highest common significance, both functional and social.* This will increase the amount of real experience of these settings and thus increase the realization of their personal meaning and value for more individuals. It will also tend to reinforce their common significance, adding to group solidarity and perhaps impeding desirable changes or shifts in value. The need for continuity in change is doubtless real but indeterminate for the moment.

7 *Increase the plasticity and manipulability of city form to the actions of small groups and individuals.* This may be one of the most effective means for increasing the personal meaning and value of the environment as well as for increasing people's sense of competence and effectiveness. It should also increase variety and the uniqueness of places. The relatively greater degree of plasticity offered by the single-family house with its private manipulable yard has undoubtedly increased the individual meaning and value of the environment, although there are system constraints on the expression of uniqueness.

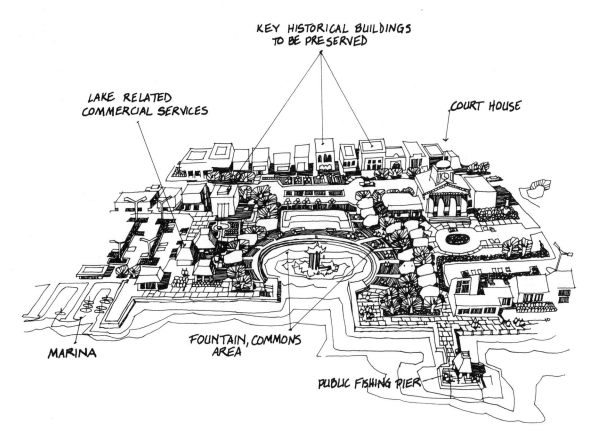

KEY HISTORICAL BUILDINGS
TO BE PRESERVED

LAKE RELATED
COMMERCIAL SERVICES

COURT HOUSE

MARINA

FOUNTAIN, COMMONS
AREA

PUBLIC FISHING PIER

A planner's eye view of a portion of a city. Note the presence of many features that Lynch and Carr would favor.
by Howard L. Deardorff

8 *Facilitate a rhythm of behavioral and perceptual constraint and release in the organization of environmental settings.* This would increase the opportunities for contrast, comparison, and the formation of new mental connections between objects and events. It would also increase the freedom of action of the individual as he moves through the environment, executing his plans. It could be accomplished by the provision of alternative routes to the same destination, contrasting in type and character, or by juxtaposing quiet places to busy ones. It requires attention to the scheduling of events within settings to enhance temporal rhythms as well as spatial ones.

9 *Adapt the form of environmental settings to facilitate the predominant plans being executed within them.* This is obviously a catch-all, but an important one. To make it operational requires that we discover what plans are actually being carried out within various typical settings and develop client-centered techniques for establishing their relative importance. I would include here such physiological requirements as microclimate, light and noise levels since they are in general relative to the types of plans being carried out. Without being able to propose specific criteria in the abstract, I could suggest, for example, that in "general purpose" environments such as town centers, settings should be structured on several levels to facilitate the execution of several types of plans (utilitarian to pleasure-seeking) without conflict.

Although these criteria do not include all the performance characteristics that city form must satisfy, I believe that they may be some of the most useful and important for design. They can be tested both by attempting to apply them to design and by further research. We should proceed on both fronts at once. ∎

Kenneth E. F. Watt
Man's Efficient Rush Toward Deadly Dullness*

Diversity is a powerful force in nature; the diversity among the members of a species makes possible adaptation to changing circumstances. Diversity also plays a role in visual preference. Watt suggests that the general trend in our society toward efficiency and productivity has led to a decline in diversity. This selection does an excellent job of communicating an intuitive feel for this concept and of showing some of the reasons for its importance. The reader, however, should watch out for a tendency toward overgeneralization. Diversity is a process component of preference, but content issues are also important. That the view out the window may have been better in former times than it is now probably has more to do with content than process. The built environment is not without diversity. Also one must guard against confusing diversity with desirability. Introducing second homes for the wealthy into the forest environment may indeed be undesirable; it is not clear, however, how it lowers diversity.

*Reprinted, with permission, from *Natural History Magazine,* February, 1972. Copyright © The American Museum of Natural History, 1972.

■   Is diversity of concern to people interested in natural history, conservation, and the environment? To answer the question fully, one must understand the exact meaning of diversity, the ubiquitous loss of diversity in the world today, and the reasons for the value of diversity.

An argument for preserving anything, particularly something rare, often turns out to be an argument in disguise for diversity. Thus, it seems worthwhile to provide natural historians with a handy kit of powerful arguments for variety because all too often they feel defenseless when confronted with the arguments of developers, which are clearly supported by short-term economic benefits, at least for a few investors.

The rapid loss of diversity in the world is a serious and pervasive phenomenon. Everywhere we look, we see examples of a large number of diverse entities being replaced by a small number of similar entities. We all know about endangered species such as birds of prey and large mammals, including all species of whales. Most of the world's commercial fish stocks are in danger, shell collectors are depleting tropical beaches and coral reefs, and pollution will annihilate commercial shellfish populations, resulting in simplification of our diets. But progressive environmental simplification is far more widespread than this. Half the butterfly species have disappeared in Holland in the last few decades. Conversion of the Russian steppe from wild plants to wheat fields has cut the number of insect species there by 58 percent.

In the economic sphere, there has been a tremendous reduction in the number of manufacturers (think of the number of automobile manufacturers in the United States in 1910). Our numerous corner grocery stores have been replaced by a small number of huge supermarkets. In many fields, large numbers of small businesses have been replaced by small numbers of large businesses, to the point where we now have close to a monopoly in the manufacture of automobiles, aircraft, and computing equipment. Similarly, in agriculture large numbers of small farms have been replaced by small numbers of gigantic farm corporations.

Textural and cultural diversity has declined in our cities, whether you compare different parts of the same city or different cities in different countries. Driving from an airport to the downtown section of a city, the signs tend to be in the same language (English) and to advertise the same products, whether one is in Rome, Beirut, or Singapore. Stores and banks seem to be stamped from a common mold.

Remarkably, the same process has occurred in the human population. An extraordinarily high proportion of the world's population is now very young. The variety once found when many human age classes coexisted in approximately equal numbers has gone.

There are too many examples of the decline of diversity for this situation to have come about by chance. There is indeed an underlying

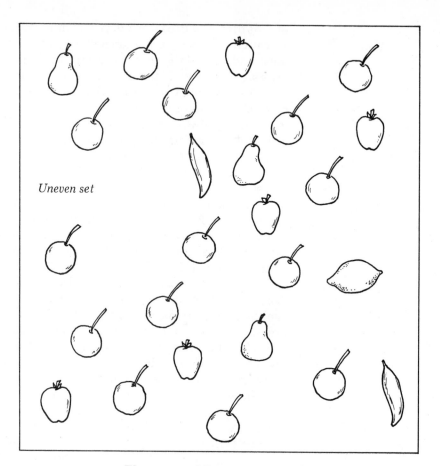

Uneven set

The concept of diversity, uneven set

explanation: we live in an age, and a culture, that puts tremendous emphasis on efficiency and productivity as desiderata for mankind. Since variety is inimical to these goals, variety has suffered and will continue to suffer. Unless powerful and compelling arguments can be offered to stop this loss of diversity, we will soon be living in a homogeneous — and boring — world.

The large number of specific arguments for maintaining the diversity of particular sets of plants, animals, or other items, all fall into four categories: (1) diversity promotes stability; (2) it insures against risks; (3) it utilizes more completely the sun's energy; and (4) it promotes the mental well-being of humans.

To understand the intrinsic value of diversity, we must be explicit as to what we mean by the concept. Diversity measures two charac-

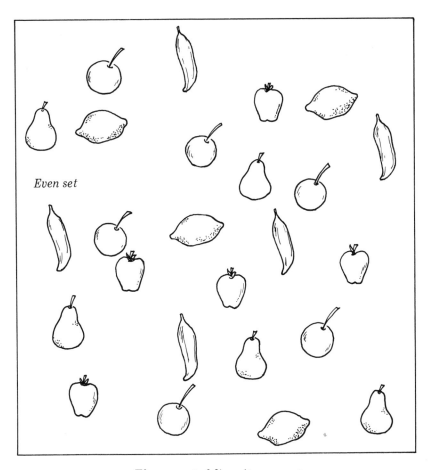

The concept of diversity, even set

teristics of any set of items: *evenness* in numbers of different items in the set; and *richness* in numbers of different items within the set.

To illustrate evenness, suppose we have two different sets comprising 25 items of five types:

Uneven Set		Even Set	
Cherries	14	Cherries	6
Apples	5	Apples	5
Pears	3	Pears	5
Bananas	2	Bananas	5
Lemons	1	Lemons	4
Total	25	Total	25

Richness depends on the number of items as well as the variety of items in a set. In the following table, the relative abundance of the first four items is the same in each set, but the second set is richer because it has both more items and rare items.

Types	First Set	Second Set
A	4	12
B	3	9
C	2	6
D	1	3
E		2
F		1
G		1
H		1
Total	10	35

In nature, an environment that is more tolerant of rarity has a larger number of species, or more richness.

Given that diversity measures both evenness and richness, can a single, simple measure combine both characteristics? In algebraic terms, we can arrive at such a measure, which will also give us a deeper understanding of diversity. Suppose we have N items in a set, divided into N_1 items of the first type, N_2 items of the second type, and so on, to N_n items of the nth and last type. Suppose N is 5, and we want to know the number of different ways we can arrange the five items in a row. The arrangement is $5 \times 4 \times 3 \times 2 \times 1$, which is typically written as $5!$ In general, the number of ways we can arrange N items in a row is $N!$ A measure of the ways in which we can arrange the items is given by

$$\frac{N!}{N_1! \ N_2! \ N_3! \ \ldots \ldots \ N_n!}$$

This can also be thought of as a measure of the variety, or diversity, within the set. By dividing the whole expression by N, we get a measure of the diversity per individual in the set. Using the first example of uneven and even sets, we get

$$\frac{1}{25}\left[\frac{25!}{14! \ 5! \ 3! \ 2! \ 1!}\right]$$

and

$$\frac{1}{25}\left[\frac{25!}{6! \ 5! \ 5! \ 5! \ 4!}\right]$$

The even set has 841 times more diversity per individual than the uneven set.

In the richness comparison, the diversity per individual is 15.6×10^{16} times greater in the richer set than in the less rich set. For those with an intuitive feeling for mathematics, this comparison will have great impact on their feelings about what mankind is doing to the planet by diminishing evenness and richness in the array of plants, animals, and everything else.

STABILITY

There are only two basic elements in all theoretical arguments as to why diversity promotes stability. The first is the idea of spreading the risk (the same idea applies when you buy insurance from the largest insurance company). If an organism feeds on many different species, the chances of all its food sources being wiped out in some catastrophe are less than if the organism feeds on a few, or only one, species. The second idea is that a system functions more harmoniously if it has more elements because it then has more homeostatic feedback loops.

This abstract language can be translated into concrete examples. The greater the variety of foods the human population has available for harvesting, hunting, or fishing, the less the likelihood of human catastrophe due to a disaster befalling a particular food species. A most chilling example was the potato famine in Ireland, where an entire human population was excessively dependent on one food species. The situation is fundamentally the same when an Indian tribe depends greatly on salmon at a certain time of year, and then something happens to the salmon population (pollution or modification of the environment in the spawning stream due to a hydroelectric installation, for example). What few people realize is that the entire human population is now setting itself up for the same situation. For example, as we rapidly deplete the stocks of more and more oceanic species through overfishing and pollution, we cut off optional food sources that we might need desperately in the future. The larger the human population becomes and the more the sources of food decline, the more precarious is our situation.

Our great preoccupation with productivity and efficiency and our lack of concern about diversity increase the precariousness of our economic lives, as well as of our food. Consider what happens when we try to maximize the manufacturing efficiency of aircraft. We are led, inexorably, to a situation in which a small group of corporations manufacture all aircraft in the United States. Each corporation is so large that it dominates the economies of the communities in which its plants are located. Thus, if a corporation meets with disaster, the community is in deep trouble. This is the case in Seattle, where Boeing sales slackened with saturation of the international aircraft market. Architectural writer Jane Jacobs discovered this principle of relating the economic stability of cities to their corporate diversity when she applied current ecological theories about the relation between diversity and stability to her urban studies.

In a most curious way, diversity appears to affect our economic, social, cultural, and political processes. For example, a slowly growing or nongrowing human population has a greater evenness of numbers in different age classes than a rapidly growing population. In a rapid-growth situation, young people are being added to the population so quickly that their numbers become unusually high relative to the numbers of older people. This strains society's ability to generate adequate educational taxes from the older group for the large younger group. It also is difficult for a rapidly growing society to create new jobs at the rate at which young people want to enter the labor force. This will be obvious as unemployment in the United States climbs above 6.0 percent of the prospective labor force when the next age class graduates high school and college in June 1972.

The more even the numbers of people in different age classes, the easier it is to maintain good communication between generations. Thus, all the present discussion about a "generation gap" has its ultimate origin in the lack of diversity in human age classes.

Many similar arguments relating diversity and different forms of stability could be put forth. But the fundamental structure of all such arguments would be the same, whether the subject is a human society or a rare plant. The reason for preserving it is that it may, in some unknown fashion, be important to the maintenance of stability in a part of the planetary ecosystem.

INSURANCE AGAINST RISK

The second class of arguments for maintaining diversity is similar to the argument for buying life insurance. You don't really want or expect to use it, but you buy it just in case. Similarly, a civilization does not expect its acts to harm the world, but just in case they are destructive it would be nice to have at hand other things to fall back on. For example, when we develop new strains of plants and animals, we do not plan on producing lines that will deteriorate in the future. We do not plan on producing strains of collie dogs in which the females will have progressively more difficulty bearing viable offspring, or strains of wheat that will succumb to rust, or berries that after many generations will no longer have much flavor. When these unintended events occur, we fall back on our "insurance policy," either by backcrossing our domestic strains to wild strains or by shifting our attention to new strains or species. But what if there are no new strains or species to replace the unsatisfactory ones?

The insurance value of diversity applies to more than just individual species or strains of plants and animals. Suppose a civilization irrigated farmland in such a fashion that long-term, irreversible destruction of the soil only showed up after a century. Suppose, further, that the entire landscape of this civilization had been managed in an identical fashion. Then when the entire landscape lost its fertility, the civilization would be without land to produce food. Further, it wouldn't even have any unmanaged land to compare with the managed lands for scientific investigations. A simple example of the importance of such comparisons is the few forest areas in Greece from which goats have been excluded. The contrast between the grazed and ungrazed lands is so startling that no argument from goat-lovers could withstand visual comparison of forested areas with and without goats.

It is tremendously important for any civilization to set aside areas where common cultivation practices are not adopted. If the same techniques are used everywhere, we can never know the long-term results of the practice. Thus, we can never know if intensive annual pesticide sprayings have long-term deleterious effects on orchards, forests, or woodlots unless we have unsprayed areas for comparison.

In short, a prudent civilization maintains the landscape under many different management strategies, including parcels of each soil and climate zone that are not managed at all. This landscape diversity has two values. First, we have a yardstick for determining if something unexpected or odd is gradually showing up in a managed area. Without the unmanaged areas, the odd or unexpected effect could be ascribed to something else, to a change in climate, for example. The unsettled arguments as to whether the changes in the landscape of the Mediterranean basin, the Middle East, North Africa, and northern India were due to climatic change or man's activities show clearly the importance of having unmanaged areas for checking. The second value of landscape diversity is that if a civilization unwittingly destroys its managed lands, it has other places on which to raise food while the destroyed areas are gradually rebuilt to productivity.

A generalization of this argument holds that an extremely prudent civilization would try to maintain other civilizations with different ideas about land use. Over the short term, the ideas of civilization A might appear vastly superior to those of civilization B. But over the long term it could turn out that the apparently "primitive" practices of civilization B were based on millennia of trial and error and incorporated deep wisdom that was unintelligible to civilization A.

FULLER USE OF ENERGY

The third argument for diversity originates in the theory of modern ecologists that any habitat contains a set of "niches," or functions, that may be filled. If only part of the niches are filled, then the sun's energy that is captured by, and flows through, a system will be less than if all the niches were filled.

Perhaps the best known and most convincing illustration of this argument comes from Africa. Research shows that a mix of native animal species uses the landscape more economically than imported livestock. Each of the different types of antelope and other game consume slightly different mixes of food plants or parts of plants, so that a whole assemblage of different species uses the landscape more efficiently than, say, beef cattle would by themselves.

The same point has been demonstrated repeatedly in analyses of the fish production per year per acre from different mixes of fish species. The more fish species there are in a body of water, the greater the gross production. Human understanding of this principle reaches its pinnacle in Oriental fish farming, where up to nine different species of carp are grown together in the set of proportions that makes best use of the resources in a pond.

MENTAL WELL-BEING

Humanity has given far too little thought to the fourth argument for preserving diversity. How much diversity in the world around us is optimal for the human mind? Might the extent of environmental diversity have any relationship to the average level of mental health in a population? Could a certain level of diversity be most satisfying — emotionally and esthetically — to the human mind because of the conditions during human evolution? Diversity in an environment may have a much deeper significance for man than is generally recognized. We know that human beings tend to hallucinate when kept in confined quarters and deprived of sensory stimuli. This could be interpreted as a protective device by the mind to provide an otherwise unavailable need. Reports have been published indicating that extremely refractory mental patients, who had not spoken to anyone in years, showed an almost miraculous response when taken to wilderness areas.

The recent popularity of skin diving as recreation may convey a deep message. It may be that the rate of incoming sensory stimuli while skin diving is optimal for the human mind. I know that after several hours of constant interruption by the phone and visitors, I almost jump with each new phone call. But I also know that I can become bored amid all this stimuli. The extremely deep satisfaction I derive from exploring the ocean edge of a tropical island may be telling me something important about my mind and all our minds. We have evolved over a very long period so that our minds can cope handily with a certain rate of incoming sensory stimuli. We find the stimuli rate we can cope with in nature because we evolved there. Either sharply higher or sharply lower rates of incoming sensory stimuli are bad for our nervous systems.

This is only anecdotal evidence, but more carefully designed and measured research leads to the same conclusion. For some years, Prof. J. Lee Kavanau of UCLA has been conducting experiments on small mammal behavior in heavily instrumented cages. These cages are wired, enabling the animal to change its environment and recording every move the animal makes and every detail of the conditions in the cage. The animals learn to control their environment by pressing levers. Kavanau has discovered that animals will press levers to select other than optimal conditions. In other words, confronted with a choice of living constantly in an optimal world but being bored, or of living in a world that is only optimal part of the time and experiencing variety, even a small rodent will opt for variety. It is reasonable to assume that humans would opt even more strongly for variety rather than constant optimality. Perhaps diversity is not merely a luxury for us. It may be something we need.

If, upon reflection, you agree with my general line of argument as to the intrinsic value of diversity, then important implications follow for many aspects of our lives. Particularly, the argument has important political implications.

For example, if diversity breeds stability, then it is worthwhile for a government to regulate the rate at which different interest groups acquire wealth and power. Undue concentration of power and wealth allows a small group of people to change the landscape to suit themselves, even though the change may not suit others. For example, wilderness mountaintops and tropical islands have been overdeveloped for second homes because the prospective profits for developers were very large relative to the total costs for society. Costs were small for the developers because they were not equitably divided within the society. If something went sour with the development — the lots didn't sell after trees were bulldozed — or if subsequent sewage and pollution control costs spiraled, then someone else, not the developer, absorbed the costs. Thus, the developer reaped a great gain from subdividing, and someone else paid the price. Given this situation it is scarcely surprising that so much of the world is being destroyed or that diversity is diminishing so rapidly.

A comparable situation exists with respect to the oceans, which our culture treats as an international "common property resource." Since no one or no one nation owns the oceans or their contents, no one has a motive for perpetuating the living diversity of the oceans. Consequently, the precious living treasures of two-thirds of the earth may be less diverse or even depleted in a short time. And there are too many links between oceanic and terrestrial life for such a loss to occur without profoundly affecting humanity.   ■

NOTE

      For additional readings, see Ellul (1964), Jacobs (1970), and Margalef (1968).

Sima Eliovson
The Japanese Garden*

People seem to prefer landscapes that facilitate and encourage both entry and exploration. A sense of spaciousness is therefore an essential component. Eliovson shows how the Japanese garden is structured to maximize the illusion of depth, thus making a limited area seem far more spacious than it really is. Mystery too plays an important role.

It is striking how a culture quite different from our own has long manipulated factors directly comparable to those that have been found to influence preference in our society. The intended effect of the Japanese garden is tranquility. Here too there are strong parallels in our society. (A number of these themes receive further attention in the last selection of the chapter.)

■   If one had to pinpoint the salient similarity between all Japanese gardens, either ancient or modern, in order to distinguish them from western gardens, one would be inclined to say that they have all been planned in order to provide the occupant of the house with a view to contemplate as he gazes outwards from his living room or from the verandah which borders it. No matter what style is followed, the one overriding aim is to create a tranquil or pleasing view so that the homeowner can relax and gaze at it while, ideally, losing himself in meditation. This is simply known as a Viewing Garden.

The Zen Buddhist garden, created chiefly with stones and sand, has a deliberately puzzling symbolism which is meant to induce philosophical thoughts while meditating, but the intention behind the

*From S. Eliovson *Gardening the Japanese Way*. London: George G. Harrap & Co. Ltd. 1971. Excerpts from pages 33–36. Reprinted by permission.

creation of every ordinary Japanese garden is to provide tranquillity so that the people of the house can obtain peace of mind and can escape from the strains of living in the contemplation of nature. As it is aesthetic to compose and not merely to scatter natural objects, such as trees, shrubs and stones around the garden, it is understood that these must be arranged with style, in a quiet, harmonious, thought-provoking composition that will continue to please over the years, throughout summer and winter.

In designing their gardens, the Japanese are influenced by the aesthetic principles that are seen in all their arts. Their use of asymmetry and space as structural elements in the composition of a picture, or in the sweep of a branch in *Ikebana* or *Bonsai,* is very important in their layout of their gardens.

Space becomes a strong element that has a shape of its own. In the same way in which it balances the placement of a flower drawn on a page, so the spaces in the garden that are formed by moss, sand or water balance the trees, shrubs and other plants that form groups.

Asymmetry is an essential part of the beauty of certain trees like maples, willows or weeping cherries. This is enhanced by pruning in the case of individual specimens. It is also effected by the placing of the tree in a strong position at the side of a garden composition, seldom centrally, or by grouping tall and short plants in a graceful way.

ACHIEVING DEPTH IN THE GARDEN

While making the main garden picture a harmonious master-piece of composition, Japanese gardeners have used the devices employed by artists in order to achieve perspective or depth when sketching in two dimensions. The Japanese gardener has learned to make the fullest use of the actual space of even the smallest garden, extending or diminishing it by the clever use of foliage, trees, rocks and water.

Perspective or depth is not used in the same way in Japanese gardens as in western gardens. The western habit of placing large trees on the boundary for privacy, with smaller trees and shrubs near the house, so that one can see into the garden, generally has the effect of making a large garden appear smaller. Trees are often used in the opposite way in the Japanese garden in order to create greater depth. While large trees may be planted on the boundary for privacy in a Japanese garden, acting as a background, trees are also planted in the foreground in order to make the garden appear larger than it is. Large trees near the house, with smaller ones in the background, give the illusion of the smaller ones being further away than they are in reality and this makes the garden appear larger. Acting on the same principle, bushes with large leaves are placed in the foreground and those with fine leaves in the background, so as to create a feeling of distance.

by Lynette T. Dobbs

Naturally, this is not a hard and fast rule, but these are useful devices to be employed when it is desired to make the garden appear larger than it is. If the garden is extremely small, the pruning down or thinning of the background trees may be practised in order to make them seem more distant, but it is always better to depend on the natural size of the slender leaves in order to enhance the feeling of distance.

When one is nearer to the trees and plants, it is easier to achieve a luxuriant woodland atmosphere and to feel closer to nature than when one looks out on to a distant panoramic view. The great landscape gardens of Europe, that depended for their magnificence on the rolling hills and recession of planes made by large trees and hedges, are difficult to emulate in present-day small gardens. The practice of placing trees, shrubs and plants around the perimeter of the garden, leaving the central lawn bare, is the natural development of the grand landscape garden, but the wonderful pastoral landscape depicted by great artists like Turner cannot be emulated in modern times, except on large estates. It would be far easier and wiser for the lover of nature, who wishes to evoke the peaceful charm of a well-designed garden, to be inspired by the Japanese-style garden and to bring the plants closer to the house, after choosing them cleverly so as to create the illusion of distance.

The illusion of distance or greater depth is created also by designing in detail those features which are nearby and treating with greater simplicity those areas which are further away. In other words, the plants and rocks nearest the house should be more elaborately arranged than those in the background, following the premise that the eye cannot see in clear detail that which is far away. By heightening this effect of distance, the garden is made to appear larger. This can be done whether one is working with rocks, plants, water or other features. Simple treatment on the far bank of a pond will make it recede further into the distance, in contrast to the large boulders and large-leaved plants in the foreground. Interesting old water-basins or lanterns in the foreground also focus attention nearest the house, while the background seems less prominent and farther away in appearance and importance. A small lantern placed in the background will seem farther away in contrast to a larger one in the foreground. Even if one does not use rocks, stone water-basins, lanterns or ornaments of any kind, one could plant a showy flowering shrub nearby that would hold one's attention, especially if it has large leaves like those of a camellia or *Aucuba,* in contrast to finer-leaved subjects, like bamboos, in the distance.

One often sees clipped bushes placed in an asymmetrical arrangement, one behind the other, in Japanese gardens so that there is a pattern made by the receding mounds of foliage. These receding planes give the illusion of distance, like mountain ranges diminishing into the distance. This illusion of distance is created by the visual impact of the scene and not by the fact that one may imagine a symbolic comparison between the bushes and mountains. It is not at all necessary to seek a meaning to these clipped bushes, but merely to appreciate their effect on the eye. The use of these receding planes, whether they are created by foliage or by rocks or by zig-zag water shorelines, all heighten the effect of depth and distance, making the small garden appear larger than it really is. Excellent examples of the use of clipped bushes to achieve interest as well as depth may be found at Sanzen-in and Shoden-ji, in Kyoto.

The obscured view is used to enhance distance as well as to create mystery. The garden viewed through a partially obscuring leafy branch or a group of slim tree trunks will not only seem to be farther away, but will become more alluring. The partially concealed view attracts the interest more than that which can be seen at a glance. The visitor is prompted to look more carefully through a half-screen of trunks or branches in order to discover what is beyond. The fact that it is vaguely seen makes it more elusive, distant, and intriguing.

by Lynette T. Dobbs

All landscape gardeners know that a garden appears larger if it is divided into portions so that the whole area cannot be seen at a glance. Nowhere is this device more apparent than in Japan, where the tiniest garden may be divided by a bamboo screen, open trellis or fence, while the paths wind into surrounding trees, a stream divides and disappears behind a hillock or a rock, and a *sozu-kakehi,* or animal chaser, is half-hidden by the luxuriant foliage. The subtle effect of hiding a little area from total view is one of the most intriguing and typical features of the Japanese garden. It has a compelling force that draws one into the garden and prompts one to discover the mystery for oneself. The half-concealed view beyond a gate in the garden invites one to explore behind the opening.

Tea-gardens in Japan are generally enclosed by fences, while rooms in the house often open on to separate enclosed gardens, no matter how tiny. These compartments develop the feeling that the garden is larger than it really is, for one feels the impulse to visit the different areas. At the same time, this gives one extra interest in the garden.

Paths are seldom straight if the effect of distance is required. A path that winds into a shrubbery, only to emerge a little later, will give the illusion that it is longer and further away than it really is. All features that are placed at an angle in a rectangular space, such as paths, swimming pools or garden beds, give an effect of greater space. In some cases they take up less space in the total area, but the chief advantage in placing them at an angle is to avoid a squat square-on look that stops the eye from looking into the distance. ∎

John B. Jackson
Front Yards*

The front yard that Jackson analyzes here at first seems strikingly different from the Japanese garden. There is less emphasis on space per se, a very different use of plant material, and apparently a quite different purpose. There is an entirely different cultural heritage. Yet in the final analysis the function of the front yard turns out to be not so different after all. It too is a reproduction of something larger, a "landscape in miniature." It too has a rich history which adds familiarity and meaning. And — although his terminology is somewhat different — Jackson's statement that the yard "exists to satisfy a love of beauty" is not that far from the tranquility the Japanese garden is intended to foster.

■   The house stands by itself, lost somewhere in the enormous plain. Next to it is a windmill, to the rear a scattering of barns and shelters and sheds. In every direction range and empty field reach to a horizon unbroken by a hill or the roof of another dwelling or even a tree. The wind blows incessantly; it raises a spiral of dust in the corral. The sun beats down on the house day after day. Straight as a die the road stretches out of sight between a perspective of fence and light poles. The only sound is the clangor of the windmill, the only movement the wind brushing over the grass and wheat, and the afternoon thunderheads boiling up in the western sky.

But in front of the house on the side facing the road there is a small patch of ground surrounded by a fence and a hedge. Here grow a dozen or more small trees — Chinese elms, much whipped and tattered by the prevailing gale. Under them is a short expanse of bright green lawn.

Trees, lawn, hedge and flowers — these things, together with much care and great expenditure of precious water, all go to make up what we call the front yard. Not only here on the western farmstead, but on every one of a million farms from California to Maine. All front yards in America are much the same, as if they had been copied from one another, or from a remote prototype.

---

*From J. B. Jackson "Ghosts at the door." *Landscape*, 1951, 1 (1), pages 3–4. Reprinted by permission. Other portions of this article appear in chapters 8 and 9.

Lawns matter

They are so much part of what is called the American Scene that you are not likely to wonder why they exist. Particularly when you see them in the East and Midwest; there they merge into the woodland landscape and into the tidy main street of a village, as if they all belonged together. But when you travel west you begin to mark the contrast between the yard and its surroundings. It occurs to you that the yard is sometimes a very artificial thing, the product of much work and thought and care. Whoever tends them so well out here on the lonely flats (you say to yourself) must think them very important.

And so they are. Front yards are a national institution — essential to every home, like a Bible somewhere in the house. It is not their size which makes them so. They are usually so small that from a vertical or horizontal distance of more than a mile they can hardly be seen. Nor are they always remarkable for what they contain. No; but they are pleasant oases of freshness and moving shade in the heat of the monotonous plain. They are cool in the summer, and in the winter their hedges and trees do much to break the violence of the weather. The way they moderate the climate justifies their existence.

They serve a social purpose, too. By common consent the appearance of a front yard, its neatness and luxuriance, is an index of the taste and enterprise of the family who owns it. Weeds and dead limbs are a disgrace, and the man who rakes and waters and clips after work is usually held to be a good citizen.

Another view of lawns
Reproduced by permission, University of Illinois

So this infinitesimal patch of land, only a few hundred square feet, meets two very useful ends: it provides a place for outdoor enjoyment, and it indicates social standing. But in reality does it always do those things?

Many front yards, and by no means the least attractive, flourish on the western ranches and homesteads many miles from neighbors. They waste their sweetness on the desert air. As for any front yard being used for recreation, this seems to be a sort of national myth. Perhaps on Sunday afternoons when friends come out from town to pay a visit chairs are tentatively placed on the fresh cut grass. For the rest of the week the yard is out of bounds, just as the now obsolete front parlor always used to be. The family is content to sit on the porch when it wants fresh air. It admires the smooth lawn from a distance.

The true reason why every American house has to have a front yard is probably very simple: it exists to satisfy a love of beauty. Not every beauty, but beauty of a special, familiar kind; one that every American can recognize and enjoy, and even after a fashion recreate for himself.

The front yard, then, is an attempt to reproduce next to the house a certain familiar or traditional setting. In essence the front yard is a landscape in miniature. It is not a garden; its value is by no means purely esthetic. It is an enclosed space which contains a garden among other things. The patch of grass and Chinese elms and privet stands for something far larger and richer and more beautiful. It is a much reduced version, as if seen through the wrong end of a pair of field glasses, of a spacious countryside of woods and hedgerows and meadow.

Such was the countryside of our remoter forebears; such was the original, the proto-landscape, which we continue to remember and cherish, even though for each generation the image becomes fainter and harder to recall.   ■

Ervin H. Zube
The Natural History of Urban Trees*

The selection provides a fascinating glimpse of the changing role of trees in the history of western cities. It is interesting to see that the urban/nature mix characteristic of so many of our cities is a relatively recent development. There are many clues here as to what people prefer. Certainly nature must be a powerful content, but that is not to say that "nature" is free of human influence. As is evident from this selection, as well as the preceding ones, things that are considered "natural" are, in fact, often highly manipulated.

■   Trees have been around for about 300 million years. Cities are thought to have started about seven to eight thousand years ago. Trees and cities, however, do not appear to have been brought together by the conscious act of design until roughly two hundred years ago.

*Reprinted by permission from *Natural History Magazine,* November 1973. Copyright © The American Museum of Natural History, 1973.

The history of urban design contains very few references to the presence or the use of trees in a public sense. There is evidence that in ancient Egypt trees were used in private gardens to provide a more salubrious environment for the wealthy or the ruling class as early as 2800–2100 B.C. But no evidence has been uncovered of the use of trees as a part of the public landscape of the city. The example of Egypt holds true through the Middle Ages and the Renaissance. The medieval city, enclosed by defensive walls, did not contain trees. The open spaces of the city were architectonic, and the only view of trees or woodlands was through an open town gate or over the walls to the landscape beyond.

Conditions changed dramatically in the eighteenth century, the impetus emanating from the seventeenth-century baroque gardens of France, which were laid out in formal geometric patterns with long axes, suggesting by their form and grand scale that man had surely mastered nature. These large gardens were designed with long, straight roadways cut through the forest. Usually radiating from several central points, the roadways provided an ideal situation for the owner while hunting: while his beaters worked their way through the woods, he was afforded a clear field of fire down each of the roadways. Thus, it was possible to go to the hunt without any discomfort.

These tree-lined roads, or pathways, which were so much a part of French gardens, strongly influenced eighteenth-century town design. They provided the pattern for what was envisioned as the ideal street layout. Washington, D.C., designed in 1791 by Maj. Pierre Charles L'Enfant, is a case in point: streets are laid out with as much concern for the field of view as for any more utilitarian, or functional, concern. The spaces and streets in both French gardens and in nineteenth-century cities such as Nancy or Bath or sections of Paris were sharply delineated either by the forest or by the planting of trees along the edges. The epitome of French garden design of the time, and undoubtedly the strongest influence on city design, was Versailles, designed between 1661 and 1674 by André Le Nôtre for Louis XIV.

Shortly thereafter trees began appearing in the London landscape. According to the architectural historian Sigfried Giedion, "Around 1800 [the] open spaces in the middle of the London squares were laid out with freely planted trees and lawns, the beginning of that luxuriant greenery which natural growth brought in due coarse of time." The image of the London squares (there were about fifteen of them by the mid-nineteenth century) was thus one of trees and grass. These were residential squares — that is, they were surrounded by housing, not by shops and markets. Some still exist today and exude the image of quiet, substantial, and comfortable residential neighborhoods. It has been suggested that the "adulation of nature" was so strong in England at this time that people felt almost a moral obligation to plant every open area.

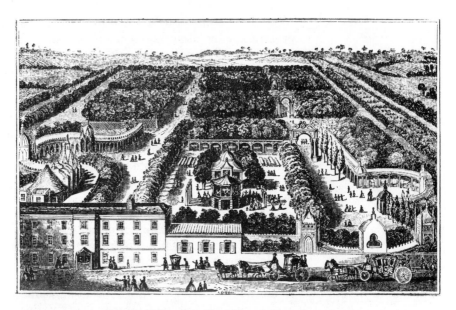

Vauxhall Gardens, London, eighteenth century
The Bettman Archive, Inc.

It was during the eighteenth century that the English romantic landscape movement reached its peak. The influence of the rigid geometry of the French gardens gave way to free-flowing lines and gently curving contours. The boundaries between garden and countryside disappeared, and the landscape image that we now call "parklike" became dominant.

Wide, tree-lined boulevards were cut through Paris under the influence of Baron Georges Eugène Haussmann in the 1850s and 60s, but they were not residentially oriented. In Haussmann's words, the tree-lined boulevards were "to disencumber the larger buildings, palaces, and barracks in such a way as to make them more pleasing to the eye, afford easier access on days of celebration, and a simplified defense on days of riot." Also according to Haussmann, they were "to assure the public peace by the creation of large boulevards which will permit the circulation of air and light but also troops." Haussmann's concept of boulevards grew out of the radiating paths and roads of the baroque garden. The baroque garden idea, however, "was to have long avenues planted with trees but devoid of houses." Considering the sixty or seventy years of French history previous to Haussmann's time, it is not the least bit surprising to find a frequently stated concern for troops and defense. After all, Haussmann worked for Prince Louis Napoleon — later known as Napoleon III — who came to power after the Revolution of 1848, a revolution that took place in the streets of Paris.

On the American scene, contrary to expectation, trees were not an integral part of New England communities from their inception. During the seventeenth century, the village green was a place for mustering the militia and herding cattle in the event of an Indian attack. Trees undoubtedly would have been discouraged because they could have provided concealment and protection for the attackers. The present popular image of a New England town center — the common of trees and grass — is a very late eighteenth- and early nineteenth-century development.

Philadelphia, a city that had been planned by William Penn in 1682 with five open squares of eight to ten acres each, which were to have only trees, was quite lacking in street trees until the end of the eighteenth century. Insurance companies would not insure houses that had trees in front of them. It wasn't until 1784 that one company — the Second Mutual Fire Insurance Company, later appropriately called "The Green Tree Company" — started accepting such clients.

An act passed in 1807 in the territory of Michigan, dealing with Detroit, called for a double line of trees on both sides of 120-foot avenues and for trees to be planted in "clumps or groves . . . of an elliptical shape" on both sides of 200-foot avenues. This act also provided for residential squares, probably similar in concept to those of London, that were to be "planted with trees or otherwise improved and ornamented."

At least a partial understanding of the changing values placed upon trees and open space in the design of some American cities in the early nineteenth century can be gleaned from the report of the commission that was appointed to select the site for the permanent capital of Mississippi in 1821. The report reads: "And even in a small town there would be a comfort, convenience and greater security against fire, as well as a fairer promise of health, all combined, by having every other square unoccupied by anything except the native trees of the forest, or artificial groves." The commissioners were discussing the merits of using a town-planning scheme in which every other block — in checkerboard fashion — would be tree-covered open space.

This conscious inclusion of trees in the design of American cities grew out of the French baroque garden and matured in the English romantic landscape movement. The design concepts of this movement were adopted at the beginning of the present century as models for numerous proposed urban beautification programs. Paris, in particular, with its broad, tree-lined boulevards became the model for plans for Chicago, San Francisco, St. Louis, Detroit, Los Angeles, and Minneapolis.

The main components of these "city beautification" plans were landscaped parks, boulevards and parkways, and civic centers. These

Under the lindens in Berlin, beginning of the nineteenth century.
The Bettman Archive, Inc.

plans, with their clearly delineated spaces and tree-lined, radiating streets were superimposing a new structure on the gridiron pattern of many American cities.

The physical structure implicit in the plans establishes a set of visual hierarchies in one's perception of the city. The importance of a street or open space is stated by its scale and by the use of trees, usually used in regular, formal patterns, to define its edges. By reading the visual clues provided by the trees and the scale, it is easy to determine which spaces are important.

The English romantic landscape movement was more significant in influencing the form outside of the center city. The movement, which started as a reaction to growing industrialism, had its strongest impact on the design of the new suburbs that sprang up in the late nineteenth century. In England and in the United States, those who could afford to escape the industrial city's concentrations of human suffering did so, and the "natural landscape" assumed a new significance. It became a symbol of all that was good, as exemplified by the writings of Thoreau, in contrast to the city, which was lacking in the qualities of nature.

Suburbs were designed with the intent of capturing the spirit of the natural landscape. Gently curving streets threaded through wooded, rolling hills. Llewellyn Park in Orange, New Jersey, dating from about 1853, was one of the earliest such suburbs. Lake Forest and Riverside, both in Illinois, Roland Park in Baltimore, and Ridley Park in Pennsylvania are other examples from the last half of the nineteenth century. These suburbs were usually developed with large lots on wooded, rolling land. When not wooded, trees were added immediately, and in abundance, to simulate natural woodland. This "natural effect" was an essential ingredient of the romantic landscape. The trees provided a natural blotter that tended to visually absorb the activities and structures of man. They provided a major element of contrast between the city, which at that time was becoming more and more industrialized in image, and its counterpart, the suburb.

The full impact of these designs on suburban development was not really felt, however, until the 1930s when the Federal Housing Administration promoted the use of curvilinear streets. These plans were based on concepts worked out at places like Llewellyn Park and Riverside. But lot sizes were usually smaller, and one other major ingredient was frequently missing in the new designs of the 1930s, 40s, 50s, and even the 60s — the trees. These subdivisions were frequently built in open fields rather than wooded areas, and little if any thought was given to the introduction of significant numbers of trees.

The London squares, the report of the commission to select a site for the Mississippi state capital, and the nineteenth-century suburbs that were a product of the attachment to the "romantic ideal," all imply that prestige or amenity value was added to the residential environment by trees. The evidence seems rather conclusive that there is a long association of trees and wooded lots with upper- and middle-class residential values in Western history. During the time of the Roman Empire, the Renaissance, or even late nineteenth-century America, those who could afford it lived on the fringe of the city absorbed by nature — although sometimes the trees were made to conform to man's idea of a more appropriate form by pollarding or topiary work. Go to almost any American metropolis today and seek out the most prestigious residential areas — you will probably find that most are in wooded sections. Names also give an indication: Forest Hills, Woodland, Lake Forest, and a host of others that either explicitly or implicitly equate trees with a quality living environment.

There is no reason to assume that long-held values of the ideal residential environment are going to change. A Louis Harris poll, which included consideration of Americans' desires in reference to lifestyles and environmental values, had 95 percent of those polled listing "green grass and trees around me" as an important environmental value. The romantic landscape movement — born in England, nurtured by the writings of Jefferson and Thoreau, and exemplified in the designs of Andrew Jackson Downing and Frederick Law Olmsted — is

Cleveland, Ohio, 1872
The Bettman Archive, Inc.

still very much a part of the American value system. As Bayard
Hooper put it in a *Life* magazine article discussing the Harris poll,
"Americans paint an almost Jeffersonian picture of their aspirations:
green grass and trees, friendly neighbors, churches, schools and good
stores nearby."

Trees can also play an important role in urban environments
where the American ideal has been difficult to achieve. In discussing a
Miami slum in 1965, two journalists wrote, "In short, the Groves' Colored Town was a slum ghetto, leaderless and neglected, where living
conditions were ameliorated to a modicum of livability only by the historical accident of low population density and the beneficent climate
which hid the rotting shacks behind a profusion of trees and flowers."

I am not suggesting that we hide our evils behind a wall of trees,
but that we consider the use of trees as a means of environmental
amelioration. Many residential streets — not necessarily slums — in
many cities are sterile, visually monotonous environments that would
be improved by street trees. The trees create a ceiling of branches and
leaves over all or part of the street, thereby changing the scale. A pattern is created by the changing shadows cast by the trees and by the
sunlight filtered through their branches onto the street and sidewalk.

These human-scale considerations, when combined with the seasonal characteristics of trees, provide a changing visual environment. Some change or environmental diversity is important to all of us.

Landscape critic J. B. Jackson in an article in *Landscape* magazine provides us with a concluding summary of the well-designed city. He envisions such a city as

one where we everywhere feel at home; it reminds us, everywhere and at all times, that we are in an environment no less natural, no less stimulating than the environment of the country dweller. Its trees and parks and lawns are more than agents of health: they tell us of the passage of the seasons, and its open places tell us the time of day. . . . If it cannot provide us with the sounds of the remoter landscape, it at least provides us with areas where the sound of human voices and footsteps are not drowned out by mechanical noises, it provides us with quiet. It cannot imitate all of nature, but it gives us archways and pools of daylight, and flights of steps and views; the splash of water in fountains, echoes and music; the breath of damp cool air, the harmony of colors and the unpolluted sun; indeed it gives us so much that our excursions into the countryside cease to be headlong flights from a sterile environment and become a conscious searching for the missing ingredients: solitude in the presence of other forms of life, space and mystery. ■

Green things too have their special claim on human attention.
by Douglas Kinsey

Rachel Kaplan
The Green Experience*

Considering how powerfully the content of the natural environment commands our attention, it is perhaps surprising that so little research has touched on this topic. Part of the problem may lie in the difficulty of defining what is meant by "nature." Greenness turns out to be less critical than one might think, and the equation of "nature" and "wilderness" also obscures a great many important relationships. Many of the themes touched on in previous selections come together here in a research context. Particularly striking, perhaps, is the importance of having nature "near by," and yet the primary relationship is one of "appreciation" rather than "use." Here again fascination plays a critical role in the relation between people and a highly valued content.

■   "Green" is shorthand. It stands for "nature," although not all nature is green. Nor does all that is green, even in the natural environment, qualify as "green" in this special sense. So there is no good longhand for it. When people tell us they chose a particular route because it was "green," they mean that it is more scenic than alternative routes, that it is relatively more natural, and that it has not been made straight and level. As such, its "greenness" would be equally attractive in the dead of winter when "white" would be a more accurate description.

The "green experience," then, refers to the encounter with the natural environment, and especially the unspectacular, everyday natural environment that comes in a variety of colors and guises. The theme is simple, perhaps obvious: The natural environment matters to people. It matters not only in the infrequent escape to far-flung poster places, but in its potential availability and accessibility as a renewable and renewing resource.

It has been said that the city-dweller is more appreciative of such "green" places — absence makes the heart grow fonder. Urban people are overrepresented in various outdoor recreation activities and in organizations oriented to the conservation of natural places. For the rural folk, nature abounds and its advantages might well be taken for granted.

But this may be a misreading of rural America. There are people in Detroit who grow corn in their driveway and talk of going back to Appalachia. Some migrants from rural places complain of never seeing a sunset. In the western part of Michigan's lower peninsula there is a county that has only a single traffic light (although there are major cities the next county over). I have gotten to know some people who live there. They have expressed no envy of my vacation in their "country." Indeed, they claim not to feel any need for a vacation. And in fact, the vacation life they see on TV is their year-round existence: fishing and hunting, growing things, a different pace, and open land. Coles (1971) describes some similarly appreciative feelings, a sense of having "an awful lot of plenty," on the part of mountain folks who, by some standards, might be said to be living in squalor. The sense of belonging, of "roots," of control over their existence and closeness to the land — these are available in the rural areas despite what may appear to be a bare subsistence livelihood. These are also dimensions that quality of life studies do not seem to index.

"Wilderness" is a term something like "green." Its legislated meaning is unlike many of its usages (Robinson, 1975). To many of my colleagues and students it is incomprehensible that people can stand in our local "Arb" and say "Isn't it wonderful, here in the wilderness, away from everything," when they are in sight of tall buildings, residences, railroad tracks, and an unpaved parking lot with cars in it. This suggests both that the word is experienced in a variety of ways, and more important, that even the urbanized, unspectacular form of nature means a great deal to people.

PICTURE PREFERENCE

Taken by itself, the anecdotal is not fully convincing. Considerable research in recent years has examined the properties of preferred "stimuli." To be rigorous in this quest, several investigators have created stimuli so that they possess certain critical properties. These artificial shapes (and sound patterns) have focused on the attribute of "complexity," and much attention has been devoted to the question of whether preference is maximized at some intermediate level of complexity. A neglected question, however, has been whether the content of the "stimuli" is in its own right an important predictor of preference.

The major purpose of a study we carried out some years ago was to see whether pictures of everyday natural and built environments were differentially liked as a function of the content of the pictures. The answer was an overwhelming "Yes." Out of the set of fifty-six slides, the ones that could be categorized as "nature" were vastly preferred by the eighty-eight freshwomen participating in the study. These nature pictures included scenes from the same Arb — grassy areas with trees,

FIGURE 1

Four of the scenes are shown here. The one on the upper left was the most preferred of the urban scenes.

denser treed views, an unpaved road, etc. The subset of slides that depicted urban settings — downtown side streets, traffic corners, tall buildings — were rated significantly lower. In fact, the only slide in the urban subset that was liked as much as any of the nature scenes was one showing a few trees against a backdrop of tall buildings in a downtown park (figure 1). To our surprise, the various residential scenes were liked least of all.

Three years later, we thought it would be interesting to see whether these participants had lost some youthful enthusiasm and had changed their ways. It was not easy to track them all down, but thirty-five came back. Among many other things, we showed them the same slides and asked them again to rate their preference for each. The re-

FIGURE 2

Examples of scenes high in mystery. The scene on the lower right in figure 1 provides another example.

sults were as before, but more so. The mean-rated preference for nature scenes showed a significant increase; for the urban scenes, the ratings declined; for the residential settings, they remained low.

Another study involved showing the same slides for very short durations, approximating the glimpses one gets of the passing scene. The differences in rated preference between viewing durations of 10, 40, and 200 milliseconds were minor, but the relative preference for the nature pictures as compared to the urban scenes was even greater than in the other studies.

This series of studies has demonstrated that nature content per se is an important characteristic of preferred scenes. (The studies are described more fully in R. Kaplan, 1975; some replications and extensions are discussed by Wohlwill, 1976.) In addition to providing strong evidence of the preference for a variety of things "green," the picture preferences have also helped in identifying factors that enhance preference in a variety of physical settings.

While we have consistently found content to be the most powerful factor in preference for different settings, a number of content-free predictors have also emerged (S. Kaplan, 1975). As far as natural settings are concerned, the most striking quality that enhances preference is what we have called "mystery" (R. Kaplan, 1973a). There are various ways for a picture or an actual place to have this quality (figure 2). A suggested path that becomes obscure as it joins the woods, a stream that meanders out of sight, a scene that is hard to make out behind some foliage — these all have a quality of enticing one to want to know more; they compel one to change one's vantage point and enter "deeper" into the scene. It is important to recognize that "mystery" is by no means a component of natural areas as opposed to urban ones. Quite the contrary. As Cullen (1961) suggests, it is a quality one may desire to introduce in designing a place. In fact, many a modern shopping center attempts to enhance mystery by elevation differences, barriers, and various other means that block a "long view." But natural scenes seem to come by a sense of mystery more readily. Linearity is not, after all, a prominent characteristic of the natural environment.

PREFERRED SETTINGS

A similar demonstration of the powerful role of the nature content is exemplified in a series of studies involving the Environmental Preference Questionnaire. This inventory includes a series of descriptions of settings and situations. It is scored for several different sources of environmental preference: cities, suburbs, nature, and some others. Several hundred people have completed this brief form. They have included the freshwomen mentioned before, participants in a garden study (R. Kaplan, 1973b), teenagers in rural and urban places (R. Kaplan, 1977b), and many others representing a broad socioeconomic spectrum. A modified form of the questionnaire administered in Sweden and in Delaware (a study in progress by Roger Ulrich of the University of Delaware) has shown essentially the same pattern of results. Consistently, the mean rating on the "nature" scale is the highest. The "nature" items include a range of everyday nature as well as some less accessible natural settings. A high score on the scale suggests that the person derives a great deal of satisfaction from the enjoyment of nature and seeks natural settings whenever possible, including when harried or under pressure.

Another source of support for the importance of nature in the immediate residential context comes from a study of the preferences of people who live along a creek or stream that is part of one of the county's "drains" (R. Kaplan, 1977a). The main purpose of the study was related to the residents' perception of the drain and of possible changes it might undergo. Here again, the findings provided strong support for the preferences of natural settings. Whether the existing situation was quite adequate or clearly needed improvement, the participants expressed a tremendous concern for "nature amenity." Once again, in addition to expressing a strong appreciation for "nature" and for "green

FIGURE 3

The upper-left scene was by far the most preferred, regardless of where residents lived. The lower-right one, by contrast, was among the least liked. The scene at lower left yielded differential ratings.

places," the participants provided some clues as to the qualities that helped make such settings particularly favorable. Here it was not a sense of mystery nearly as much as it was a sense of orderliness. Pictures showing the drain or creek kept well in bounds, with the edge of the water well defined and the grassy areas finely textured, were definitely the most preferred (figure 3). As Jackson (1951) points out, the green area immediately surrounding one's home holds a special status.

In all these studies, as well as in the anecdotal material, two characteristics are consistently present. The natural environments are distinctly unspectacular, and they are appreciated for their "thereness." The "green" aspect is important, but the people are not doing much in it or with it. What matters is the mere presence of the natural material. In Little's (1975) descriptions of what mattered to residents in suburban, urban, and farm areas, this theme is strongly felt. The presence of a tree outside the window, the small piece of open land, the river — these are often cherished and sought.

BACKYARD NATURE

Many natural settings are appreciated for their "thereness." There are also many green places that provide the setting for involving and gratifying activities. The striking success of the Backyard Wildlife Program (Davis, 1973) provides one example of this. The National Wildlife Federation initiated a program to encourage the use of small backyards as miniature refuges and asked people to write them reporting species they had seen and what they had done to facilitate wildlife. Evidently, the participation was far more voluminous and widespread than they had anticipated. Here again is an opportunity to have an encounter with nature that is both strongly involving and encourages active participation.

Gardening is another activity where the nature experience goes beyond the "thereness" and is intrinsically involved with the nature content. As Vogt (1966) mentioned a decade ago, this activity reached more than half the population. With the sharp increase in community gardens (Bureau of Outdoor Recreation, 1975), and gardening in general, there is probably no single activity that is nature-based and so widely shared by the population. Quite in addition to the tangible benefits brought forth from this plot of land, gardening provides an opportunity for fascination. It is an activity that provides knowledge and requires it; it has an orderliness, but the order is embedded in uncertainty and change (R. Kaplan, 1973b).

While gardening offers such pervasive benefits, their effects are shown even more dramatically in the context of gardening projects associated with public housing. People for whom so many things are not going well, for whom despair is a way of life, might hardly be expected to find comfort in flowers. The evidence is to the contrary.

The story of how flower boxes transformed "the worst block" (Mann, 1973) may sound a bit unreal, but they are consistent with the effect Lewis (1972; 1977) has so sensitively documented. The New York City Housing Authority has sponsored its annual Tenant Gardening Competition for well over a decade by now. The participation figures for 1975 (provided by Beatrice Friedman, Director of Special Services) indicate that "about 14,000 people, from nursery-age children to senior citizens, participated in the Competition." These amounted to 964 groups from throughout the city. Over 80 percent of these were flower gardens. (Vegetable gardens were added to the competition about a year earlier.)

But more important than numbers are the intangible benefits derived from this competition. Lewis tells of the community arrangements fostered in the spirit of guarding the cherished growing things. Tenants were organized enough to have window-watch shifts from upper floors and to mobilize ground-floor "co-workers" in the event that protective action was needed. He tells of elaborate themes and schemes where the flowers led to the adjacent areas. Of course one would not want the sidewalk littered beside one's treasured plants. In one of the neighborhoods Lewis observed, a red-and-white color scheme was extended from the flower patch to the adjacent wall. Even a window box project led to a dramatic increase in maintenance and repair in one neighborhood. In suburban areas one might call these efforts "beautification." In the public housing context, they reflect a sense of identity; the stigma of the situation is reduced. Self-esteem has a rare opportunity to be nurtured.

SMALL SOLUTIONS   The green experience is pervasive. Nature matters to people. The examples are endless and involve innumerable nooks and crannies in people's lives. They also provide hints of countless small changes that can make the human condition just a little more satisfying.

Zube (1973) has commented on the treelessness of many suburban tracts. The lack of plantings around some of the newest, costliest architectural monuments in our cities and on many campuses suggests that some people believe the stonework matters more to people than a view of a growing plant. It might be interesting to ask, for example, how much office space one would be willing to trade for the view of a tree outside the window. (Assuming, of course, one has a window.)

The assembly workers who rush off during their lunch hour, driving madly for several miles to reach a spot with some trees, also tell a story. There they sit for but a few moments to eat their lunch, before rushing back again. Here too a little attention to natural elements might have a disproportionate impact. (For some other examples of the importance of natural elements in ameliorating urban stress, see Stainbrook, 1968.)

On the everyday scale there are countless opportunities for creating a greater exposure to natural, living things. Many of these would have a high (though intangible) payoff for little expenditure. This is not a call for hiring more gardeners and staffs to maintain the plantings. Many times one could tap people's intrinsic desire to nurture growing things and to participate in the management of things that influence their own lives. I am told that somewhere, someone noticed that flower plantings beside bus stops are always kept weeded.   ■

NOTE
    Work on this paper was supported, in part, by the Forest Service, USDA (North Central Forest Experiment Station, St. Paul, Minn.).

7 Stress and the Failure of Preference

Among the characteristics of the environment that seem to create problems are crowding, confusion, coercion, and noise. These lead to a variety of reactions which, in turn, raise other problems. People may become insensitive and distrustful, constantly on guard, and withdraw from the offending environment whenever possible. The result can be a decline in communication, in trust, in helpfulness, in receptivity to people and ideas — in other words, to a decline in many of the essential ingredients of human community.

Linking stress with the failure of preference may seem to put too much emphasis on the preferred and the uncomfortable. Humans, after all, often find themselves in places and situations that fall short of the ideal. Humans are also known to be adaptable. We are constantly confronted with circumstances we had not expected and find ourselves in places that do not "make sense." But we negotiate the terrain, we make do; we hardly even comment on the fact that here again is a nonpreferred environment. To the extent that humans do indeed continuously make their way in less than optimal situations, what are the costs of being such adaptable animals?

COSTS AND CONSEQUENCES

The causes of nonpreference are in many ways easier to identify than are the consequences. Blatant effects such as mortality and rate of reproduction have been documented in some of the research involving animals. But psychological consequences on the human scale are subtle enough that many studies have staunchly reported no negative effects when it is quite possible that the problem lies in the research itself, and the timing of the measurements, rather than in a lack of consequences. After all, the costs associated with nonoptimal environments are not necessarily discernible at the instant one is encountering such situations. Perhaps because of such delays one often fails to associate a painful state of mind with the conditions that helped cause it.

The costs and consequences of such situations manifest themselves in diverse ways. Some of these may be considered positive manifestations, or coping strategies (the focus of the next two chapters). By and large, however, the consequences reflected in the selections here are the more negative, less desirable ones.

The costs of living in a nonpreferred environment are complex and interactive. People may become less willing to venture forth, less likely to find and utilize the resources available in the surrounding environment. They may interact less with one another, impairing the sense of community. An individual in a crowded or otherwise nonpreferred environment lives with an often uncomfortable state of mind and often limited capacity to solve problems. Such an individual may also experience a constrained physical environment and a social environment where people are insensitive and uncaring. It is hardly surprising that humans under such conditions display an increased irritability, a greater preponderance of behavior that others would regard as "aggressive."

The irritability and aggression characteristic of many crowded situations has, as the ethological material in this chapter suggests, some interesting adaptive implications. These reactions, probably common to many circumstances of crowding, may well have served a useful function at one time. By encouraging wider spacing of individuals, the distribution across the available space is made more uniform. Similarly, migration into as yet unoccupied space is encouraged. But when available space runs out and this source of stress is added to many others already at hand, this once beneficial tendency seems somehow less benign.

The selections in this chapter, taken as a whole, create a rather grim impression. Descriptions of the debilitating effects of what for many people constitutes their ordinary, everyday environment hardly make exhilarating reading. The intent of these selections is not to discourage, however, but to provide an urgently needed basis for analysis. Problems generally have to be identified and understood before they can be solved. Through the exploration of a variety of costs in a variety of settings, the chapter may contribute to the needed insights.

"This drawing – an almost arbitrary selection of subject matter – is taken from the chaotic table on which I'm working. I have organized the composition to the extent that it no longer is uncomfortable, but I've kept it complex enough to be interesting (maybe even mysterious). I suspect the magic balance point on that scale of richness and clarity (Dionysus and Apollo) is an individual matter. To know that point for yourself is an important part of self-knowledge. But alas, as soon as you think you know it, it shifts" (Douglas Kinsey).

SOME SOURCES OF STRESS

What kinds of things lead to an environment or situation being less than optimal? In terms of the analysis in the previous chapter, when is there likely to be failure in making sense and when is the likelihood of involvement severely reduced? Environments where making sense is difficult have sometimes been said to create an "overload"; those that fail to call forth involvement have been said to cause an "underload." It is important to recognize that, despite the connotations of "overload" and "underload," it is possible for an environment to *both* make little sense and fail to be involving. Also, there is no meaningful "optimal" or "just right" point somewhere in the middle between overload and underload. The environment cannot be a frozen scene in which everything is in perfect balance. Rather, the goal is an adequate degree of both components. In a rough and ready sort of fashion, both of these terms are useful, as long as they are not taken too literally, or too seriously.[1] But the consequences of environments with such deficiencies, whatever they are called, can be far from trivial. They can be destructive of human functioning, and the cause of considerable pain and stress.

When environments fail to call forth sufficient involvement, people suffer from too little stimulation. Underabundance can be a problem. While most of the selections in this chapter do not address this issue, it came up repeatedly, albeit obliquely, in chapter 4. Surely the effort people are willing to expend to avoid having too little stimulation speaks to the power and pervasiveness of this component in the human makeup. An environment that neither provides stimulation nor permits it to be sought would surely be stressful. Examples of this can be found among humans of all ages. Teenagers seek adventure with an urgency that borders on addiction. Similarly, although at the other end of the spectrum, many elderly also experience such deprivation. In all such instances the larger cost must be taken to include not only the pain endured by the bored, but the human loss that is an inevitable side-effect of any such underutilization.

On the "overload" side of the ledger, many of the problems can be described in terms of overabundance. But what exactly is there too much of? A good deal of research has addressed itself to the causes and consequences of crowding, both in humans and other animals. Does a sheer abundance of people in itself reduce the ability to make sense of one's environment? Or does it matter whether the crowd can be differentiated in some way? Is it the number of people or their density? Is it the number of people or the number of groups of people?

It is an irony of human functioning that (beyond some minimum, of course) the larger the number of people an individual comes in contact with, the less preferred the environment is likely to be and the more damage is likely to be done to the social fabric. People are inherently interesting stimuli. They are difficult to ignore and, as such, will tend to be distracting as their frequency increases. While people thus rate high on the involvement side of the ledger, they are hard to make sense of if they are not familiar. A stranger has a simultaneous threat potential and attraction potential. Strangers elicit strong attention without a clear-cut mandate for action. The more people one encounters, the fewer one is likely to know, probably on an absolute as

Tiger
© *King Features Syndicate Inc. 1973*

well as a relative basis. Thus, the greater the number of strangers, the more difficult the environment. At the same time, even a crowded neighborhood or ethnic enclave need not entail substantial coping efforts and strain as long as the people involved are not strangers.

In other aspects of the environment, too, an overabundance may lead to problems. While these are directly attributable to an increase in the number of people, they are stressors quite apart from that source. Noise constitutes one such situation. Here again the problem is not as simple as it at first may seem. Not only are some noises more disturbing than others, but it turns out that an individual's sense of control over the situation greatly influences the degree of stress involved. While residential traffic brings with it many other problems as well as noise, it certainly constitutes a concrete and pervasive example of the stressful potential of uncontrollable noise.

Often overload is a by-product of a basic difficulty of comprehending and dealing with the environment. Perhaps a useful framework for talking about this failure of making sense is in terms of being lost, both literally and figuratively. Lynch earlier mentioned how powerful a cognitive fear being lost can be. In fact, even the thought of becoming lost can prevent people from venturing forth on uncharted land. Hall (1971), in a paper on environmental communication, discusses residents of a Chicago ghetto sufficiently baffled by the city to have never left the block where they were born. Orleans (1973) carried out a cognitive mapping study of the Los Angeles area. While there were indeed people with a good grasp of the entire city, he also found an ethnic community whose residents were totally lacking in spatial information beyond their own small neighborhood. Transportation planners have been slow to recognize the relationship between these "getting lost" concerns and the information that people would require to make maximal use of the available lines. It is likely that the resources of many a great city are simply unavailable to many of its residents.

NOTE
    1. Such terms as "overload" and "stress" are used here in an informal sense, following what has become common usage. These same terms have been used in a technical sense as elements in theories of the effects of crowding. For some thoughtful criticisms of this technical usage and discussions of alternative conceptualizations of crowding and the related issues of territoriality, privacy and personal space, see Evans and Eichelman (1976) and Stokols (1976).

Edward O. Wilson
Density and Aggressive Behavior*

    This selection and Napier's, which follows, examine the reaction to density from an evolutionary perspective. Aggressive reactions are often thought of in purely negative terms. These papers show the adaptive value such reactions can have as a spacing mechanism. Whether they are still adaptive in a world that is increasingly space-short and people-plentiful is of course a separate question. (Note that these analyses of reactions to density depend upon the idea that tendencies to behave in certain ways can be inherited. Readers who are uncomfortable with this idea may find it helpful to refer back to chapter 1, where this matter was first discussed.)

■   This brings us to the subject of the crowding syndrome and social pathology. Leyhausen (1965) has graphically described what happens to the behavior of cats when they are subjected to unnatural crowding: "The more crowded the cage is, the less relative hierarchy there is. Eventually a despot emerges, 'pariahs' appear, driven to frenzy and all kinds of neurotic behaviour by continuous and pitiless attack by all

*Excerpted from E. O. Wilson "Competitive and aggressive behavior" in J. F. Eisenberg and W. S. Dillon (Eds.) *Man and Beast: Comparative Social Behavior.* Washington, D.C.: The Smithsonian Institution Press, 1971. Pages 200–201; 209–210. Reprinted by permission.

others; the community turns into a spiteful mob. They all seldom relax, they never look at ease, and there is a continuous hissing, growling, and even fighting. Play stops altogether and locomotion and exercise are reduced to a minimum." Still more bizarre effects were observed by Calhoun (1962) in his experimentally overcrowded laboratory populations of white rats. In addition to the hypertensive behavior seen in Leyhausen's cats, some of the rats displayed hypersexuality and homosexuality and engaged in cannibalism. Nest construction was commonly atypical and nonfunctional, and infant mortality among the more disturbed mothers ran as high as 96 percent.

Such behavior is obviously abnormal. It has its close parallels in certain of the more dreadful aspects of human behavior. There are some clear similarities, for example, between the social life of Calhoun's rats and that of people in concentration and prisoner-of-war camps, dramatized so remorselessly, for example, in the novels *Andersonville* and *King Rat*. We must not be misled, however, into thinking that because aggression is twisted into bizarre forms in conditions of abnormally high density, it is therefore nonadaptive. A much more likely circumstance for any given aggressive species, and one which I suspect is true for man, is that the aggressive responses vary in what can properly be called a genetically programed manner. At low population densities, to take one conceivable example, all aggressive behavior may be suspended. At moderate densities it may take a mild form such as intermittent territorial defense. At high densities territorial defense may be sharp, while joint occupancy of land is also permitted under the regime of dominance hierarchies. Finally, at extremely high densities, the system may break down almost completely, transforming the pattern of aggressive encounters into "social pathology." Whatever the specific program that slides individual responses up and down the aggression scale, however, each of the various degrees of aggressiveness is adaptive at an appropriate level of population density — short of the rarely recurring pathological levels. In sum, it is the total *pattern* of responses that is adaptive and has been selected for in the course of evolution.

Is aggression in man *really* adaptive? From the biologist's point of view it certainly seems to be. It is hard to believe that any characteristic so widespread and easily invoked in a species, as aggressive behavior is in man, could be neutral or negative in its effects on individual survival and reproduction. To be sure, overt aggressiveness is not a trait in all or even a majority of human cultures. But in order to be adaptive it is enough that aggressive patterns be evoked only under certain conditions of stress such as those that might arise during food shortages and periodic high population densities. It also does not matter whether the aggression is wholly innate or is acquired partially or wholly by learning. We are now sophisticated enough to know that the capacity to learn certain behaviors is itself a genetically controlled and therefore evolved trait.

CONCLUSIONS   Competition is widespread but not universal in animal species. Current ecological theory predicts that there are several easily obtained conditions under which competition could be permanently avoided. It is not surprising, therefore, that in numerous instances empirical studies have either failed to uncover evidence of competition or else have revealed it to be of secondary importance.

Aggressive behavior among members of the same species without competition is improbable. Aggression is only one of several competitive techniques that have been documented in animal species. Among the species that engage in competition, the more overt forms of aggression are less common in the vertebrate species than in the invertebrates. A small minority of invertebrate species employ killing and even cannibalism as normal competitive techniques, but the occurrence of such behavior seems to be extremely rare in vertebrates.

Within the species that engage in competition and aggression, these phenomena nevertheless tend to be suspended in periods of low population density and accentuated as population density increases. Aggressiveness is viewed as a pattern of adaptive response — most commonly increasing along the ascending scale of population density — rather than as a "neurotic" response to "abnormal" stresses.

The idea that man's immediate ancestors, the primitive Hominidae, were territorial and very aggressive may be true. But the evidence from comparative studies of primate sociology is wholly inconclusive on this point, and ecological correlation can no longer be invoked with any degree of confidence to argue the matter either way.

Some degree of aggressiveness in man is nevertheless probably adaptive — that is, genetically programed by means of natural selection to contribute to fitness in the narrow reproductive sense. This complex trait cannot be assumed to be due to a useless or harmful genetic residue left over from prehistoric times. It is more plausibly viewed as a trait that has been adaptive within the past few hundreds or, at most, thousands of years. Some of its components might even have *originated* during historical times, since both theoretical considerations and empirical studies on animal populations show that some behavioral traits can evolve significantly within ten generations or less. ∎

John Napier
Violence and Overcrowding*

■   The Russells have said much the same thing in their book *Violence, Monkeys and Man* (1968). Violence, as they clearly demonstrate, is not some ultimate and irreducible feature of the universe, but a reaction of all mammals exposed to stress, the principal etiology of which is overcrowding. Violence and aggression are adaptive phenomena that serve to counter the extreme danger to the species of overpopulation. As the Russells say, if we can reduce overcrowding we can diminish violence. The remedy is there, but is mankind capable of taking the hint and accepting all that it entails in the way of compulsory birth control? Overpopulation may not lead to world starvation as Malthus prophesied; mankind is more likely to jostle itself to death. This is one of the lessons that has been learned from ethological studies of living primates.   ■

Lou McClelland
Crowding and Territoriality†

This selection reviews research with both animals and humans on the interrelated topics of crowding, density, and territory. The contrast between the suggestiveness of the animal research and the often inconclusive character of the human research in this area has been striking. One hopes that the issues McClelland raises will guide and inspire more definitive studies in this important area.

■   Many animal species, including humans, live primarily in groups, or at least within communicating distance of one another. For

*From John Napier *The Roots of Mankind.* Washington, D.C.: The Smithsonian Institution Press. 1970. Page 221. Reprinted by permission.
†This is the first publication of this article. All rights reserved. Permission to reprint must be obtained from the author and publisher.

these species, the advantages of group living — protection from predators, group food attainment, and localization of resources — outweigh the disadvantages of contagion and increased competition. Group life has a tremendous effect on the behavior of the individual animal; discussed here are two of these effects: participation in a system of social organization, and reaction to the presence of too many fellow species members.

TERRITORIALITY AND SOCIAL RANK
Animal Studies

If a species of animals is to survive, the food supply must not be overused to such an extent that it cannot replenish itself, and individual animals must not eliminate each other in competition for food and mates. In response to these two survival requirements territorial and social rank systems have evolved in which animals compete in ritualized fashion for the social goals of territory and status rather than directly for food and mates. In such systems possession of territory or high rank allows the animal access to resources; animals without territory or status disperse to other, less desirable environments or receive resource access only after the needs of those with higher priority are fulfilled. Intraspecies aggression is limited, because individuals refrain from entering territories where fighting might occur or engage in ritualized dominant-subordinate behavior patterns rather than in actual combat.

The relationship between territoriality and social rank systems is most intriguing; many species seem to display aspects of both systems simultaneously. The relationship is summarized by the adage "His home is his castle"; that is, an animal on his own territory is dominant. This dominance diminishes in proportion to distance from the home territory. Thus, the social ranking, or hierarchy, is relative, dependent upon location. Only on "neutral ground" equally unfamiliar to all can an absolute hierarchy with invariant dominance relations be established. A newcomer without territory is clearly at a disadvantage under such a system. A correlated finding is that more dominant animals (as determined on neutral grounds) gain larger territories. In other words, space itself becomes a status symbol. The stronger, more aggressive animals are more carefully avoided by others, leaving them a larger space, whether the territory be fixed or portable.

Human Territoriality

Although the territorial behavior of humans is certainly not identical to that of other animals, it is in many ways analogous, being exhibited in similar fashion and serving similar needs. Men clearly organize themselves in social-status ranks; just as clearly, they occupy and defend territories in space and time.

The forms of human territories are, of course, extremely varied. Size may range from a school desk to a continent; group size from one (or less than one, if people are divided into the roles they play) to millions. Territories may be defended physically, legally, verbally, or not at all; they may be clearly bounded or fade from a central point; be permanent, weekly, monthly, or temporary; be fixed or portable, as the work on personal space (Sommer, 1969) indicates. The area may consist of contiguous space, or points and paths, or of totally discontinuous spaces; these may be occupied all, some, or even none of the time. A most important extension of territoriality in humans is to objects, other people, and ideas. Patent and copyright laws are formal systems designed to aid in the defense of nonphysical territories such as ideas and inventions.

The relationship between social status and territoriality in humans is strikingly similar to that in other animals. Status, in fact, is usually *measured* in terms of possession of property (both space and objects, especially money); space allotments both indicate and reinforce status. Another important correlate of high status is mobility; the wealthy man not only has the means to move to various places, he is dominant wherever he may be. Conversely, the low-status person is dominant only in a limited physical space, and then perhaps only by acknowledging the dominance of others by such means as rent. The newcomer to an area is generally lowest in status, as with animals.

Experimental work confirms the theoretical link between territoriality and status in humans. For example, Esser, Chamberlain, Chapple, and Kline (1965) ranked twenty-two psychiatric patients on status and then observed their spatial behavior in the ward, in terms of "territories" (spots in which a patient spent at least 25 percent of waking time) and rooms avoided (places in which a patient spent less than 5 percent of the time). The seven high-status patients had neither territories nor avoided areas; rather, they were free to occupy any space they wished. The seven middle-status patients occupied territories in high-contact, desirable locations; those of low status had territories in secluded, undesirable locations. Both low and middle groups avoided some rooms. Fighting with other patients and staff was correlated with recent admission or changes in drug therapy, and continued until a patient either reached a high-status position or attained a territory.

CROWDING AND DENSITY
Animal Studies

Research on crowding in animals stems from a basic interest in population regulation. Animal populations do not increase without limit, but rather vary in cyclic fashion about a stable mean. Although the factors listed by Malthus — resource availability, predators, and disease — do act to limit population growth, another factor, a "density-dependent behavioral endocrine mechanism," is the "perfect" method (Christian, 1963) of regulating population growth; that is, if the external factors do not limit growth, the internal mechanisms will.

Since the presence of such a self-regulating system was established, research has centered on two questions: What is it about density that causes the effects of "crowding?" How does it operate? While the first question is of central interest to this discussion, the answer to the second is also important, for it provides the mechanism for study of the first.

As established by field and laboratory research, the internal population-regulating mechanism is an endocrine response like that elicited by other stressors. The anterior pituitary is stimulated to secrete adrenocorticotrophin (ACTH), which in turn stimulates the adrenal cortex. The effects of this and related endocrine responses are several: suppression of antibody production and of inflammation reaction, decreased resistance to disease and infection, a slowing in the rate of maturation and diminution of gonadal activity: in females, failures of fertilized ova to implant, reabsorption of blastulae, small litter size, and inadequate lactation; in males, a general slowing of sexual development. These changes act to reduce population size by raising the mortality rate, lowering the birth rate, and decreasing the rate of recruitment of young into the adult population. (See Christian, 1963; Thiessen, 1964; and Thiessen and Rodgers, 1961, for reviews.) This very general knowledge of the endocrine mechanisms is sufficient to establish a paradigm or method for the study of what it is about density that causes the "crowding" effect: we vary the components associated with density until the ones that result in the population-lowering physical effects are isolated. In other words, we work backwards from effect to cause. Studies on confined rodent populations and in the field using this paradigm have produced the conclusions summarized below.

The critical factor in producing the endocrine response is "social competition" or "social density," which is not identical to spatial density. Rather, two major components contribute to the effect:

1 The *number* of animals and social interactions. When density is held constant, endocrine effects are related to the number of animals present, not to space per animal.

2 The *quality* of the social interactions. If the individual members of a population are socially compatible, more crowding can be tolerated.

Compatibility is affected by many factors, including the natural aggressiveness of the species, introduction of aliens into the population, and the presence of a stable social hierarchy. In fact, any genetic, group history, or situational factor that limits aggressive and competitive activity serves to weaken the effect of group size on endocrine reactions and allows greater population growth in a given space.

The two factors of number and quality of social interactions combine in a multiplicative fashion to create the stress that causes the endocrine response. Thus, Christian (1963) defines crowding as "any change in a population which results in increased social competition," through increased numbers of animals with constant behavior, or increased aggression within a group of animals. Spatial density is important *only* when it assures contact among animals by making territorial systems impossible or increasing competition for resources.

The adverse effects of social competition are not distributed evenly over all members of a population; the more dominant the animal, the less effect of crowding it suffers. This phenomenon is not a function of amount of fighting or degree of wounding; in fact, the effects of stress have been found in animals merely anticipating, but not participating in, a physical confrontation with a more dominant animal. The mechanisms by which dominant animals are protected from the effects of social density are not genetic; rather, the dominant animal simply experiences less "social strife" and competition for resources than do subordinate members of the group.

Although the simple relation "crowding is stress, which causes endocrine reactions" has proved very useful for studying the components of crowding, it is probably not entirely correct. In addition to the physiological responses so easily measured, behavioral changes also occur. Withdrawal, passivity, hyperactivity, and most especially abnormal sexual and maternal behavior are characteristic of crowded populations. In fact, these changes sometimes occur without the usual physiological changes, leading Thiessen (1964) to state: "Behavior is the most sensitive index to density, and is regulated in part independently of pituitary-adrenocortical-gonadal involvement."

The Human Situation

Research on the effects of crowding on humans has for several ethical and practical reasons not closely followed the paradigm of the animal research. Instead, it has developed along two rather independent main lines: the effects of living in crowded housing (long-term crowding), and the effects of time spent in crowded public settings (short-term crowding).

Long-Term Crowding   Not all of the many studies of the effects of long-term crowding are of sufficient methodological quality to merit attention; seven studies — four correlational, three experimental — have been selected for discussion here. The correlational studies (Booth and Johnson, 1975; Galle et al., 1972; Freedman et al., 1975; and Mitchell, 1971) attempt to examine the relationship between crowding and various pathologies (as suggested by the animal literature) over individuals or groups of people such as census tracts, with statistical controls for the confounding effects of socioeconomic status, ethnicity, income, and/or education. The experimental studies compare individuals randomly assigned to varying housing conditions on a semipermanent basis (school year, prison term).

All the correlational studies except that of Mitchell (1971) include measures of two types of crowding: crowding within the neighborhood or city, measured as people per residential acre; and crowding within the dwelling unit, usually measured as people per room or square feet per person. When the results from the various studies are taken together, the following picture emerges.

1 Neighborhood or city crowding, or large numbers of people per acre, has no independent relation to pathologies such as mental illness, mortality, and impaired family relations. In other words, the evidence does *not* point to any negative effects of living in large, dense cities.

2 Household crowding *may* have a small adverse effect on the development of certain pathologies, especially if the resident is confined to his dwelling by poverty or lack of outside access, or if interaction with strangers is forced. In other words, if housing conditions (including, but not restricted to, density) require large numbers of unpleasant social interactions, pathology may result, just as in the animal model.

The three experimental studies to date have focused primarily on the effects of group size on satisfaction and behavior. Valins and Baum (1973; Baum, Harpin, and Valins, 1975) compared students (at SUNY, Stony Brook) assigned to dormitories designed with *suites* (three two-person rooms arranged around a common bath and lounge) or *corridors* (twenty-seven two-person rooms along a long hall, sharing one bath and lounge); the two dormitory designs had equal per student density. Compared to suite residents, corridor residents felt more crowded, felt crowded with fewer others present, avoided social interaction with other residents and with strangers (in a laboratory setting), and did not form as readily into functioning groups. Aiello, Epstein, and Karlin (1975) compared Rutgers University dormitory students assigned to live either two or three to a room. (All rooms were of equal size, designed for two, so density and group size varied together.) Residents of the triple rooms were less satisfied with their living arrangements and showed more arousal on behavioral (but not physiological) measures. Female triple rooms were very unstable, with six or seven breaking up before the year's end; this was not true for males.

D'Atri (1975) compared prisoners (71 percent white, average sentence length seven months) assigned to one-man cells or to twenty-to-thirty-man dormitories. Dorm residents had substantially higher blood pressures, which D'Atri interprets as indicative of stress. The dorms were preferred by the prisoners. Thus, these three studies have found substantial negative effects of increased group size on a wide range of physiological, psychological, and behavioral variables. Although the "relative deprivation" of the tripled-up Rutgers students (living in rooms designed for two) undoubtedly was at least partially responsible for the negative effects they experienced, the other two studies suggest again that unavoidable interaction (unavoidable because the dorm residents must share common facilities and because the prison dorm is a closed environment) with many (unrelated) others can cause pathologies and/or efforts to adapt by minimizing social contacts.

An observational study of the !Kung Bushmen of southwest Africa (Draper, 1973) reinforces these conclusions. Although the !Kung population density is very low (one person per ten square miles), within widely separated camps of thirty to forty people, density and intensity of interpersonal interaction are extremely high. The within-camp situation had no negative effects on health or disposition and seemed to be enjoyed by the residents. Draper pointed to the individual's ever present and often used option of moving to another camp and the virtual absence of chance encounters or interactions with strangers as conditions facilitating accommodation to the high density.

Short-Term Crowding   Interest in the effects and processes of short-term crowding by research psychologists has led to at least twenty experimental laboratory studies since 1970 (virtually none before that); because they vary on so many dimensions (task, dependent and independent variables, levels of density, etc.) they will not all be described in detail here. The general paradigm or method of these studies is: subjects, in groups of four to ten, are randomly assigned to conditions varying in space and/or group size (and possibly in other ways such as room temperature, nature of the task, or subject characteristics); they are "crowded" or "not crowded." While in the group, the subjects may fill out written forms, discuss an assigned topic, play a game, compete or cooperate, or do nothing. During and/or after the crowding, measurements on dependent variables such as task performance, attitudes toward the group, arousal, and nonverbal behavior are taken.

Two examples illustrate the paradigm: In Marshall and Heslin (1975), 284 subjects (college students) were assigned, in groups of four or sixteen, to rooms of sixteen, sixty-nine, or 228 square feet. For ninety minutes they worked as groups on a "paragraph unscrambling" task requiring participation of all group members. While still in the experimental room, the subjects each completed verbal scales assessing liking of others in the group, evaluation of the group as a whole, their general feelings (good-bad, sad-happy, etc.), and desire to remain in the group. In Dooley (1975), 227 male college students were assigned to groups of one, three, or nine subjects, and placed in a six-and-a-half-by-twelve-foot room set up as a "grocery store" with "products" on "shelves." For forty minutes they participated in a marketing task, competing with one another for speed and accuracy of "best-buy" judgments. Subjects then moved to individual cubicles for assessment of the dependent variables: aftereffects of stress on behavior, perceptions of crowding, irritability, attitude toward others in the group, and enjoyment.

At present the vast disparities in methods and in results across the several laboratory studies make the drawing of any very definitive conclusions difficult. However, several basic issues have emerged:

1 Is "spatial density" (resulting from less space for an equal number of people) equivalent in its effects to "social density" (resulting from more people in an equal space)? In other words, does crowding mean having to deal with a large number of others, or having others in a very close proximity, or both? An answer to this question is just now becoming clear: density, or lack of space, is important *only* at extreme values. Thus when six experimental subjects must sit for thirty minutes in a four-by-four-foot room, density has a negative effect! At more normal levels of density, number of people is a far more important factor in determining feelings of crowding.

2 Is the animal model relevant to human behavior? In confined animal populations, high levels of social stimulation or social competition lead to arousal and withdrawal. Freedman, Klevansky, and Ehrlich (1971) made the first attempt to relate this model to humans. High school students, in groups of five or nine, were assigned to rooms of 35, 80, or 160 square feet. The subjects spent three hours in discussion of an assigned topic, four different individual written tasks, an oral concentration task, and a group task. Arousal was measured by contrasting performance on easy and complex (novel solution) tasks (high arousal produces improved performance on easy tasks, lowered performance on complex tasks). No effects of room or group size on either type task were found, leading the surprised authors to conclude that "density per se does not function as an ordinary arousing stimulus," and that the animal model must not apply to humans. Of course, the animal model does *not* posit that "density per se" has any effects at all, but that social stimulation, (which was virtually absent in this experiment) does. More recent experiments have attempted to

"*I want to see people eaten by sharks just as much as the next fellow, but I don't think I can hack this line!*"

© 1975 by NEA, Inc.

© 1970 by NEA, Inc.,

Reprinted by permission of Newspaper Enterprise Association.

manipulate social stimulation rather than only density. Some of these studies have found negative effects of crowding, but such effects are not always found and are mild when they are. Why should this be? It is difficult to give human experimental subjects *too much* social stimulation; they seem to consider the "high crowding" conditions of the experiments to be challenging, interesting, fun, or even funny — but not stressful. Thus, although the animal model has received some support from laboratory work on human adults, more definitive tests, conducted under more natural conditions, are necessary.

3 Can the results of the laboratory studies be generalized to "real life"? Such generalizations are hampered by three factors: (1) all but two of the studies used subject populations restricted to high school or college students; (2) in all studies the subjects knew they were subjects whose behavior was under observation, knew they were in the experimental setting for a relatively short, clearly finite time period, and were assigned to perform some activity of no inherent interest or consequence for their own lives; and (3) in all but four of the studies, subjects were separated into same-sex groups, a situation not particularly representative of the "real world." Thus, even if definite conclusions could be drawn from the laboratory studies, their application must await confirmation from studies using other subject populations; unaware, involved subjects; and real-world settings.   ■

Barrie B. Greenbie
Social Territory, Community Health, and Urban Planning*

This paper is too rich, too diverse in content and perspective to fit neatly in any one chapter. It is included here because of the kinds of costs of unsatisfactory environmental arrangements it considers. Many people will dismiss other indicators of stress as minor annoyances; physical illness is much harder to ignore. In addition to this issue, Greenbie's analysis should be appreciated for its synthesis of concepts from the animal literature and problems of planning, and for its perceptive treatment of coping strategies that will be considered in greater detail in the next chapter.

■   Sociological research has established the harmful effects of disrupting ethnic and other social structures in the central city. Proposals to redistribute urban poor in middle-class suburbs may repeat these errors. Cassel and others have correlated various diseases with disordered social relationships that often accompany migration. Physical and social stress are shown to be least harmful to all classes when familiar group support is present; also the effects are most severe on individuals with lowest social status. Where a strange population is introduced into the territory of an indigenous one, social health and stability require protection of the cultural integrity of both groups. Legal and institutional changes of this sort should be accompanied by careful application of what might be called current anthropology or human ethology.

*Reprinted by permission of the *Journal of the American Institute of Planners,* Vol. 40, No. 2, March 1974. Pages 74–82.

The effects of human population growth, in one way or another, have become the central problem of our time. In this country a number of widely acknowledged warnings have appeared, beginning with Ehrlich's "Population Bomb" (1968), and most recently followed by Meadows (1972) and the report of the Commission on Population Growth and the American Future (1972). The continued deterioration of both our urban and our natural environment has lent increasing urgency to the need to control, restrict, or reorganize the impact of people on resources.

This has, of course, always been the primary concern of planners. But, ironically, relatively little consideration has been given to the question of the effect of the *impact of people on other people*. The magnitude of the problems and their relative universality lead planners to think of human beings as aggregations of essentially similar entities, divided at best into certain crude — very crude — categories, such as income level, age, occupation, or race. Despite the current fashion for "social," as opposed to "physical," planning, social considerations continue to be framed in terms of very material economic needs, and a traditionally physicalist view of health. A century after Sigmund Freud and Charles Darwin, much of what has been learned about the nature of man as a unique being and man as another animal is still largely ignored in the framing of public policy.

MIGRATION AND DISRUPTION

One aspect of population growth in particular that is insufficiently considered is the effect of *migration* on people, as individuals and as groups. Toffler (1971) has observed that changes of all sorts now take place much more rapidly than the human mind can cope with them, bringing about what he has called "future shock." One of the most disturbing forms of change for many people is a constant change in social milieu, the familiar "cultural shock" which Toffler has paraphrased. In such situations *cultural shock* and *future shock* combine, and we have ample evidence that the shock can be great indeed.

For many years thoughtful observers have warned that the mass relocations of poor people, as a result of urban renewal and relocation in high-rise public housing projects, have been disrupting intricate social relationships which contribute to the stability of the various ethnic, racial, and cultural groups affected (Jacobs, 1961; Anderson, 1964). The degree to which such policies have contributed to the unrest, crime, violence, dope addiction, and general social breakdown in large American cities can only be guessed at, but the social cost of failure to understand the relationships involved must be staggering. The dollar cost to taxpayers has recently been illustrated by the partial demolition and final abandonment of the notorious (and former prize-winning) Pruitt-Igoe housing project in St. Louis.

More than ten years ago, Herbert Gans (1962) examined the social relationships among working class Italians in what was then an "Urban Village" in Boston's West End, later to be destroyed in the name of "renewal." Marc Fried (1963) followed up Gans's study with a most sensitive investigation of the effect of dislocation on the lives of these people, eloquently entitled "Grieving for a Lost Home." Fried noted that the emotional effects were very similar to grief for a lost person. Rainwater (1966b) examined the destructive impact on the lives of low-income people of relocation in the St. Louis high-rise Pruitt-Igoe project. The last two studies and a number of others, showing intricate connections between physical space and established social relationships, have been brought together by Gutman (1972) in his *People and Buildings*. But perhaps the most convincing examination of this whole problem has been Newman's (1972) brilliantly quantified empirical study of the relationship of residential design to crime and what he calls "Defensible Space."

HOMOGENEITY OR DIVERSITY

These questions have special urgency in regard to two alternatives which are increasingly being considered by social and physical planners. One of these is the legal assault on so-called exclusionary zoning to permit increased construction of low-income development in middle-class suburbs (Davidoff et al., 1970; Downs, 1973). This policy is also generally recommended by the Commission on Population Growth and the American Future. The other is revival of the heterogeneous *new town,* to which Congress has given impetus by Title 7 of the Housing Act of 1970. Implicit in any program to increase the social heterogeneity of a community, whether by introducing new populations into old ones, or by planning new cities from scratch, is the democratic axiom that the breaking down of social barriers between subcultural segments of the population is in and of itself a public good.

There is obvious justification for such a viewpoint. Clearly the complex social interactions and intricate webs of cooperation required by modern technological societies also require a high degree of communication across socioeconomic lines, and the elimination, in so far as possible, of prejudice, hostility, and fear, based on ignorance of other lifestyles. In particular, the social wastefulness and cruelty of racial barriers hardly need reiteration. But the incontestable social value of reducing barriers to human communication, understanding, and cooperation does not necessarily suggest that indiscriminate mixing of populations will achieve such a result. There is much evidence that the opposite is true, that protection of ethnic and other social constellations, and respect for the self-defined boundaries or spatial arrangements which identify them, are an indispensable condition for human cooperation and wellbeing (Glazer and Moynihan, 1963, 1970; Gans,

1961; Hall, 1966; Sommer, 1969; Greenbie, 1971, 1973; Goffman, 1971; Novak, 1972; Levine and Campbell, 1972; Suttles, 1968, 1972).

One may expect this to be particularly true in countries, such as the United States, which, because of immigration, have emerged without the unifying influence of a long-established, preindustrial culture. There is also reason to believe that opposition to the homogeneity of the suburbs, which has been so much deplored in current popular and academic literature, is based on an unrealistic stereotype of suburbia (Berger, 1960; Dobriner, 1963; Wood, 1959; Clark, 1966; Gans, 1967; Donaldson, 1969; Greenbie, 1969). It is quite probable that this homogeneity, for all its limitations, may contribute to the stability which makes such communities a focal point for new low-income housing policies on the one hand, and an implicit, if not overt, model for new towns on the other. Whether or not this is so, it is clearly of the utmost urgency that current policy and planning be based on as accurate an understanding as possible of how human beings mix well and safely and in what ways mixing produces negative consequences.

HIGH DENSITIES AND DISEASE

I will examine some theories that the social dislocations that result from forced mixing under the wrong conditions, as well as from overcrowding under certain circumstances, may not only contribute to social problems, but also to physical disease. For more than a century, reformers and city planning theorists have looked upon high densities as the chief evil of modern cities. Ebenezer Howard's classic formula for new town planning was subtitled "Nothing Gained from Overcrowding." From nineteenth-century utopian reformers to the present day, most writers on the subject of slums have attributed their worst effects to conditions imposed by high densities. A conspicuous exception has been Jane Jacobs (1961), who took the opposite position, ascribing the chief virtues of cities to high densities. Her insights into modern city life have made a most important contribution to urban knowledge, but this aspect of her theory has been severely challenged by most urbanists. In the field of public health, the prevalence of disease has been associated with crowding, on the general theory that disease-bearing germs and pollutants have a greater opportunity to build up under such conditions.

The grim statistics of poverty have long showed a correlation between certain kinds of disease and low socioeconomic status. In this country these statistics show up conspicuously among the black population. It is generally assumed that poor physical conditions, such as sanitation and exposure, as well as poor nutrition due to limited food budgets, are the primary cause. The evidence correlating crowding with certain types of poverty, and poverty with social and physical pathologies of all sorts is immense, but the nature of the processes involved has been far from clear.

For instance, McHarg and his students mapped a number of physical, mental, and social disease variables for the city of Philadelphia. They found that all of these increased toward the city center and correlated highly with each other. The incidence of disease did not, however, correlate directly with poverty per se, although both poverty and disease of all sorts were concentrated toward the city center, but disease did correlate with high densities (McHarg, 1969). On the other hand, Dubos (1968a) notes that some areas like Holland and Hong Kong which have the highest densities in the world also have the highest levels of physical and social health. He feels that the greatest danger to human life, and particularly to human culture, may lie in the fact that man can adapt to conditions which among societies of other animals would normally limit population growth (1968b).

From a wide range of animal studies we have corroborating evidence that crowding does correlate with physical, psychological, and social breakdown, and that this is a primary means of population control, particularly where the consequences of such breakdowns are reflected in inability to mate and rear young (Calhoun, 1952, 1968, 1971; Wynne-Edwards, 1962). One of the generalities often used in connection with the negative effects of high densities is the concept of "stress," and stress is often assumed to be the result of interactions between individuals and each other or individuals and their environment per se.

STRESS AND CULTURAL DISLOCATION

Studies of John Cassel and his associates at the University of North Carolina School of Public Health have used behavioral references from other species in examining disease patterns in our own, and he has concluded that the destructive consequences of crowding do not derive from either *densities* or *stress* per se, but rather from the particular *kind of stress* that arises from the disordered social relationships which normally accompany extreme densities. These are particularly acute in human beings when familiar customs, status hierarchies, and emotional group support systems based on specific cultures are disorganized through enforced migration (Cassel, 1961, 1970, 1971; Nuckolls and Cassel, in press).

Animal ethologists have shown that when an intruder approaches a conspecific's home territory, a ritualized set of behaviors will be initiated on both sides (Lorenz, 1966, 1967; Wynne-Edwards, 1962; Tinbergen, 1953, 1961, 1967). Under normal conditions, behaviors will go on until the intruder retreats or the proprietary animal yields up his territory. In either case, the behavior of one animal is dependent on a predictable response from the other one; in other words, the behavior is reciprocal and may be called a form of communication. This has led Tinbergen (1951) to describe aggression among animals as a form of social behavior. However, if for some reason one animal doesn't respond predictably to the other, the confused animal will tend to indulge in behavior which is quite bizarre; he will do inappropriate things like pulling up grass, attempting to copulate, or even lying down and going to sleep. Lorenz describes this as *displacement* behavior, which in his theory performs the function of diverting aggressive energy into harmless forms. Cassel notes that a more common consequence of failure to get a proper response is that the animal will continue to repeat the behavior, and that this is accompanied by very marked changes in powerful neuro-endocrine processes and the distribution of crucial hormones in the animal's body. It is these physiological concomitants of failure to get a proper social response to conventional behavior signals which, in this theory, lead to making the body vulnerable to various insults, such as a disease-bearing virus, or a functional breakdown, like stomach ulcers.

Human beings communicate not only by spoken words and written symbols but by very subtle changes in gesture and inflection, facial expression, or bodily movements, most of which will vary considerably from one culture to another (Hall, 1959). Cassel believes that although the disorganization of the social cues which individuals depend on to relate properly to others will almost always result from crowding in animals, among humans it may show up in both crowded and uncrowded situations. He notes, however, that even among animals, crowding will be tolerated much better among litter mates than among strangers. For lower-class humans, migration is most likely to result in movement from lower to higher density areas, but in Cassel's view it will be the changed social situation, and not the density, that is most critical.

DISEASE CYCLES AND IMPLICATIONS

Cassel (1971) examined the history of disease patterns which accompanied the industrial revolution. Tuberculosis has been a prime example of a disease which is associated with crowding, poverty, and unhealthful living conditions. He notes that this disease rose sharply for seventy-five to one hundred years after the beginning of industrialization in Britain and the United States, and then started to fall spontaneously between 1850 and 1900, fifty to one hundred years before effective means of treating it became available. Furthermore the rate of decline in this disease has not changed significantly following new drugs for its treatment. As tuberculosis began to decline, it was replaced by malnutrition syndromes, such as rickets and pellagra, which also peaked, and, for reasons only partially understood, also began to decline. These in turn were replaced by childhood diseases, which waxed and waned, "largely but not entirely" due to immunization and improved sanitary conditions. A new cycle introduced an increase in duodenal ulcers, particularly in young men, to be replaced in the present time by epidemics of heart disease, cancer, arthritis, diabetes, and mental disorders, some of which have already peaked and declined. Cassel believes these cycles cannot be attributed entirely to developments in medical practice. Apparently they do not correspond to equivalent fluctuations in crowding, either, which as a general phenomenon has continued to increase more or less constantly.

He has looked at data from military camps, for instance, where upper respiratory disease is common. The agent responsible is Adenovirus 4, and the orthodox explanation is that crowding in barracks and elsewhere facilitates the spread of the virus, but he notes that the virus is equally present in schools and colleges, where it is rarely implicated in similar infections. Examination of military camps revealed that the permanent staffs were not involved in the outbreaks under study, but *only the recruits*. When the latter were immunized against Adenovirus 4, they continued to experience the same amount of respiratory illness, now associated with a *different* virus. Even more importantly, studies at a Marine base found that there was a definite cycle of the disease during the eight week basic training period, in which the number of respiratory infections increased from the first to the fourth week, decreased during the fifth and sixth, and rose again during the last two (Cassel, 1971).

Data from epidemiology shows furthermore that increases in diseases do not always take place in the crowded cities, but that often the reverse is true, and that this cannot always be explained by improved health services in the city. An example is the greater preponderance in rural areas of streptococcal infections, for which there is no known preventative. Urban data for tuberculosis show that it is not more prevalent among people who are most crowded, but rather among people who are socially isolated in what must be considered relatively low densities, on a person per room basis. A study in Britain found the tuberculosis rate among lodgers living alone was three to four times as high as among families living in otherwise similar conditions (Cassel, 1971).

CASSEL'S FOUR PRINCIPLES   Cassel believes that data from both human and animal studies of crowding can best be examined in terms of four principles: The first is the hypothesis that "the social process linking high population density to enhanced susceptibility to disease is not crowding per se but *the disordered relationships that in animals are inevitable consequences of such crowding*." (My italics.) The clear implication of this hypothesis is that for human beings crowding may facilitate *social disorganization,* but will not necessarily produce it. Cassel's second general principle is that not all members of a population will be equally *susceptible* to these processes, and that the most *dominant individuals* will show the *least effects,* while the subordinate ones will show the most extreme responses. His third principle is that two types of buffers will cushion the individual against the consequences of social disorganization, one *biological,* the other *social.* The biological buffer is the capacity of all living organisms *over time* to adjust psychologically and physiologically to new circumstances. The social cushion is the strength of *group support* given by familiar conspecifics. The fourth principle he advances is that the consequences of social disorganization in these terms do not directly cause a specific illness, but rather they enhance susceptibility to disease in general, and that it will be a matter of which disease agents, independent of social factors, happen to strike at any particular place at any particular time (1970a).

These principles are supported with considerable evidence from his own and others' research. Supporting the first hypothesis is a great deal of information linking various indicators of social or family breakdown, such as divorce or sudden unemployment, to various diseases. It is supported conversely by the examples already given of very crowded societies which do not have a high incidence of disease but which are also very stable socially. The second principle is supported by similar data which shows a high correlation of illness to low social status and to job positions which occupy a subordinate role in society. The biological adaptability in the third principle is confirmed by experience with animals raised in crowded conditions, as compared with those moved into them after maturing in less crowded ones. In humans the incidence of lung cancer (when controlled for cigarette smoking) is actually higher among farm-born people who move to air-polluted cities than for lifetime urban residents, despite greater exposure of the latter to cancer-producing agents. The group-support hypothesis is reinforced by studies of rats, for instance, where peptic ulcers caused by electric shocks are much less likely in animals who are shocked in the presence of litter mates than those who are stressed that way alone. In humans, stress induced by being given unsolvable problems to solve was much greater in a group of strangers than in a group of friends. There is much evidence that diseases such as tuberculosis are more common among marginal people who, for one reason or another, are deprived of meaningful and stable social contacts. The final principle that disturbances in group relationships will not lead to specific illnesses (such as job frustration causing ulcers), but rather to a susceptibility to disease in general, is supported by data which show that those regions having highest death rates, for instance from cardiovascular disease, also have higher than expected death rates from all causes.

It is apparent that all such phenomena are interrelated. Studies in Scotland, for instance, show that male red grouse who failed to obtain territory were also unable to make a pair bond with females, generally were prone to various illnesses, failed to protect themselves from predators, and did not survive the winter (Watson and Moss, 1971).

STATUS, CROWDING, AND CHANGE

If Cassel's theories are correct, we may conclude that the mechanism which enables man to remain healthy at densities higher than most animals could tolerate, also enables man to structure his environment and his social relationships conceptually, as suggested by Calhoun (1971) and Esser (1971, 1972). In a very real sense, it is probably not densities that cause a person to feel more or less crowded, but *what he thinks being crowded is,* and the effect this has on his social interactions. Crowding does not only affect the amount of interaction, but also changes the nature of the interaction. At the same time, a person's concept of status and of family or other in-group relations will be very critical in determining how he adjusts both to crowding and to change. A study by Christenson and Hinkle (1961) showed a much lower incidence of disease among a group of managers who had completed college, as compared with those doing the same job for the same pay who had only completed high school. The college graduates were generally sons of high-status managers and white-collar workers from middle-class neighborhoods; the non-college managers were children of working-class immigrants. One may assume that not only did social class status play a role in this phenomenon, but also the symbols of middle-class life, which would normally be part of the managerial world. Cassel and an associate made a series of studies of two groups of rural mountaineers who had moved to urban areas and taken industrial jobs in factories. The groups were similar in age and other factors, but one had recently migrated from the mountains, while the others were the children of factory workers who had previously come from the same mountain coves. It was hypothesized that the second generation workers would be better prepared than the first group for the expectations and demands of industrial living, and would, therefore, exhibit fewer signs of ill health. Health was measured according to the Cornell Medical Index and various indices of sick absenteeism. As predicted, the highest health scores and lowest absenteeism was from the group whose parents had been employed in industry before them (Cassel and Tyroler, 1961).

The second principle of Cassel, that social disruption hits hardest on the least dominant, will also be compounded because the shift will often be accompanied by a loss of status, if only because the person becomes a newcomer and, even when potentially a leader, will have to establish that fact in a new group. In any case, it is the least dominant who are most likely to be forced to migrate. The third principle, that time and group unities provide buffers, is a function of migration under such circumstances; the group is left behind, and the instability result-ing from the first situation may force continued migration which will not permit the healing adaptations in one situation long enough for new codes to be established. In any case, these may often require more than one generation, especially in people with limited educational, and therefore limited conceptual, resources. So the three principles become negatively reinforcing, and lead inevitably to the fourth, a propensity for disease.

To test the proposition that health is correlated negatively with changes in life situation and positively with group support, Cassel and his colleagues did a study of young women having their first pregnancy (Nuckolls and Cassel, in press). They developed a score system which incorporated such changes as moves to a new community, and family breakups, which in other studies have shown a high correlation with illness. These were combined with what the researchers called a "social asset" score, which included whether or not the woman wanted the pregnancy and how much support she felt she had from husband, fam-ily, and community. They found that ninety percent of the women who had high life-change scores and low social-asset scores developed pregnancy or postpartum complications, whereas of those with equally high life-change scores, but high assets, only thirty percent had dif-ficulties. Significantly, the *adequacy of social assets was irrelevant where life-change scores were low.* Cassel also notes a study of immi-grants to Israel, which found that those who migrated as families had much better health records than those who did so as individuals.

In view of the fact that our core cities are more and more popu-lated not only by poor, low-status, minority people crowded into slums, but also by people who have recently migrated from rural areas, this is pretty crucial information for planners to chew on. It is particularly crucial in terms of the dissolution of family life that so often accom-panies rural to urban migration, aggravated by lack of housing and the inability of male heads-of-households to find work. It may help to ex-plain why our present welfare program fails to offer even a palliative for this kind of poverty.

MOVING THE POOR TO THE SUBURBS   Now that the arrogance of well-intentioned ignorance has helped many of our large cities to become virtually uninhabitable, we are faced with propositions that may, if what I will call "Cassel's Syn-drome" is not carefully considered, extend the same disastrous policies to the suburbs. Whatever else they may or may not be, these have, at least until recently, tended to be stable communities. That, of course, is why they are being looked to by reformers who have given up on the central city. Many of the campaigns to relocate core city poor are based on a legal assault on what is called "exclusionary" zoning. As the

Davidoffs (1970), and more recently Downs (1973) have noted, present residential patterns in most metropolitan areas represent an unworkable and unbalanced distribution of populations in relation to resources, both economic and natural. But if we look at the problem closely, it is not the "exclusionary" nature of zoning that is causing the trouble, but exclusion in the *wrong places*. What *is* needed, of course, is a restructuring of the way residential communities are organized around centers of employment, transportation, commerce, and available space, with due regard to the eco-system. But the rhetoric of these projects, with terms such as "snob zoning" and an "open society," seems to me not only to be wide of the real mark, but self-righteous, troublemaking, and likely to make a difficult problem harder to solve.

Zoning originated in an attempt to bring form to an otherwise formless urban environment. It did so precisely because the forces which shaped earlier communities were no longer operative. In general it has proved to be a crude and blunt instrument, mangling the physical environment and permitting no subtleties, either in human or nonhuman relationships. But the fact that it has proved to be a poor solution on the one hand, and that it has led to a new problem of community structure on the other, does not mean that it can be breached like a castle wall without recognizing and respecting the more constructive purposes it was designed to accomplish in the first place.

Social Mixing

Jane Jacobs and others have made an excellent case for social diversity of all kinds, and there is no question that under proper conditions social heterogeneity is a prerequisite for cross-cultural cooperation and for civilization in any real sense. The achievement of such conditions may certainly be regarded as a primary object of planning. But rarely are plans for social mixing accompanied by consideration in careful detail of who is to be mixed with whom, how, where, and under what conditions. If a chemist advanced the proposition that a "mix" per se is good, we would call him mad! If a cook advanced such a notion, we would go elsewhere to eat. Yet the evidence we have looked at suggests that some people mix well and some do not, that the same people can mix safely and happily under some conditions but not under others, and above all that he who would intrude one group into another's territory had better be prepared to guarantee the safety of both if his egalitarian predictions prove false.

Established presuburban old towns contain a real measure of social diversity precisely because that diversity holds at least some common features. Everyone, or almost everyone, knows everybody else, and shares not only a common geographical space, but a common conceptual territory as well. The modern zoned subdivision attempts to cope with the fact that in our socially, economically, and physically mobile world, diversity is accompanied by widely disparate conceptual territories carried by continually shifting groups to new places, and that therefore the only way that a common set of references can be established is through considerable social stratification based on externalities.

If particular land use and building laws are an expression of a conventional culture, and are relied on to preserve a predictable and intelligible environment, and if, in the name of social justice, these are to be radically altered, we may well ask what is to take their place? What sort of cultural institutions will immigrate with those for whom geographical doors have been opened? Is the middle class, in being forced to yield many of its own conventions, expected to welcome alien ones? Is this, with the best of intentions, possible? If so, what sort of cultural trade-offs or compromises can be negotiated, and how? To what extent when social systems mix are they mutually reinforcing or mutually destructive?

New Laws and Institutions Needed

In the general pattern of United States history, whatever equality of opportunity there has been for succeeding generations of immigrants has resulted in acceptance of middle-class conventions, including housing patterns, by those who moved up the socioeconomic ladder. Now the immigration of city poor to the middle-class countryside is being proposed as a conscious and deliberate assault on the status quo. It is being proposed in some cases on the ideological grounds that the status quo is immoral. This is predictably perceived by the middle-class territory holders exactly as what it is claimed to be, an invasion. Under such circumstances, laws and institutions to resolve contests must be imposed. There is a very real question as to whether the abrupt and forceful dislocation of community norms in the case of the middle class will prove to be any more salutary for society as a whole than such dislocations have proved to be in the case of the urban poor. But can the *imposition* of new norms, via changed laws and institutions, be limited to the middle classes on the site? Will not something have to be imposed on the new *immigrants*? And if so, will *what* is imposed on them be any more likely to provide satisfactory environments than the impositions of public housing authorities and relocation agencies back in the city core? Who is to determine the nature of the imposed institutions, and how will the determination be made, if the collective opinion of the existing community is made invalid?

Let us suppose the culture of the new residents is one which involves a lively street life, and some care has been taken in the physical design of the new residences to provide opportunity for it. How will the attendant noise and general commotion fit in with the internalized lifestyle of many middle-class nuclear families? What of differences in manners and general deportment, especially as regards the behavior of children (which can cause a problem even in socially homogeneous communities)? To what extent will the inevitable conflicts result in voluntary withdrawal on all sides into culturally segregated enclaves, replacing big city ghettos with small city ghettos? To what extent will this raise the question Newman addresses regarding abdication of responsibility for the affairs of the community, and consequent opportunity for criminal behavior? In short, what sorts of socially organizing principles can or cannot be written into the new laws and institutions which will preserve the stabilizing functions of the older, indigenous ones.

These questions are answerable in principle, but it is unlikely that the answers will be available prior to assaults on the laws and institutions that bring about the changes that make them necessary. Certainly much more careful, systematic, perceptive, and *empathetic* research will be needed than now appears to be going on, and what is going on should find its way more readily into public policy making. If the official rhetoric regarding the "public welfare" and an "open society" continues to provide the conceptual framework for research, it seems likely that the right questions will not be asked.

CONCEPTUAL TERRITORIES

Elsewhere (Greenbie, 1973) I have suggested that the fewer conceptual resources people have, the more, rather than less, dependent they will be on relationships which are defined by geographical space. For sophisticated urban man, conceptual territories may be provided by professions, hobbies, and religious or political organizations, which can substitute for physical territory. Such people may be relatively indifferent to physical design and location. The poor and cultural minorities will be most likely to need secure physical-cultural boundaries. To intrude them heedlessly, in the name of improving their lot, into territories where residents have more conceptual, as well as physical, resources, can be expected to benefit only the most able and conceptually agile among them. On the other hand, they will be well received only by those whose conceptual territories, or self-images, are, in one way or another, secure from invasion.

In a most interesting, ongoing study of migration in an Argentine village, R. W. Wilkie (1972) has found that the portion of the population most able to cope with change through migration was a part — and only a part — of what he defined as its *middle class.* (The entire village, a peasant community, would be called by most sociologists lower class.) Wilkie observed that the upper and lower class in this village were conservative for different reasons, the upper because it was oriented to peer group expectations, and the lower because it lacked confidence in its ability to cope with new environments. In addition, a portion of the middle class also resembled these groups.

CONCLUSIONS   We who propose, devise, and administer laws and institutions are very likely to come out of the professional middle class. We may in some cases be people of little formal education, but who nevertheless have had tremendous conceptual resources of some sort. We will be most likely to organize space and events in abstract, conceptual, intellectual terms. We will continually model environments on our own needs for intellectual complexity, projecting as a universal good what is in fact a minority point of view, even if a most important one. We can afford to be relatively indifferent to other people's needs for secure physical-cultural territory, because we have other resources. We can moralize about the "greed" of affluent groups whose security depends on material welfare, because we have other symbolic ways of maintaining status and power. Yet our problem is, like that of everybody else, how to bring about environments which will enable all of us at least to survive, let alone live happily together.

Wherever mass migrations occur, the interests of two opposing parties must be considered, and constructively provided for; the cultural integrity of the incoming people and the territorial integrity of the proprietary group. The law and its institutions can provide a structure for appropriate compromise, but the negotiation and arbitration will have to be personal and particular in each case. Because modern society requires cross-cultural communication and cooperation on an *intellectual* basis, spaces and social mechanisms for this must be created. On the other hand, studies by ethologists have shown that nonhuman animals gain a psychological advantage on their own territory (Wynne-Edwards, 1962; Leyhausen, 1965, 1971; Lorenz, 1966), which enables them to defend themselves against larger, stronger, and more dominant creatures who would prevail on neutral ground. For human beings also, on the most primitive level of experience, this appears to hold true (Ardrey, 1966, 1970). Physical-social buffers are therefore essential. The first requirement for a healthy change of milieu, whether physical or social, is the assurance of emotional security based on *conceptual territory,* that is, native culture. The second is opportunity for it to recombine with others and evolve safely into something new.

Since legal and institutional mechanisms cannot create these by edict, but can only discover them, changes in laws and institutions must be preceded by what might be called current *anthropology,* or better, *human ethology.* It must be applied in a creative manner that can only be described as *art.*   ■

NOTE
1. Part of the research on which this article has been based was supported by Grant No. A 71-I-26 from the National Endowment for the Arts.

Stanley Milgram
The Experience of Living in Cities*

To the extent that the city confronts people with a very high level
of distraction, being able to ignore otherwise interesting stimulation
becomes a vital skill if one is to continue to function. Milgram does not
question whether people are capable of doing this, but rather looks at
the costs of being insensitive to many things that humans ordinarily
find of interest.

■   When I first came to New York it seemed like a nightmare. As soon as I
    got off the train at Grand Central I was caught up in pushing, shoving
    crowds on 42nd Street. Sometimes people bumped into me without apol-
    ogy; what really frightened me was to see two people literally engaged in
    combat for possession of a cab. Why were they so rushed? Even drunks on
    the street were bypassed without a glance. People didn't seem to care
    about each other at all.

This statement represents a common reaction to a great city, but
it does not tell the whole story. Obviously cities have great appeal because of their variety, eventfulness, possibility of choice, and the
stimulation of an intense atmosphere that many individuals find a desirable background to their lives. Where face-to-face contacts are important, the city offers unparalleled possibilities. It has been calculated
by the Regional Plan Association that in Nassau County, a suburb of
New York City, an individual can meet 11,000 others within a ten-
minute radius of his office by foot or car. In Newark, a moderate-sized
city, he can meet more than 20,000 persons within this radius. But in
midtown Manhattan he can meet fully 220,000. So there is an order-
of-magnitude increment in the communication possibilities offered by
a great city. That is one of the bases of its appeal and, indeed, of its
functional necessity. The city provides options that no other social arrangement permits. But there is a negative side also, as we shall see.
        Granted that cities are indispensable in complex society, we may
still ask what contribution psychology can make to understanding the
experience of living in them. What theories are relevant? How can we
extend our knowledge of the psychological aspects of life in cities

*Excerpted and reprinted by permission from S. Milgram "The experience of living in
   cities." *Science,* 13 March 1970, 167, 1461–1464, 1468. Copyright 1970 by the American Association for the Advancement of Science.

through empirical inquiry? If empirical inquiry is possible, along what lines should it proceed? In short, where do we start in constructing urban theory and in laying out lines of research?

Observation is the indispensable starting point. Any observer in the streets of midtown Manhattan will see (1) large numbers of people, (2) a high population density, and (3) heterogeneity of population. These three factors need to be at the root of any sociopsychological theory of city life, for they condition all aspects of our experience in the metropolis. Louis Wirth (1938), if not the first to point to these factors, is nonetheless the sociologist who relied most heavily on them in his analysis of the city.[1] Yet, for a psychologist, there is something unsatisfactory about Wirth's theoretical variables. Numbers, density, and heterogeneity are demographic facts, but they are not yet psychological facts. They are external to the individual. Psychology needs an idea that links the individual's *experience* to the demographic circumstances of urban life.

One link is provided by the concept of overload. This term, drawn from systems analysis, refers to a system's inability to process inputs from the environment because there are too many inputs for the system to cope with, or because successive inputs come so fast that input A cannot be processed when input B is presented. When overload is present, adaptations occur. The system must set priorities and make choices. A may be processed first while B is kept in abeyance, or one input may be sacrificed altogether. City life, as we experience it, constitutes a continuous set of encounters with overload, and of resultant adaptations. Overload characteristically deforms daily life on several levels, impinging on role performance, the evolution of social norms, cognitive functioning, and the use of facilities.

The concept has been implicit in several theories of urban experience. In 1903 George Simmel (1950) pointed out that, since urban dwellers come into contact with vast numbers of people each day, they conserve psychic energy by becoming acquainted with a far smaller proportion of people than their rural counterparts do, and by maintaining more superficial relationships even with these acquaintances. Wirth (1938) points specifically to "the superficiality, the anonymity, and the transitory character of urban social relations."

One adaptive response to overload, therefore, is the allocation of less time to each input. A second adaptive mechanism is disregard of low-priority inputs. Principles of selectivity are formulated such that investment of time and energy are reserved for carefully defined inputs (the urbanite disregards the drunk sick on the street as he purposefully navigates through the crowd). Third, boundaries are redrawn in certain social transactions so that the overloaded system can shift the burden to the other party in the exchange; thus, harried New York bus drivers once made change for customers, but now this responsibility has been shifted to the client, who must have the exact fare ready. Fourth, reception is blocked off prior to entrance into a system; city dwellers increasingly use unlisted telephone numbers to prevent individuals from calling them, and a small but growing number resort to keeping the telephone off the hook to prevent incoming calls. More subtly, a city dweller blocks inputs by assuming an unfriendly countenance, which discourages others from initiating contact. Additionally, social screening devices are interposed between the individual and environmental inputs (in a town of 5000 anyone can drop in to chat with the mayor, but in the metropolis organizational screening devices deflect inputs to other destinations). Fifth, the intensity of inputs is diminished by filtering devices, so that only weak and relatively superficial forms of involvement with others are allowed. Sixth, specialized institutions are created to absorb inputs that would otherwise swamp the individual (welfare departments handle the financial needs of a million individuals in New York City, who would otherwise create an army of mendicants continuously importuning the pedestrian). The interposition of institutions between the individual and the social world, a characteristic of all modern society, and most notably of the large metropolis, has its negative side. It deprives the individual of a sense of direct contact and spontaneous integration in the life around him. It simultaneously protects and estranges the individual from his social environment.

Many of these adaptive mechanisms apply not only to individuals but to institutional systems as well, as Meier (1962) has so brilliantly shown in connection with the library and the stock exchange.

In sum, the observed behavior of the urbanite in a wide range of situations appears to be determined largely by a variety of adaptations to overload. I now deal with several specific consequences of responses to overload, which make for differences in the tone of city and town.

SOCIAL RESPONSIBILITY

The principal point of interest for a social psychology of the city is that moral and social involvement with individuals is necessarily restricted. This is a direct and necessary function of excess of input over capacity to process. Such restriction of involvement runs a broad spectrum from refusal to become involved in the needs of another person, even when the person desperately needs assistance, through refusal to do favors, to the simple withdrawal of courtesies (such as offering a lady a seat, or saying "sorry" when a pedestrian collision occurs). In any transaction more and more details need to be dropped as the total number of units to be processed increases and assaults an instrument of limited processing capacity.

The ultimate adaptation to an overloaded social environment is to totally disregard the needs, interests, and demands of those whom one does not define as relevant to the satisfaction of personal needs, and to develop highly efficient perceptual means of determining whether an individual falls into the category of friend or stranger. The disparity in the treatment of friends and strangers ought to be greater in cities than in towns; the time allotment and willingness to become involved with those who have no personal claim on one's time is likely to be less in cities than in towns.

Bystander Intervention in Crises   The most striking deficiencies in social responsibility in cities occur in crisis situations, such as the Genovese murder in Queens. In 1964, Catherine Genovese, coming home from a night job in the early hours of an April morning, was stabbed repeatedly, over an extended period of time. Thirty-eight residents of a respectable New York City neighborhood admit to having witnessed at least a part of the attack, but none went to her aid or called the police until after she was dead. Milgram and Hollander, writing in *The Nation* (1964), analyzed the event in these terms:

> Urban friendships and associations are not primarily formed on the basis of physical proximity. A person with numerous close friends in different parts of the city may not know the occupant of an adjacent apartment. This does not mean that a city dweller has fewer friends than does a villager, or knows fewer persons who will come to his aid; however, it does mean that his allies are not constantly at hand. Miss Genovese required immediate aid from those physically present. There is no evidence that the city had deprived Miss Genovese of human associations, but the friends who might have rushed to her side were miles from the scene of her tragedy.
>   Further, it is known that her cries for help were not directed to a specific person; they were general. But only individuals can act, and as the cries were not specifically directed, no particular person felt a special responsibility. The crime and the failure of community response seem absurd to us. At the time, it may well have seemed equally absurd to the Kew Gardens residents that not one of the neighbors would have called the police. A collective paralysis may have developed from the belief of each of the witnesses that someone else must surely have taken that obvious step.

Latané and Darley (1969) have reported laboratory approaches to the study of bystander intervention and have established experimentally the following principle: the larger the number of bystanders, the less the likelihood that any one of them will intervene in an emergency. Gaertner and Bickman of The City University of New York have extended the bystander studies to an examination of help across ethnic lines. Blacks and whites, with clearly identifiable accents, called strangers (through what the caller represented as an error in telephone dialing), gave them a plausible story of being stranded on an outlying highway without more dimes, and asked the stranger to call a garage. The experimenters found that the white callers had a significantly better chance of obtaining assistance than the black callers. This suggests that ethnic allegiance may well be another means of coping with overload: the city dweller can reduce excessive demands and screen out urban heterogeneity by responding along ethnic lines; overload is made more manageable by limiting the "span of sympathy."

In any quantitative characterization of the social texture of city life, a necessary first step is the application of such experimental methods as these to field situations in large cities and small towns. Theorists argue that the indifference shown in the Genovese case would not be found in a small town, but in the absence of solid experimental evidence the question remains an open one.

More than just callousness prevents bystanders from participating in altercations between people. A rule of urban life is respect for other people's emotional and social privacy, perhaps because physical privacy is so hard to achieve. And in situations for which the standards are heterogeneous, it is much harder to know whether taking an active role is unwarranted meddling or an appropriate response to a critical situation. If a husband and wife are quarreling in public, at what point should a bystander step in? On the one hand, the heterogeneity of the city produces substantially greater tolerance about behavior, dress, and codes of ethics than is generally found in the small town, but this diversity also encourages people to withhold aid for fear of antagonizing the participants or crossing an inappropriate and difficult-to-define line.

Moreover, the frequency of demands present in the city gives rise to norms of noninvolvement. There are practical limitations to the Samaritan impulse in a major city. If a citizen attended to every needy person, if he were sensitive to and acted on every altruistic impulse that was evoked in the city, he could scarcely keep his own affairs in order.

Willingness To Trust and Assist Strangers   We now move away from crisis situations to less urgent examples of social responsibility. For it is not only in situations of dramatic need but in the ordinary, everyday willingness to lend a hand that the city dweller is said to be deficient relative to his small-town cousin. The comparative method must be used in any empirical examination of this question. A commonplace social situation is staged in an urban setting and in a small town — a situation to which a subject can respond by either extending help or withholding it. The responses in town and city are compared.

TABLE 1   Percentage of entries achieved by investigators for city and town dwellings (see text)

Experimenter	Entries achieved (%)	
	City*	Small town†
Male		
No. 1	16	40
No. 2	12	60
Female		
No. 3	40	87
No. 4	40	100

*Number of requests for entry, 100. † Number of requests for entry, 60.

One factor in the purported unwillingness of urbanites to be helpful to strangers may well be their heightened sense of physical (and emotional) vulnerability — a feeling that is supported by urban crime statistics. A key test for distinguishing between city and town behavior, therefore, is determining how city dwellers compare with town dwellers in offering aid that increases their personal vulnerability and requires some trust of strangers. Altman, Levine, Nadien, and Villena of The City University of New York devised a study to compare the behaviors of city and town dwellers in this respect. The criterion used in this study was the willingness of householders to allow strangers to enter their home to use the telephone. The student investigators individually rang doorbells, explained that they had misplaced the address of a friend nearby, and asked to use the phone. The investigators (two males and two females) made 100 requests for entry into homes in the city and 60 requests in the small towns. The results for middle-income housing developments in Manhattan were compared with data for several small towns (Stony Point, Spring Valley, Ramapo, Nyack, New City, and West Clarkstown) in Rockland County, outside of New York City. As table 1 shows, in all cases there was a sharp increase in the proportion of entries achieved by an experimenter when he moved from the city to a small town. In the most extreme case the experimenter was five times as likely to gain admission to homes in a small town as to homes in Manhattan. Although the female experimenters had notably greater success both in cities and in towns than the male experimenters had, each of the four students did at least twice as well in towns as in cities. This suggests that the city-town distinction overrides even the predictably greater fear of male strangers than of female ones.

The lower level of helpfulness by city dwellers seems due in part to recognition of the dangers of living in Manhattan, rather than to mere indifference or coldness. It is significant that 75 percent of all the city respondents received and answered messages by shouting through closed doors and by peering out through peepholes; in the towns, by contrast, about 75 percent of the respondents opened the door.

Supporting the experimenters' quantitative results was their general observation that the town dwellers were noticeably more friendly and less suspicious than the city dwellers. In seeking to explain the reasons for the greater sense of psychological vulnerability city dwellers feel, above and beyond the differences in crime statistics, Villena points out that, if a crime is committed in a village, a resident of a neighboring village may not perceive the crime as personally relevant, though the geographic distance may be small, whereas a criminal act committed anywhere in the city, though miles from the city-dweller's home is still verbally located within the city; thus, Villena says, "the inhabitant of the city possesses a larger vulnerable space."

Civilities

Even at the most superficial level of involvement — the exercise of everyday civilities — urbanites are reputedly deficient. People bump into each other and often do not apologize. They knock over another person's packages and, as often as not, proceed on their way with a grumpy exclamation instead of an offer of assistance. Such behavior, which many visitors to great cities find distasteful, is less common, we are told, in smaller communities, where traditional courtesies are more likely to be observed.

In some instances it is not simply that, in the city, traditional courtesies are violated; rather, the cities develop new norms of noninvolvement. These are so well defined and so deeply a part of city life that *they* constitute the norms people are reluctant to violate. Men are actually embarrassed to give up a seat on the subway to an old woman; they mumble, "I was getting off anyway," instead of making the gesture in a straightforward and gracious way. These norms develop because everyone realizes that, in situations of high population density, people cannot implicate themselves in each others' affairs, for to do so would create conditions of continual distraction which would frustrate purposeful action.

In discussing the effects of overload I do not imply that at every instant the city dweller is bombarded with an unmanageable number of inputs, and that his responses are determined by the excess of input at any given instant. Rather, adaptation occurs in the form of gradual

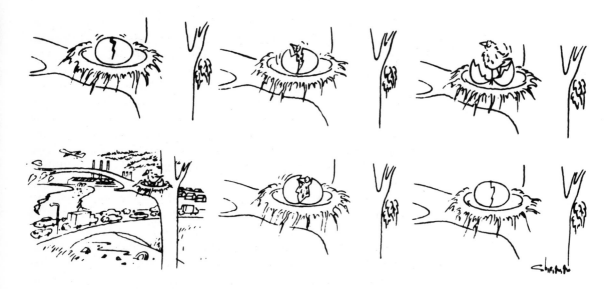

Courtesy, Vahan Shirvanian

evolution of norms of behavior. Norms are evolved in response to frequent discrete experiences of overload; they persist and become generalized modes of responding.

Overload on Cognitive Capacities: Anonymity

That we respond differently toward those whom we know and those who are strangers to us is a truism. An eager patron aggressively cuts in front of someone in a long movie line to save time only to confront a friend; he then behaves sheepishly. A man is involved in an automobile accident caused by another driver, emerges from his car shouting in rage, then moderates his behavior on discovering a friend driving the other car. The city dweller, when walking through the midtown streets, is in a state of continual anonymity vis-à-vis the other pedestrians.

Anonymity is part of a continuous spectrum ranging from total anonymity to full acquaintance, and it may well be that measurement of the precise degrees of anonymity in cities and towns would help to explain important distinctions between the quality of life in each. Conditions of full acquaintance, for example, offer security and familiarity, but they may also be stifling, because the individual is caught in a web of established relationships. Conditions of complete anonymity, by contrast, provide freedom from routinized social ties, but they may also create feelings of alienation and detachment.

CONCLUSION

I have tried to indicate some organizing theory that starts with the basic facts of city life: large numbers, density, and heterogeneity.

These are external to the individual. He experiences these factors as overloads at the level of roles, norms, cognitive functions, and facilities. These overloads lead to adaptive mechanisms which create the distinctive tone and behaviors of city life. These notions, of course, need to be examined by objective comparative studies of cities and towns. ■

NOTE

1. Wirth's ideas have come under heavy criticism by contemporary city planners, who point out that the city is broken down into neighborhoods, which fulfill many of the functions of small towns. See, for example, H. J. Gans, *People and Plans: Essays on Urban Problems and Solutions* (Basic Books, New York, 1968); J. Jacobs, *The Death and Life of Great American Cities* (Random House, New York, 1961); G. D. Suttles, *The Social Order of the Slum* (Univ. of Chicago Press, Chicago, 1968).

Donald Appleyard and Mark Lintell
The Environmental Quality of City Streets: The Residents' Viewpoint*

Because of its understatement this elegant paper might not be fully appreciated. It is a landmark study, an unequivocal demonstration of the impact of the physical environment on human behavior and human experience. At one level it points out that too much traffic bugs people, leading them to stay off the streets, or to leave the neighborhood if they can. Perhaps this is something already known, already obvious. On the other hand, traffic may be such an everyday, pervasive phenomenon that it tends to be taken for granted, ignored as far as issues of cost are concerned. But the paper makes it clear that traffic is indeed a source of stress, and a serious one at that. In addition, traffic undermines some of the very coping mechanisms that would otherwise be available for dealing with environment problems.

Unavoidably, this paper also raises the matter of the automobile and the costs it extracts. An interesting discussion of the automobile as the most destructive single factor as far as urban life and urban structure is concerned can be found in Barbara Ward's *The Home of Man* (1976).

*Reprinted by permission of the *Journal of the American Institute of Planners*, Vol. 38, No. 2, March 1972. Pages 84–101. The tabular presentations of the results have been deleted here.

■   Field interviews and observations were carried out on three similar San Francisco streets with differing traffic levels to determine how traffic conditions affected the livability and quality of the street environment. All aspects of perceived livability — absence of noise, stress, and pollution; levels of social interaction, territorial extent, and environmental awareness; and safety — were found to correlate inversely with traffic intensity. Traffic increases were also accompanied by the departure of families with children from these streets. Responses were nevertheless muted for a number of probable reasons, including environmental self-selection, adaptation, and lack of a target for resentment. The study is presently being replicated on a larger scale. Meanwhile, interim policies and standards are proposed.

Protests and research about the environmental and social impact of transportation systems have paid most attention to the problems created by new freeways through urban areas. But while these are the more dramatic instances of traffic impacts, the rapid growth of vehicular traffic has swamped residential streets in cities across the United States and in other countries. Traffic on city streets may affect as many, if not more, people than traffic on freeways. In San Francisco, approximately 60 percent of the city's major streets (those with a daily traffic volume of over 10,000 vehicles) are lined with residences.[1]

Studies of urban streets (such as the current TOPICS program of the Federal Highway Administration) have concentrated almost exclusively on increasing their traffic capacity, through devices such as street widening, signalization, and one-way streets, with no parallel accounting of the environmental and social costs of these alternatives. Wilfred Owen (1969) recently directed attention to the role that city streets play in the environmental quality of cities as "the main corridors and front parlors" of the city, but even he did not point out that people also have to live along city streets. To our knowledge, the only empirical studies of life on city streets, apart from some studies of traffic noise and a Michigan study of the economic and environmental effects of one-way streets (Michigan, 1969), have been those carried out in Britain since the Buchanan Report (Her Majesty's Stationary Office, 1963 and Chu, 1971).[2]

The investigation reported here is a small-scale attempt to identify the environmental concerns of those who live on city streets in San Francisco. It is a pilot study using observation and open response interview techniques, and does not pretend to statistical significance. The results, however, are suggestive. The project grew out of the San Francisco City Planning Department's concern over increasing traffic on the city's streets and the side effects of street widenings and other proposed changes in the street system. It was one of a series of studies of environmental conditions made in San Francisco during 1969 and 1970 (San Francisco City Planning Department, 1969–70).

FIGURE 1

Heavy street

STUDY STREETS   Of the street blocks selected for a general study of street living three streets are reported upon here to serve as a model of the research approach and because they contrast the effects of traffic on similar types of streets. The street blocks chosen were adjacent north-south residential streets in the northern part of the city (figures 1, 2, 3).

TRAFFIC   The major environmental differences between the streets were their traffic levels. The first street, which we shall call HEAVY STREET, was a one-way street with synchronized stop lights and a peak hour traffic volume (at the evening rush hour) of 900 vehicles per hour (average 15,750 vehicles over twenty-four hours). The second street, MODERATE STREET, was a two-way street with a peak traffic flow of 550 vehicles per hour (average 8,700 vehicles over twenty-four hours); the third street, LIGHT STREET, had a volume of only 200 vehicles at peak hour (average 2,000 vehicles over twenty-four hours).[3]

Speeds on all streets could rise to forty-five miles an hour or more, but only on HEAVY STREET was the speed controlled by the synchronized lights. Traffic volumes had increased on HEAVY and MODERATE STREETS ten years earlier when they were connected to a freeway at their southern terminal. Through traffic was dominant on MODERATE and HEAVY STREETS, and traffic composition included more trucks and buses on HEAVY STREET than on the others.

FIGURE 2

Medium street

POPULATION

The three study blocks were part of a residual Italian neighborhood that also included other white residents and a small but growing Oriental minority. By social class, education, and income the streets were relatively homogeneous. Contrasts, however, occurred in age, family composition, ownership, and length of residence.

LIGHT STREET was predominantly a family street with many children. Grownup children were even returning to bring up their own children there. One-half of the people interviewed were homeowners, and the average length of residence was 16.3 years. HEAVY STREET, at the other extreme, had almost no children on its block. It was inhabited mostly by single persons of all ages from twenty years upward, with many old people, especially single elderly women. The average length of residence on HEAVY STREET was 8.0 years, and people were nearly all renters. Rents were also somewhat higher on HEAVY STREET, averaging $140 a month among our respondents, whereas those on LIGHT STREET averaged $103. MODERATE STREET stood in between. Average length of residence here was 9.2 years and the average rent was $120 (table 1).

ENVIRONMENT

The three streets were typical San Francisco streets, with terrace houses or apartments built up to the building-line, very few front yards and very few gaps between the houses. The architectural style ranged

FIGURE 3

Light street

from Victorian to modern. The buildings were finished in either wood, stucco, or brick and were of white or light colors. They were pleasant-looking blocks. The streets were each fairly level, with a slight gradient to the south. They were close to various shopping and community facilities.

STUDY DESIGN   Two sources of information were used in the study. Detailed interviews lasting about an hour were held with twelve residents on each block, composed of three equal age categories, the young (under twenty-five), the middle-aged (twenty-five to fifty-five), and the elderly (over fifty-five). This was not a very large sample but since they represented about 30 percent of the households on each block, their attitudes were probably representative of those on the three blocks. Second, systematic observations and, where possible, objective measurements of pedestrian and traffic activity on the streets were carried out.

The study design stemmed from earlier papers by Appleyard and others (Appleyard and Lynch, 1967; Appleyard and Okamoto, 1968) which proposed environmental criteria to be used in transportation system design. The criteria identified in the earlier studies were hypothetical in nature and for this investigation were slightly modified to cover the probable concerns of those living on urban streets. Five major criteria categories were employed to describe the character

TABLE 1   Street Profiles

Street Characteristics:	Heavy Street	Moderate Street	Light Street
Peak hour traffic flow (vehicles/hour)	900	550	200
Average daily traffic flow (vehicles)	15,750	8,700	2,000
Traffic flow direction	one-way	two-way	two-way
Vehicle speed range (mph)	30-50	10-45	10-35
Noise levels (precentage of time above 65 decibels at the sidewalk)	45%	25%	5%
Accidents (per annum over a 4 block length)	17	12	...
Land uses	Residential (apartment blocks, apartments)	Residential (apartment blocks, apartments, single family homes), corner store	Residential (apartments, single family homes), corner store, small business
Street width (feet)	69	69	69
Pavement width (feet)	52	41	39
Sidewalk width (feet)	8.5	14	15
Average building height (no. of storeys)	3.5	3.0	2.5

Interview Sample:	Heavy Street	Moderate Street	Light Street
Mean household size (no. of people)	1.5	2.6	2.7
Percentage renters	92%	67%	50%
Mean household income ($1,000's)	6.6	8.1	10.0
Mean income/member of household	4.4	3.1	3.7
Mean number of school years completed	14	13	15
Mean length of residence (years)	8.0	9.2	16.3
Mean rents ($ per month)	140.00	120.00	103.00

Source: Traffic statistics and accident counts were obtained from the San Francisco Department of Public Works, Traffic Engineering Section. All other information came from interviews, summer 1969.

and day-to-day use of the street and the concerns and satisfactions of the residents. The interview was introduced as a survey of what the resident thought of his street, inviting suggestions for its improvement. The residents were not told that we were primarily interested in the effects of traffic.

The criteria categories were:

1   Traffic hazard: concerns for safety in the street associated with traffic activity.

2   Stress, noise, and pollution: dissatisfaction with noise, vibration, fumes, dust, and feelings of anxiety concerning traffic.

3   Social interaction: the degree to which residents had friends and acquaintances on the block, and the degree to which the street was a community.

4   Privacy and home territory: the residents' responses to intrusion from outside their homes, and the extent of their sensed personal territory or turf.

5   Environmental awareness: the degree to which the respondents were aware of their physical surroundings and were concerned for the external appearance of the buildings and the street.

Each question in the interview was related to one of the above categories, though some answers had relevance to more than one. The answers were independently rated on a five-point scale as "environmental quality" ratings by the interviewer and another member of the study team according to a general description of each criterion. Disparate judgments were discussed and a consensus rating was eventually recorded. No attempt was made to weight the responses in terms of their overall importance to the residents, although this report emphasizes the main points of concern for the residents as expressed in the interviews. To make these findings more understandable, we have graphed the responses in cartoon form.

So far, a public report on the study has met with considerable response in San Francisco. The general concerns of the study, and many of the individual conclusions, have been featured in the local press and on television. Furthermore, the officially adopted San Francisco "Urban Design Plan" (San Francisco, City Planning Department, 1971) incorporates many of the recommendations for limiting through traffic on residential streets and creating "protected residential areas."

TRAFFIC HAZARD   Accident counts were equally high on HEAVY and MODERATE STREETS (means of seventeen and twelve accidents per year over a four-block length).

The danger of traffic was of concern to inhabitants on all three streets, but especially so on HEAVY STREET (ratings 3.7, 3.8). These findings are not surprising, since the need for "safe intersections" was the most repeated concern in a concurrent citywide survey of city residents (Kaplan et al., 1969).

HEAVY STREET is a one-way street with synchronized stoplights which enable bunches of vehicles, already with momentum from traveling downhill, to travel through at speeds of up to fifty miles an hour. The fast speeds were frequently mentioned in the responses. The very heavy traffic volumes on HEAVY STREET made it unsafe for children, and even for people washing their cars. For residents trying to maneuver out of their garages, a one-way street had advantages over a two-way street, since the driver only has to look one way, but getting a car into a garage can be more difficult since the driver either has to swing across the traffic flow or pull to one side and wait for a lull. Excessive speed was the cause of most of the perceived traffic safety problems, especially on HEAVY STREET. Residents, seeing a large number of cars speeding down the hill, would wait for someone to make a false move or would listen for the screeching of brakes. Several residents wanted the speed limit on HEAVY STREET reduced.

LIGHT STREET, with only a small amount of through traffic, had problems of a different nature. It tended to attract the occasional hotrodder who was, in some instances, a greater menace than the steady stream of traffic on HEAVY STREET. He appeared without warning, often jumping the stop signs at intersections, and was extremely dangerous for children playing in the street. Another problem on LIGHT STREET was the temptation to park where it was immediately convenient. Delivery trucks often parked on the corner when making deliveries to the grocery and blocked the view down the cross street for motorists approaching the intersection.

Residents of MODERATE STREET perceived less safety problems arising from traffic than did the residents of HEAVY STREET. However, they were concerned about traffic dangers. As one respondent put it, "There have been some accidents and I am taking precautions."

Apart from the direct effects of traffic on the feelings of safety, there were some indirect effects. The continuous presence of strangers on HEAVY STREET, even though they were in automobiles, evinced some feelings of fear. One young housewife had frequently been "hassled" from passing cars, and some of the older ladies on HEAVY STREET were "afraid to stop and chat."

As can be seen from the aggregated ratings, there was a consistent trend through all age groups to consider LIGHT STREET as being safe, MODERATE STREET as being neither safe nor unsafe, and HEAVY STREET as being unsafe. (See figure 4).

STRESS, NOISE, AND POLLUTION

Measurements of noise levels were made on all three streets. The sound levels were determined through the use of Sound Survey Meters, utilized at four periods during a weekday; early morning (6:30 to 8:30 A.M.), late morning (11:00 A.M. to 12:30 P.M.), late afternoon (5:00 to 6:00 P.M.), and early evening (7:00 to 8:00 P.M.). In each measurement period, fifty consecutive measurements were made at fifteen second intervals at corner and midblock locations on each street. To translate these measurements into a useful measure of average conditions, the percentages of time that the noise exceeded certain A-weighted decibel levels [dB(A)] were calculated. From these we computed a traffic noise index,[4] a recognized measure of noise problems, which can be used to predict probable dissatisfaction due to noise. (Griffiths and Langdon, 1968).

On HEAVY STREET, noise levels were above sixty-five decibels 45 percent of the time and did not fall below fifty-five decibels more than 10 percent of the time except in the early morning. These noise levels were so high that the traffic noise index read right off the scale. The two-minute sample sound level recording in figure 5 illustrates the uneven character of noise due to the waves of cars that flowed down the street, and to the occasional noisy vehicle which exceeded seventy decibels.

On MODERATE STREET, sound levels were above sixty-five decibels 25 percent of the time. By the traffic noise index, the noise level (6.5) would be rated as "definitely unsatisfactory." On LIGHT STREET, the quietest of the three, sound levels rose above sixty-five decibels only 5 percent of the time, meaning that one-half of the residents would consider the noise level "unsatisfactory" and one-half "satisfactory."

The two-minute sample sound level recordings on MODERATE STREET show that the noise levels tended to be more variable than on HEAVY STREET but in the same range, whereas the sound level chart on LIGHT STREET shows an ambient noise level much lower than the other two streets.

After the danger of traffic itself, traffic noise, vibrations, fumes, soot, and trash were considered to be the most stressful aspects of the environment on these three streets. On HEAVY STREET, the noise was so severe that one elderly couple was forced to try to catch up on sleep in the daytime. Many, especially the older people, were unable to be objective about the other characteristics of their street because these stresses totally colored their perceptions of their environment. Adjectives such as "unbearable," or "too much" or "vulnerable" were typical of the responses.

As with traffic hazard, the large mass of vehicles was not always the major problem. It was often the lone individual or the unusual vehicle that disturbed the situation. This was certainly true of HEAVY STREET, where the large majority of cars were reasonably quiet and passed by at a smooth even flow. The real offenders were sports cars, buses, and trucks. The steady drone of traffic was certainly bad, but the random deep-throated roar of a bus or large truck, with the accompanying shudder that rattled every window, unnerved the most hardened resident, especially when it continued day and night. The screeching of brakes at the intersections added to the distress.

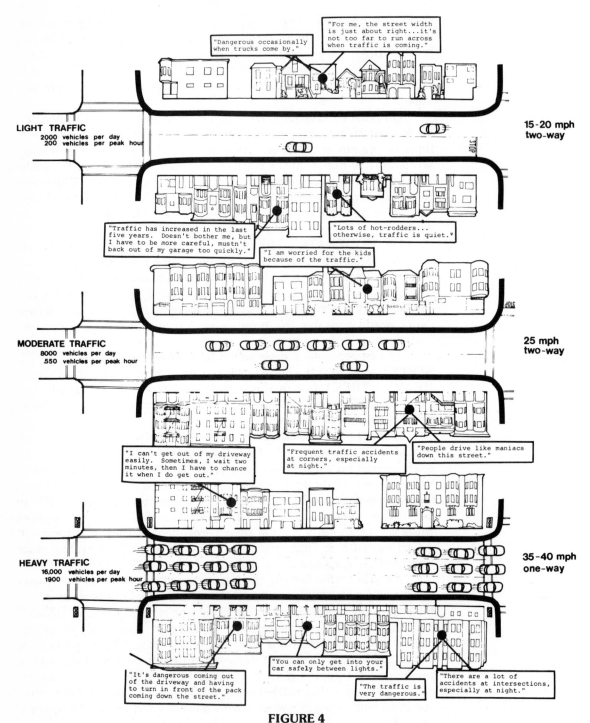

FIGURE 4

Traffic Hazard

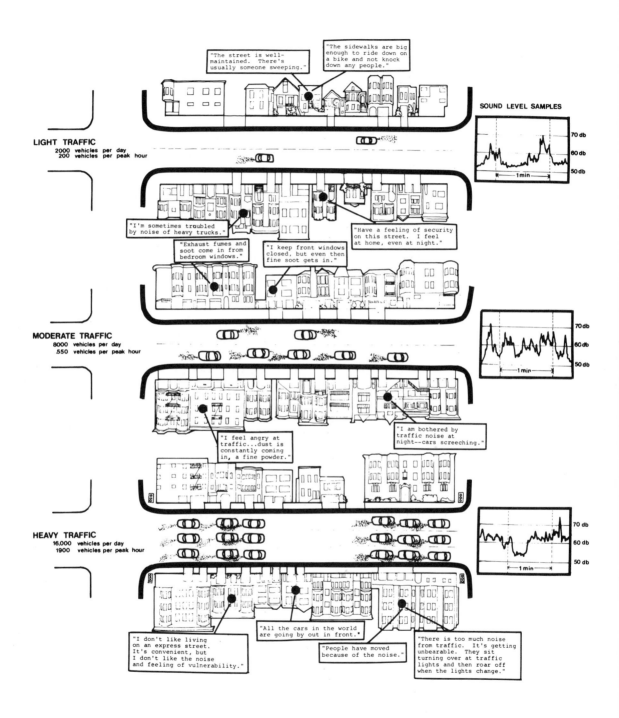

FIGURE 5

Noise, stress, and pollution

Residents on HEAVY STREET had petitioned for a sign prohibiting trucks and buses. The sign was installed, but it did not mention buses. It was small, the same color as the background, and was seldom seen. In any case, the law was not enforced, so truck drivers had learned to continue on their way with impunity. Noise problems were not so acute on MODERATE STREET, where people were more bothered by the fumes, dust, and soot which penetrated into their living rooms and bedrooms. LIGHT STREET had a few complaints of occasional noise.

Other Forms of Pollution

The condition and cleanliness of the buildings on the three streets was generally high. Maintenance and clean appearance were clearly important to all the inhabitants. HEAVY STREET was constantly on show to outsiders who were traveling through it, and the owners of the buildings were careful to maintain a high standard of cleanliness despite the "disgusting amount of litter." The *appearance* of a quality environment was therefore maintained — and paid for through higher rents — but because the street did not encourage people to be outgoing, tenants were reluctant to accept responsibility for the street itself. Therefore, they avoided picking up trash and were slow to defend the street against vandalism and abuse.

On MODERATE STREET, concerns for trash, dust, and soot, where specifically referred to, were more pronounced than on HEAVY STREET. This street was going through a difficult stage. Traffic and traffic problems were increasing, and there was no clear demarcation between public territory, which was the responsibility of the city, and local territory, which might have been the responsibility of the residents. People in parked cars had been observed dumping the contents of ash trays and beer cans into the gutter. Even so, it was still seen as a "good respectable place to live" and sidewalk maintenance by the local inhabitants helped to keep up the appearance of the street.

LIGHT STREET was very seldom seen by outsiders and so the issue of maintenance was a local matter. This street was also seen to be changing and residents had noticed signs of deterioration. As one resident put it, "The quality of [LIGHT STREET] is getting better in that people take great care of their properties, but worse in that there is more traffic and more cars on the street." Indeed, the responses showed that many inhabitants took an interest in looking after the cleanliness of the street, and some had planted their own trees.

The only other inconvenience mentioned was the crowded parking conditions. Many suburban commuters and users of the nearby shopping center were parking on all three streets and taking up parking spaces of the residents. In response to questions concerning the adequacy of street lighting, garbage collection, and street cleaning, respondents considered the three streets to be without serious problems.

In reaction to all these issues, each age group found HEAVY STREET more severe, and the old- and middle-aged groups found MODERATE STREET worse than LIGHT STREET. The only exceptions were residents under twenty-five, who were more critical of LIGHT STREET. People on LIGHT STREET tended in many cases to be more aware and more critical of their street, while those on MODERATE STREET were more apathetic.

SOCIAL INTERACTION

Residents were asked a series of questions about the friendliness of the street, the numbers of friends and acquaintances they possessed, and the places where people met. Each respondent was shown a photograph of the buildings on the street and asked to point out where any friends, relatives, or acquaintances lived.

On LIGHT STREET, inhabitants were found to have three times as many friends and twice as many acquaintances on the street itself (9.3 friends and acquaintances per person) as those on HEAVY STREET (4 per person). The diagrammatic network of social contacts in figure 6 shows clearly that contact *across* the street was much less frequent on HEAVY STREET than on LIGHT STREET. The friendliness on LIGHT STREET was no doubt related to the small amount of traffic, but also to the larger number of children on the street and the longer length of residence of the inhabitants. The statements of the inhabitants corroborate this.

On HEAVY STREET, there was very little social interaction. With few if any friends (0.9 per respondent) the residents did not consider it a friendly street. Although it might be argued that this was primarily a consequence of the life style of those living on HEAVY STREET, the sense of loneliness came out very clearly, especially in the responses of the elderly. As for MODERATE STREET, residents felt that the old community was on the point of extinction. "It used to be friendly; what was outside has now withdrawn into the buildings. People are preoccupied with their own lives." Some of the families had been there a long time, but the number of longtime residents was diminishing. As other respondents put it, "It is half-way from here to there." "An in-between street with no real sense of community." There was still a core of original Italian residents lamenting that "There are no longer any friends around here." The average number of friends and acquaintances per respondent was only a little higher (total 5.4 per person) than on HEAVY STREET.

There were sharp differences between age groups. The middle-aged residents on the three streets possessed a similar number of friends, although those on LIGHT STREET had more acquaintances. This age group was probably more mobile and better equipped to make friends than the other groups. The young and old, on the other hand, who had many less social contacts on HEAVY STREET than on

LIGHT STREET, appeared to be more affected by the amount of traffic, especially in establishing casual acquaintanceship with neighbors in the street.

From the notations of street activities drawn by the subjects on the map of the streets (see figure 6), it can be seen that LIGHT STREET had the heaviest use, mostly by teenagers and children. MODERATE STREET had lighter use, more by adults than by children, and HEAVY STREET had little or no use, even by adults. The few reported activities on HEAVY STREET consisted of middle-aged and elderly people walking on the sidewalks but seldom stopping to pass the time of day with a neighbor or friend. Reports on MODERATE STREET indicated that the sidewalks were more heavily used by adults, especially be a group of old men who frequently gathered outside the corner store. Children and some teenagers played on the sidewalks, mostly on the eastern side of the street (probably because most of their homes were on the eastern side and they didn't like to cross the road except at the crossings). On LIGHT STREET, people used the sidewalks more than any other part of the street, but children and teenagers often played games in the middle of the street. Children also used the sidewalks extensively because of their gentle gradient and their width. Again, a corner store acted as a magnet for middle-aged and elderly people, and a tennis store across the road attracted a small group of young adults. Front porches and steps on LIGHT STREET, and to a certain extent on MODERATE STREET, were used for sitting, chatting with friends, and, by children, for play. The residents of HEAVY STREET regretted their lack of porches.

In conclusion, there was a marked difference in the way these three streets were seen and used, especially by the young and elderly. On the one hand, LIGHT STREET was a lively close-knit community whose residents made full use of their street. The street had been divided into different use zones by the residents. Front steps were used for sitting and chatting, sidewalks by children for playing, and by adults for standing and passing the time of day (especially round the corner store), and the roadway by children and teenagers for playing more active games like football. However, the street was seen as a whole and no part was out of bounds. This full use of the street was paralleled by an acute awareness of the physical environment (as will be described in the section on environmental awareness).

HEAVY STREET, on the other hand, had little or no sidewalk activity and was used solely as a corridor between the sanctuary of individual homes and the outside world. Residents kept very much to themselves so that there was no feeling of community at all, and they failed to notice and remember the detailed physical environment around them. MODERATE STREET again seemed to fall somewhere

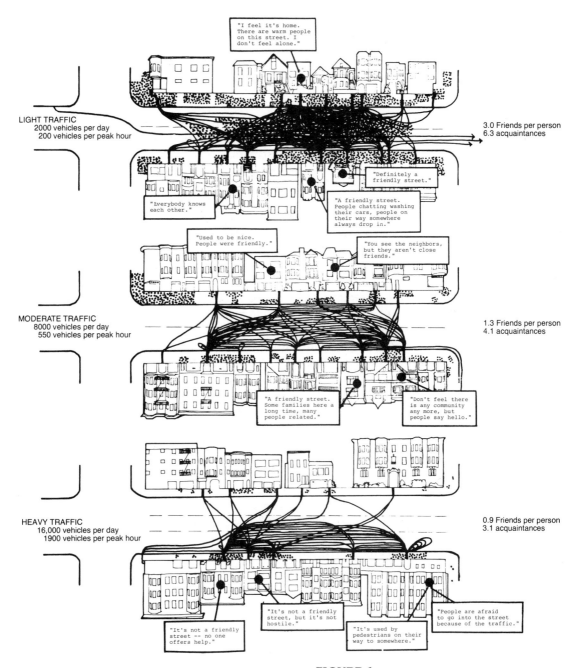

FIGURE 6

Social interaction. Lines show where people said they had friends or acquaintances. Dots show where people are said to gather.

between the two extremes. It was still quite an active social street, although there was no strong feeling of community. Most activity was confined to the sidewalks, where a finely sensed boundary separated pedestrians from traffic. . . .

PRIVACY AND HOME TERRITORY

A number of questions were asked to gauge whether inhabitants felt they had sufficient privacy, and whether they had any feelings of stewardship over their streets.

In their responses, residents of LIGHT and MODERATE STREETS, especially middle-aged residents, evidenced great pride in their homes and streets. On HEAVY STREET there was little peace and seclusion, even within the home, and residents struggled to retain some feeling of personal identity in their surroundings.

Perception of individual privacy was high throughout this area, perhaps because of the feeling of "privacy and seclusion that exists in any middle class area," as one respondent put it. Inevitably, in a tight-knit community like the one that existed on LIGHT STREET, life on the street tended to intrude more into a person's home than it would on a less friendly street, but the residents had achieved a good balance wherein they maintained their own household privacy and yet contributed to the sense of community. As one woman enthusiastically put it, "Only happiness enters in." Children and young people often preferred the lack of seclusion because they liked to be part of things. On LIGHT STREET a satisfactory balance had been achieved between a feeling of privacy and contact with the outside world. Even on HEAVY STREET residents occasionally enjoyed the street activity. ("I feel it's alive, busy, and invigorating.") However, for the majority, the constant noise and vibration were a persistent intrusion into the home and ruined any feeling of peace and solitude.

Figure 7 shows the residents' conceptions of personal territory. Even though legally a householder's responsibilities extend to the maintenance of the sidewalk immediately outside his building, residents on MODERATE and LIGHT STREETS considered part or all of the street as their territory. However, the HEAVY STREET resident's sense of personal territory did not extend into the street, and for some, mostly renters in the large apartment blocks, it was confined to their own apartment and no further. This pattern of territorial space corresponds to the pattern of social use of each street. The contrast between the territorial restrictions of those living on HEAVY STREET and the territorial expansiveness of those on LIGHT STREET is one of the more salient findings of the study. The residents on LIGHT STREET are quite similar in this respect to those West End Italians in Boston who considered the boundaries between house and street space to be quite permeable (Fried and Gleicher, 1961). In sum, HEAVY STREET

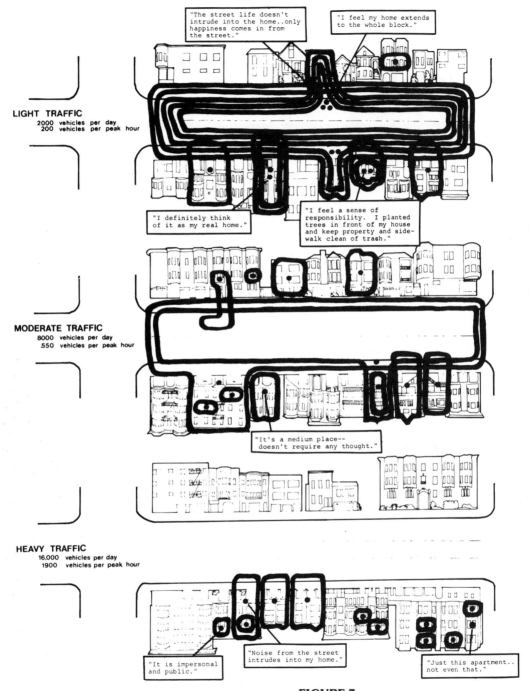

FIGURE 7

Home territory. Lines show areas people indicated as their "home territory."

was seen as considerably less private than the other two streets, especially for those most confined to the street, the young and the old.

ENVIRONMENTAL AWARENESS

Street dwellers were each asked to recall all important features of their street, to judge whether their street was in any way different from surrounding streets, and to draw a map of their street.

The responses to the questions were much richer in content — and more critical in character — on LIGHT STREET than on the other two streets. This can be partly explained by the greater differentiation of front yards and smaller houses; but it clearly stemmed from an increased awareness of the street environment by the residents themselves.

Interest in the street as evidenced by the maps drawn varied by age group. LIGHT STREET had tremendous appeal for children, who recalled individual buildings, front yards, steps, particular parked cars, manhole covers, telegraph poles, and even the brickwork setting around the base of a tree. Many of these detailed elements were obviously encountered during their play on the street. On MODERATE STREET, where there was less street activity, the maps of children and young people were accordingly less rich.

Middle-aged people on the other hand seemed to have a more complete impression of their street. Their recollections included combinations of buildings, sidewalks, the roadway, and the traffic itself. For them, LIGHT STREET was seen as a collection of individual buildings with differences in front yards and porches. MODERATE STREET was much more straight-walled. Residents had accurate memories of driveways, pedestrian crossings, and road markings (possibly because it was seen as a traffic route with finely defined boundaries).

HEAVY STREET was seen overwhelmingly as a continuous traffic corridor, straight-sided without a break for cross streets, and packed with cars. The traffic itself was an easily identified characteristic of the busier street.

As for the responsiveness of the street environment to the needs of the street dwellers, LIGHT STREET once more showed up well. Two trees had been planted in the sidewalk, other plants were thriving in the occasional front yard, and flower boxes were prevalent. On HEAVY STREET, the sidewalks were too narrow to allow anything to grow except the very small bushes that flanked the doors of one or two apartment buildings.

STUDY CONCLUSIONS

1 The intensive traffic conditions on HEAVY STREET led to both stress and withdrawal. Those people who found the traffic conditions intolerable, especially those with children, had moved elsewhere, and the people who lived there at the time of the survey had either withdrawn from the street or had never become engaged in it. They only used it when they had to, they had few local friends and acquaintances, and they had become oblivious to the street as a living environment. If they could, they lived at the backs of their houses. For those who treated HEAVY STREET as a transient residence, this condition was tolerable. Those who had to treat it as a permanent residence because they were too old or too poor to leave suffered.

In contrast, those who lived on LIGHT STREET were very much engaged with their street. They saw it as their own territory. Their children played on the sidewalk and in the street. They had many friends and acquaintances (over twice as many on the average as those on HEAVY STREET), they noted many more features of the street when they were asked to make a drawing of it, and they were generally much more aware of their street. Despite all this, the rents on HEAVY STREET were higher. Perhaps the apartments on that street, because of their higher exposure and turnover, were more available to a transient population.

The living conditions of those who lived on MODERATE STREET lay somewhere in between the other two, but the residents' levels of satisfaction were lower than their middle position might suggest.

From our results we can state some hypotheses about the apparent effects of traffic on the environmental and social quality of these streets (figure 8). These hypotheses should be tested in later studies.

a Heavy traffic activity is associated with more apartment renters and less owner-occupants and families with children. The income levels of the residents are in a similar range.

b Heavy traffic is associated with much less social interaction and street activity. Conversely, a street with little traffic, and many families, promotes a rich social climate and a strong sense of community.

c Heavy traffic is associated with a withdrawal from the physical environment. Conversely, residents of the street with low traffic show an acute, critical, and appreciative awareness of and care for the physical environment.

2 There are some exceptions to the above conclusions. Many respondents on MODERATE STREET had chosen that street for its livable environment. MODERATE STREET, however, was changing from a quiet residential street into a major traffic corridor. Therefore, the residents there were often more dissatisfied than those on HEAVY STREET. Their original expectations for the environment were higher and their disappointment was therefore greater.

On LIGHT STREET some respondents perceived the occasional hot-rodder as worse than the traffic on HEAVY STREET for similar

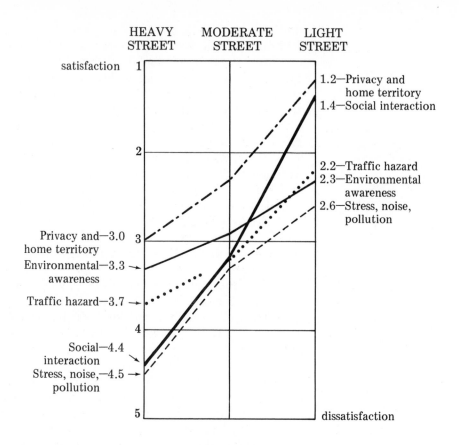

FIGURE 8

Environmental Quality
Note: *The following interview questions were chosen to represent the "environmental quality" criteria illustrated in this figure.*

*Traffic hazard: What is traffic like on this street, how would you describe it?
Does it bother you at all?*

*Stress, noise, and pollution: Is there anything that bothers you or causes you
nuisance on and around this street?*

Social interaction: Where do people congregate on the street, if at all?

*Privacy and home territory: Where do you feel that your "home" extends to: in
other words, what do you see as your personal territory or turf?*

*Environmental awareness: Do you find your street and the life that goes on
there interesting? Do you get bored by life on this street, do you find it
monotonous?*

reasons. When people expect traffic to be heavy, their behavior adapts to the situation and traffic is tolerated. When they expect it to be light, a hot-rodder is especially intrusive. In conclusion, people were dissatisfied with the streets with lighter traffic when their environmental expectations were not realized either through an environmental decline from a previously higher quality or from deviant traffic behavior.

3 The appearance of environmental quality was found to be quite different from the environmental quality as revealed by the comments of the residents. HEAVY STREET was well maintained and appeared to be of high quality to the outsider (for example, to the city urban design staff in earlier field surveys of the area). The residents were aware of its high status, yet the presence of heavy traffic lowered its quality below that of more modest-looking streets.

4 The pattern of interview responses suggested that the issues of safety, stress, condition, pollution, privacy, and territoriality, followed closely by neighborliness, were of primary concern to the inhabitants of all the streets. Issues such as sense of identity, environmental interest, appropriateness, and individual self-expression were not considered important if the other issues were seen as problems.

5 The general trend was toward increased traffic on each of the three streets, with the prospect that the environment of each street would decline further.

DISCUSSION OF CONCLUSIONS

Objective observations of environmental quality, through traffic flow and noise counts, showed that environmental conditions on HEAVY STREET were particularly severe. Though complaints were numerous, however, they were not so strong as one might reasonably expect. There had been very little public complaint or protest by any group. Why was this?

One major reason appears to be that the erosion of environmental quality had been subtle and slow, taking place over a period of ten years or more. During this time the workings of *environmental selection* and *environmental adaptation* had been allowed to operate. These are important phenomena to consider in measurements of response to environmental quality.

1 The workings of *environmental selection* may be stated as follows: an environment tends to be selected by those groups who find it most amenable, and to be rejected by those who find it least amenable. Hence, when traffic increased on HEAVY STREET, families with children moved away, and single people and couples whose local environmental needs were less but who valued accessibility tended to replace them. The principle does not work perfectly, however. Those who are unable to select their preferred environment through lack of financial, informational, or psychological resources become "locked in" to certain environments, and are therefore likely to suffer the most from changing environmental quality. On HEAVY STREET the older people, finding it too costly and too much effort to move, experienced severe discomforts, and the families who had to remain on MODERATE STREET experienced the loss of friends. Similar predicaments face lower income populations.

People may select a less than ideal environment for reasons other than lack of resources. Many make a *compromise,* sacrificing amenity for the benefits of, for example, an easily available apartment or accessibility to other parts of the city. The apartments on LIGHT STREET had less turnover so they were seldom on the market. Others make *errors of judgment.* Visually HEAVY STREET is a well-maintained high quality street. Therefore, an apartment hunter might be deceived. Another kind of error is the *inability to predict future deterioration.* When many of the present inhabitants moved in to HEAVY and MODERATE STREETS conditions were good. Since then they have worsened.

2 By *environmental adaptation* we mean that those who remain in one environment for a length of time will become adapted (or resigned) to it whether or not it is or has been pleasant, especially if they see no future change in sight. Evidence for this phenomenon can be found in this study, especially in some of the more indifferent responses on HEAVY STREET. Such evidence can also be found in the research literature in this field (Sonnenfeld, 1966; Wohlwill, 1966). Those with low expectations or aspirations may be content with any environment.

Besides private adaptation, there appears to be a more publicly oriented defensive kind of adaptation. Most people are stuck with the choices they have made. When an interviewer arrives at the door and asks if there is anything they dislike about their environment, people may not wish to complain even though they may privately acknowledge that their environment is unsatisfactory. They may refuse to complain in order to keep up their social image and the sales value of their property, or through reluctance to admit that they have limited resources or have made an error of judgment.

Individual and family adjustments to a deteriorating environment were further muted because there was no clear public target for resentment, only the individual automobiles and trucks. No particular agency was threatening the environment or initiating changes. This worked both ways; residents' hopes were not raised that anything would be done about their problem, but neither were their frustrations focused sufficiently for them to band together in protest.

Despite the private nature of the adjustments and the slowness of the deterioration, a majority of the inhabitants were still well aware of their plight, as their comments tell.

One final and more positive finding of this study was what it told us of life on a "good" residential street, namely LIGHT STREET. Since we cannot hope to improve urban environments without some positive goals to work toward, LIGHT STREET performs a critical function.

ENVIRONMENTAL PROPOSALS

1 Policy usually has to be made without the benefit of adequate research, and this study is no exception. The strongest proposal resulting from the study was the designation in the adopted Urban Design Plan (San Francisco City Planning Department, 1971) of "protected residential areas" throughout San Francisco (figure 9). These are areas which will be protected from through traffic by policies such as the improvement of public transit; the concentration of traffic on the city's main arteries by increasing their capacity through separated grades, selective widening, parking controls, and so on; and the blocking of through traffic by devices such as rough pavement surfaces, "necking down" entrances, bending alignments, landscaping, lighting and sidewalk treatment, all of which would slow traffic down to a residential pace (and incidentally provide more street recreation space).

2 On streets where traffic flows and speeds could not be reduced, ways of ameliorating conditions were proposed. These included sidewalk protection by means of trees, low walls, hedges, and so on; the provision of alternative play spaces to divert children's activities away from the dangerous street; the protection of residences from glaring street lights, car lamps, and the view of passing vehicles through the planting of trees; the clear definition of parking spaces; and the encouragement of inhabitants to exercise some interest in their own front yards and sidewalks through provisions and subsidies for private planting, benches, and the like.

ENVIRONMENTAL STANDARDS

Environmental conditions on residential streets will not be improved unless means of determining acceptable and unacceptable conditions are available. Present planning thought is running against the formulation of standards, as planners have come to realize the variability of population needs and situations and the difficulties of scaling environmental conditions. Yet without standards or specific guidelines, planning controls will remain amorphous and ineffectual. There is an urgent need at the very least to articulate unacceptable environmental conditions for particular groups. These conditions might be couched in the form of environmental performance standards.

The field of noise abatement, which has progressed quite far in trying to set environmental standards related to behavioral response, has encountered some difficulties. Simple decibel ratings (for example, forty-five decibels as a tolerable level inside residences) have to be modified by the "duration, frequency, substantive content of the sound and individual differences" (U.S. Department of Housing and Urban

FIGURE 9

Development, 1969). The Traffic Noise Index (Griffiths and Langdon, 1968), developed in Britain, attempts to take a few of these factors into account. The Buchanan Report (Her Majesty's Stationary Office, 1964) identified "vulnerable" populations. But what about standards which will allow people to feel comfortable on sidewalks, or to cross the street, which encourage neighborliness, allow privacy and an ample sense of personal territory, or which promote care and interest for the physical environment of the street? These are even more difficult measures to scale. The effort to measure pedestrian crossing delay times as an indicator of residential quality, which was used in the *Kensington Environmental Management Study* (Greater London Council, 1966), was an interesting attempt in this direction. The work reported here is not substantial enough to develop such indicators, but this is the direction of our research.[5]

RESEARCH IMPLICATIONS

The results of this study are suggestive but obviously unrepresentative. Our a priori groupings of issues under criteria headings proved a useful way of organizing the interviews and observations. More studies examining larger numbers of street conditions and types of population are clearly required. Such studies should use more structured questionnaires that would allow subjects to make their own ratings and selections from adjective and other check lists (Craik, 1968; Shaffer, 1967). They should also use a more comprehensive set of observable environmental indicators (such as pedestrian delay times, counts of street activity, closed windows, drawn blinds, parked cars, trash, flower boxes, and other signs of personal care) and a finer assessment of traffic variables (including flows at different times of day and night, speed levels, traffic composition, traffic control signals, and so on).

Multivariate analyses of interviews, traffic composition, and environmental indicators would then allow us to understand the ways in which factors tend to cluster, and to develop predictive models from regression analyses of response to various conditions. With such models, indices (similar to the traffic noise index) could be established to predict subjective responses to environmental phenomena such as levels of privacy, neighborliness, street identity, stress, and sense of safety for residential streets. The ability to predict the flow and speed of traffic from environmental conditions, given the desire lines operating in an area, would allow the control of speeds and flows at environmentally acceptable levels. We know that signs alone do not control speed. What are the effects of rough surfaces, trees, "necking down" streets, and street bends on these traffic variables?

Finally, more extensive surveys to assess the numbers of people who actually live under the deteriorated environmental conditions of streets with heavy traffic are needed. In a recent book, J. M. Thompson (1970) calculated that one million people in London would be living within 200 yards of the proposed motorway system. The implication was that one million people would be suffering from a deteriorated environment. Such accounts of conditions in a U.S. metropolitan area might have a significant impact on the allocation of investment to environmental improvements. ■

NOTES

We are indebted to the San Francisco Department of City Planning (Director, Allan Jacobs) for supporting this project through an urban planning grant from the U.S. Department of Housing and Urban Development, under the provisions of Sec. 701 of the Housing Act of 1954, as part of their Urban Design Study, and for permission to use the drawings. Elizabeth Seltzer assisted with the drawings and Hugo Blasdell carried out the noise surveys and analysis.

1. Estimated from Report no. 4, San Francisco City Planning Department (1969–70).

2. For example, the Barnsbury Environmental Study (Great Britain, Ministry of Housing and Local Government, 1968) and the Pimlico Precinct Study (City of Westminster, 1968).

3. All traffic statistics were obtained from the San Francisco Department of Public Works, Traffic Engineering Section.

4. The traffic noise index is a function of the 50 percent noise level and the difference between the 10 percent and 90 percent levels.

$$TNI = L_{50} + 4(L_{10} - L_{90}) - 30$$

This figure has been shown to correlate with expressions of annoyance. Our budget did not allow us to take the customary hourly samplings over the full twenty-four-hour period.

5. A study of a larger residential area in Oakland, California, is now under way supported by small grants from the U.S. Department of Transportation and the National Institute of Mental Health.

David C. Glass and Jerome E. Singer
Some Effects of Uncontrollable and Unpredictable Noise*

In a series of important studies, Glass and Singer have shown that even uncontrollable and unpredictable noise does not interfere with task performance. Subsequently, however, there is a substantial deficit. Apparently people who have gone through this experience suffer a loss of their capacity to fend off distraction. (In terms of the approach outlined in the attention and fascination paper [chapter 4], contending with noise would require inhibition to hold down the potentially disruptive cognitive activity the noise would otherwise produce. The distraction-suppression mechanism could only provide the needed inhibition for so long — eventually it would become fatigued. The mechanism would then be less effective in blocking potential distraction until it had the opportunity to recover.)

The Glass and Singer research has shown another interesting relationship with regard to what influences stress. Some participants in their research were in a "controllable" noise condition. While they too performed tasks amid loud noise, they had a button they could press if they had all they could take and wished to terminate the noise. The stress for these people turned out to be considerably less, even though very few pressed the button. Apparently having the button available answers the otherwise troublesome question "What if I can't take it and want to get out of here?" In other words, the uncertainty of the situation is reduced in an important respect and the proportion of the individual's limited capacity devoted to the problem is thus reduced. There is, one might say, less lookahead required. Less voluntary attention, in turn, is required to carry out some additional task. The same argument, of course, applies to any circumstance of helplessness. Seligman's *Helplessness* (1975) provides many fascinating examples of comparable magnitude. A problem that appears to have a solution is necessarily more compact and manageable than one that appears insoluble. (Many of the issues presented here are further examined in the context of control as a coping strategy in the paper by Sherrod and Cohen in the next chapter.)

*Excerpted from "Experimental Studies of Uncontrollable and Unpredictable Noise." *Representative Research in Social Psychology.* 1973, 4, pages 165, 176, 179–180. Reprinted by permission of the University of North Carolina.

■   This paper examines the influence of noise and related environmental stressors on a variety of behavioral and psychophysiological processes. Though seemingly obvious, these effects are difficult to demonstrate. For, in time, people simply learn to ignore noise. However, the proposition that man is adaptable has an important corollary; namely, man pays a price for adaptation that is observable in behavior (cf. Selye, 1956; Dubos, 1965; Wohlwill, 1970).

This paper describes a series of laboratory and field experiments concerning behavioral effects and aftereffects of exposure to unpredictable and uncontrollable high-intensity noise. Both tolerance for frustration and quality of task performance in human subjects were impaired following stimulation by unpredictable noise. Even though physiological adaptation occurred to an equivalent degree under predictable and unpredictable noise, adverse aftereffects were greater following exposure to the latter type of noise. Subsequent experimentation suggested that unpredictable noise has these effects because the individual believes he cannot determine onset and/or offset of the stressor. The perception of control over unpredictable noise was manipulated in our research, with the result that frustration tolerance and post-noise task performance were appreciably improved. We concluded that psychological factors, not simply physical parameters of noise, are the determinants of adverse aftereffects of noise exposure. Further evidence was adduced suggesting possible mechanisms for the ameliorative effects of perceived control. However, the major thrust of our results is that while man adapts to unpredictable stressors, behavioral residues occur that are inimical to his subsequent functioning. There is a "psychic cost" for exposure to unpredictable and uncontrollable aversive events in spite of the fact that individuals seem able to adapt to a variety of stressors.

PERCEIVED CONTROL AND HELPLESSNESS

But what specific stress-reducing mechanisms are aroused by the manipulation of perceived control? In answering this question, we reasoned that inescapable and unpredictable noise confronts the individual with a situation in which he is powerless to anticipate and affect the occurrence of the stressor. We may thus describe his psychological state under these circumstances as one of helplessness (Janis, 1962; Lazarus, 1966; Seligman, Maier, and Solomon, 1971). Such a mechanism provides a nice explanation of the relationship between unpredictable and uncontrollable noise and deleterious aftereffects. If the impact of a repeatedly presented aversive event is greatest where feelings of helplessness are maximal, it follows that adverse aftereffects will also be maximal. Our working thesis is that exposure to uncontrollable noise produces feelings of helplessness which interfere with later functioning. Perceived Control subjects label their situation as one in which they have control over their environment and, therefore, are not helpless. By contrast, No Perceived Control subjects do not develop these expectations.

Subsequent performance after noise stimulation is affected in a way that is consistent with prior experience, when control was or was not perceived as available. Presumably, the helpless group not only experiences the aversiveness of unpredictable noise per se, but also the "anxiety" connected with their felt inability to do anything about it. Perceived Control subjects, on the other hand, are exposed only to the stress of the noise itself; they do not experience additional anxiety produced by feelings of helplessness. We tentatively conclude, therefore, that unpredictable noise produces more adverse aftereffects than predictable noise because unpredictability leads to a sense of helplessness in individuals who are unable to control and/or predict the onset and offset of noise.

OTHER COGNITIVE FACTORS

The importance of unpredictability and lack of perceived control in determining noise aftereffects led us to examine the influence of additional cognitive factors on reactivity to noise. In one study, we found that "relative deprivation," under certain circumstances, can modify the consequences of a noise stressor. When people are relatively deprived with respect to noise — they believe others are undergoing less noise — they show greater aftereffect deficits. Conversely, when they believe that others are undergoing more severe noise, people show less deficits from noise. It is both fascinating and ironic to note that stress aftereffects decline when others are perceived to be in more stressful circumstances, but increase when others are ostensibly experiencing less stress.

In another experiment, a choice of whether or not to experience noise also affected the severity of aftereffects. When people are required to work under noisy conditions, they suffer deficits of a given level of severity; if, however, people work under noisy circumstances as a consequence of a free and informed decision on their part, the aftereffects of noise are appreciably reduced.

The necessity of the noise, whether it occurred as an unavoidable concomitant of an important activity or whether it was gratuitous, was also investigated in our research. It is presently equivocal whether this factor influences noise-produced aftereffect performance; however, there are indications that an adequate test has not yet been made of the effects of necessity.

PROLONGED EXPOSURE TO NOISE

All of the studies described up to this point were carried out in the laboratory. The aftereffects of prolonged noise exposure cannot easily be investigated within this type of research context. However, this limitation was at least partly overcome in a recent field study conducted in New York City (Cohen, Glass, and Singer, 1972). Expressway traffic was the principal source of intermittent noise. It was assumed that subjects, fifty-four elementary school boys and girls, had minimal control over this noise source. Initial decibel measurements in a highrise housing development built over an expressway permitted the use of floor level as an index of noise intensity in the children's apartments.

The study showed inverse relationships between the children's verbal skills and the noisiness of their apartments. Children living on lower floors of the thirty-two-story buildings showed great impairment of auditory discrimination and reading ability than those living in higher-floor apartments, where noise level was in fact lower. Auditory discrimination mediated the association between noise and reading deficits, and length of residence in the building increased the magnitude of the correlation between noise and auditory discrimination. Additional analyses ruled out explanations of the result in terms of social class variables and physiological damage. It would appear that there are indeed negative aftereffects of prolonged exposure to noise.

OTHER STRESSORS

Noise has been the principal stressor used in our research. However, we do not believe our findings or interpretations hinge upon characteristics unique to noise. The pattern of results obtained with noise — almost universal adaptation followed by adverse aftereffects as a function of cognitive factors surrounding noise exposure — has been obtained with other stressors. For example, data from two laboratory experiments using electric shock demonstrated that adverse behavioral consequences were reduced if this form of stimulation was both predictable and controllable (Glass and Singer, 1972; Glass, Singer, Leonard, Krantz, Cohen, and Cummings, 1972). Still other research from our laboratories has indicated that these two variables (predictability and controllability) produce similar effects with social stressors (e.g., bureaucratic frustration and arbitrary discrimination), thereby permitting the general conclusion that deleterious aftereffects of stress are probably a function of the unpredictability of aversive stimulation and the belief that one has little control over stimulus occurrence. ■

8 Coping Strategies: Choice and Control

A relatively straightforward strategy for making the informational environment manageable would seem to involve choosing preferred settings. In other words, even though the environment as a whole may be difficult to comprehend and may provide little grounds for involvement, one might feel at home in some smaller portion of it. Ideally one would come to know this portion of the environment thoroughly and thus find it comprehendible and supportive.

Choice is a frequently employed, and in principle highly effective, strategy. Preferred environments are sought, and often discovered, at many environmental scales. Choice of residential location (even when others might consider it nothing but a slum), the decision to migrate to another city, state, or nation, even the selection of a vacation site are examples of this strategy. At a still smaller scale is the choice involved in a shopping trip or other foray into the environment to utilize available resources. But this means of coping — so pleasing from the perspective of Rational Man — is flawed by the very deficiencies that undermine the Rational Man position: ignorance of alternatives, and the difficulty of obtaining the needed information within a reasonable period of time and with a reasonable amount of effort. Further, the best available environment, especially given limited resources, may not be satisfactory. And environments change, particularly as many people make the same choice. Thus, even when one has the capability to opt for it, choice is rarely effective for long without some element of control. And the less adequate the settings available for choice are, the more critical becomes the factor of control.

And environments change, particularly as many people make the same choice.
Reprinted by permission of Newspaper Enterprise Association.

Choice and control thus often act as complementary strategies. Together they create a pattern of coping that has striking similarities to the behavior called "territorial" in other animals. The concept of territory has a special place within an informational framework. It refers not only to a spatial configuration that individuals or groups regard as theirs, but also to other arrangements less clearly spatial and less clearly circumscribed. In fact, one might say that territory refers to any circumstance where "knowing" and "caring" are jointly important. Territory would thus exist any time there is a well-developed cognitive map with associated positive feelings. It is a domain within which recognition and prediction can be carried out with confidence and ease. It is valued for the way it facilitates making sense, for the opportunity for choice and control it provides, as well as for the many positive associations it comes to have.

Control is sometimes of the environment, sometimes of the behavior of others, and sometimes of the flow of information. It can be exerted at an individual and at a group level; it also can be strongly influenced through design and planning. There is an inherent conflict in the application of the control strategy at different levels of organization. At an individual level, control is closely related to privacy. It suggests a domain where one can do what one pleases, away from the influence of others. Given privacy, one need not worry about the uncertainty created by the behavior of others. Likewise, one need not be concerned with the obligation to be predictable in their presence.

But one needs others for many reasons. Certainly in human prehistory, hunting for big game and securing food required group effort and a concern for each other. Humans manifest their social dependencies in many other respects as well. Safety, information, child care, and the like often involve other people. Such needs, however, can not be fulfilled by "random" others. The necessity of keeping the group's behavior somewhat predictable has led to arrangements of mutually dependent people often called "community." Such arrangements sacrifice a certain amount of privacy and freedom in exchange for assistance of various kinds. Together a group can defend a territory against threats that individuals would be unable to handle. Together a group can exert social control over behavior deemed undesirable, as well as determine who is to have access to "their" environment. (For an interesting analysis of the relationships between territory and community, see Edney, 1976.)

The very existence of community depends on the control of information. The larger the group, the more difficult this becomes. With too many people to become familiar with, the very basis of group control is undermined. One cannot check the intentions of intruders if one cannot recognize who does and who does not belong.

Different settings would seem to make varying demands on the trade-off between privacy and community. In order to maintain a reasonable level of privacy while at the same time facilitating the sharing of certain information, various compromise arrangements have evolved. Yancey, for example, speaks of "semipublic space." Interaction between people in such spaces is limited. One can recognize others and share information without having to divulge more than one wishes. In a similar vein, Feldt distinguishes between a friend and a neighbor:

> So, the neighborhood we are speaking of is rather loose, is not necessarily friendly, but does contain people who are tolerant of each other and know each other's faces. They may not know each other's names. That does not seem to be a vital ingredient. Such a neighborhood is not characterized

by coffee klatching and all those invasions of privacy which characterize some suburban developments and some urban developments. It is, rather, a loose but functional grouping of people who can assist each other on occasion, who have established criteria of social etiquette which would allow them to resolve boundary disputes and troubles among children, and other territorial problems in a reasonably civilized fashion. It is a vague grouping. We don't mean anything tight, warm, friendly, or intimate. We mean a true urban kind of a phenomenon which is not caught up in any kind of romanticized rural ideals. It appears important to us to consider this for a number of reasons revolving around what we think a decent kind of a neighborhood — a well-designed form of neighborhood — could do in an urban society. We think there are a number of potential benefits to society which can be generated from such urban neighborhood.[1]

As Feldt suggests, physical design can play an important role in influencing the control of information and the development of community. Physical design can help establish clear boundaries of a given portion of the environment. Since behavior must be observed if it is to be subject to social control, visual access is another important factor. The number of families using a given stairwell, for instance, is a design decision with direct implications for the control of information. It should be noted here that the high-rise apartment building, which systematically violates many of these principles, has proved acutely unsatisfactory as a living environment not only in the United States, but throughout western Europe as well. For a thoughtful discussion of these parallel disasters, and their role in the "search for community," see Ward's (1976) *The Home of Man*.

One further informational element in the operation of a community must be examined. It is not only essential to recognize who belongs in one's community. It is also necessary to predict their likely behavior. Such prediction is easiest if the others are perceived as similar to oneself. The greater the number of people involved, the harder it will be to know each individually, and the more important the factor of perceived similarity is likely to be. Perhaps for this reason, the most reliable settings for strong communities are places such as small towns, rural "hollows," and ethnic enclaves in urban areas.[2]

Choice and control are not only available to the wealthy and the powerful. In fact, as many of the selections make abundantly clear, a sense of community can be achieved along the entire spectrum of economic means. The cognitive structures of even the poorest can translate to what Coles calls "an awful lot of plenty." On the other hand, as the Pruitt-Igoe fiasco poignantly illustrates, denial of opportunities for cognitive clarity is more likely to befall the poor. In this light, Newman's insights into ways to permit control as a coping strategy, even under extreme residential pressures, is of major significance. His solutions illustrate ways to introduce spacing mechanisms (Kummer), to help demarcate territory (Jackson's hedgerows on a different scale), and to understand the conditions that can make a tenement a home.

NOTES

1. Excerpt from "Some Dimensions of Residential Development" presented by Allan G. Feldt at "Planning the Future Residential Environment." Tenth Annual Conference of the Organization of Cornell Planners. 1967. Quoted by permission.

2. Greenbie's paper included in the previous chapter makes a number of pertinent points concerning the role of social territory and the interdependence of familiarity and community.

Robert Sommer
Territory*

This selection highlights not only the pervasiveness of territorial feelings and territorial behavior, but also its positive psychological contribution. Some people either deny or are embarrassed by territoriality in humans. Yet, as Sommer points out, territory can be related to feelings about home, to the need for roots, and to various manifestations of human cooperation. The need to create order in the environment and the comfort of familiarity are involved here, as well as the rather explicit operation of choice and control.

■   The recent volume *African Genesis* by Ardrey (1961) has reawakened interest in the possibility of territorial behavior among humans. More than forty years earlier Craig had written, "With animals as with men, the cause of a quarrel is very commonly a coveted territory," while Heape (1931) considered the recognition of territorial rights as "one of the most significant attributes of civilization." The ecologist Burt believed that the display of property ownership "reaches its highest development in human species," and later used the obviousness of human territoriality as an argument that territories also

*From R. Sommer "Man's proximate environment." *Journal of Social Issues,* 1966, 22, 60–63. Reprinted by permission of the Society for the Psychological Study of Social Issues and the author.

exist among animals, while Ardrey and more recent writers argue in the reverse direction — since territorial behavior is an agreed fact among animals, it likely exists among humans. Jung (1965) believes that territories are psychologically important and cannot be replaced by anything else; he maintains, "Each person should possess his own piece of land, then the old instincts would flourish again," and speaks of territoriality as part of the human need for roots. Scott (1965) considers territoriality (along with the development of dominance and subordination) as devices for the control of aggression and observes that in our society the violation of territory is considered a serious crime. Hediger notes the resemblance between hedge rows, fences, and flower beds in human communities and territorial boundaries in the animal kingdom. Numerous studies of neighborhoods have emphasized the special emotional attachment people feel for their homes and the space immediately around it. Fried and Gleicher write:

> [This space] is territorial in a more profound sense: that individuals feel different spatial regions belong to or do not belong to them and, correspondingly, feel that they belong to . . . specific spatial regions or do not belong (1961, p. 313).

Territorial ownership in human society is a complex affair. To simplify it by equating territory with legally owned property would exclude territoriality from the tens of millions of city dwellers who occupy but do not own property. The owner may be a board or corporation rather than an individual. The concept of a shared territory however, such as that found in baboon society, is not applicable, since corporation stockholders tend to be an aggregation, most of whom have never seen the property in question, rather than a face-to-face group.

The most logical extension of the *territory* concept is to define it as an area controlled by an individual, family, or other face-to-face collectivity. The emphasis in this definition is on physical possession, actual or potential, as well as defense. Since human communication is based largely on symbols, territorial defense relies more on symbols such as name plates, fences, and personal possessions than on physical combat or aggressive displays. However, teenage gangs have territories, and bloody battles have resulted when one gang invaded another's "turf." Salesmen have, and actively defend, their individual territories. One criterion of territoriality is, to use Ardrey's phrase, the home team always wins. According to Lorenz (1938) an animal on its own territory will fight with more vigor, while other writers (e.g., Tinbergen, 1939) maintain that a male on its own territory is almost undefeatable against other males of the species. This is not necessarily identical with the "home cage effect" observed in captive animals. It has been reported for fish, lizards, mice, chickens, and monkeys that the "owner" of a cage, even if it has been there only a short period, is usually victorious over a newcomer. Nice (1941) notes that the home cage effect is found among children "at play and in school." There has been little systematic study of the "home cage effect" among children, although there is ample anecdotal material describing the difference between children's behavior at home and away from home.

In view of the increasing mobility of families, and the lessened use of the home for family functions, further investigation of the effects of familiar environments on children's behaviors seems warranted. Defining home range statistically on the basis of a particular criterion of occupancy and defining territory on the basis of instinctive displays, boundary markings, and biological functions permits research into human and animal biotopes without unwarranted assumptions as to instinctive bases for such preferences. This lends some semantic clarity to studies of favored seating places in restaurants, meeting rooms, and classrooms as well as habitual pathways and routes.

The habitat or locale to which an organism is attracted through some combination of learning, imprinting, and instinct is called a biotope. The exact mechanisms for biotope preference have not yet been specified. Humans become attached to particular areas. During the Second World War Russians from the Great Steppes were confined in mountain resorts in Switzerland and were most unhappy. Pygmies from the covered primeval forest feel exposed and helpless in a clearing, while European settlers feel trapped and depressed under the constant jungle cover. The Saskatchewan prairie dweller begins to feel uncomfortable in the scrub brush zone and distinctly unhappy when he reaches the forests of the pre-Cambrian shield.

It would appear that the process of biotope formations is similar to imprinting. Miller (1962) placed a series of screens in the middle of a half-mile long section of one creek. He took trout from above this half-mile section and trout from below this section and transferred them to the enclosure. The next fifty days were spent in bringing trout into the enclosure which meant that some fish were there only a few days, some a few weeks, and some almost the entire fifty days by the time the experiment ended. Then the screens were removed so that trout would return home if they wished. Three weeks later it was found that fish that had been detained thirty days or more were still in the enclosure area but those who had been in the enclosure for less than thirty days had all moved away. He also found that none of the fish made a mistake. All trout from downstream went downstream and all those from upstream went upstream. As far as arriving in their previous location is concerned, the trout were not quite so clever. The upstream fish did reasonably well; more than half were found in their original pools and the rest simply hadn't gone far enough. The fish whose homes lay downstream made a much poorer showing, some of them appearing just to be drifting, but at least they went in the proper direction. There have been few systematic attempts to experimentally manipulate environmental exposure and make biotope preference a dependent variable under natural conditions. Again the hazards of generalizing from studies of wild animals under natural conditions to man or even domestic animals are evident.

Staehelin (1954) and Esser et al. (1965) have both been interested in the extent to which actions of mental patients resemble the behavior of captive animals. This is not a new thesis since many critics of institutional life have equated cells, wards, and cages. A woman confined in prison wrote, "I began to pace up and down the cell as man in confinement and caged animals have done since the world began" (Henry, 1952). Ellenberger (1960) has made a thought-provoking comparison of the mental hospital and the zoo. Staehelin believes that territorial drive and dominance order among mental patients are instinctive biological phenomena brought to the surface because of the psychosis. Esser has made a detailed analysis of the ecology of a research ward of mental patients. Using continuous observation of where each patient is at any moment, he considers a place where a patient spends 75 percent of his time as that patient's territory. Esser is currently relating territorial occupancy to the dominance hierarchy among the patients. Unfortunately the present practice of studying such behavior in mental institutions tends to associate territorial drive with psychosis and leaves unanswered the role of incarceration per se in spatial behavior. ■

John B. Jackson
Fences and Hedges*

Fences and hedges are physical manifestations of territorial concerns. Jackson appreciated their positive function and regretted the cultural influences that seemed to be curtailing their use in the early fifties — an era known for its emphasis on cooperation and conformity. Whether or not individualism is making a comeback, the view from an airplane approaching an airport in many parts of the United States suggests that fences and hedges have not disappeared from the face of the land.

*From J. B. Jackson "Ghosts at the door." *Landscape,* 1951, 1 (1), pages 7–9. Reprinted by permission. Other portions of this article appear in chapters 6 and 9.

■   To hedge in, to fence in; the language seems to shift in meaning and emphasis almost while we use it. Until not long ago neither of those words meant to keep in. They meant to keep out. A fence was a de-fense against trespassers and wild animals. The hedge was a coveted symbol of independence and privacy. Coveted, because it was not every farmer who could have one around his land.

Like the lawn and the tree, the hedge is something inherited from an ancient agricultural system and an ancient way of life. The farming of the Middle Ages is usually called the open-field system. Briefly, it was based on community ownership (or community control) of all the land — ownership by a noble amounted to the same thing — with fields apportioned to the individual under certain strict conditions. Among them were rules as to when the land was to lie fallow, what day it was to be plowed, and when the village cattle were to be allowed to graze on it. Much modified by social and economical revolutions, the open-field system still prevails over much of northern Europe. Fences and hedges, as indications of property lines, naturally had no place in such a scheme.

In the course of generations a more individualistic order came into being, and when for several good reasons it was no longer desirable to have the cattle roaming at will over the countryside the first thing to appear, the first change in the landscape, was the hedge. With that hedge to protect his land against intruders of every kind, the individual peasant or farmer began for the first time to come into his own, and to feel identified with a particular piece of land. He did not necessarily own it; more often than not he was a tenant. But at least he could operate it as he saw fit, and he could keep out strangers.

Each field and each farm was defined by this impenetrable barrier. It served to provide firewood, now that the forests were gone, shelter for the livestock, and a nesting place for small game. Most important of all, the hedge or fence served as a visible sign that the land was owned by one particular man and not by a group or community. In America we are so accustomed to the fence that we cannot realize how eloquent a symbol it is in other parts of the world. The Communist governments of Europe do realize it, and when they collectivize the farms they first of all destroy the hedgerows — even when the fields are not to be altered in size.

The free men who first colonized North America were careful to bring the hedge and fence with them, not only to exclude the animals of the forest, but as indications of the farmers' independent status. Hedges and fences used to be much more common in the United States than they are now. One traveller in Revolutionary New England enumerated five different kinds — ranging from stone walls to rows of upended tree stumps. In Pennsylvania at the same period fields were often bordered with privet. As new farms were settled in the Midwest every field as a matter of course had its stone wall or hedge of privet or hawthorn, or permanent wooden fence. And along these walls and fences a small wilderness of brush and vine and trees soon grew, so that every field had its border of shade and movement, and its own wildlife refuge. The practice, however inspired, did much to make the older parts of the nation varied and beautiful, and we have come to identify fences and hedges with the American rural landscape at its most charming.

As a matter of fact the hedge and wooden fence started to go out of style a good hundred years ago. Mechanized farming, which started then, found the old fields much too small. A threshing machine pulled by several teams of horses had trouble negotiating a ten-acre field, and much good land was wasted in the corners. So the solution was to throw two or more fields together. Then agricultural experts warned the farmers that the hedge and fence rows, in addition to occupying too much land, harbored noxious animals and birds and insects. When a farm was being frequently reorganized, first for one commercial crop then another, depending on the market, permanent fences were a nuisance. Finally Mr. Glidden invented barbed wire, and at that the last hedgerows began to fall in earnest.

There were thus good practical reasons for ridding the farm of the fences. But there was another reason too: a change in taste. The more sophisticated landscape architects in the mid-century strongly advised homeowners to do away with every fence if possible. A book on suburban gardening, published in 1870, flatly stated: "that kind of fence is best which is least seen, and best seen through." Hedges were viewed with no greater favor. "The practice of hedging one's ground so that the passer-by cannot enjoy its beauty, is one of the barbarisms of old gardening, as absurd and unchristian in our day as the walled courts and barred windows of a Spanish cloister."

Pronouncements of this sort had their effect. Describing the early resistance to the anti-fence crusade during the last century, a writer on agricultural matters explained it thus:

> Persons had come to feel that a fence is as much a part of any place as a walk or a wall is. It had come to be associated with the idea of home. The removal of stock was not sufficient reason for the removal of the fence. At best such a reason was only negative. The positive reason came in the development of what is really the art-idea in the outward character of the home . . . with the feeling that the breadth of setting for the house can be increased by extending the lawn to the actual highway.

Utilitarian considerations led the farmer to suppress the fences between his fields; esthetic considerations led the town and city dwellers to increase the size of their lawns. Neither consideration had

Courtesy of Etoile Holzaepfel

any influence on those who had homesteaded the land, lived on it and who therefore clung to the traditional concept of the privacy and individualism of the home. The front yard, however, had already become old-fashioned and countrified fifty years ago; the hedge and picket fence, now thought of as merely quaint, were judged to be in the worst taste. Today, in spite of their antiquarian appeal, they are held in such disrepute that the modern architect and the modern landscapist have no use for either of them; and they are not allowed in any housing development financed by FHA.

Why? Because they disturb the uniformity of a street vista; because they introduce a dangerous note of individualistic nonconformity. Because in brief they still have something of their old meaning as symbols of self-sufficiency and independence. No qualities in twentieth-century America are more suspect than these.   ■

Clayton C. Denman
Small Towns Are the Future of America*

> The sense of community is an enormously valuable asset in any human settlement. Denman discusses the advantages of small-scale settlements in aiding comprehension and hence control and hence community. His comparison of small towns and urban patterns constitutes a valuable commentary on how far-reaching the effects of scale can be. (The Denmans have been codirectors of the Small Towns Institute and edit its monthly news journal, *Small Town,* which continues to be an invaluable resource for those who doubt that economies of scale apply to the quality of life.)

■   Recent concern with environmental pollution has pointed up crucial reasons for considering small towns an important part of America's future. Those of us who live in rural communities or small cities are relatively free of the problems that come from crowding and overpopulation. We already enjoy life styles much like those which city planners and urban engineers hope to create in the future, perhaps in "new towns" now being proposed as a way of relieving urban population pressures. Small town residents whose communities are in a state of economic decline have a simple problem to alleviate compared to the urban dweller's task of finding solutions to crime, smog, and overpopulation.

Most of the 72 million people now living outside of urban complexes enjoy low crime rates, minimum air and water pollution, and less social decay than the majority of Americans living in big cities. We all know that small towns do have serious problems of poverty and unemployment, but these conditions are largely a result of economic pressures and technological change and not the result of overpopulation and lack of rational planning for change. It took protests and even riots before the cities started planning; and then it was through the efforts of private organizations such as Urban America Inc., the National Alliance of Businessmen, and the Urban Coalition that the fight for remedial programs was undertaken as soon as it was.

*Reprinted with permission from C. C. Denman "Small towns are the future of America." *Congressional Record* — Extension of Remarks. March 16, 1970, E2025, E2026.

To the urban planner of today, small towns seem to be existing in a state of apathy regarding their own problems, a view which has led some analysts to suggest that if small towns are to be revitalized, the leadership will have to come from the cities. If these people are right, it will not be because small town leaders are not capable of their own planning, but because they have not organized to make themselves heard in the policy-making centers of this country. In fact, as a group, small town leaders were active in pointing out and solving problems long before urban planners became aware that cities were headed for disaster. The main reason for this is that small towns have retained a sense of community — the essential social ingredient that enables men to work together. This is something that cities have lost, something that they try to re-create in "new towns"; it is also a reason that they are hungrily eyeing our small towns as places to direct their unwanted populations.

Most of us will welcome new members to our communities, especially if they are accompanied by small industries fleeing overcrowding and decay. But I also suggest that we retain control over the process of redevelopment; that we must have funds for retraining and housing, for expanded public and private utilities, for preventing a repetition of pollution that fouls the cities, and for the necessary expansion of educational facilities.

PRESENT CONDITIONS

Many small towns suffer from conditions of economic and population decline — factors which contribute significantly to poverty and decay of housing and business properties, to poor educational and medical facilities, and to continued unemployment. I might point out, however, that these conditions are a result of economic and technological changes created in, and for, urban needs. Agricultural technology is a product of urban industry and city-oriented marketing and pricing systems. High paying jobs — the "better opportunities" of educational advertising — are creations of urban demands for goods and services. These and similar conditions have all combined to stimulate outmigrations from small towns and farms, leaving behind people more dedicated to rural life styles than to visions of vast wealth. Some of us are, like myself, returnees to small towns, some are struggling small town businessmen, some are retired, and many are living in poverty conditions as a result of technological unemployment. All of us, however, have chosen to maintain small town life styles; to save these values we must now adapt them to modern conditions in our society. This should be our job, not that of those who have already failed in the cities.

I would agree that housing in many small towns is in need of replacement, and that incomes, educational facilities, medical services, and public utilities need improvement. But we should not allow city-oriented planners to equate rural or small community life styles with poverty, nor to demean the average small town dweller for not having aspirations for a $450 a month "middle income" apartment.

Small towns are good places to live precisely because they lack the pressures of cities; because they offer a more personal and serene atmosphere; and, I repeat, have a sense of community and cooperation. All citizens benefit from closer association with the elderly, with young people, with farmers, businessmen, with teachers and with one another. These are some of the factors that have attracted the attention of city planners, as well as the more often expressed reason of open space.

In the past, government policy and attention was focused almost exclusively upon the cities. Urban conditions had resulted in riots, rising crime rates, unemployment for minorities; school, housing, employment, and transportation crises; as well as an increasing breakdown of traditional family living and rebellion among youth. No one seemed to realize that a major cause of these urban problems was increasing population pressures on an urban system that was designed for much smaller numbers and for the life styles and technology of the past century.

Increasing urban population was not only a result of a rising birth rate after World War II, but of a massive out-migration of young people, farmers, and especially unskilled minorities from rural areas. Most of this migration was a direct result of change in technology, but a good proportion of it was in response to a false belief that a better life was to be attained in the cities. We now know that the city offered millions greater hardships than it did answers to dreams. It also left many small towns with decreasing populations; small businesses, schools and town governments with new problems; and a self-fulfilling prophecy that small town and rural America were on the decline.

MYTHS AND FACTS ABOUT THE SMALL TOWN

It wasn't too many years ago that small towns were looked upon as the backwaters of America, as places forever alien to the progressive and exciting life in the cities. Small towns have suffered from this mythological image fostered by negative thinking in such novels as Sinclair Lewis's *Main Street* and Edgar Lee Masters's *Spoon River Anthology,* two early twentieth-century literary works which presented small towns in a light of "conformity, stupidity, loneliness, and physical ugliness," in addition to ideas about an entrenched elite who ran the community from behind the scenes.

These beliefs were perpetuated by many professional community studies that did not go far enough to understand the diversity that exists in every community. Even Robert Lynd's classic study of

Middletown in the 1920s and 1930s failed to point out that the economic conditions producing poverty and a confirming class structure had their roots, not in the small town community, but in the reflection of urban conditions on agriculture and small town industry. It was not until the publication of Aaron Wildavsky's book *Leadership in a Small Town* (1964) that even the objective social scientist began to understand the diversity of interest and process in small communities.

In the past ten years, however, these out-of-date myths have rapidly dissolved. Academic researchers are now aware of diversity in small communities, and the average American has come to look with favor upon life in our small towns. A recent study conducted for the National Rural Electric Cooperative Association showed that most Americans think positively toward people in rural communities: 81 percent think small community dwellers are warm and friendly toward others, and only 7 percent think city people are this way. Nearly 65 percent think small town merchants are more honest, and only 6 percent think city merchants are more honest. When asked about emotional differences, 83 percent thought that city people were more tense and pressured in their daily lives, and only 5 percent thought small town and rural residents were more tense and pressured. About 22 percent of the people surveyed thought there were no differences between urban and rural community life.

In fact, this study indicated that 82 percent of all Americans would prefer to live in rural communities if they could find suitable employment opportunities. Other studies show similar impressive results. A 1968 Gallup Poll indicated that only 18 percent of Americans would choose to live in cities, while 56 percent would prefer to settle in rural areas if the same economic opportunities were available to them as in the city. A study of University of Nebraska graduates in agriculture now working outside of that state showed that 60 percent desire to return to Nebraska if suitable employment were available.

The prospective of these studies strongly indicates that small towns have been the victims of the urban myth and of an unchallenged faith that technological developments were a contribution to human progress to which men had to adapt their lives even if it meant a change from satisfying social environments to the chaos of the modern city. The desire to return to rural America indicates a shift in our values from a blind faith in technology to a realization that men must live together in a social context before technological progress can become meaningful. As further proof of the truth of this premise, we are on the threshold of a concern with environmental conditions that will eventually include the quality of living as an integral part of economic profits; and economists are increasingly feeding social costs into cost-benefit formulas.

Our communities will share in this new awakening to the values of quality in both our natural and social environments. We are finally realizing that small towns, even though they have serious problems, represent the basic life styles to which a majority of Americans aspire. Furthermore, most small towns and rural communities exist in more ecologically balanced environments than do cities. If we can come to better understand these conditions and improve upon them where they are headed in undesirable directions, we can proudly present our towns as models which cities have only begun to think about. A small town free from environmental threats and still maintaining its sense of social community will have a prime asset for attracting both population and industry that can no longer tolerate the deterioration of urban services, as well as declining physical and social environments. The people who left the small towns and farms of America in the last two decades are fast discovering that the economic and psychological pressures that led them to the city in a search for greater abundance are melting away before the realities of social and environmental crises.

THE SENSE OF COMMUNITY

We have already touched upon some of the important factors which make small towns good places to live today and to build upon for a more livable future.

One of these important features is what I have called the "sense of community," a critical need for human beings living together and sharing even minimum values, goals, and expectations of the good life. In recent years, planners and policy makers alike have discovered that most small towns have never lost this desirable feature, even though many of them have sharply declined in population and economic viability. Heavily funded federal urban programs have many times tried to recreate in cities the social values associated with community. Most of them have failed to reach this goal. In fact, many city programs such as urban renewal, freeways, and public housing, have probably destroyed more functional communities than they have aided. The result is social disorganization seen by all of us as higher crime rates, decreasing respect for schools and other public institutions, juvenile delinquency, drug abuse, and a host of other socially disruptive conditions. We now depend upon formal law enforcement agencies rather than community pressures to hold these disruptions in check.

Without the sense of community, there is no sense of social commitment to fellow citizens, no longer a relationship between people that can be channeled into making our social and physical environments better places in which to live. Small towns still have a sense of community — even if we are sometimes apathetic, we at least know who is active and who is not — and we can use this sense of community as a foundation upon which to build for a more prosperous future.

With an absence of social community in the cities, many human values are no longer transmitted by the group in which growing up takes place. Children tend to learn only the more artificial values of mass media, the schools, and of course the inexperience of their peers. What is missing is not so much abstract truth, but knowledge of how human groups live together; for no longer do the young, the mature, and the aged share common interests.

Thus in cities there is no longer a blend of the enthusiasm and energy of the young, the experience of their parents, the wisdom of grandparents, all focused into a goal of realizing an "American Dream." Urban life has dispersed this interlinking between these basic assets that all societies — whether primitive hunters or modern industrial —have shared.

It has been these attributes of community and the interlinking of the contributions of young and old that has built our country. Where these tend to break down, as we have seen them do in the cities, our society gives way to despair, lawlessness, splintered family life, and other forms of disorganization. Small towns have not been entirely immune from this process, and they are vulnerable during periods of decline as well as growth. Therefore it will take a measure of vigilance to avoid the loss of community values as towns begin a regrowth in the seventies. Most of us are already familiar with the loss of community solidarity when small towns decline. Signs of a dying community are numerous, and they affect everyone. The loss of economic and social institutions can be the initial cause of decline, eventually leading local residents to become dependent on services from other communities. Young people leave for opportunities elsewhere, small businesses fail to interest fresh management, industries stand still or close, maintenance of stores and houses ceases. Absence of young families means no prosperous schools, so necessary to attract new industry. Even those who choose to retire in such a place find retail facilities closing and community services faltering.

Although the loss of the sense of community in the city leads to crime, poverty, and disorder, it is not as critical for survival there as it is in a small town. A city's services are far more diverse than those of small towns, and citizens can always trade in another district. Public services are always available from a distant governmental source; but in the small town there is little appeal to outside agencies. The solution to the problem is to retain the sense of community, and to maintain the ability and motivation to work together for mutual benefit. ■

Robert Coles
The Edge of the Hollow*

Here a strong sense of choice — despite considerable pressure — and a thorough knowledge of place combine to create a sense of rooted-ness, a sense of belonging that provides identity and support. Coles's sensitive observation and reporting effectively communicate the tightly linked themes of territory and community. (Billy, mentioned in the first paragraph, appears in the Coles selection in chapter 9.)

■   On the map, Martin County in Kentucky looks a short distance from Logan County, West Virginia, but ordinary maps tell little about high, nearly impassable hills and mountains and valleys that run north to south rather than east to west — and therefore form a barrier to someone moving across rather than up and down the Appalachians. Marie Lewis is a seven-year-old girl who lives in Martin County, not too far from Inez, the county seat. Marie's father is a good deal better off than Billy's. Mr. Lewis has a full-time job as a bus driver and school custodian. He works for the county's school board, and considers him-self extremely fortunate to do so. Jobs are short in the county, and a steady job makes one secure beyond the comprehension of outsiders. George Lewis's salary by national standards is low, very low; in 1969 it placed him among the nation's poor, among those who make less than $3,000 a year. Yet, as he himself put it: "When others see no money at all, and you get your check every week, you're doing pretty good."

Little Marie, as her father calls her, is almost a picture-book child. She has blond, curly hair, blue eyes, a round face with pink cheeks, and a sturdy body, though even at seven she carries herself like a lady — perhaps like the gentle, sensitive schoolteacher she wants to be. She has such a teacher in school, and she idolizes her. And if little Marie someday does become a teacher, she will substantially consoli-date her father's rise in position or class or whatever. Her parents realize this. They see few if any jobs available for their sons, but Marie might indeed be able to become a teacher, unless she marries young, has children, and forgets the whole idea.

"I'd like to have a family — a girl and a boy; but not a lot of chil-dren like they do up the hollow. We live right at the foot of the hollow,

*From Robert Coles "A domain of sorts." *Harper's* (November, 1971). Pages 118–122. Copyright 1971 by *Harper's Magazine*. Reprinted by permission (Other portions of this article appear in chapters 4 and 9.)

and we see them all going by, and there are too many of them. My daddy says one thing they could do, since they don't have the money, is stop having all those children, one after another. Susan — she sits beside me in school — must have ten brothers and sisters, I think. She says we live in a real fancy house, and how come my daddy gets to make all the money, and I told her he works hard and he's up before all of them in that hollow."

Marie lives in a modest bungalow, but as she said, the house is luxurious compared to some of the cabins up the hollow, which rises and rises behind the Lewises' house. Still, the Lewis family is poor. They are not townspeople, but by their own description they are "people just lucky enough to get out of the hollow." They are *at* but not *in* the hollow. They enjoy electricity and a furnace and running water. They have a television set and a radio and a refrigerator and an electric stove. They don't have much money for furniture, nor do they drive a car. They will be paying off the house they have built for years and years and years, and it is all the property they have and hope to have.

Marie can be a little casual and even humorous as she talks about things up in the hollow, for all the sadness and misery to be found there. She can point out to her worried and pitying listener that schoolmates of hers, from homes as poor as any in America, nevertheless smile and laugh and jostle one another and get fresh and nasty and tease one another and have fights, "good fights," she calls them, sometimes serious and fierce ones, then make up and become helpful and kind and thoughtful — to everyone, which certainly includes her: "I'd like to marry someone from this county. We have the best people in the world here. The boys can do anything. They can climb every hill, I know they can. They can hunt and fish better than people who live in other places. I know from what my father says. If you go to the cities in Ohio and states like that, you don't know what the people are like. They talk different and they think different. A lot of them don't go to church, and they're mean to you, unless you're in their family; and they don't help you out the way we do here to everyone who comes by, so long as he means well."

Like a good social scientist (not to mention a person with common sense), Marie talks about the social distinctions she observes, from the grossly apparent ones to others that are decidedly subtle: "The history book the teacher reads to us says our country is made up of different kinds of people, and they come from all over the world, but then in a book about Kentucky she read to us, it said we're mostly the same here in the mountains. I don't agree we're all the same here, and neither does my daddy, because if you look around in school and in church and if you go with my daddy on the bus when he picks everyone up, you'll see we're not the same.

"There's a girl Sally who doesn't want to be a teacher or a nurse or anything. She says she doesn't want to come to school, but her mother tells her she should go just long enough to read and write a little, but not too much. There's a girl Betty who is sick, real bad sick she is, and she should go to a doctor in Inez, and Daddy says she belongs in Lexington, where they have a big hospital, but she's never seen a doctor, and the teacher tried twice to have the nurse come over, but each time Betty didn't come to school that day, and the nurse said she couldn't go up the hollow and she didn't know which house it was that Betty lived in, and the teacher didn't know either. Betty told me one day that the doctors get you sicker, and her daddy has her eating herbs and things, and she'd been prayed over a lot, and she'll be getting better soon, she believes. My mother said it's a shame, and besides Betty being sick there's her whole family: they're all sick with one trouble or another, and they don't have money, and Daddy says they're in the worst shape it's possible to be, and the father is always drinkin'-mad and fightin'-mad, my daddy says. Jamie is her kin, I believe, Betty's kin; and he's maybe nine or ten. He's real good with guns. He can shoot sharper than anyone else, everyone says. Jamie says he's got to know how to shoot, and they're always shooting up there, and not only at animals. They're feuding, feuding real bad all the time, and with liquor it gets worse. They go running up the road and they'll take a shot or two at the first house they come to. They don't dare come down to us and do that, because they know the sheriff would come and have them in jail so fast they wouldn't know what happened to them. Daddy says they fight and drink up the liquor they make because they have to fill up the day, and anyone would surely be unhappy if he didn't have his work and there was no money and all the sickness they have up in the hollow. They're always tossing their mess into the creek — a lot of glass and paper and everything. The dogs go swimming, and they'll get scraps of food if there are any, but food is scarce up there, so they don't throw it away.

"Once the teacher called me over, and she said I was being real nice because I shared my cookies with the kids, and my mother packed me extra ones, because I told her I felt bad eating, when others have nothing to eat. I told her they're hungry from up there, and they need better clothes than they have. I give them the cookies, but they're not going to be saying thank you all the time, and I'm glad they don't! You have to keep your chin up, and not bow and scrape, and people don't like to be asking for favors all the time. Sally said her mother told her not to take anything for free and not to go asking favors of people, and she should have her pride. Sally said her mother told her, 'To hell with people feeling sorry for us, because if they try, they'll get shot real fast around here.'

"Sally takes my cookies though. We'll eat my cookies and she'll tell me she's glad we live where we do, because our house is a good beginning for the hollow, and we're lucky Daddy has the job he's got. I know that's right, because if I was Sally, I wouldn't be thinking of going on to the high school, either.

"When they took in their corn, Sally came down with some, because they grow it and we don't. She said she wanted to thank us for the cookies at school, and the corn was just picked and ripe as can be and real sweet, and her mother said they knew we were good to Sally and they wanted to be good to us. Later, when she had left, my daddy said I should never forget that people in Martin County are the best people in the world, and even if they've got almost nothing except what they grow, they don't go begging and stealing and they don't do much borrowing either. They'll take something and let a favor be done, then they'll keep it in their mind, and when the moment is a good one, then they'll go and pay the favor back. He's told me that a few times, Daddy has —not to forget Sally bringing up the corn. I don't. I won't."

ON ACCOUNT OF THE MACHINES

What of the Sallys who by the thousands live up those hollows and creeks, the poorest of the poor, those whose minds and hearts and souls have significantly given way, having suffered beyond any reasonable limit, even where people know how to take hardship in their stride? They are the families and the children whose extreme condition — of life and limb and spirit — has been described by Appalachian people themselves. Sally, for example, can spell out unselfconsciously and even casually some of the distinguishing characteristics that set her apart, say, from Herbie, a boy of eight who lives not far away in the same hollow: "Herbie's daddy had a job in the mines, but then he got fired because they were closing down the mines, some of them, and laying off people on account of the machines. They had some money during the time he was working, and my daddy says once you've had money you never can forget it. Herbie says his daddy can't recall the last time he saw a paycheck, but you can see his folks went and got things with the money — the television and the stove and the refrigerator. In our place there's no electricity, none — so we couldn't have television or a refrigerator, even if we had the money to buy them. We don't need electricity. We have the stove. All we need is wood for it, and my daddy goes and finds coal up the hollow and digs out the pieces. The trouble is a lot of the time he's under, real bad under, and then we have to do his chores, and my mother will be crying and then we all start and it's then I wish I was staying down the hollow, maybe with Herbie and his folks — they're the best people you could meet."

When her father goes "real bad under," he has been drinking too much. Her mother tries hard to stop "the old man's habit," as she refers

*A sketch of a modest dwelling from the
Appalachian portion of Kentucky.*
by Douglas Kinsey

to him and his drinking. After a while, though, she also starts drinking, first slowly but then with a certain desperate acceleration that strikes terror into the minds of her seven children, who run for cover — to the woods and to kinfolk down the hollow.

Sally's parents live as far up the hollow as one can go. From their cabin one can see a truly splendid view of the Appalachians: the hills close by and far; the low-hanging white clouds and the higher gray clouds; the mist or the drizzle or the fog; and, near at hand, everywhere the green of the trees. The cabin is black, tar-paper black, and stands on four cement blocks. It lacks curtains but does indeed possess that old stove, the place where life-giving food is prepared and life-preserving heat is given off. Near the stove there are three beds with mattresses but nothing else. Ten human beings use the mattresses: Sally's grandmother, her parents, and the seven children in the family. The cabin possesses a table but only one chair to go with it, and two other old "sitting chairs," both of which are battered and tattered, with springs in each quite visible.

The children sit and eat outside under the trees, or inside on the floor, or near the house on the ground; or else they walk out in front of the house, in which case they often remain standing or hunch over their food. The children commonly use their hands to eat, or share a limited number of forks (four), spoons (five), and knives (seven) with their parents and grandmother. The children also share clothes: two pairs of shoes, both in serious need of repair, two ragged winter jackets, and three very old pairs of winter gloves. The children, let it be said, also share something else — the hollow: its hills and land, its vast imposing view, its bushes and shrubs and plants and animals and water and silence and noise, its seclusion and isolation, and also its people — for Sally a whole crowded, complicated sustaining world.

What I have learned from Sally's life (and her words and her) does not require me to say that a good deal of it is unsatisfying — to her, never mind me. She does not need me to express her central longing that her family find a more coherent, valuable kind of existence. Sally and children like her made it very clear to me that on the one hand they very much like certain things about mountain living, and on the other hand they are troubled and confused and even badly hurt (yes, they *know* they are hurt) by the hunger pangs they experience, the sickness that goes untreated, and, perhaps worst of all, the sight of what their suffering does to their parents. Those Appalachian parents certainly do take notice of their children's suffering — partly because they are parents, and also because they are traditionally proud and defiant people. Children notice their parents noticing, and Sally herself can talk about that kind of watching and counterwatching as it goes on among bruised and offended people, unwilling to let go of their sense of dignity and self-respect, and unwilling also to let go of their love for their ancestors, for their homes, their land, their conventions: "There's nothing that gets my daddy going worse than liquor. Once he told my mother he was going to start drinking because he was upset as bad as he could be, because he'd been down the hollow and over to the welfare people and it was the first time he'd gone and it was going to be the last, even if he starved to death. I guess they didn't give him anything. They said they were sorry. They said there's no money for most people, and that's all they can do in the office there.

"Daddy was more upset that he'd gone over to them than that they had refused him; I know that, because he said so all morning. I've never seen him so fightin'-mad, and he said he was, and we all got more and more scared. My mother told us we'd better go out to the woods and play, and she would take care of everything. Then before we left he looked at me and my sister and he raised up his hand, and I got scared he might come over and take it out on us —but no, he didn't do anything. He told me I was good and he was glad I was good, and he said the day would come when he'd be able to bring home clothes for us and I'd look pretty. He said I already do, but if you have a dress, it helps. Then he said I could go outside and my mother said to go, and I went.

The next thing I knew he was drinking and he started screaming real bad after a while. I believe a lot of the time he gets himself upset on account of us, and then he'll go and take to the liquor he makes.

"I wouldn't want to live any other place. What do you do if there's no hill you're on — if it's flat like they show you in the books in school? If I could change anything I wanted, I'd tear down that place Daddy and his friends use to make the liquor. I'd just have the hill here, where we live, and the other ones, to go and look at. I'd have us living in a different house, maybe like Marie's. Then we'd all be happier. I know that. Then I think my daddy might stop his drinking and never start again, like he'll promise us each time that he's going to do."

STALEMATE

Mountaineers look upon life as a sort of stalemate, in which there is plenty of good as well as plenty of bad, plenty to hold onto as well as plenty to wish for, and, as a result "an awful lot of plenty" to be high-strung about, unsettled about, feel torn about. Faced with such thoroughly mixed feelings, mountaineers stand fast and try to persist. In the words of Marie's father, they "stick it out, last it out." Stick out and last out what, one wonders? Does he mean the obvious lack of material things and opportunities? That, yes; but more is at stake than some of us on the outside realize. Marie's father says, "As I see it, up there in the hollow it's real bad — yes, with Sally and her people. But there's plenty they just don't want to lose, an awful lot of plenty, I'll tell you. People come in here and they don't know that. I heard on the TV a man saying we're supposed to be suspicious up in the mountains, and we don't trust no one, except ourselves. What a lot of hooey he had in his mouth, saying that. Sure we're not going to like someone if he comes in here and tells us we're a bunch of damn fools, and we should do this and that and everything they want us, and then we'll be all right.

"Hell, this is our country. We made it. We came here and we stayed because we loved it, and no one's going to get us out — except, I guess, if we're going to starve right to death, and then we'll be gone anyway. But I think we're friendlier here than in those cities you see all the time on the TV, where they pay no mind to anyone but themselves. I'm no expert on anything, except driving a bus and making sure those schools stay warm in the winter and as clean as they can, what with all the kids messing things up every day; but you can walk up any hollow or creek in Kentucky and West Virginia and you'll hear people picking on the guitar and listening to the radio and they'll stop and talk with you, and if you want to stay for supper, that's fine. Now, if you do, they're not going to go and spit on themselves and hold out their hand and say, 'Look here mister, give us a few pennies out of your big fat wallet.' No sir, they're going to put out their best for you, and they're going to show you they've got a lot to put out, that's right.

"Sure, we need more, a hell of a lot more, and you must have figured that out by now. But no one's going to get us feeling kindly by coming on first thing with a lot of that lousy pity stuff you hear on the TV — about the poor people of Appalachia! Hell on that! Hell on it! They start with that and the next thing I know I'm ready to tell them to take themselves and their charity and go try it on someone else, because that's not what a decent, God-fearing man wants, no it's not. You can get suspicious, like they say we are. The coal people come in here, and they're tearing up everything they can get their hands on, and maybe they'll give you the money, the wages, but sure as hell they get more out of it than all of us ever will, and then the next thing you know they're gone, and all we have for it is that they've torn up a whole mountain and what's left of the mountain is falling down on us in a landslide, and we're supposed to get out, fast. If you don't get suspicious over that, then you're not right in your head. Then you know they've been taking our timber away, by the hillful, since way back, and right in front of our eyes that's what's been happening since I guess Abraham Lincoln or someone was President. So, why shouldn't we go and tell our children to watch out when some big-smiling city slicker comes here with a dozen lawyers standing guard over him?

"Sure we're afraid of them all coming here; we can smell the trouble before it gets to the first hill in Kentucky —or over in West Virginia. But if they came to us and wanted to bring in some work here, and it didn't mean tearing up the whole country, and it didn't mean eating up our lungs, then we'd be just like any American — glad to have a job, you bet your life. We'd want to sit here and be ourselves, of course. We wouldn't want to act like some of the people you see on television. We wouldn't want to dress as they do, and talk as they do, no matter how much money we made. We'd want to live as we do. But we'd be working, and that would sure be a welcome change hereabouts."

Many of us on the "outside" have yet to convince a man like Marie's father that we really understand what we claim is obvious to us; for he thinks we would only pity him and his kin, even as we pity the children of sharecroppers and of migrant farmers. Our pity will give very little to anyone, and it enrages the mountaineers — who know very well what kind of justice they require and what justice we in America have so far done and not done.   ■

Jane Jacobs
Contrasting Perceptions of a Community*

This selection is from a book written quite a few years ago. Planners have learned to see things differently in the intervening years. However, Rational Man still carries considerable weight, raising some doubt as to how well Jacobs's message has been absorbed. Another dimension of the problem raised here, the expert versus the people, is still very much with us. What one knows is always a powerful factor in what one sees. Since what the planner knows and what the local resident knows about the same neighborhood differ substantially, the consequent perceptions of need also diverge. When the planners' perceptions are translated, unchecked, into policy, the local residents are unlikely to perceive either an improvement in their chosen neighborhood or a gain in their capacity to control their lives.

■   Consider, for example, the orthodox planning reaction to a district called the North End in Boston. This is an old, low-rent area merging into the heavy industry of the waterfront, and it is officially considered Boston's worst slum and civic shame. It embodies attributes which all enlightened people know are evil because so many wise men have said they are evil. Not only is the North End bumped right up against industry, but worse still it has all kinds of working places and commerce mingled in the greatest complexity with its residences. It has the highest concentration of dwelling units, on the land that is used for dwelling units, of any part of Boston, and indeed one of the highest concentrations to be found in any American city. It has little parkland. Children play in the streets. Instead of super-blocks, or even decently large blocks, it has very small blocks, in planning parlance it is "badly cut up with wasteful streets." Its buildings are old. Everything conceivable is presumably wrong with the North End. In orthodox planning terms, it is a three-dimensional textbook of "megalopolis" in the last stages of depravity. The North End is thus a recurring assignment for M.I.T. and Harvard planning and architectural students, who now and again pursue, under the guidance of their teachers, the paper exercise of converting it into super-blocks and park

*From *The Death and Life of Great American Cities,* by Jane Jacobs. Copyright © 1961 by Jane Jacobs. Reprinted by permission of Random House, Inc. and Jonathan Cape Ltd. Pages 8–11.

promenades, wiping away its noncomforming uses, transforming it to an ideal of order and gentility so simple it could be engraved on the head of a pin.

Twenty years ago, when I first happened to see the North End, its buildings — town houses of different kinds and sizes converted to flats, and four- or five-story tenements built to house the flood of immigrants first from Ireland, then from Eastern Europe and finally from Sicily — were badly overcrowded, and the general effect was of a district taking a terrible physical beating and certainly desperately poor.

When I saw the North End again in 1959, I was amazed at the change. Dozens and dozens of buildings had been rehabilitated. Instead of mattresses against the windows there were Venetian blinds and glimpses of fresh paint. Many of the small, converted houses now had only one or two families in them instead of the old crowded three or four. Some of the families in the tenements (as I learned later, visiting inside) had uncrowded themselves by throwing two older apartments together, and had equipped these with bathrooms, new kitchens and the like. I looked down a narrow alley, thinking to find at least here the old, squalid North End, but no: more neatly repointed brickwork, new blinds, and a burst of music as a door opened. Indeed, this was the only city district I had ever seen — or have seen to this day — in which the sides of buildings around parking lots had not been left raw and amputated, but repaired and painted as neatly as if they were intended to be seen. Mingled all among the buildings for living were an incredible number of splendid food stores, as well as such enterprises as upholstery making, metal working, carpentry, food processing. The streets were alive with children playing, people shopping, people strolling, people talking. Had it not been a cold January day, there would surely have been people sitting.

The general street atmosphere of buoyancy, friendliness and good health was so infectious that I began asking directions of people just for the fun of getting in on some talk. I had seen a lot of Boston in the past couple of days, most of it sorely distresssing, and this struck me, with relief, as the healthiest place in the city. But I could not imagine where the money had come from for the rehabilitation, because it is almost impossible today to get any appreciable mortgage money in districts of American cities that are not either high-rent, or else imitations of suburbs. To find out, I went into a bar and restaurant (where an animated conversation about fishing was in progress) and called a Boston planner I know.

"Why in the world are you down in the North End?" he said. "Money? Why, no money or work has gone into the North End. Nothing's going on down there. Eventually, yes, but not yet. That's a slum!"

"It doesn't seem like a slum to me," I said.

"Why, that's the worst slum in the city. It has two hundred and seventy-five dwelling units to the net acre! I hate to admit we have anything like that in Boston, but it's a fact."

"Do you have any other figures on it?" I asked.

"Yes, funny thing. It has among the lowest delinquency, disease and infant mortality rates in the city. It also has the lowest ratio of rent to income in the city. Boy, are those people getting bargains. Let's see . . . the child population is just about average for the city, on the nose. The death rate is low, 8.8 per thousand, against the average city rate of 11.2. The TB death rate is very low, less than 1 per ten thousand, can't understand it, it's lower even than Brookline's. In the old days the North End used to be the city's worst spot for tuberculosis, but all that has changed. Well, they must be strong people. Of course it's a terrible slum."

"You should have more slums like this," I said. "Don't tell me there are plans to wipe this out. You ought to be down here learning as much as you can from it."

"I know how you feel," he said. "I often go down there myself just to walk around the streets and feel that wonderful, cheerful street life. Say, what you ought to do, you ought to come back and go down in the summer if you think it's fun now. You'd be crazy about it in summer. But of course we have to rebuild it eventually. We've got to get those people off the streets."

Here was a curious thing. My friend's instincts told him the North End was a good place, and his social statistics confirmed it. But everything he had learned as a physical planner about what is good for people and good for city neighborhoods, everything that made him an expert, told him the North End had to be a bad place. ■

J. Douglas Porteous
The Pathology of Forced Relocation*

The story of Boston's West End is, along with the Pruitt-Igoe story in the following selection, probably the best known example of what happens when the planning process ignores the human factor. The vital role that community and territory play in the well-being of these mistreated citizens is painfully obvious. Here we see the impact of the absence of choice and the absence of control.

■   The physical removal, often against their will, of large numbers of inner-city people has social and psychological as well as economical repercussions. To illustrate this, the case of the West End of Boston will be discussed in some detail. The renewal of the West End has become a *cause célèbre* in planning circles, has led to much rethinking by urban planners, and has probably been more intensively studied than any other renewal project.

In the 1950s about 10,000 people inhabited the West End's forty-eight-acre site in the heart of Boston. Like the still extant North End nearby, the West End was inhabited largely by low-income immigrants, over 40 percent of whom were of Italian origin. As with similar inner-city areas, it was characterized by high densities, mixed land uses, aged tenements, many small shops and businesses, and a communal life lived as much in the street as indoors (Whyte, 1955). Gans, who spent much time in the area, recorded it as a socially tight multigenerational ethnic ghetto with strong internal linkages but little significant social contact with Boston as a whole. In short, the West End was inhabited by *Urban Villagers* (Gans, 1962).

Boston's city fathers viewed the West End as a suitable site for urban renewal because of its location close to downtown, adjacent to the high-class area of Beacon Hill, and with a frontage on the Charles River. The chief motives for public renewal were a desire to replace the tenement-dominated skyline with a prestigious high-rent complex which would bring in much more municipal income and would hopefully induce a spiral of private renewal. The area was recommended for renewal in 1949, but did not receive federal approval until 1957. Soon

*From J. Douglas Porteous *Environment and behavior: planning and everyday urban life*. Copyright 1977 by Addison-Wesley Publishing Company, Reading, Massachusetts. Pages 288–290.

afterwards demolition began, and within a decade the area had become the site of office blocks, government centers, luxury apartments, and extensions of the Massachusetts General Hospital.

Every West Ender who was renewed out of the area was guaranteed space in the luxury apartments built on the site. In financial terms, this was not a realistic alternative. Moreover, only about 15 percent of the displaced persons found replacement housing, including public housing, through the aid of renewal officials. Most dispersed to other areas of Boston with the same high density and mixed land use environment as the West End (Hartman, 1966). Such replacements of so-called slum housing by luxury apartment towers have been condemned as less slum clearance than slum shifting or slum relocation, and as "land grabs aided by government subsidies and the powerful privilege of eminent domain" (Higbee, 1960, p. 86). Little wonder that among blacks urban renewal is identified, bitterly, as "negro removal."

Forced relocation has identifiable effects. Several reports on the West End indicate that many of its inhabitants had strong attachments to the area and did not wish to leave. What the relocatees lost was a mutually supportive physical and social environment where the high density and mixed land uses facilitated interaction among friends and relatives. About 90 percent of the inhabitants identified themselves as West Enders (Ryan, 1963). West Enders perceived a sharp geographical and social boundary between their territorial home base and other parts of the city; a girl who married a non-West Ender and left the area was said to have "married outside." For male West Enders, the salient social relationships were the family-kinship group and the "hanging group" which hung around a local corner or bar. Both these networks were strongly based on propinquity.

Forced relocation from this environment proved disruptive and disturbing for many. The loss of close spatial links with friends and relatives and the loss of a feeling of enclosure and safety were very apparent. Hartman (1963) found that 76 percent of the West Enders had unreserved positive feelings about the area, and reported potential relocatees as saying:

> I love it. I was born and brought up here. I like the conveniences, the people, I feel safe. . . . I'm going to miss it terribly.

and

> I loved it very much. It was home to me. I was very happy. Everyone was nice. All my relatives lived there.

Gans also reports the feelings of persons about to be relocated:

> I wish the world would end tonight. . . . I'm going to be lost without the West End. Where the hell can I go?

and

> It isn't right to scatter the community to the four winds. It pulls the heart out of a guy to lose all his friends.

Fried (1963), in a study of the effects of relocation on women, found that among those who had previously reported liking living in the West End "very much," 73 percent showed evidence of extreme grief. Even 34 percent of those who were ambivalent or negative about the West End grieved severely for their lost home area. The grief syndrome included vomiting, intestinal disorders, crying spells, nausea, general sadness, and depression. This reaction is similar to the characteristics of grief and mourning for a dead person, but in this case is related to the loss of both spatial identity and group identity following forced residential relocation. Gans tells of West Enders returning both during and after the demolition to walk through the rubble-strewn streets of their former home. ■

William L. Yancey
Architecture, Interaction, and Social Control*

Here community, analyzed in terms of informal social networks, is shown to be greatly influenced by physical design. Yancey is careful to demonstrate that social class requirements for such networks differ; for lower-class needs the design of Pruitt-Igoe was particularly unfortunate. Semipublic space is seen by Yancey as playing a key role. It is in such places that informational exchange takes place, and this, in turn, is essential to the formation and maintenance of social networks. It is evident that space does not cause such exchanges — but space properly arranged can play an important enabling role.

■   In this paper we will argue that the architectural design of the Pruitt-Igoe Housing Project, located in St. Louis, Missouri, has had an atomizing effect on the informal social networks frequently found in lower- and working-class neighborhoods. Without the provision of semipublic space and facilities around which informal networks might develop, families living in Pruitt-Igoe have retreated into the internal

*"Architecture, Interaction, and Social Control: The Case of a Large-Scale Public Housing Project," by William L. Yancey is reprinted from *Environment & Behavior,* Vol. 3, No. 1 (March 1971) pp. 3–21, by permission of the Publisher, Sage Publications, Inc.

structures of their apartments and do not have the social support, protection, and informal social control found in other lower- and working-class neighborhoods.

It is clear that social and economic factors, particularly the level and stability of incomes and occupations, are major determinants of the life styles of the poor. Yet there is also evidence which indicates that the physical environment in which families live, in particular the design and condition of dwelling units, has an effect on the manner in which they live (Schorr, 1963; Wilner et al., 1962).

Among the effects of architectural design which have been identified by previous research is that of the physical proximity of dwelling units on the development of informal relationships between families. Gans (1963) has pointed out that the effects of proximity on informal relationships is somewhat contingent on differences in life styles exhibited by various groups. Gans's research indicates that it cannot be assumed that a particular architectural design will have the same effect on all social groups. The presence or absence of a particular design should have a variant effect on the total social life of a particular group, depending on the interdependence of the architecturally related behavior to other dimensions of the group's life. More specifically, we should find that the architectural relationships between dwellings and the effects of such spatial relationships on the social relationships that develop between families will have varying degrees of significance, depending on the importance of informal neighboring relationships in a particular social group.

In this paper, we will argue that informal networks among neighbors are an important means by which the urban lower and working classes cope with poverty and deprivation and that these networks are at least in part dependent on the semipublic space and facilities that are present in many working- and lower-class neighborhoods. Finally, we will review results of an ethnographic study of the Pruitt-Igoe Housing Project which indicate the nature of the consequences stemming, in part, from the absence of such space and facilities and the networks that might otherwise have developed.

SOCIAL CLASS AND INFORMAL NETWORKS

There is some ambiguity in the sociological literature concerning the importance of informal networks among different social classes. On the one hand, there are authors who argue that the frequency of neighboring and sociability is particularly prevalent in upper- and middle-class suburbs (Whyte, 1956; Bell and Boat, 1957; Fava, 1957). On the other hand, studies of the urban working and lower classes have shown rather strong interpersonal networks of neighbors and strong attachment to neighborhoods (Bott, 1957; Young and Wilmott, 1957; Gans, 1962; Fried and Gleicher, 1961; Fried, 1963; Suttles, 1968).

Careful reviews of these studies indicate that there is a difference in the character of social relationships with neighbors found in the middle class as compared to the working and lower classes. While neighboring is found to be frequent in both areas, "the intensity of social interaction tends to decrease as one moves from working class areas to upper income bracket residential suburbs" (Herberle, 1960, p. 279).

Illustrative of this debate are the results of a survey directed by John McCarthy and myself in Nashville and Philadelphia. The survey was taken in what were principally lower- and working-class neighborhoods in the two cities, with a smaller proportion of what might be considered lower-middle-class respondents. A total of 1178 interviews were completed, 712 in Nashville, and 466 in Philadelphia. Approximately equal numbers of these were with black households (576) and white households (602). Samples were systematic, rather than random, and were not designed so as to be representative of either city.

Using a scale developed by Wallin (1953), we found no relationship between casual neighboring relationships and social status.[1] In contrast to these results were those obtained when we asked our respondents to tell us how far away their closest friends lived. In this case, lower-status respondents were more likely to have friends living nearby than were those of higher status.[2]

These results conform to statements by Alan Blum (1964) and Rudolf Herberle (1960), suggesting that once the distinction is made between casual acquaintances and relatively high levels of interdependence, lower-class respondents are more closely tied to their neighbors. Among the lower class, friends are more likely to be neighbors. While, among the middle class, one might be friendly with his neighbors, friendships are more likely to be based on common interests, rather than upon physical proximity[3] (see Gans, 1961).

There is also considerable literature suggestive of the functions of informal networks for the lower and working class. Marc Fried's (1963) research on the depressing effects of urban renewal and relocation, particularly for families who had strong personal ties to the Boston West End, is illustrative. Gerald Suttles's recent research in Chicago's Adams area documents the manner in which the development of neighborhood networks based on physical proximity, age, sex, and ethnicity provided social and moral norms, as well as a means of integration into the larger groups. He writes

> Within each small, localized peer group, continuing face-to-face relations can eventually provide a personalistic order. Once these groups are established, a single personal relation between them can extend the range of such an order. With the acceptance of age grading and territorial usu-

fruct, it becomes possible for slum neighborhoods to work out a moral order that includes most of their residents [Suttles, 1968, p. 8].

A recent study of an all-white slum neighborhood in St. Louis found similar informal networks. Of particular interest here, and complementing the work of Suttles (1968), is the finding that the level of personal integration into networks was strongly related to the perception of human dangers in the environment. Persons who were not integrated into such networks were more likely to express concern over allowing their children out of the house, felt that they were vulnerable to strangers entering the neighborhood, felt unsafe on the street at night, and felt that children in the neighborhood were out of control (Wolfe et al., 1968).

There are also some indications that the presence of ecologically local networks is more important to lower- and working-class urban dwellers than to their middle-class counterparts. Herbert Gans has noted that the move to suburban areas by middle-class families results in part in having more privacy from neighbors than they had in inner-city apartments. Gans's research suggests that, for the middle class, the move to suburban areas results in few changes in life style that were not intended. He writes: "They are effects, not of suburban life, but of the larger cultural milieu in which people form their aspirations" (1963, p. 192).

The limited consequences of moving to suburbs by middle-class families stand in sharp contrast to those reported by Marris (1962) and Young and Wilmott (1957). These studies of the relocation of lower- and working-class communities indicate that the move to suburbia resulted in significant and unintended changes in their life styles. No longer available in the suburban housing estates were the amenities of the slum — the close proximity to work, the pub, and to friends and relatives. They changed their way of life and began focusing energies more sharply on their homes and jointly pursued family lives, and much less on separate activities by husband and wife participating in sex-segregated peer groups.

In addition to the ethnographic evidence on the relative importance of ecologically local informal networks, there is considerable research indicating that, much to the dismay of urban renewers, lower- and working-class populations are as satisfied with their neighborhoods as are members of the middle class (Foote et al., 1960; Fried, 1963). Our recent survey in Nashville and Philadelphia indicated that there was no relationship between social status and neighborhood satisfaction. Over 60 percent of our respondents were satisfied with their neighborhoods, no matter what their social and economic status.

The works of Fried (1963), Gans (1962), and Foote et al. (1960)

also indicate that among the lower and working classes, neighborhood satisfaction is rather closely tied to the presence of informal networks of friends and relatives. Results from our survey support this proposition. Without social class controls, we found no relationship between the proximity of friends and neighborhood satisfaction. When we controlled on the social class, we found that neighborhood satisfaction was related to the proximity of friends in the lower socioeconomic group, while there was no relationship in the higher-status respondents.[4]

These survey data suggest that, not only are the existence and integration into ecologically local informal social networks significant for the lower and working classes, but our results go slightly beyond the earlier studies in that they are suggestive of the relative importance of such networks for different social and economic levels. While social and economic factors are the principal variables that determine the life styles of the poor, they have developed ways of coping with and adapting to poverty, thus making the condition less oppressive. We have argued that among these adaptations is the development of ecologically local informal neighborhood relationships. When these are disrupted, or a community is designed which makes their development almost impossible, we should expect to see their importance made manifest by other differences that emerge in the life styles of a particular group. The Pruitt-Igoe Housing Project community is illustrative of one such group.

THE CASE OF PRUITT-IGOE

The Pruitt-Igoe Housing Project consists of forty-three eleven-story buildings near downtown St. Louis, Missouri. The project was opened in 1954, had 2762 apartments (many of which are currently vacant), and has as tenants a high proportion of female-headed households, on one form or another of public assistance. Though originally containing a large population of white families, the project has been all-Negro for the past several years. The project community is plagued by petty crimes, vandalism, much destruction to the physical plant, and has a rather widespread reputation as being an extreme example of the pathologies associated with lower-class life (Demerath, 1962; Rainwater, 1966a, 1966b).

Pruitt-Igoe represents, in its architectural design, an extreme example of a national housing policy whose single goal is the provision of housing for individual families, with little knowledge about or concern for the development of a community and neighborhood. Unlike normal slums, with their cluttered streets and alleys, Pruitt-Igoe provides no semiprivate space and facilities around which neighboring relationships might develop. There is a minimum of what is often considered "wasted space" — space within buildings that is outside of individual family dwelling units. An early review of the project's design

Courtesy of William L. Yancey

(Architectural Forum, 1951) praised the designers for their individualistic design and the absence of such wasted space between dwelling units.

Walking into the project, one is struck by the mosaic of glass that covers what were grassy areas and playgrounds. The barren dirt, or mud when it rains, is constantly tracked into the apartments. Windows, particularly those on the lower floors, are broken out. The cost of replacing glass in vacant apartments led the Housing Authority to cover many with plywood. Streets and parking lots are littered with trash, bottles, and tin cans. Derelict cars provide an attractive source of entertainment for children. Fences around "tot lots" are torn; swings, sliding boards, and merry-go-rounds are noticeably unpainted, rusted, and broken.

Within the buildings themselves, the neglect is more apparent. Entering the buildings via one of the three stairwells, one is struck with the stale air and the stench of urine, trash, and garbage on the floors. One is also struck by the unfinished construction — the unpainted cinderblocks and cement. These unfinished walls in the stairwells are decorated with colorful graffiti.

The alternative route into the building is the single elevator. The elevator is used as a public restroom, as well as a means of transportation up into the buildings. Even though it is mopped every morning, the smell of urine is noticeable throughout the day. Many individual building elevators are without handrails and in need of painting; all have the reputation of breaking down between floors.

On the fourth, seventh, and tenth floors, there is an open gallery, or hall, the only level public space within the building, one side of which is lined with broken windows and steel gratings. Next to the incinerator, open garbage is often found on the floor. The laundry rooms, located off the gallery, are sometimes used as lavatories. We observed residents and officials urinating in them.

The physical danger and deterioration of Pruitt-Igoe is but a reflection of the more pressing human dangers. Residents of Pruitt-Igoe continually expressed concern with being assaulted, beaten, or raped. We were frequently warned of such dangers and told that we should never enter buildings alone and should stay out of the elevators, especially after dark. We were told stories of people being cut by bottles thrown from the buildings and warned never to stand immediately outside of a building. In addition to the physical violence, there was also the danger to one's self — the verbal hostility, the shaming and exploitation from children, neighbors, and outsiders (see Rainwater, 1966a).

One of the first things pointed out by the residents of Pruitt-Igoe was the distinction between "private" space within apartments and the "public" space and facilities. In our early interviews with families, we asked what they liked about living in the housing project. Almost without exception, what they liked was limited to the physical space and amenities within the family unit. Characteristic of these interviews is the following exchange:

Interviewer: How do you like living here in Pruitt-Igoe?
Respondent: I like living here better than I like living on O'Fallon Street [in a private housing slum] where we had a first floor, but did not have heat provided in the winter and windows were broken out. We did have an inside toilet, but no modern plumbing — we had no water. I like living here because it's convenient.
Interviewer: What do you mean by "convenient?"
Respondent: The apartment itself — it's easier to take care of and to clean. Although the paint on these walls holds dirt badly, the Housing Authority does furnish the paint. We don't have a choice of what kind of paint, but I painted the walls. It's real convenient here, especially in the wintertime. It's always so nice and warm here, and I only have one rent to pay. I don't have to pay for gas and electricity and all that. I just pay once. I like that. I like this apartment, it's good for the kids. Here we have separate rooms.
Interviewer: Each child has a separate room?
Respondent: No, but this way the children have a bedroom and the parents have a bedroom. It gives them and us more freedom.

Courtesy of William L. Yancey

When the interviewer changed the focus of the interview by asking, "How do you feel about this building?" the character of the interview changed.

Respondent: Well, I don't like being upstairs like this. The problem is that I can't see the kids. They're just too far away. If one of them gets hurt, needs to go to the bathroom, or anything, it's just too far away. And you can't get outside. We don't have any porches.

And there are too many different kids around here. Some of them have parents, some do not. There are just a variety of families. Some have husbands, some not.

If it weren't for the project police, the teenagers would take over. I've got some children that are teenagers, but I still think they are the most dangerous group.

This pattern of responses repeats itself throughout our research. The results of a survey taken in the housing project indicate that 78 percent of the residents were satisfied with their apartments, while only 49 percent were satisfied with living in the project. This pattern of satisfaction and dissatisfaction with one's dwelling unit as compared to one's neighborhood is exactly the opposite of that found in most studies of housing and neighborhood satisfaction. In contrast with Pruitt-Igoe, slum dwellers generally are dissatisfied with their specific dwellings, while satisfied with their neighborhoods.[5] In Pruitt-Igoe, the familiar aspects of slum living, such as fires and burning, freezing and cold, poor plumbing, dangerous electrical wiring, thin walls, and overcrowding of children and parents into single rooms are somewhat abated. *Yet the amenities of lower-class neighborhoods are apparently lost.*

Complementing the pattern of satisfaction with apartment and neighborhood, and again in sharp contrast to the research reviewed above, informal social networks did not form in the corridors and stairwells of Pruitt-Igoe. Residents of the projects had a similar number of friends as in other lower-class populations, yet these friendships bore little or no relationship to the physical proximity of families to each other.

In Pruitt-Igoe, relationships with neighbors ranged from occasional friendship and helping patterns to (more frequently found) open hostility or isolation. As one woman explained when we asked about troubles in the project:

> I think people bring trouble on themselves, but like the kids — see, the kids get fighting and the parents they get into it too. Now us, we mind our own business. I say little to the people across the hall. We don't have any friends in the building. Most of our friends are from work. Some of them we have known for a long time.

Still another replied, when asked about her neighbors:

> They are selfish. I've got no friends here. There's none of this door-to-door coffee business of being friends here or anything like that. Down here, if you are sick you just go to the hospital. There are no friends to help you. I don't think my neighbors would help me and I wouldn't ask them to anyway. I don't have trouble with my neighbors because I never visit them. The rule of the game down here is *go for yourself.*

THE CONSEQUENCES OF ATOMIZATION

Gerald Suttles notes that in the Adams area in Chicago, conflict between residents in the area results in the reinforcement of the small informal group. He writes (1968, p. 228):

> Individuals in the Adams area achieve a positive association with co-residents of the same age, sex and ethnicity primarily because conflict with other persons forces them together into small face-to-face groupings. Otherwise, people might remain almost wholly isolated, associate indiscriminately, and be dependent on such dyadic relations as they could form.

Of particular interest here is his discussion of the sequence through which such groups develop. New residents of the area restrict their children's movement to the areas immediately around or close by their homes. As a result, small and continuous face-to-face associations develop around the immediate proximity of the home. They provide

Courtesy of William L. Yancey

means of controlling children and provide "assurances that relieve their apprehension." Conflict with persons outside these small groups forces the residents to "throw their lot in with a definite group of people" (Suttles, 1968, p. 228).

In a similar manner, mothers in Pruitt-Igoe attempt to keep their children in close proximity to their apartments. Yet in contrast to the slum, the architectural design of the project is such that as soon as a child leaves an apartment he is out of his mother's sight and direct control. There are no areas within buildings, except the galleries (which cannot be seen from the apartments and which are shared by some twenty families) in which children can play. As one mother explained:

> I find that I can't keep up with the children when they leave the house to play. When they go out they play with just anybody; there are some people in the project who raise their children and some who don't. I want to have control over who they play with and when so many people live in one place you just can't choose your kid's playmates. If we were in a house I could keep them in a yard and see who they play with.

Mothers fear the early introduction and socialization of their children into sex and other troubles. They also see the adults in the housing project as being irresponsible, deviant, and beyond control.

Said one:

> They tell their children one thing and go out and do the very opposite. They see kids in a fight and rather than break it up, will get into it themselves.

Yet attempts to control children who are members of unknown families frequently resulted in conflict between adults. Thus one woman reported:

> I used to watch the kids in this building. In the beginning I tried to discipline them. I'd tell them every time I found them doing something mischievous what was wrong and what was right. But kids don't like that; their parents don't like it. They don't want somebody else to discipline their children. They put the blame on you. Watching children is dangerous.

Another explained that after she had "made one of the neighbor's boys do right," his mother came and said she was going to bring a gun.

The conflict is further escalated when one of the two adults calls the police. As one woman explained, after she was told the police had been called because her son had gotten into a fight:

> Well, I'm not going to get shook because the police are coming. They always come to this house and tell me how bad my children are. It's too bad the parents had to call the police and could never take the time to come up and talk to me first.

Apparently without the informal networks, informal social control that might otherwise be based on the small social group is not strong enough to resolve such conflicts. Thus, as a means of resolving what might otherwise have been a relatively small complaint, a more powerful authority — the policeman — is called upon. This, in turn, further exacerbates the atomization that exists.

Our interviews and observations with families in the housing project contain many references to the police. A sample survey of the Pruitt-Igoe Housing Project showed that over 90 percent of the residents of the project indicated that there should be more policemen patrolling the area. As one lady explained:

> In other projects they have enough policemen, but not here. You put lights in and they take them out, or the police never turn them on. They have policemen but they don't do any good. They are not here long enough. They used to have auxiliary policemen down here. But as soon as they took them away there was all kinds of raping and stealing all over the project. It has turned into a jungle.

Other features of the architecture, apart from the lack of semi-public space and facilities, have contributed to the fears that characterize the community. The design of the stairwells is such that they represent almost completely uncontrolled space. They are public in the

Courtesy of William L. Yancey

sense that anyone can enter them without being challenged, yet they are private in that no one is likely to be held accountable for his behavior in the stairwell. This lack of accountability is particularly prevalent in the center stairwell, where a small anteroom separates the individual apartments from the stairwell. This room creates a buffer zone between the totally private apartment and the stairwell. Pruitt-Igoens fear this stairwell more than the others, and it is said to be used by teenagers as a relatively private place in which they can engage in sexual intercourse. As one teenager explained, "All you have to do is knock out the light on the landings above and below you. Then when someone comes, if they are not afraid of the dark, they stumble around and you can hear them in time to get out."

The isolation, the lack of accountability for entry into the stairwells, and the fears that are centered around them are somewhat interdependent with the lack of informal networks. Given the number of families who have rights to this space, it should not be surprising that strangers can enter it without being challenged. While interviewing in lower- and working-class neighborhoods, one often encounters persons on the street who question you as to where you are going. After an introduction, such persons often give interviewers instructions as to where a family can be found, when they will return home, or how to get through an alley to an apartment. Later, when such an interviewer returns and introduces himself, he often gets a response such as, "Oh yes, you were here earlier." During our three years of intensive research in

Pruitt-Igoe, such an experience never occurred. The presence of outsiders was noticed by the residents, but they were never challenged.

Absent from the architectural design of Pruitt-Igoe is what has sometimes been referred to as wasted space. We choose to call it "defensible space." In lower- and working-class slums, the littered and often trash-filled alleys, streets, and backyards provide the ecological basis around which informal networks of friends and relatives may develop. Without such semipublic space and facilities, the development of such networks is retarded; the resulting atomization of the community can be seen in the frequent and escalating conflict between neighbors, fears of and vulnerability to the human dangers in the environment, and, finally, withdrawal to the last line of defense — into the single-family dwelling unit. The sense of security and control that is found in other working- and lower-class neighborhoods is not present.

There are at least two alternative hypotheses which might be used to explain the atomized nature of the Pruitt-Igoe community. The first of these stems from the research and literature on social stratification, which rather clearly show that the level of interpersonal trust is lower in the lower class than in any other segment of the population. Thus, it is argued that Pruitt-Igoe, being representative of the lowest class, is therefore a community of people none of whom trust one another. A comparison of Pruitt-Igoe's residents' responses to questionnaire items measuring the level of trust indicates that, while they are less trustful than are persons of higher status, they are not different from other lower-class populations (see Rainwater and Schwarts, 1965).

Perhaps a more credible hypothesis, one which might be termed the "police state" theory, stems from the public nature of life in public housing. Over 50 percent of the residents are on some form of welfare assistance. Welfare workers and housing authority officials maintain a rather close scrutiny of their clients who might otherwise break one of the many rules governing residence in the project. Under such a "police state," residents of the project may fear that becoming friendly with neighbors will result in their being turned in to the authorities. We observed neighbors calling the police about one another, as discussed above, and some families complained that neighbors had reported them to the housing authority or welfare office for an infraction of one of their rules.

Without a comparative study of Pruitt-Igoe with another housing project with a similar population, similar reputation, and similar administration by caretakers, it is difficult to adequately judge the effects of architecture per se. David Wilner's study of public housing in Baltimore shows, in contrast with Pruitt-Igoe, that with an architectural design which facilitated interpersonal interaction by the provision of common space and facilities, an increased amount of neighboring, visiting, and mutual aid was found among persons moving from a slum into a public housing project (Wilner et al., 1962, p. 161).

We obviously believe that architecture does have an effect on the manner in which the poor cope with poverty. And we further suggest that designers of housing for the poor, rather than viewing the space between dwelling units as something to be avoided or reduced as far as possible, should provide semipublic space and facilities around which smaller indentifiable units of residence can organize their sense of "turf." Designers should minimize space that belongs to no one and maximize the informal control over the space required to get from one dwelling to another. In a word, if housing must be designed for the ghetto — if we must reconcile ourselves to not being able to change the social forces which produce the world of danger that lower-class families experience — the architect can make some small contribution by facilitating the constructive adaptations that have emerged as a means of defense against the world of the lower class. ∎

NOTES

1. When status was measured by education, we found a positive, although weak, relationship. When status was measured by income, we obtained the opposite results.

Neighboring and Social Status. Percentage of each status group scoring "high" on neighboring items:

Education Completed			Weekly Income		
0–7 yrs	25.2	(306)	00–$59	41.2	(240)
8–11 yrs	33.8	(409)	60–129	29.9	(421)
12 yrs	33.8	(225)	$130+	28.6	(318)
College	30.7	(192)			

2. *Friends' Distance and Social Status.* Percentage with first friend living on same block:

Education Completed			Weekly Income		
0–7 yrs	43.7	(300)	00–$59	40.7	(231)
8–11 yrs	31.6	(415)	60–129	29.3	(413)
12 yrs	26.8	(220)	$130+	19.9	(311)
College	14.5	(186)			
Probability	.0074		.0027		

Similar results were obtained with each of three friends.

3. We also found that higher-status persons are more likely to have friends whose occupations are similar to their own, in level of prestige, than are members of the lower and working classes.

4. *Neighborhood Satisfaction and Proximity of First Friend by Social Status.* Percentage satisfied with neighborhood:

		Distance in Blocks	
	0-4	*5-25*	*26+*
(Total Sample)	72.9(541)	69.4(264)	70.0(240)
Education Completed			
0–8 yrs. LO	74.8(262)	76.0 (71)	71.0 (60)
9–12 yrs MD	70.0(203)	61.9(126)	63.2 (87)
College HI	77.3 (66)	67.3 (61)	78.2 (78)

As these data reveal, without social and economic controls there is little or no relationship between friends' distance and neighborhood satisfaction. Yet when we control on the level of education, we find that there is a relationship in the lower class, but not in the middle class.

Similar results were obtained with the second- and third-friend responses and when social status was measured by income and occupation. The levels of significance, beyond the .05 level, are not always achieved, but in every case the pattern of a stronger relationship between the proximity of friends and satisfaction with neighborhood is found in the lower-status groups.

5. A survey taken in the private slum neighborhood directly adjacent to Pruitt-Igoe found the more usual pattern of satisfaction with housing and neighborhood. The results of this and a survey taken in Pruitt-Igoe are presented below.

	Percentage Satisfied	
	Pruitt-Igoe	*Adjacent Slum*
with apartment	78	55
with project living	49	
with neighborhood	53	74
	(n=154)	(n=69)

In more recent years, vandalism and lack of maintenance have resulted in the deterioration of the plumbing and heating of the building. Thus these data, if gathered more recently, would probably not be found to be as striking as they were when this study was done in 1965.

AUTHOR'S NOTE: *This paper is based in part on research supported by grants from the National Institute of Mental Health, Grant MH-09189, "Social and Community Problems in Public Housing Areas," and from the Urban and Regional Development Center, Vanderbilt University. Many of the ideas presented stem from discussions I have had with the directors of the Pruitt-Igoe research – Alvin Gouldner and Lee Rainwater. This paper was presented at a Symposium on Environmental Perception at the meetings of the American Psychological Association at Miami Beach, Florida, on September 5, 1970.*

Alternatives to Fear —
Review of Oscar Newman's
*Defensible Space**

Newman's imaginative, analytic treatment of the conditions supportive of community in low-income housing is a classic in the area of human/environment relations. It is all too easy to deny the connection between physical design and human behavior. This unfortunate conclusion is understandable given the complexity of the causal chain that Newman has uncovered. Crime is not reduced because of the arrangement of space. Rather it is the arrangement of space that makes it possible for residents to comprehend and become involved in what goes on in their building. They in turn come to know each other and to exert control over their common space. It is this social control then that is directly connected to the reduction in crime. There is, of course, a close connection here to Yancey's analysis of a relatively comparable situation. [A recent volume that extends and concretizes the ideas presented in *Defensible Space* is Newman's *Design Guidelines for Creating Defensible Space* (1975).]

■   The much publicized failures of St. Louis's Pruitt-Igoe housing proved that even well-intentioned "ideal" housing projects have serious flaws that encourage crime and vandalism. Many attempts are being made to understand, and thereby end, design of such problem-prone areas. One major study is now a book, *Defensible Space* by Oscar Newman, published this month by The Macmillan Company. An architect, Newman is director of the New York University Institute of Planning and Housing. The study, called The Project for the Security of Design of Urban Residential Areas, measures the effects of the physical layout on the residents' vulnerability to crime. Funding came, not from any government housing agency, but from the National Institute of Law Enforcement and Criminal Justice of the U.S. Department of Justice.

In the course of their research, Newman and his team visited many housing projects across the country, checking them against their "defensible space." Emphasis was placed on low-income housing, since greater income brings with it the possibility of added security measures. The most comprehensive source of data was the computerized records of New York City Housing Authority; its files note every occurrence of crime or vandalism, including complaint, location, time, persons involved and apprehension rate. Such a wealth of statistics, gathered for all projects under the nation's largest housing authority (150,000 units in five boroughs), coupled with the diverse nature of the locations, sites, populations and configurations of projects made that source invaluable.

Crime and vandalism rates have soared with the increased housing developments of large cities. The study and Newman's book attempt to make clear observations of the projects' physical characteristics that might encourage criminal activity. In oversimplified terms, the problem is getting a person to and from his or her living quarters without the fear (or occurrence) of crime or harassment. This includes the resident's safety and sense of well-being on project grounds and in lobbies, elevators, stairs, corridors and apartments. All of these areas, short of the actual living unit, have been covered in Newman's book. A few sacred cows, prized by some architects, planners, sociologists, housing officials and builders, have been dispatched along the way.

One widely accepted tenet is that large, shared open areas around project buildings are desirable. On the assumption that every resident could use these areas for recreation and leisure, open space requirements often have been met by building higher and assembling superblocks. The automobile, seen as an anathema, has been banished from the inner space and through roads removed. Since main building entrances are often designed to face away from perimeter streets and into the shared space, their use requires a circuitous route from the street, parking or public transportation. This, and the absence of general traffic, makes the center of the project the most feared part of the grounds. Even at its busiest, anonymity makes it a no-man's-land in large projects. It is avoided at night because it provides opportunities for criminal violence without observation. The same lack of possible surveillance, either formal or casual, carries similar implications for entrance lobbies, and from there to elevators and corridors.

Most public housing allows no amenities, and hold-the-line budgets have no room in the ledger book for fear or its causes. Land-use economics produces more and more high-rise housing. Long double-loaded corridors dictated by elevator grouping economics, combined with fire stair requirements, often provide a criminal with multiple escape routes.

The goal of building more units has overpowered scrutiny of the means. More units mean less recognition of strangers by residents, and less involvement. From less involvement comes less feeling of control over any part of the project outside the individual's apartment, and fewer attempts to cope.

Newman also notes a very definite negative identity attached to public housing. By their very design, most projects reinforce feelings of self-deprecation in their residents, and express a form of helpless isolation. This stigma is a flag that invites exploitation by others, continuing the occupants' downward interest spiral.

Still another self-perpetuating trouble source is the normal criteria for site selection. Often relegated to the most undesirable land by economic and sociopolitical pressures, projects cannot even begin existence without absorbing adjacent ills. Surrounded by high crime areas, the best aspirations falter.

Newman defines the goal of defensible space concepts as design that "returns to the productive use of residents the public areas beyond the doors of individual apartments: the hallways, lobbies, grounds, and surrounding streets — areas which are now beyond the control of inhabitants." He lists four elements of physical design that contribute, separately or together, to the creation of secure environments.

1   Territorial definition of space in developments reflecting the areas of influence of the inhabitants. This works by subdividing the residential environment into zones toward which adjacent residents easily adopt proprietary attitudes.

2   Positioning apartment windows to allow residents to naturally survey the exterior and interior public areas of their living environment.

3   Adopting building forms and idioms that avoid the stigma of peculiarity which allow others to perceive the vulnerability and isolation of the inhabitants.

4   Enhancing safety by locating residential developments in functionally sympathetic urban areas immediately adjacent to activities that do not provide continued threat.

Of the four mentioned elements, some can be incorporated in existing developments through carefully designed modifications. Others, such as location and siting, might be impossible to correct, but all, Newman feels, should play major roles in new project planning.

"Defensible space," he writes, "can be made to operate in an evolving hierarchy from level to level in the collective human habitat — to extend from apartment to street. It is a technique applicable to low-density rowhouse groupings as well as to developments composed of high-rise apartment buildings. The small cluster of apartments at each floor of a multistory building is the first level beyond the apartment unit where occupants can be made to extend the realm of their homes and responsibilities. The second level is the common entry and circulation paths within their buildings. The third level is the clustering of buildings which define a project's grounds and its entry. The final level in the hierarchy occurs when the housing development stakes its claim on the urban streets surrounding the housing development."

TERRITORIALITY

Newman readily acknowledges that territoriality, as a basis for a new rationalism in housing design, has been recognized by the work of Jane Jacobs and Elizabeth Wood, among others. Historically, it has been most clearly stated by the single-family house, with explicit or implied buffers and boundaries. Within those boundaries, a very strong sense of ownership and involvement exists. Any stranger would be expected to justify his presence there, and the resident readily adopts maintenance responsibilities.

To the apartment dweller, however, limits of influence are often defined by the apartment door. Corridors shared by many units are felt to be public spaces not controlled by anyone. Newman cites evidence that increasing the number of units per hallway to that usually found in high-rise, double-loaded corridor schemes eliminates almost all territoriality. Because of the inability to distinguish a potential intruder from a neighbor's expected visitor, no challenge of his presence occurs. This effect, multiplied by a number of floors, makes elevators and lobby areas increasingly public. In simple terms, then, reducing the number of people sharing a given access space increases the chance of spotting suspicious visitors, as well as increasing the pride of collective maintenance.

Number is very important in almost every consideration for defensible space, Newman emphasizes: "At various scales of subdivision — from number of apartments per hallway, apartment units per building, and number of buildings per project — there appears to be a rule which says that the lower the number, the better." Walkup buildings can easily and economically be subdivided, with each stair serving a limited number of units. Elevator buildings are more difficult; grouping elevators provides the tenants with shorter waiting times but, at a sacrifice in waiting time, elevators can be separated to serve fewer units per floor. As pointed out throughout the study, high-rise elevatored housing often has the least defensible space potential.

The principle of territoriality extends to the lobby and grounds. Again, subdividing the building's occupants can have its effect, since the fewer the people who share an entrance, the greater their protective attitude about it. If the entrance grounds are also treated in a manner indicating that they lead to a nonpublic area, so much the better. Such indicators could be earth mounding, a few steps, symbolic or actual gateways, a change of walkway material or texture, or any device which indicates that, past that point, any ambiguous activity might be questioned. Newman cites examples of increased territoriality in projects with such semipublic differentiation, as shown by increased resident use for sitting and talking. This and other aspects of territoriality are reinforced by building configurations that define areas that might be adopted as extensions of proprietary spaces.

NATURAL SURVEILLANCE

Another factor in creating defensible space that can work alone but is best reinforced by territoriality is that of surveillance. The knowledge, by both resident and intruder, that constant observation is possible, can allay fears and deter crime. If windows, doors and plan configurations make it possible to monitor activities outside the unit, both the inside and the outside spaces provide a greater feeling of security. Further, Newman notes, "This may have some self-fulfilling attributes in that residents, feeling that an area is secure, will make more frequent use of it and so further improve its security by providing the safety which comes with intensive use. However, experience has shown that the ability to observe criminal activity will not, by itself, impel the observer to respond with aid to the person or property being victimized."

The decision to act, he explains, will also depend on the presence of the following conditions: the extent to which the observer has a developed sense of his personal and proprietary rights and is accustomed to defending them; the extent to which the activity observed is understood to be occurring in an area within the sphere of influence of the observer; identification of the observed behavior as being abnormal to the area in which it occurs and therefore warranting response; the observer's identification with either the victim or the property being vandalized or stolen; the extent to which the observer feels he can effectively alter (by personal or collective response) the course of events being observed.

Surveillance should not be seen as a panacea, Newman warns, as it still works best coupled with territorial subdivision. If there is no feeling of *effectiveness,* mere observation cannot be relied on for total crime prevention. Even so, "most crime in housing occurs in the visually deprived semipublic interiors of buildings: the lobbies, halls, elevators and fire stairs," he says. He has found that, by providing the means of surveying these areas, a design can go a long way toward decreasing anxiety and making a project less palatable to criminals.

Lobby surveillance, as noted earlier, is severely hampered when main entrances are in obscure locations, when elevators and mailboxes are tucked around a corner in a blind spot, or both. A related lack of security on adjacent streets has been found, since observation works both ways. Common planning of the large central open areas advocates interrupting paths and walks by curves or angles. At points of curvature or intersection, it is common to plant shrubs or trees which, Newman points out, provide natural hiding places for criminals. Each of these potential trouble spots gives the resident little or no chance to anticipate what lies ahead of him.

IMAGE AND MILIEU   Problems of the stigma attached to public housing are some of the most difficult, due to a variety of less tangible, or at least less talked about, causal relationships. It is customary that American government-sponsored housing projects, says Newman, "for a variety of reasons seldom articulated, are designed so that they stand out and are recognized as distinctively different residential complexes. It is our contention that this differentiation serves in a negative way to single out the project and its inhabitants as easy *hits*. The idiosyncratic image of publicly assisted housing, coupled with other design features and the social characteristics of the resident population, makes such housing a peculiarly vulnerable target of criminal activity." Closing through internal streets serves to increase that vulnerability.

One facet of the negative image is the distinctiveness of building height, project size, materials and amenities. Because of their height and number, most of the buildings are extremely visible. Exterior materials are often mean and devoid of any saving touches of quality. Balconies or other amenities are out of the question. Newman does not imply that public housing is built cheaply. "In fact," he points out, "the cost per square foot of public housing at times equals the cost per square foot of luxury high rise housing. Public housing, built by a housing authority, is usually built extremely carefully, with good attention to detail and meticulously supervised construction." Still, the distinction often remains clearly expressed.

Another recognizable shortcoming of public housing is the institutional, vandal-proofed interior treatment. In Newman's view,

> This attitude toward interior finishes and furnishings creates an institutional atmosphere, not unlike that achieved in our worst hospitals and prisons. Even though the materials are in fact stronger and more resistant to wear, tenants seem to go out of their way to test their resistance capacities. Instead of being provided with an environment in which they can take pride and might desire to keep up, they are provided with one that begs them to test their ability in tearing it down. In the long run, even the institutional wall tiles and vandal-resistant radiators at Pruitt-Igoe met their match.

Signs of the effect that these depressing surroundings have on residents cannot be ignored, says Newman.

Our interviews with tenants have led us to the unmistakable conclusion that living units are assessed by tenants not only on the basis of size and available amenities, but on the basis of the lifestyle they symbolize and purport to offer. Building prototypes, from rowhousing to high rise, symbolize various forms of class status. The small, two-story rowhouse unit totaling 1200 sq ft, with a couple of hundred feet taken away by an interior staircase, is universally held by tenants to be more desirable than the 1000-sq-ft apartment in an elevator building, equipped with more modern conveniences. As with most of American society, low-income groups aspire to the lifestyle symbolized by this housing prototype and by the suburban bungalow. They view the rowhouse as more closely resembling the individual family house than the apartment within a communal building. A piece of ground adjacent to a unit, provided for the exclusive use of a family, is cherished and defended, regardless of how small.

By gentlemen's agreement, public housing must never approach the luxurious in appearance, even though it may cost more per sq ft. It must retain an institutional image. Unfortunately, this practice not only "puts the poor in their place," but brings their vulnerability to the attention of others. Parallel to this, and much more devastating, is the effect of the institutional image as perceived by the project residents themselves. Unable to camouflage their identities and adopt the attitudes of private apartment dwellers, they sometimes overreact and treat their dwellings as prisoners treat the penal institution in which they are housed. They show no concern for assisting in the care, upkeep and maintenance of the buildings, no inclination toward the decoration of their apartment units with paint or curtains.

Newman goes on to quote Lee Rainwater (in a 1966 *AIP Journal* article, "Fear and the House-as-Haven in the Lower Class"):

Finally, the consequences for conceptions of the moral order of one's world, of one's self, and of others, are very great. Although lower class people may not adhere in action to many middle class values about neatness, cleanliness, order and proper decorum, it is apparent that they are often aware of their deviance, wishing that their world could be a nicer place, physically and socially. The presence of nonhuman threats conveys in devastating terms a sense that they live in an immoral and uncontrolled world. The physical evidence of trash, poor plumbing and the stink that goes with it, rats and other vermin, deepens their feeling of being moral outcasts. Their physical world is telling them that they are inferior and bad just as effectively perhaps as do their human interactions.

Newman's conclusion: "A resident who has resigned himself to not caring about the conditions of his immediate surroundings — who has come to accept his ineffectualness in modifying his condition — is not about to intercede, even in his own behalf, when he becomes the victim of a criminal."

Juxtaposition with influences outside or at the periphery of the project grounds may have various effects. Public streets around a project are almost universally identified by residents as safer than interior project paths and walks. Relationships between projects and commercial, park or school facilities need careful weighing, Newman feels. It is necessary to evaluate the adjacent activity in terms of its nature, intended users, its identification with area residents, periods of activity and the frequency of the presence of concerned authorities. Proponents of the theory that commercial development adds safety through activity and numbers may or may not be right, depending on these variables. If store owners and staff add security by concerned surveillance, for instance, the entire area may benefit, at least during business hours. Its effectiveness, however, should still be checked by the other principles to ascertain that inactive periods do not produce detrimental effects. New York City Housing Authority Police list higher crime rates for projects near commercial streets.

If parks meet the discussed qualifications of surveillance, and become identified as part of a project's territorial influence, they can be an asset. The opposite can be true, Newman finds, if its park spaces are ambiguous or too openly public. The potential for becoming an unobserved hangout, or a collecting area for alcoholics or drug traffic is too great. Most surveyed projects that were located next to activities such as high schools, junior colleges, game rooms or hamburger joint hangouts had problems . In some New York, Philadelphia and Cleveland projects bordering high schools, for example, students make heavy use of the enclosed fire stairs for selling and taking drugs. In such cases, Newman has found correspondingly high incidence of harassment, burglary and loitering in halls and lobbies of the nearest units.

DESIGN UNDERSTANDING

Newman expects architects and planners to have difficulty with two categories of the defensible space mechanisms: the design image in housing environments and juxtaposition of housing with other activities in the urban setting. Of the architect, then of the planner, he says,

> If his client is rich and well educated, his tastes may be similar to those of the architect. But if the client comes from a low- or middle-income background, it is most likely that he will aspire to the tastes of the class immediately above him, and probably those in vogue ten and twenty years ago.
>
> Architects are chagrined and sometimes express moral indignation when they find their low-income clients rejecting a housing project designed in the most current professional idiom, asking instead for something that looks quaintly middle class. But this middle-class look is the client's image of arrival — his symbol of status. The well-meaning architect who worked hard at designing buildings, which he knows will please his peers and receive recognition in the professional journals, for some incomprehensible reason finds himself accused of giving the poor "funny houses."
>
> In a similar way, for decades after the original utopian physical

planners first set down rules for segregating different activities and functions in designing new cities, urban designers have been fighting for the re-integration of shopping and institutional facilities with housing. Now with this fight almost won, it appears that someone else is again advocating their segregation. The facts however cannot be easily dismissed. The matter is one of scale: at which level is the segregation to occur? It is possible within the frames of our guidelines to juxtapose schools and shops with housing so as to create the desired walking distance milieu, while at the same time providing for the territorially intact residential enclave.

SOME OBSERVATIONS

Any attempt to summarize the points covered in Newman's book would be unfair to the book, its author and the study team. Nevertheless, a few passages from chapter 8 of Defensible Space *are included below as a brief recap:*

Paradoxically, at a time when we are all just learning to open up — to question the value of the individual pursuit of wealth at the expense of society — the idea of a defensible space environment may be interpreted by some as a methodology for restriction and closing down. At a time when the Western world seems to have approached acceptance of the notion of an open society with accompanying open institutions, it is strange to find one of its proponents advocating what may appear as a retrenchment tactic. It is sad to have to conclude that the free and fertile soil of the liberalized imagination may also have nurtured the seeds of its own restriction. The challenge to the establishment's rights, methods and motives is being used by elements in our society who, unlike the questioning liberal, have no constructive objectives to achieve — they are content simply with "ripping-off" who and what they can.

It is strange, then, to find the enlightened middle class fleeing to the ghettos of suburbia, fleeing from the liberalized atmosphere it has worked at creating in the cities; stranger still to observe their flight and apparent content with leaving behind an immobile population far more vulnerable to the ravages of criminals, addicts and abusive agents of authority. For the middle class, criminal assault is a survivable nuisance. For the poor and working class, it may mean a total wipe-out: a life's work gone; a psychological disaster. For our low-income population, security in their residential environment — security from the natural elements, from criminals, and from authority — is the first essential step to liberation.

We are concerned that some might read into our work the implication that architectural design can have a direct causal effect on social interactions. Architecture operates more in the area of "influence" than control. It can create a setting conducive to realizing the potential of mutual concern. It does not and cannot manipulate people toward these feelings, but rather allows mutually benefiting attitudes to surface. We are advocating a program for the restructuring of residential developments in our cities to facilitate their control by the people who inhabit them.

The past few years have witnessed efforts by the Federal Government, in partnership with large corporations, to apply large-scale technological and financial methods to the mass production of housing

Van Dyke Houses. The expansive central grounds area is underdeveloped for productive use. High-rise buildings are isolated from one another, and because of their positioning serve no effective surveillance function in monitoring activity on project grounds.

Courtesy of Oscar Newman

(as in Project Breakthrough). One danger is all too clear: in our concern for coming to grips with the problem of providing mass housing, we may be moving into a period where technological and economic acumen in the provision and construction of buildings have become ends in themselves. A parallel empirical and theoretical breakthrough is necessary in defining the social and psychological constraints with which these new forms will have to reckon. It is our hope that this initial study will serve as the first of many steps in this direction.

TWO ON A STREET   Graphic evidence of the effects of defensible space may be seen in a comparison of the Brownsville (1947) and Van Dyke (1955) projects in New York City. Paired for Newman's study because of their similar project size and population composition, the two Brooklyn projects are located across the street from each other. Both house approximately 6000 persons, and have exactly the same density: 288 persons per acre. Crime and vandalism are common to both, but there the similarities end.

The Brownsville buildings are three to six stories high and cover 23 percent of the available land, while Van Dyke buildings are a mix of three-story and fourteen-story buildings covering 16.6 percent of the site. Of the total Van Dyke population, 76 percent occupy the high-rise slabs.

Brownsville Houses – Sketch of a typical entry. Exterior areas are under possible observation from apartments and the street, providing security and increasing resident use and responsibility.
Courtesy of Oscar Newman

Van Dyke lacks many defensible space characteristics found in Brownsville Houses. Site and building scale differences, for instance, make Van Dyke's monolithic appearance even more forbidding. Large open spaces separate the buildings, while at Brownsville, small manageable zones are defined by building placement and relationships. The open center of Van Dyke, separated from and unrelated to the buildings, is a sharp contrast to the small, human-scale areas adopted and monitored by Brownsville residents.

Entrance to all buildings at Van Dyke is from the project interior, allowing no observation from the street. Small doors, with undifferentiated site conditions, each serve 112 to 136 families. Most of the Brownsville entrances are just off public streets, in semidefined areas serving the nine to thirteen families using each door. Unlike Van Dyke, the Brownsville entry space is used by the families as an extension of their territory.

Building interior arrangements of the two projects produce very different attitudes in both occupants and police charged with their protection. Van Dyke's double-loaded corridors, serving eight families per floor, are decidedly public spaces which are not considered safe as children's play areas. Outside the apartment, therefore, no areas of extended territoriality exist, and there is very little communication between families, even on the same floor. At Brownsville, six families occupy a floor, and are grouped into two sets of three units around a common vestibule. Skip-stop elevators and an open central stair assure vertical communication, and parents allow children to play in the halls and stairs. By the simple device of leaving apartment doors ajar (not advisable at Van Dyke), parents keep an auditory "watch."

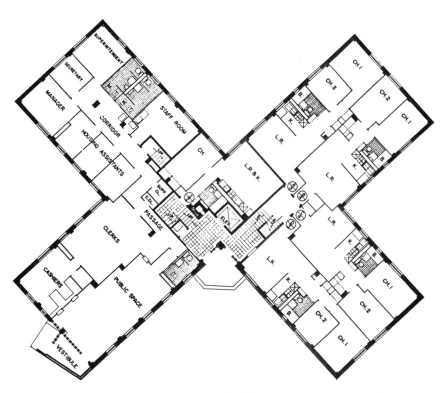

Brownsville Houses. Six-story elevator buildings have an exposed staircase allowing for vertical communication. Six units on a floor are divided into two sections by a door. Each grouping of three units shares a common vestibule and staircase. Apartment doors are frequently left open, children play in halls near apartments, and loud noises are responded to immediately.

Courtesy of Oscar Newman

Attitudes held by and about the police show distinct differences in the two projects. Due to the permissive apathy characteristic of Van Dyke's interior and exterior circulation routes, an officer patrolling in that project meets with little or no cooperation. Because of the impossibility of covering all of the areas conducive to crime, the number of open escape routes and the lack of residents' concern, the police soon adopt a callous attitude. The police and the residents share an acute pessimism about police effectiveness at Van Dyke. Newman's study shows, however, that the same police and the Brownsville tenants have more optimistic expectations, and a more friendly relationship. Reinforced by concerned residents, police are more readily summoned and perform their duties more effectively.

Results of these differences show up in the housing authority statistics: Van Dyke has had 66 percent more total crime incidents, over 2½ times as many robberies (264 percent), 60 percent more

Comparison of crime incidents

Crime incidents	Van Dyke	Brownsville
Total incidents	1189	790
Total felonies, misdemeanors and offenses	432	264
Number of robberies	92	24
Number of malicious mischief	52	28

Source: New York City Housing Authority Police Records, 1968.

Comparison of maintenance

Maintenance	Van Dyke (constructed 1955)	Brownsville (constructed 1947)
Number of maintenance jobs of any sort (work tickets) 4/70	3301	2376
Number of maintenance jobs, excluding glass repair	2643	1651
Number of nonglass jobs per unit	1.47	1.16
Number of full-time maintenance staff	9	7
Number of elevator breakdowns per month	280	110

Source: New York City Housing Authority Project Managers' Bookkeeping records.

Comparison of physical design and population density

Physical measure	Van Dyke	Brownsville
Total size	22.35 acres	19.16 acres
Number of buildings	23	27
Building height	13–14 story 9–3 story	6 story with some 3 story wings
Coverage	16.6	23.0
Floor area ratio	1.49	1.39
Average number of rooms per apartment	4.62	4.69
Density	288 persons/acre	287 persons/acre
Year completed	1955 (one building added in 1964)	1947

Source: New York City Housing Authority Project Physical Design Statistics.

felonies, misdemeanors and offenses, and 72 percent more repair maintenance work than Brownsville.

Newman does not yet claim that all data provide absolute proof of the effect of physical design on crime and vandalism. Still, he notes,

> In summary, it seems unmistakable that physical design plays a very significant role in crime rate. It should also be kept in mind that the defensible space qualities inherent in the Brownsville design are there, for the most part, by accident. From a critical, defensible space viewpoint, Brownsville is far from perfect. The comparison of the crime and vandalism rates in the two projects was made using gross crime data on both projects. Twenty-three percent of the apartments at Van Dyke consist of three-story walkup buildings serving a small number of families. It is likely that comparative data on crime rates in the low building versus the towers at Van Dyke would reveal significant differences. This would make the comparison of crime rates between Van Dyke and Brownsville even more startling. ∎

Hans Kummer
Spacing Mechanisms in Social Behavior*

Control of the behavior of the members of one's group can be quite different from the control exerted outside the group. Kummer looks at these two aspects of social control in the context of evolution. Particularly intriguing is his analysis of the relatively elaborate pattern of intragroup control. He sees the distance between members of a group as the outcome of two conflicting factors, one tendency to hold the group together and the other tendency to keep its members apart. Such competing influences, while facilitating subtle adjustments, often yield a rather uneasy equilibrium that is not lacking in tension.

∎   This symposium has been stimulated by the theory that human social behavior has a biological basis inherited from nonhuman ancestors. The theory implies that cultural developments of social behavior

*Excerpted from Hans Kummer "Spacing mechanisms in social behavior" in J. F. Eisenberg and W. S. Dillon (Eds.) *Man and Beast: Comparative Social Behavior*. Washington, D.C.: The Smithsonian Institution Press. 1971. Pages 230–233. Reprinted by permission.

are possible only within the limits set by our behavioral heritage. If this is true, research on these limits of our behavioral adaptability is of first-rate importance. In my view these limits exist beyond any reasonable doubt; but where exactly are they?

Some human ways of handling social space resemble common animals techniques. We may experience attraction and, at short distance, repulsion. It has been shown for at least one sample (Sommer, 1959) that the preferred distances among women may be smaller than those among men. We feel an urge to interpret very close distances by communicating our intentions. In a crowd we tend to act and feel like the crowd. We may seek privacy behind visual screens; in addition, we reduce social stimulation by clothing and deodorants (Hall congratulates man for being a microsmat). Nations defend "territories." Individuals may give an angry look to intruders on their premises. Approaching the center of another person's private area reduces our self-confidence. An executive therefore meets an esteemed visitor at the door of his office, but he awaits at his desk a subordinate whom he wishes to reduce in status. Armies and business organizations seem to operate by a formalized dominance. Since these groups are too large to allow personal experience of all individual ranks, status is marked by brass on shoulders and by titles on office doors. Enemies may be as necessary to the cohesion of some human groups as they are to some animal groups. The human inhibitions that secure the integrity of territorial property and social ties resemble those found in primates, although for some reason human inhibitions must often be reinforced by ancestral spirits or courts. Relative position in space is used on the battlefield and to separate incompatible dinner guests. The human male, like other primate males, is more apt to leave the group, to wander, and to explore than the human female.

Examples of such similarities between man and animals (*some* animals, that is) could be amplified almost *ad libitum*. Many of them will not withstand scrutiny, but in their totality they make it more probable that we inherited much of our spatial behavior from prehuman ancestors than that we invented the same patterns all over again on the cultural level. Assuming for the moment that this is so, we shall be most interested, in relation to present human problems, in the flexibility of such behavior, that is, in the limits within which it may safely be altered *beyond* the range of known cultural variation.

The study of primate behavior offers some hopes that spacing behavior may be relatively open to environmental influence. Aggressive spacing, territoriality, and closed groups are not engrained, pervading attributes of the primate order. They appear here and there in varying intensity, often with little relationship to taxonomic positions. They seem to be common primate potentials which, however, appear and disappear relatively fast in evolution. Man's closest relatives for instance, the great apes, are relatively unaggressive; they do not defend territories, and their groups are open to strangers. We do not know whether this resembles our own ancestral condition. If it does, we have, in a relatively short period, swung toward the opposite (Reynolds, 1966) approaching the style of macaques and baboons.

More relevant to man's problems is the flexibility observed within the same species. The vervet monkey is territorial in some areas but not in others (Gartlan and Brain, 1968). Gibbons, naturally organized in territorial pairs, are not territorial in small cages but breed there nevertheless. One of our recent field experiments has demonstrated a high flexibility of spacing behavior in baboons. Transferred into a group of anubis baboons, a hamadryas female reverts her spacing behavior. After half an hour she no longer approaches an attacking male but flees like an anubis female. The reverse experiment is yet more instructive; an anubis female in a hamadryas troop learns, within one hour, to approach the male who attacks her although it is almost certain that none of her ancestors behaved this way. But the really interesting lesson of this experiment is that most anubis females, after learning the new behavior to perfection, suddenly escaped the herding male and left the troop for good. Learning was not enough; these females had gone beyond some limit of their behavioral adaptability. They provide a model case of what I meant by the "limits within which behavior can be *safely* altered."

CONCLUSIONS

Let me conclude by characterizing the evolutionary stage of spacing mechanisms at which primates leave off and man, perhaps, takes over. The use of ecological resources requires animals to space-out, and aggression provides the principal means to do so. In primates, selective pressures introduced the life in permanent groups. The spacing problem thus took two different forms: Groups still had to keep apart for ecological reasons, but group members had to remain together. Nearly all subsequent refinements in the handling of social space were designed for intragroup use, as checks on the factors that tend to disperse. In comparison, intergroup relations could safely be left at an archaic state, with territorial behavior as the only major elaboration. Intergroup relations in man still show archaic traits. Social behavior in foreign politics certainly falls short of the standards of the average citizen.

In considering spatial behavior in modern man we must keep in mind that space and distance in themselves are socially meaningless. What matters is the behavioral potential of a spatial arrangement. Being far apart means having time to respond, being close means having to respond at short notice. Being between two other animals prevents their interaction. These implications of a spatial situation entirely depend on two factors: the participants' speed of movement and the range of their means of communication. Both factors remain constant in animal societies and their importance is easily overlooked. But both speed and the range of communication undergo drastic changes in our own species. A total application of electrical technology would make our arrangement in space socially irrelevant, except at the one-to-ten-meter level of a cocktail party. This development would by itself close the chapter of spacing behavior in technical man, were it not for another behavioral heritage. Behavior is easily redirected and transferred to new objects and contexts. Territorial tendencies, for example, can reemerge in the handling of information. Crowding and privacy are now possible without any connection to meters and miles, but our responses to them remain. Our attention should follow the old mechanisms into the new media. ■

Leon A. Pastalan
Privacy as an Expression of Human Territoriality*

Here territory is analyzed at the level of the individual. Note the pervasive role of information flow in defining different aspects of privacy. An important factor in information flow is the presence of other people. There is a group-imposed requirement that one behave predictably; what one does, in other words, should not add to the information load. Thus, a major advantage of privacy is the relief from monitoring one's own behavior, from behaving the way others expect one to.

■ The need to test directly the concept of human territoriality at this juncture of its development without excessively drawing on the experiences of nonhuman territorial studies seems imperative.

There have been at least two historical examples of social science disciplines being unduly influenced by data taken from the physical sciences and enthusiastically applied to the human condition. One

*From L. A. Pastalan "Privacy as an expression of human territoriality" in L. A. Pastalan and D. H. Carson (Eds.) *Spatial behavior of older people*. Institute of Gerontology, University of Michigan-Wayne State University. 1970. Pages 88–93; 95–97. Reprinted by permission.

needs only to recall the difficulties engendered when the theory of uni-linear evolution dominated the thinking of leading anthropologists. The influence of plant and animal ecology on urban sociology in the 1920s and 1930s is another example of the conceptual mischief that can be done when the findings of one science are applied in analogous terms to that of another. Urban sociology, for instance, oriented itself to the geophysical aspects of the city rather than to its social life. Too much of the ecological study of the city was devoted to the establishment of the properties of various zones — natural areas, habitats, and the like — and too little attention was paid to the life that produced these properties. Exhaustive studies were made of the scene of the crime but the criminal was largely ignored. The ecological theory of the city was, in part, betrayed by the premature demand to make the science immediately autonomous, exact, and mature by utilizing propositions tested by other sciences in entirely different contexts.

The urgency to avoid these same kinds of pitfalls has led to the call for initiating a systematic study of human territoriality in terms of establishing its own conceptual framework. Because of its unique human behavioral states, privacy may constitute a basic form of human territoriality and thus should be examined for its rich potential of generating empirical and theoretical data.

Privacy may be defined as the right of the individual to decide what information about himself should be communicated to others and under what conditions (Westin, 1967). Despite cultural and subcultural differences found in the elaboration and satisfaction of privacy needs, Westin (1967) has established four basic states of privacy along with their related functions: solitude, intimacy, anonymity, and reserve.

Solitude as a state of privacy is where an individual is separated from the group and freed from the observation of other persons. He may be subjected to jarring physical stimuli, such as noise, odors, and vibrations. His peace of mind may continue to be disturbed by physical sensations of heat, cold, itching, and pain. He may believe that he is being observed by God or that Big Brother is secretly watching. Solitude is the most complete state of visual privacy that individuals can achieve.

In the second state of privacy, *intimacy,* the individual is acting as part of a small unit that claims and is allowed to exercise corporate seclusion so that it may achieve a close, relaxed, and frank relationship between two or more individuals. Typical units of intimacy are husband and wife, the family, a friendship circle, or a work clique. Whether close contact brings relaxed relations or abrasive hostility depends on the personal interaction of the members, but without intimacy, a basic need of human contact would not be met. Again, such interaction is made possible through controlling visual and other types of sensory informational flow through the use of barriers, sound deadening materials and other assorted environmental props.

The third state of privacy, *anonymity,* occurs when the individual is in public places or performing public acts but still seeks, and finds, freedom from identification and surveillance. He may be riding a subway, attending a ball game, or walking the streets; he is among people and knows that he is being observed. But unless he is a well-known celebrity, he does not expect to be personally identified and held to the full rules of behavior and role that would operate if he were known to those observing him. In this state, the individual is able to merge into the "situational landscape." Knowledge or fear that one is under official observation in public places destroys the sense of relaxation and freedom that men seek in open spaces and public arenas.

Reserve, the fourth and most subtle state of privacy, is the creation of a psychological barrier against unwanted intrusion. This occurs when the individual's need to limit communication about himself is protected by the willing discretion of those surrounding him. Most of our lives are spent not in solitude or anonymity but in situations of intimacy and in group settings where we are known to others. Even in the most intimate relations, communication of the self to others is always incomplete and is based on the need to hold back some part or parts of one's self as either too personal and sacred or too shameful and profane to express. This circumstance gives rise to what Simmel called "reciprocal reserve and indifference," the relation that creates a mental distance to protect the personality (Wulf, 1950). The manner in which individuals claim reserve and the extent to which it is respected or disregarded by others is at the heart of securing meaningful privacy.

The related functions of privacy can also be grouped into four headings, (Westin, 1967) personal autonomy, emotional release, self-evaluation, and limited and protected communication.

PERSONAL AUTONOMY

Our society professes a fundamental belief in the uniqueness of the individual, in his basic dignity and worth as a human being and in the need to maintain social processes that safeguard his sacred individuality (Shills, 1959). Psychologists and sociologists have linked the development and maintenance of this sense of individuality to the human need for autonomy — the desire to avoid being manipulated or dominated wholly by others. Autonomy is threatened by those who are not, for one reason or another, discretionary in their intrusions and do not recognize or choose to ignore the importance of privacy, or feel that the casual and uninvited help they may be rendering compensates for the violation. The elderly suffer more than most from this kind of intrusion.

The autonomy that privacy protects is also vital to the development and maintenance of individuality and consciousness of individual choice in life. Leontine Young (1966) has noted that without privacy there is no individuality. Who can know what he thinks and feels if he never has the opportunity to be alone with his thoughts and feelings. The individual's sense that it is he who decides when to "go public" is crucial to the idea of autonomy.

EMOTIONAL RELEASE

Life in society generates such tensions for the individual that both physical and psychological health demand periods of privacy for various types of emotional release. At one level, such relaxation is necessitated by the pressure of playing roles. Goffman (1959) has noted that individuals are like actors on the dramatic stage, where roles can be sustained only for reasonable periods of time and no individual can play indefinitely, without relief, the variety of roles that life demands. There have to be moments "off stage" when the individual can be himself — e.g., tender, angry, irritable, lustful, or whatever. Such moments may come in the solitude of a locked private study; in the intimacy of family, or peers; in the anonymity of park or street; or in a state of reserve while in a group. Privacy in this aspect gives individuals a chance to lay their marks aside for rest. To be always "on," as Goffman says, would destroy the human organism.

Still another aspect of release through privacy arises in the management of bodily functions. Alexander Kira (1967) points out that the bathroom is often the only room in the house offering security from intrusion. Although poverty, for instance, may produce crowded conditions which tend to deny privacy for bodily functions for certain groups in our society, it is not accidental that surveillance of such functions by outsiders is practiced with social approval only in total institutions such as jails, hospitals, monasteries, and the like. (Westin, 1967)

Finally, emotional release through privacy plays an important part in individual life at times of loss, shock, or sorrow.

SELF-EVALUATION

Every individual needs to integrate his experiences into a meaningful pattern and to exert his individuality on events. To carry on such self-evaluation, privacy is essential. At the intellectual level, individuals need to process the information that is constantly bombarding them, information that cannot be processed while they are still on the go.

Privacy serves not only a processing but a planning need by providing a time to anticipate, to recast, and to originate. Studies of creativity show that it is in reflective solitude or even "day-dreaming" during moments of reserve that most creative nonverbal thought takes place.

A further contribution of privacy to self-evaluation is its role in the proper timing of the decision to move from private reflection or intimate conversation to a more general publication of acts and thoughts.

LIMITED AND PROTECTED COMMUNICATION

Privacy for limited and protected communication has two general aspects. First, it provides the individual with opportunities he needs for sharing confidences and intimacies with those he trusts — spouse, family members, personal friends, and close associates at work. In its second general aspect, privacy through limited communication serves to set necessary boundaries of mental distance in interpersonal situations ranging from the most intimate to the most formal and public.

Psychological distance is used in crowded settings to provide privacy for the participants of group and public encounters. For example, withdrawal into privacy is expressed by facial expressions, bodily gestures, and by verbal conventions such as changing the subject. It is also exhibited through personal devices which exclude others present, such as private words, jokes, winks, and grimaces (Bates, 1964).

In work situations, mental distance is necessary so that the relations of superior and subordinate do not slip into an intimacy which would create a lack of respect and an impediment to work efficiency. Thus, physical arrangements shield superiors from constant observation by subordinates, and social etiquette forbids conversations or off-duty contacts that are "too close" for the work relationship. Similar distance is observed in relations between professor and student, parent and child, minister and communicant, and many others.

Viewing the behavioral states and functions of privacy within the foregoing framework, it seems plausible to posit that privacy is a distinctly human manisfestation of territoriality. Further credence is given to this proposition when viewed in terms of the Altman definition of human territoriality. Altman states that human territoriality encompasses temporally durable, preventive, and reactive behaviors including perceptions, use and defense of places, people, objects, and ideas, by means of verbal, self-marker, and environmental prop behaviors in response to the actual or implied presence of others and in response to properties of the environment, and is geared to satisfying certain primary and secondary motivational states of individuals and groups (Altman, 1968).

Let us pursue this idea by attempting to link the properties of the definition to the behavioral states of privacy in some sort of systematic fashion. Altman asserts that there are four distinct categories included in the definition: (1) behavior forms; (2) situational contexts; (3) antecedent factors; and (4) organismic factors. It will be recalled that

TABLE 1   Privacy states and definitional properties of territoriality

	Territoriality			
Privacy	Behavior Form	Situational Context	Antecedent Factors	Organismic Factors
Solitude	Physical withdrawal from view from primary and secondary associates as well as the public; verbal reports; full range of occupancy and defense responses	Environmental props to control informational flow, location; single person	Pressures of multiple role playing, role incompatibility; interpersonal incompatibility; defeat	Relief from visual observation; self-evaluation; to unmask and be oneself; to perform bodily functions
Intimacy	Physical seclusion from secondary associates and public; anticipatory preventive responses; full range of occupancy and defense responses	Environmental props to control informational flow location; small group	Role relations and interpersonal compatibility or incompatibility	Need for close, relaxed, frank relationships; egalitarian; sharing of confidences
Anonymity	Psychological and physical blending with the public; defense through self-markers and verbal reports	Informational flow is controlled through merging into the situational landscape; use of open space, mass numbers of people and objects	Role responsibilities demanding full adherence to expected behavior; anonymous relations	Need to escape personal identification and responsibility of full rules of behavior and role; anonymous sharing of confidences
Reserve	Psychological barrier against unwanted intrusion; defense through self-markers and verbal reports	Control of informational flow through self-restraint and willing discretion of associates	Reciprocal reserve and indifference; mental distance to protect the personality	Need to limit communication about the self

there are also four behavioral states of privacy: (1) solitude; (2) intimacy; (3) anonymity; and (4) reserve.

The relationships between privacy states and the definitional properties of territoriality can be seen in simple matrix form in table 1.

Conceptually, perhaps the most valuable aspects of viewing the behavior related to the states of privacy as a fundamental form of human territoriality is that it releases us from dealing with territoriality only in terms of occupation and defense responses. It also suggests the potential of using privacy as an organizing principle in working out linkages between territorially related behavior and general human behavior.

To emphasize this last point, it should be remembered that privacy is neither a self-sufficient state nor an end in itself. It is basically an instrument for achieving individual goals of self-realization. As such, it is only a part of the individual's or group's complex and shifting system of social needs, part of the way persons adjust their emotional mechanisms to the barrage of personal and social stimuli that are encountered environmentally. Individuals have needs for disclosure and companionship and group affiliation; at another moment, the intimacy of family or close friends; at another, the anonymity of the city street, or the movie; and at still other times, to be totally alone and unobserved. To be left in privacy when one wants companionship is as bad as the inability to have privacy when one wants it (Westin, 1967). ∎

From Research News, *1975, Vol. 26, Nos. 5/6, p. 10. Reprinted by permission of the Institute of Gerontology, The University of Michigan-Wayne State University.*

Drury R. Sherrod and
Sheldon Cohen
Density, Personal Control, and Design*

Here Sherrod and Cohen demonstrate the importance of control in ameliorating the stress of such adverse environmental properties as high density and low predictability. The cognitive perspective is central to their analysis: the way the person perceives or interprets the situation is the essential determinant of its influence.

■   High-density environments are often — but not always — uncontrollable environments. This distinction may be the key in understanding the circumstances under which density adversely affects behavior. In addition it suggests a number of design-related interventions that can increase the controllability and livability of environments.

High density determines the perceived controllability of environments in two ways. First, the close presence of others can restrict and interfere with the attainment of one's goals. Second, when high density involves the close presence of *strangers,* the environment is not only restricting but also unpredictable — a possible source of irritation or surprise — and thus potentially uncontrollable. Under other circumstances, high density may not be perceived as uncontrollable at all. For example, if goal attainment is not an important issue or if the others present are not strangers, people may experience no loss of control in high-density environments.

The distinction between the effects of density, on the one hand, versus those of control and predictability of environments, on the other, is helpful in clarifying the confusing results of crowding research. Studies of density by itself have found few effects on human behavior. In contrast, studies of uncontrollable environments have produced a variety of ill effects on human behavior. Thus, it may not be high density per se, but only uncontrollable high density which is responsible for the negative effects popularly associated with crowding and sometimes observed in research on human density. In a practical sense this could be a very fortunate finding. While high density is no

*Based on paper presented at Environmental Design Research Association Meeting, Vancouver, 1976. This paper will also appear in J. R. Aiello (Ed.) *Residential crowding and design.* New York: Plenum. Reprinted by permission.

doubt an unavoidable fact of life for most urban dwellers, controllability is a perceived relationship between self and environment. As a perceptual or cognitive phenomenon, controllability can be altered and fostered by a variety of cognitive, social, and environmental factors. As a result, the effects of "uncontrollable" density can be reduced without reducing density itself. The present paper is an attempt to distinguish between density and controllability in the research literature. In addition, we hope to show how controllability of environments can be increased by taking account of user needs at several stages in the design process.

RESEARCH ON HUMAN DENSITY

Research on the effects of human density is beginning to accumulate. Although differences in density manipulations, measures, and mediators make the findings difficult to compare, tentative conclusions are possible. One conclusion based on numerous correlational and experimental studies is that density by itself has fewer and smaller effects on human behavior than anyone expected (see Cohen, Glass, and Phillips, in press, for review). [Ed. Note: cf. McClelland's paper in chapter 7.] Overall, several studies — which primarily deal with families residing in high-density dwellings — have found no negative effects of density strong enough to register consistently on measures of crime, physical or mental health, and social disorganization.

Do these finding of well-controlled correlational studies suggest that density is unlikely to affect human behavior adversely in any context? We think not. When the focus of researchers shifts from general populations to specific subgroups low in environmental control, density effects do emerge. Also, laboratory studies suggest that high density does exert negative effects on behavior in certain situations and on certain kinds of tasks.

In contrast to the studies of residential density, research dealing with population subgroups low in environmental control has revealed pathological effects of internal density. Thus, Cohen et al. (in press) argue that the evidence for pathological effects of high density is largely limited to populations such as the young (Booth, 1975), the lower class (Mitchell, 1971), ship crews (Dean, Pugh, and Gunderson, 1975) and prisoners (D'Atri, 1975) — all groups with limited environmental control. Similar results have also been reported for college dormitory residents who were tripled in two-person rooms and presumably lacked control over their social interactions (Baum, Harpin, and Valins, 1974).

Recent laboratory research also suggests that the high density can have detrimental effects on human task performance, despite Freedman's (1975) well-publicized argument to the contrary. While several studies have found no effects of short term high density on *simple* task performance (Freedman, Klevansky, and Ehrlich, 1971; Sherrod, 1974; Worchel and Teddlie, 1976; Evans, 1976; Rodin, 1976), two recent studies have shown that density can adversely affect *complex* task performance. Evans (1975) found that subjects in a high-density laboratory setting performed less well on a dual information processing task than low-density subjects, and Paulus and his colleagues (Paulus, Annis, Seta, Schkade, and Matthews, 1976) demonstrated that high density interferes with human maze learning. In addition, several studies have found that high density produces negative aftereffects on a measure of frustration tolerance (Sherrod, 1974; Evans, 1975; Dooley, 1976). Thus, while it is clear that short-term high density does not affect simple task performance in the laboratory, high density does seem to affect complex task performance, to reduce post-crowding frustration tolerance, and to interfere with verbal problem solving when combined with personal space invasion.

COGNITIVE FACTORS IN HUMAN DENSITY

What do the above situations have in common that may account for the effects of high density? We believe that they are all situations where controllability is important. The laboratory studies provide a clear demonstration of our point. Strangers in a crowded laboratory may be perceived as unpredictable, and thus potentially uncontrollable. According to a recent theoretical paper by Cohen (in press), the unpredictability of others is likely to impede complex but not simple task performance. Cohen argues that unpredictable and uncontrollable environments require close monitoring so that individuals may protect themselves from potential threat or surprise. Such monitoring of the environment demands attentional capacity that would otherwise be available for high information processing needs, such as complex task performance. Thus, unpredictability may disrupt complex task performance but not affect performance on less demanding tasks. Similarly, strangers who are invading an individual's personal space also increase the unpredictability of an environment, perhaps more seriously than strangers merely in close proximity. Consequently, the unpredictability of personal space invasion may impede performance on a cognitively demanding task such as verbal problem solving.

Crowded environments also have a second effect, as we noted at the outset of this paper. Crowding not only increases unpredictability of environments but also restricts freedom and constrains behavior, in effect producing a sense of helplessness. According to Seligman's theory of learned helplessness (1975), uncontrollability diminishes motivation by setting up an expectancy that an individual's responses are independent of outcomes — in other words, that responses don't matter. As a result, organisms emit fewer responses, and this tendency can generalize to subsequent situations. Consequently, high density may create a sense of learned helplessness that could influence responses on postcrowding measures that are sensitive to motivational deficits, for example, a measure of frustration tolerance.

Each of the three performance situations in which high density has produced negative effects — i.e., complex task performance, personal space invasion, and postcrowding frustration tolerance — may therefore be interpreted as resulting from environmental unpredictability or uncontrollability rather than density per se. Two studies provide direct support for this interpretation. In the first, Rodin (1976) demonstrated that children from high-density environments performed in a laboratory setting as if they were "helpless."

In the second study, Sherrod (1974) showed that a perception of control can reduce the aftereffects of short-term laboratory crowding. In this study, subjects were exposed to either high or low density. Some of the high-density subjects were informed that they could leave the crowded room whenever they chose in order to work in another less crowded room. Although no subjects actually left the crowded room, subjects with perceived control over crowding performed better on postcrowding measures of frustration tolerance than subjects who had no control.

Indirect support for the assertion that perceived control can reduce the effects of crowding can be found in several other studies. Schopler and Walton (1974) found that Internals (people who generally feel in control of themselves and their environments) felt less crowded in a high-density setting than Externals (people who feel controlled by the environment). Similarly, Karlin, Epstein, and Aiello (1975) found that Internals were less influenced by group processes in a crowded environment than Externals. Also Baum, Harpin, and Valins (1975) found that members of cohesive groups felt less crowded in high-density dormitories than people who aren't members of cohesive groups. If we assume that cohesive groups allow for greater predictability and consequent controllability of one's environment, then this study fits in well with our perspective. Finally, Worchel and Teddlie (1976) found that when crowded people are distracted from attending to the close proximity of other persons by the presence of attractive wall posters, they experience the environment as less crowded and perform better on verbal puzzle-solving tasks. In this experiment, when subjects' attention was diverted from the presence of other people in the crowded environment, it is possible that subjects then felt less concerned about the issue of control than subjects whose attention was not distracted. Each of these studies, then, provides some indirect support for our perspective regarding human density and control.

EFFECTS OF PERSONAL CONTROL

Controllability also has independent effects on human behavior above and beyond the effects of density. The belief in one's ability to control the environment has been clearly shown to have a variety of important psychological effects. In their work on urban stress, Glass and Singer (1972) found that individuals who had some perception of control over loud noises, electric shock, or frustrating bureaucracies performed better on measures of frustration tolerance and attention to detail than did subjects who had no perception of control, even though none of the subjects with perceived control ever actually exercised their options and escaped the environmental stressors.

From another perspective, Seligman and his colleagues (cf., Seligman, 1975) have demonstrated that both animals and humans tend to give up in a free response situation if they have experienced prior uncontrollable aversive stimulation. Not only do such individuals tend to give up when their continued responses could actually bring about relief from stress, they even fail to learn when environmental contingencies have changed and their responses could finally be successful. In contrast, when individuals are exposed to prior escapable aversive stimulation, they easily learn that subsequent situations are also escapable and they quickly emit the necessary responses.

In still another approach to the control issue, de Charms (1968) has argued that uncontrollable situations cause individuals to see themselves as "Pawns" of the environment, while persons who feel in control of the environment come to see themselves as "Origins." A self-perception as an Origin or a Pawn affects one's general sense of competence and motivation for behavior. Pawns respond with passivity across a variety of situations as if they were helpless, while Origins emit a high level of voluntary responses, in the belief that they can successfully manipulate the environment. These theories suggest that a sense of controllability may not only reduce the effects of uncontrollable high density, but also may serve to alter an individual's expectations about the value of voluntary responses and to influence one's self perceptions as a competent human being.

PERSONAL CONTROL AND THE DESIGN PROCESS

If the perceived relationship between self and environment can produce such profound consequences in the laboratory, a relevant question then becomes, to what extent is it possible to increase people's perceptions of controllability in real-world settings. As we noted at the outset of this paper, while crowding is often an unavoidable physical fact, perceived control is an alterable cognitive phenomenon. It is important to emphasize that the belief in one's ability to control the environment need not imply the ability to actually implement control. Perceived control *may* result from actual control, but it can also result from prior control experiences, from information suggesting that control is potentially available, from self inferences, or from any social or physical intervention that makes the environment appear more manageable or predictable. Perceived control may even be illusory, but its effects on human behavior can be significant, as numerous experiments have shown.

We believe that an individual's sense of control over the environment can be enhanced in a variety of ways. Environments can not only be physically designed so as to make them more controllable, they can also be made to *appear* more controllable as a result of social and cognitive interventions. [Ed. Note: While these comments may make it appear that a cognitive or informational perspective sanctions deception, quite the opposite is the case when a broader perspective is considered. Humans value information; they likewise would be expected to value reliable sources of information. The converse, however, is also likely. In other words, humans strongly dislike being lied to. A source that has lost its credibility is, effectively, a source no longer. This can make deception an unacceptably costly proposition.]

A major issue in designing more controllable environments is a problem that can be labelled "environment-function fit." Simply put, when the environment fits well with the functions to be performed there, the environment is manageable; if there is not a good fit, the environment is less manageable, less controllable. To determine environment-function fit, designers must take into account the demands of the tasks and behaviors to be performed in the environment. For example, what will be the effect of environmental distractions on task performance? How important is social support and communication, and to what extent does the environment allow for this? While it is impossible to outline all relevant factors for any particular environment, the essential point is that an advance analysis be made of the task functions and social functions to be performed in the environment. Manageable environments are predictable and controllable, while "nonfitting" environments deprive one of perceptions of control.

The best way of assessing potential environment-function fit is to go directly to the users — not the administrators and managers, but the users. Not only should uses and patterns of behaviors be observed and surveyed, but the users should also be directly involved in planning and specifying the design needs. [Ed. Note: This issue is discussed further in the last chapter.] User participation in the design process allows a sense of personal control over the environment. Even if users choose not to participate, they can still benefit from the opportunity.

Other design factors relate more specifically to high density. As we pointed out earlier, density can increase unpredictability in environments and can create feelings of helplessness by restricting behavioral options. While unpredictability is probably not a significant factor within the home, where others are generally well known, density may nevertheless produce feelings of helplessness, as demonstrated by Rodin's experiment. Perhaps a design feature which could increase feelings of control in residential environments would be to build "escape rooms" — private nooks or enclosed nodules — when economically feasible. Even when the space is not in use, its mere availability could ameliorate some effects of density. Such private spaces might be included in apartment houses or dormitories in the form of small private rooms that residents could reserve for reading, writing, or just a time to be alone.

Outside the immediate family, unpredictability becomes a factor that can influence the effects of crowding. For example, the greater the number of tenants in a building, or the more apartments on a corridor, or the more people who must use a recreational area, then the less likely are residents to know each other well and the more unpredictable are the others to whom one is exposed. However, friendship formation and predictability can be increased by building smaller apartment houses, breaking up long corridors, and decreasing the number of people served by a recreational area. Such practices would foster community, decrease anonymity, and make environments more predictable and controllable. In addition, by encouraging the development of cohesive groups, such environemnts may actually cause people to feel less crowded, as demonstrated by the research of Baum, Harpin, and Valins.

Other features can be incorporated into the larger urban environment to increase perceptions of control. As Lynch (1960) has argued, urban environments are more "codable" when they include salient features such as well-defined neighborhoods, landmarks, points of interest, and clear pathways. Such features allow individuals to form clearer cognitive maps of an area, facilitate information processing, increase predictability, and enhance perceptions of control. In addition, as Jacobs (1961) has argued, when buildings and communities are designed to encourage the use of streets and sidewalks, a sense of community develops and the streets become safer. From our own perspective, when the streets are friendlier and safer, they are less threatening and more predictable.

In summary, we have suggested a number of ways that predictability and controllability of environments can be increased. The research suggests that greater perceptions of controllability can influence a wide range of behaviors. Moreover, controllability may be the single most important factor that mediates the effects of crowding. As we have argued throughout this paper, the effects of crowding depend upon the behaviors being performed in an environment as well as the individual's appraisal of the environment as controllable or uncontrollable. In a real sense, the most important determinant of human behavior may not be the physical environments we inhabit, but the cognitive environments we perceive.   ■

NOTE
    Preparation of this paper was supported by a grant from the National Science Foundation (SOC 75-09224). The authors are indebted to Dan Stokols for his comments on an earlier draft.

9 Coping Strategies: Interpretation

Relative to a human's capacity to perceive, to explore, to comprehend, and to remember, the universe is complex and uncertain to a degree that can only be considered awesome. It is difficult to know what to do; it is easy to be overwhelmed.

Many times the strategies of choice and control are not in themselves appropriate. Some things are too uncertain for choice and some too powerful for control. Natural hazards provide a ready example, but many other less dramatic and more frequent events are equally pertinent. The seasons seem to have been a major force in the experience of early humans, and they are not irrelevant even today. Accident and disease continue to take their toll despite modern technology. "The race is not to the swift nor the battle to the strong, but time and chance happen to them all" is a biblical perspective that has lost little of its force over the ensuing two thousand or more years.

But humans are conceptual creatures. They approach the awesome and the unmanageable very much like they approach anything else — with an effort to build cognitive maps, to comprehend, to make sense. Making sense is, as we have noted before, an achievement. It is a blend of discovery and invention involving a creative act — or, as is more often the case, a synthesis of a whole host of creative acts. In the process, structure is created, and a focus is established. Some things are emphasized, others ignored. The world, or a part of it, becomes that much simpler and that much less overwhelming.

Since humans are capable of choice and control, a conceptual solution would ideally relate these strategies to the world. One not only needs to know what to do in various circumstances; one needs to know what choices are available, what aspects of the world are even susceptible to human control. The legend lettered on a simulated wood plaque in souvenir shops across the land is not without point:

> God, grant me the serenity
> to accept the things I cannot change
> the courage
> to change the things I can
> and the wisdom
> to know the difference.

The general strategy of simplifying and organizing the universe, of translating it into human scale and human terms, is here called "interpretation." Some interpretive strategies are based on insights and creative explanations that each individual develops. More often, however, they stem from a more widely shared basis. The problem of uncertainty, the threat of overload, and the pain of helplessness have likely been human concerns for as long as there have been humans. One means of coping, likely to be equally ancient, involves shared and agreed upon interpretations of the world, ways of thinking about problems, and ways of behaving. Since humans are group-living animals, such agreements not only made the environment less overwhelming, they also made each other's behavior more predictable. In addition to such agreed upon conceptions, cultures tend to structure the environment and to provide opportunities to learn about it.

The selections in this chapter provide examples of group-shared conceptual solutions to the problems of a world that is full of uncertainty and unpredictability. These cultural conceptions offer explanations for a great range of phenomena that serve a variety of functions. They help make sense of what otherwise would be mystifying and frightening; they make order by imposing structure on what might otherwise seem random and incoherent. They provide guidelines for separating the important from the to-be-ignored. Such explanations help structure the way one sees things and the actions one chooses to take. Thus, ascribing cause to an omniscient power, or to a microscopic "brainless" organism, are both examples of interpretation. Each has implications for coping and each enhances cognitive map building.

In the modern world numerous factors have tended to undermine both the emergence and the transmission of useful, shared interpretations. Environments are changing at a dizzying pace. Many environments are also less observable, less accessible, harder to learn from than they once were. Concern for safety, changes in transportation patterns, an emphasis on size and efficiency in production and marketing

— all these have tended to separate people from essential aspects of the world they live in. (Several selections in the next chapter, notably the interview with Wurman and the piece by Carr and Lynch, also speak to these issues.)

In addition, people with distinctly different understandings about the world and different conventional guides to behavior have been thrown together in the same community. Further, problems of rapidly increasing size have often led to rationalized, explicit (and often ad hoc) means of handling problems that were once dealt with in an intuitive, integrated, relatively coherent system of beliefs and directives for behavior.

One particular manifestation of such rationalized solutions is discussed by Alexander in the last selection. The conceptual — and orderly — view of the city in the planner's mind can lead to a physical environment not well suited to the support of human life. This paper, like the Jacobs paper that precedes it, demonstrates how important interpretations are by showing how damaging inappropriate ones can be. While there are many possible interpretive solutions to any given problem, and in general there is no "best" solution, it does not follow that all interpretive solutions are equally appropriate as far as their effects on humans are concerned. Both Alexander and Jacobs consider interpretations of patterns of human habitation that are seemingly reasonable on the surface, but whose impacts on the built environment are actually misfortunes, perhaps disasters.

Robert Coles
Names Written in a Bible*

An important vehicle for communicating understandings of the world is parents. What is communicated is not only information about how to interpret the world, but about oneself as well. Membership in a knowledge-sharing community is an important source of identity, and the more so when the community is rooted in history as well.

---

*From Robert Coles "A domain of sorts." *Harper's* (November 1971). Pages 117–118. Copyright 1971 by *Harper's Magazine*. Reprinted by permission. Other portions of this article appear in chapters 4 and 8.

■   At the edge of Logan County, West Virginia, by Rocky Creek, lives Billy Potter, age eight. Billy is tall for his age, with blue eyes and black hair. He has a strong face. His forehead is broad, his nose substantial and sharp, his chin long. Billy is large-boned and already broad-shouldered. He is thin, much thinner than he was meant to be. His teeth are in fearful condition, giving him pains in the mouth, and he suffers from dizzy spells; but his cheeks are red and he looks like the very picture of health.

"If I had to choose a time of the year I like best," Billy told me one day when we were talking, "then I'd choose the winter. It's hard in the winter, and you're cold and you shiver, even near the fire; but the creek looks the best, and we all have the most laughing and fun then. My daddy says he's in a better mood in winter than any other time, because there's no place to go, and we just get buried in Rocky Creek, and we have the big sled we built and we go hunting, and it's a real job you have, fooling those animals and catching them, what with the snow and a lot of them hiding and some of them only out for a short time. A lot of time there's no school, because you can't get in here and you can't get out. We play checkers and cards and we take turns picking the guitar and we have the radio with all the music we want, except if there's a bad storm out there. Daddy teaches us how to cut wood and make more things than you can believe. Each winter he has a new plan on what I'm to make out of wood with my knife. He says he's my teacher when there's no school.

"For me, this is the best place to be in the whole world. I've not been to other places, I know; but if you have the best place right round you, before your eyes, you don't have to go looking. I hear they come from all over the country to look at the mountains we have, and Daddy says he wouldn't let one of them, with the cameras and all, into the creek, because they just want to stare and stare, and they don't know what to look for. He says they'll look at a hill, and they won't even stop to think what's on it — the different trees and the animals and birds. The first thing he taught us was what to call the different trees and bushes and vines. He takes us walking and he'll see more than anyone else. He knows where the animals live and where they're going and why they want to go over here and there. He's taking my brother Donald around now. Then he comes home and tells us that Donald is learning — or else he's not learning all he should.

"If I left here and went to live in a city, I'd be losing everything — that's what I hear said by my father and my uncle and cousins. We've been here so long, it's as long as when the country was started. My people came here and they followed the creek up to here and they named it Rocky Creek; they were the ones, that's right. In the Bible we have written down the names of our kin that came before us and when they were born and when they died, and my name is there and I'm not going to leave here, because there'd be no mention of me when I get married and no mention of my children, if I left the creek." ■

Robin Fox
The Cultural Animal*

Although culture is sometimes cast as an alternative to biology, something in the biology of humans must incline them toward the creation, transmission, and dependence on culture. Fox not only explores this issue in an engaging fashion; he also provides a list of cultural activities that is colorful and thought provoking. A survey of this list shows how closely interwoven are issues of choice, control, and interpretation in what we call culture.

■   At least two monarchs in history are said to have tried the experiment of isolating children at birth and keeping them isolated through childhood to see if they would spontaneously produce a language when they matured. The Egyptian Psammetichos, in the seventh century B.C., and later James IV of Scotland, in the fifteenth century A.D. Both, it seemed, did not doubt that untutored children would speak, although King James's hope that they would speak Hebrew was perhaps a little optimistic.

I do not doubt that they *could* speak and that, theoretically, given time, they or their offspring would invent and develop a language despite their never having been taught one. Furthermore, this language, although totally different from any known to us, would be analyzable by linguists on the same basis as other languages and translatable into all known languages. But I would push this further. If our new Adam and Eve could survive and breed — still in total isolation from any cultural influences — then eventually they would produce a society which would have laws about property, rules about incest and marriage, customs of taboo and avoidance, methods of settling disputes with a

*Excerpted from J. F. Eisenberg and W. S. Dillon (Eds.) *Man and beast: comparative social behavior*. Washington, D.C.: Smithsonian Institution Press. 1971. Pages 283–285; 295–296. Reprinted by permission.

minimum of bloodshed, beliefs about the supernatural and practices relating to it, a system of social status and methods of indicating it, initiation ceremonies for young men, courtship practices including the adornment of females, systems of symbolic body adornment generally, certain activities and associations set aside for men from which women were excluded, gambling of some kind, a tool- and weapon-making industry, myths and legends, dancing, adultery, and various doses of homicide, suicide, homosexuality, schizophrenia, psychosis and neuroses, and various practitioners to take advantage of or cure these, depending on how they are viewed. I could extend the list but this will suffice.

In short, the new Adam and Eve would not only produce, as our monarchs suspected, a recognizable human language, but a recognizable human culture and society. It might not be in content quite like any we have come across: Its religious beliefs might be different, but it would have some; its marriage rules might be unique (I doubt it), but it would have them and their type would be recognized; its status structure might be based on an odd criterion, but there would be one; its initiation ceremonies might be unbelievably grotesque but they would exist; its use or treatment of schizophrenia might be bizarre, but there it would be. All these things would be there because we are the kind of animal that does these kinds of things.

In the same way, in a zoo one can rear infant baboons who know nothing of the state in which their ancestors and wild cousins lived, and yet when they reach maturity they produce a social structure with all the elements found in the wilds and of which they have no experience. Their capacity to produce a unique "language" is of course much more limited than that of our hypothetical naive group of humans, but in both cases the basic grammaticality of behavior will be operative. In the same way that a linguist could take our Garden of Eden tribe and analyze its totally unique language, so an anthropologist would be able to analyze its totally unique kinship system or mythology or whatever, because the basic rules of the universal grammar would be operating.

(Actually in the interests of accuracy I should add a rider here to the effect that the experiment might be impossible to perform. It is one of the ground rules of the universal behavioral grammar of all primates — not just humans — that if you take young infants away from maternal care at a critical period they will grow up to be very disturbed indeed and may well perpetuate this error by maltreating their own children in turn. Thus our experiment may well produce a group of very maladjusted adults and the whole thing founder rather quickly. But at least this gives us one element of the universal system: Some method has to be found of associating mother and child closely and safely during certain critical periods. If isolated during critical periods, not only can the animal not learn *anything* at all, it loses the potential to learn at any other time. It has to learn certain things at certain times — true of language and of many other areas of behavior.)

The model of behavior sees the human actor as a bundle of potentialities rather than a *tabula rasa:* potentialities for action, for instinct, for learning, for the development of unconscious habits. These potentials or predispositions or biases are the end product of a process of natural selection peculiar to our species. One consequence of this view is that much of the quasi-instinctive cultural behavior of man can be studied in much the same way and by much the same methods as ethologists study the truly instinctive behavior of other animals. Many strands of investigation seem to be leading in this direction at the moment.

The kind of overall investigation that emerges from this theoretical position would utilize primarily three kinds of data: Data from human behavior both contemporary and known in history; data on animal behavior, particularly that on wild primates; data on hominid evolution with special attention to the evolution of the brain. Eventually data from genetics — molecular genetics, behavior genetics, and population genetics — will have to be included. But this is perhaps jumping ahead too far. At the moment the best we can say is that we should be prepared to use genetic data when we become sophisticated enough to incorporate it.

We began with the theme of human uniqueness and should end with my point that our uniqueness has to be interpreted in the same way as the uniqueness of any other species. We have to ask "How come?" How did culture get into the wiring? How did the great constructors operate to produce this feature, which, like everything else about us, is not anti-nature, or superorganic, or extrabiological, or any of the other demagogic fantasy-states that science and religion imagine for us? Darwin did not banish mind from the universe as Butler feared; indeed, he gave us a basis for explaining how mind got into the universe in the first place. And it got there — as did every other natural and biological feature — by natural selection. The tool-making animal needed mind to survive; that is, he needed language and culture and the reorganization of experience that goes with these. And having got the rudiments and become dependent on them, there was no turning back. There was no retreat to the perilous certainty of instinct. It was mind or nothing. It was classification and verbalization, rules and laws, mnemonics and knowledge, ritual and art, that piled up their pressures on the precarious species, demanding better and better brains to cope with this new organ — culture — now essential to survival. Two related processes, thought and self control, evolved hand in hand, and their end product is the cultural animal, which speaks and rules itself because that is the kind of animal it is; because speaking and self-discipline have made it what it is; because it is what it produces and was produced by what it is.   ■

■   The whole of human life, it can be said, is a dialogue between us and our environment . . . a sequence of questions and responses. We pose questions to the universe by what we do, and the universe, by its response, informs us of whether or not our actions fit into its laws. When we husband the earth and manage it wisely, we are rewarded with health, beauty, permanence, and productivity. But when we abuse and degrade the earth, we reap disease, ugliness, impermanence, and barren harvests.

Our smaller transgressions evoke limited or mild responses. But large transgressions evoke general, threatening, and possibly violent responses. And now, the very universality of the environmental crisis indicates the universality of our transgressions. It is no less than the philosophy of materialism which is being challenged . . . and the challenge comes not from a few saints and sages, but from the environment.

Now this is a new situation. At all times and in all societies and in all parts of the world, the saints and sages have warned against materialism and pleaded for a more realistic order of priorities. The languages have differed and the symbols have varied, but the essential message has always been the same. . . .

We must redirect our science and technology. *Not* abandon, but redirect them. As things now stand we have foolishly shaped a technology which drives us into giantism, infinite complexity, vast expensiveness, and violence. We must devise a new technology that will help us move in the opposite direction . . . towards smallness, simplicity, low cost, and non-violence.   ■

— E. F. Schumacher*

*Excerpted from a Plowboy Interview with E. F. Schumacher in *The Mother Earth News,* Issue No. 42. Copyright © 1976 by The Mother Earth News®, Inc., P.O. Box 70, Hendersonville, N.C. 28739. Excerpted by permission.

John B. Jackson
After the Forest Came the Pasture*

Fairy tales set in the forest have a rather ambivalent tone. The forest is clearly important; at the same time it is undeniably threatening. Jackson shows the ecological importance of the forest at an earlier time. The pasture stands for the forest domesticated, and the lawn in turn stands for the pasture. Perhaps by stories of menace in the forest we explain to ourselves the necessity of replacing it with pasture. As the forest diminishes we shall require a fresh collection of fairy tales with a different story to tell.

■   For almost a thousand years after the collapse of the Roman Empire the history of Europe was the history of a slow and persistent deforestation. When the Classic civilization began to die, Europe ceased to be one unit and became two. The region around the Mediterranean preserved a good deal of the Roman heritage; for the most part its population did not greatly change; and the land remained under cultivation. But for several reasons the entire northwestern portion of the Empire — Great Britain, the Lowlands, northern France and western Germany — began to revert to wilderness. Roads, towns, cities and farms were gradually abandoned, fell into ruin, and in time were hidden by brush and forest. The peoples whom we call the Barbarians and who later moved in from the East had thus to reclaim the land all over again. They were obliged to take back from the forest by main force whatever land they needed for farms and pastures and villages. They were pioneers no less tough than those who settled our own West. Their numbers were so few and their means so primitive that every lengthy war and every epidemic saw much newly cleared land revert to undergrowth once more. It was not until a century ago that the last wastelands on the continent were put under cultivation. The whole undertaking was an extraordinary phase of European history, one which we know very little about. How well it succeeded is shown by the fact that Holland, now a land of gardens, originally meant "Land of Forests."

*From J. B. Jackson "Ghosts at the door." *Landscape,* 1951, 1 (1), pages 5–7. Reprinted by permission. Other portions of this article appear in chapters 6 and 8.

Could this incessant warfare with the forest fail to have an effect on the men who engaged in it? Does it not help to explain an attitude toward nature quite unlike that of the peoples farther south? The constant struggle against cold and solitude and darkness, the omnipresent threat of the wilderness and the animals that lived in it in time produced a conviction that there was no existing on equal terms with nature. Nature had to be subdued, and in order to subdue her men had to study her and know her strength. We have inherited this philosophy, it sometimes seems, in its entirety: this determination to know every one of nature's secrets and to establish complete mastery over her; to love in order to possess and eventually destroy. It is not a point of view which has worked very well here in the West. If we had thought more in terms of cooperation with a reluctant and sensitive environment, as the Mediterranean people still do, and less in terms of "harnessing" and "taming," we would have not made such a shambles of the southwestern landscape.

That aggressive attitude is however only part of what the earliest farmers in northern Europe bequeathed us. Since they created the human landscape themselves and under great difficulties, they had a deep affection for it. They looked upon the combination of farmland and meadow and forest as the direct expression of their way of life. It was a harsh and primitive landscape, just as by all accounts it was a harsh and primitive way of life, but it was not lacking in a sentiment for the surrounding world, nor an element of poetry. The perpetual challenge of the forest stirred the imagination as did no other feature in the environment. It was the forest where the outlaw went to hide, it was there that adventurous men went to make a new farm and a new and freer life. It teemed with wolves, boars, bears and wild oxen. It contained in its depths the abandoned clearings and crumbling ruins of an earlier civilization. It was a place of terror to the farmer and at the same time a place of refuge. He was obliged to enter it for wood and game and in search of pasture. For hundreds of years the forest determined the spread of population and represented the largest source of raw materials; it was an outlet for every energy. Its dangers as well as its wealth became part of the daily existence of every man and woman.

When at last it was removed from the landscape our whole culture began to change and even to disintegrate. A Frenchman has recently written a book to prove that the decline in popular beliefs and traditions (and in popular attitudes toward art and work and society) in his country was the direct outcome of the destruction a century ago of the last areas of untouched woodland. If he is correct, how many of those traditions can be left among us who have denuded half a continent in less than six generations? The urge to cut down trees is stronger than ever. The slightest excuse is enough for us to strip an entire countryside. And yet —there is the front yard with its tenderly cared for Chinese elms, the picnic ground in the shadow of the pines, and a mass of poems and pictures and songs about trees. A Mediterranean would find this sentimentality hard to understand.

The old ambivalence persists. But the reverence for the forest is no longer universal. Our household economy is largely free from dependence on the resources of the nearby forest, and any feeling for the forest itself is a survival from childhood associations. Until the last generation it might have been said that much of every American (and northern European) childhood was passed in the landscape of traditional forest legends. Time had transformed the reality of the wilderness into myth. The forest outlaw became Robin Hood, the vine-grown ruins became the castle of Sleeping Beauty. The frightened farmer, armed with an ax for cutting firewood, was the hero of Little Red Riding Hood and the father of Hänsl and Gretl. In a sense, our youngest years were a re-enactment of the formative period of our culture, and the magic of the forest was never entirely forgotten in adult life. Magic, of course, is part of every childhood; yet if a generation grew up on the magic of Superman and Mickey Mouse and Space Cadet instead, if it lived in the empty and inanimate landscape which provides a background for those figures, how long would it continue to feel the charms of the forest? How long would the Chinese elms be watered and cared for?

After the forest came the pasture, and the pasture in time became the lawn. When a Canadian today cuts down trees in order to start a farm he says he is "making land." He might with equal accuracy say that he is "making lawn," for the two words have the same origin and once had the same meaning. Our lawns are merely the civilized descendants of the medieval pastures cleared among the trees. In the New Forest in England a "lawn" is still an open space in the woods where cattle are fed.

So the lawn has a very prosaic background, and if lawns seem to be typically northern European — the English secretly believe that there are no true lawns outside of Great Britain — that is simply because the farmers in northern Europe raised more cattle than did the farmers near the Mediterranean, and had to provide more feed.

As cattle and sheep-raising increased in importance, the new land wrested from the forest became more and more essential to the farmer; he set the highest value on it. But to recognize the economic worth of a piece of land is one thing: to find beauty in it is quite another. Wheat fields and turnip patches were vital to the European peasant, yet he never, as it were, domesticated them. The lawn was different. It was not only part and parcel of a pastoral economy, it was also part of the farmer's leisure. It was the place for sociability and play; and that is why it was and still is looked upon with affection.

The common grazing land of every village is actually what we mean when we speak of the village common, and it was on the common that most of our favorite group pastimes came into being. Maypole and Morris dances never got a foothold in northern America, and for that we can thank the Puritans. But baseball, like cricket in England, originated on the green. Before cricket the national sport was archery, likewise a product of the common. Rugby, and its American variation football, are both products of the same pastoral landscape, and golf is the product of the very special pastoral landscape of lowland Scotland. Would it not be possible to establish a bond between national sports and the type of terrain where they developed? Bowling is favored in Holland and near the Mediterranean — both regions of gardens and garden paths. A continental hunt is still a forest hunt; the English or Irish hunt needs a landscape of open fields and hedgerows. Among the many ways in which men exploit the environment and establish an emotional bond with it we should not forget sports and games. And the absence among certain peoples of games inspired by the environment is probably no less significant.

In the course of time the private dwelling took over the lawn. With the exclusion of the general public a new set of pastimes was devised: croquet, lawn tennis, badminton, and the lawn party. But all of these games and gatherings, whether taking place on the common or on someone's enclosed lawn, were by way of being schools where certain standards of conduct, and even certain standards of dress were formed. And in an indefinable way the lawn is still the background for conventionally correct behavior. The poor sport walks off the field; the poor citizen neglects his lawn.

Just as the early forest determined our poetry and legend, that original pasture land, redeemed from the forest for the delectation of cows and sheep, has indirectly determined many of our social attitudes. Both are essential elements of the proto-landscape. But in America the lawn is more than essential; it is the very heart and soul of the entire front yard. We may say what we like about the futility of these areas of bright green grass; we may lament the waste of labor and water they represent here in the semi-arid West. Yet to condemn them or justify them on utilitarian or esthetic grounds is to miss the point entirely. The lawn, with its vague but nonetheless real social connotations, is precisely that landscape element which every American values most. Unconsciously he identifies it with every group event in his life: childhood games, commencement and graduation with white flannels or cap and gown, wedding receptions, "having company," the high school drill field and the Big Game of the season. Even the cemetery is now landscaped as a lawn to provide an appropriate background for the ultimate

Courtesy of Charles W. Cares

social event: How can a citizen be loyal to that tradition without creating and taking care of a lawn of his own? Whoever supposes that Americans are not willing to sacrifice time and money in order to keep a heritage alive regardless of its practical value had better count the number of sweating and panting men and women and children, pushing lawn-mowers on a summer's day. It is quite possible that the lawn will go out of fashion. But if it does it will not be because the toiling masses behind the lawn-mower have rebelled. It will be because a younger generation has fewer convivial associations with it; has found other places for group functions and other places to play: the gymnasium, the school grounds, the swimming pool or the ski run. It will be because the feeling of being hedged in by conventional standards of behavior has become objectionable. ■

Albert E. Parr
The Child in the City: Urbanity and the Urban Scene*

Some cultural interpretation is not transmitted through storytelling or other forms of instruction; rather, it is developed by each member of the culture through observation of important activities. Parr writes of another time and another place within the framework of western culture where such observation readily occurred. Such opportunities are considerably harder to come by in our contemporary setting. Many children have little or no conception of where their food comes from, what adult work looks like, and the many other aspects of the larger picture of how things fit together that could be so readily learned under favorable conditions.

■   Planners, critics, and defenders of the metropolis seem divided over the question as to whether the texture of life and the structure of society are being rapidly and drastically altered by our evolving cities, for better or for worse, or whether the basic pattern and aims of urban existence are not changing at all, merely using new vehicles for old functions and purposes. The dispute often resembles a conflict of cults rather than rational debate based upon clearly stated and verifiable premises. It is particularly rare to find any contestant offering a full and clear description of the state of affairs that presumably was or was not the urban condition that is now in transformation. A more common ploy is to try to divine our destination, which is then retrospectively claimed to be where we have always been, or wanted to be — or have never been before — even though it may have looked otherwise, either way.

One of the problems is, of course, that modern sociology is itself a child of the twentieth century which it attempts to study. The students therefore came upon the scene too late to gather data of their own on the point of departure for the social evolution of the age we live in. A brief recollection of certain urban experiences of a child born when the century was born may contribute at least one statistic towards the accumulation of a bench mark from which the tides of change may be measured.

*From A. E. Parr "The child in the city: Urbanity and the urban scene." *Landscape*, Spring 1967, pages 3–5. Reprinted by permission.

Until I reached the age of five we lived a short commuter distance outside of a town of about 75,000 on the west coast of Norway. Not as a chore, but as an eagerly desired pleasure, I was fairly regularly entrusted with the task of buying fish and bringing it home alone. This involved the following: walking to the station in five to ten minutes; buying ticket; watching train with coal-burning steam locomotive pull in; boarding train; riding across long bridge over shallows separating small-boat harbor (on the right) from ship's harbor (on the left), including small naval base with torpedo boats; continuing through a tunnel; leaving train at terminal, sometimes dawdling to look at railroad equipment; walking by and sometimes entering fisheries museum; passing central town park where military band played during mid-day break; strolling by central shopping and business district, or, alternatively, passing fire station with horses at ease under suspended harnesses, ready to go, and continuing past centuries old town hall and other ancient buildings; exploration of fish market and fishing fleet; selection of fish; haggling about price; purchase and return home.

I do not intend to claim that this was usual for a four-year-old boy on his own. Rather was it due to very unusual parents. The point is that such experiences were possible and permissible at that time while they would be utterly unthinkable today, due in no small measure to the hazards introduced by automobile traffic, among other causes.

When I was five we moved into the town itself, and I started to kindergarten and elementary school soon after. The days would go as follows: off to school with other children joining the morning stream of white-collar pedestrian males ranging from clerks to shipowners, usually not walking with our elders but unavoidably exposed to overhearing adult conversation and observing adult behavior; soon passing a small botanical garden and greenhouse and a large building housing a substantial museum of natural history and a fair museum of history and ethnography; passing, also, a great architectural variety of residences; then the railroad terminal and the building opposite which houses the fisheries museum previously mentioned, and also, on higher floors, a museum of decorative arts, a small city art gallery and the exhibition halls of the art association; past the central park with the music stand to the school, which shared a block with the fire station, city prison and an historic but still functioning public building. These were the days of two work periods with a long midday break. During the break the morning route was reversed, with stops to listen to the military band, to pay visits to museums (in my case) and to seek other adventures. At this time the stream would include some women, and it would cross a flow of blue-collar workers moving in the other direction. In the afternoon the pedestrian procession would go back again, but now with a considerable number of wives on errands of their own, starting out with, or more or less at the same time as, their husbands, and proceeding to the same parts of town, sometimes accompanied by their children, there being no afternoon elementary school. When spending free time in our own neighborhood, I had only about 300 feet to walk to watch activities in a booming shipyard; about 1000 feet farther along came the public aquarium; and immediately beyond that was the seawater moat protecting the naval station, where sticklebacks nested in the seaweeds; sculpins, gobies and small flounders darted about and could be watched for hours. In another direction it was about 300 feet to ferry stairs where I could fish, about 600 feet to a large dock and coal depot, and many rocky, still vacant lots to explore. There were also frequent visits unaccompanied, back to the natural history and history museum. This is actually only a very incomplete list of how things were around 1905–1907.

Gutheim has suggested that if we are to have cities it must be because they make men. Whether or not we stipulate that this is the purpose of their existence, no one can deny that the cities among their other functions also serve as nurseries for future generations. Today probably all psychologists agree that the character, personality and future potentials of the individual are usually determined in all their basic features before, perhaps even long before, the child becomes a teenager. Before attempting to distill the essentials from this recital of childhood memories it therefore seems best to call attention to the fact that children in the first dozen years of their lives may well have to be considered the most important segment of the urban population. One or two centuries ago such a statement might have been merely a sentimental generalization of parental affections or the expression of a romantic devotion to the welfare of a future world of which we would not be a part. But with the life expectancies of today, our own comforts and pleasures will be in a large measure dependent upon more than one generation of adults raised from children born after we ourselves first saw the light of day. It is time to stop fooling ourselves about the place of children in our lives. What the city does or does not do to the children must be a matter of equal concern to the most realistic egotist and the most visionary altruist.

References to man's increased mobility run like a bad refrain through all the literature on urban planning. Sixty years ago the mobility of a child in first grade was not very different from that of its parents, and its autonomous daily orbit was virtually identical with that of its elders. Today the mobility of the adult is greatly increased, but one never sees any mention of the corollary fact that the child's mobility has simultaneously been greatly reduced, largely as a result of the hazards introduced by the new means of adult locomotion. The child's daily orbit has been even more sharply curtailed than its mobility. It seems the ideal of all urban designers to place the schools as near the homes as possible and with the simplest route between them, at the same time as urban growth is pushing residential precincts and school districts farther and farther away from the centers of history and of current affairs. A child's exposure to the life of the city two to four times daily has become a thing of the past.

Sixty years ago the orbits of men and women were also essentially the same. Automobile transportation has greatly increased the mobility of both, but has also separated the orbits of housewives from those of husbands and of women workers in business, industry, government and the professions. This reduction of urban experience shared in common by men, women and children also reduces their ability to communicate with each other.

There is no doubt in my mind that the daily morning promenade to school and office greatly extended the influence of the male adults upon the children, not by direct communication so much as by the child's observation of adult speech and behavior among adults. The separation of orbits has destroyed this feature of urban childhood.

The opportunity to find and to join people with the same interests and attitudes is today often extolled as one of the great virtues and attractions of the metropolis. This may be true in the age of the automobile. But in the pedestrian era one of the greatest virtues of the city was that it did not permit the degree of withdrawal into the circle of the like-minded which now seems to have become so desirable. Cities were proudly referred to as "melting pots" and "mixing bowls." My own memories tell me that the four pedestrian parades each day were an important instrument of this mixing process that spun the warp of our social fabric. There can be a lot of communication without the exchange of words. Those that you see or "run into" several times a day may become friends or remain your enemies, but can no longer be thought of as alien devils in the dark, with all the vicious feelings that complete ignorance between antagonists is likely to encourage. Bumping bumpers is not a good substitute for rubbing shoulders.

For us children in particular, the institution of domestic servants added immeasurably to the bonds of understanding that made one community without uniformity out of a great diversity of people in a wide variety of circumstances. Often it served in a three-way relationship. A maid from the outer islands might give us a warm insight into the life of a fisherman and his kin, as well as an appreciation of the urban workers among whom she made her friends in town. And her uncontrived mediation would of course operate in both directions. Vacuum cleaners and washing machines do not have quite the same effect.

This is not to be construed in any way as an argument for a return to the past. But must we always be so faint-hearted that it is necessary for us to forget the merits of any system we want to condemn on the balance of its assets and liabilities? Whatever else they did and suffered, house servants also performed important functions as human lines of communication in the warp of a nation.

The individualistic architectural diversity on the way to school has for most children been replaced by a walk, if not a ride, within the monotonous anonymity of new housing developments, and the twice daily autonomous plunge into the heartland of urbanity has become a rare and guided event during the early years of life.

It is commonly assumed that the greatest cultural opportunities are generally enjoyed by the inhabitants of the metropolis. And again we have to contend with reasoning based upon the exclusion of the child from the logical premises of current rationalizations about the urban condition. As our cities increase in size their cultural institutions tend to grow larger, or more select in their quality, or both. But these establishments scarcely ever multiply in proportion to the expansion of the community. For the adults the resulting greater distances may be compensated for by their increased mobility, but even this is a very questionable assumption. Highest per capita museum attendance is, for example, not found in the largest cities. But for a child, with his reduced autonomous mobility, the opportunity for frequent and independent visits to cultural treasures and centers of informal education are virtually eliminated by the urban spread. While electronic surrogates have valuable uses of their own, they are in no sense adequate substitutes for self-directed experience of the real thing. I am quite confident that any objective investigation of the urban ecology of children would prove the average metropolitan child to be culturally underprivileged by comparison with the youngsters growing up in medium-to-small cities with a modicum of cultural interests and attainments.

The one shining exception to the rule of growth without proportionate multiplication is provided by the public library system, which may be considered to occupy an intermediate place between the cultural institutions of entirely optional and informal attendance and the educational system of formally scheduled and required studies. If the cultural institutions could be persuaded to adopt a pattern of dispersal similar to that of the libraries and schools, it would help to restore some of the childhood opportunities that have been lost in megalopolis, but no such remedy is available for the loss of exposure to the urban milieu of history.

In the childhood I have described we walked with history every day, not merely among the rather perfunctory reminders of scattered

by Lynette T. Dobbs

and protected historical houses and monuments, but in churches and commercial structures still carrying on their normal functions of centuries past: in squares before or around public buildings still in active use in the conduct of public affairs; past residences still occupied in a perfectly normal manner without evidence of self-consciousness. When towns become cities, residential quarters tend to shift away from the central area and the everyday contacts with the past during the years of childhood become infrequent experiences organized and guided by one's elders. The population explosion has watered the wine of history. There is, so to speak, less history per capita than the world has ever had before, less opportunity for the average person to identify his own life with that of the past, through a sense of acting it out on the same stage, using some of the same props.

These comments and recollections are offered as a contribution to our awareness of the nature and dimensions of some of the differences between childhood life in an old and small but thriving city at the beginning of the century, and childhood existence today in the family precincts of a modern metropolis, in order to show that these are not differences that can be blandly discounted by our urban fortune-tellers bent on proselytizing us for their own favorite version of the future.

This is not the place for a detailed analysis and evaluation of the consequences of our altered circumstances, but one broad generalization suggests itself as a possible warning of danger. So many of the changes that are taking place — through increased adult mobility, the replacement of domestics by mechanical appliances, the dilution of history and other developments including automation in commerce and industry — seem to have the effect of reducing the warp of society while increasing the woof, and a heavy woof in a slender warp does not provide a strong fabric.

When some of our planners now envision a diffusion of our cities over the countryside, with destruction of the dichotomies that once distinguished the rural from the urban, what they preach and foresee will probably prove less of a dispersal of urbanity through the provinces than of an urban conversion to provincialism. But it should not be beyond our abilities to avoid such an outcome if we honestly acknowledge the changes that are taking place, and do not merely disclaim the damages, but seek compensations for our losses, while continuing to improve upon our gains.   ■

Eliot Wigginton
Foxfire 3: Introduction*

Here Wigginton describes the process of coping with success. This does not constitute a contradiction in terms; even desirable events can have undesirable effects as far as one's purposes are concerned. Indeed, there is reason to believe that humans are, both by their constitution and culture, better able to cope with difficulty than with its absence. What Wigginton describes could be viewed as an attempt to cope with something that our culture does not prepare us for. A multitude of choices and patterns of control are involved, but guiding the entire effort is interpretation, a story, if you will, of what one is trying to achieve, of what the motives of others are, of what is likely to happen under certain circumstances, and so on.

This selection has another relationship to interpretation. The Foxfire project is itself a vehicle for preserving and sharing the interpretive patterns that once guided the lives of people living in south-

ern Appalachia. Since the students involved in this project often redis-
cover their own heritage in the process, it is also an example of the
importance of interpretive content to identity, to the ability to explain
to oneself who one is.

■   In the spring of 1976, *Foxfire* magazine will be ten years old. By
all the normal standards of measurement, we should have plenty to
celebrate, for *Foxfire* has not only survived, but is being called one of
the most dramatically successful high school projects in sight.

By 1976, our first book will have sold well over a million copies.
The second book will be right behind it. The telephone in our office
rings constantly, bringing requests from film and TV producers, advertising executives, and free-lance writers and photographers. I receive
hundreds of letters a year inviting me to speak before various organizations, serve on various boards, lend my name to various proposals or
proposed proposals, or accept various jobs. Scores of visitors come
through our tiny office with no more reason that "just wanting to see
where it's done," or wanting us to introduce them to some "real mountain people." Not long ago, a stranger came huffing the half mile up the
mountain to my log house, where a couple of kids and I were spending a
Saturday adding a porch, took a picture of us with his Instamatic, and
then struggled back down the mountain.

I accept several invitations a year to speak. Almost invariably in
the question-and-answer period that follows the presentation, the
same question comes up. It goes something like this: "Did you ever
dream when you started the project that all this success would happen?"

I usually laugh and answer, "No, never." And that's true. I sometimes don't see how we made it past our second issue. But at a recent
talk, something perverse in my character or my mood made me answer, "Say you're a high school teacher who wants to reach his students in a very special way. You start a project with them, and in the
early days, you all do everything together. When you walk across the
campus, as often as not a kid will come charging up from behind and
tackle you, laughing crazily as you roll, wrestling, scattering books
and papers across the grass.

"Your project prospers. Your name is in lots of papers and before
lots of folks. You come back on campus after a successful four-day
speaking engagement, and a kid stands before you looking down, scuffing his feet at something imaginary in the dirt, and says, 'Gee, you're
not around much any more.'

"Are you still successful? Do you have anything to rejoice about
except notoriety and a stack of invitations? Is that success?"

I think about that a lot now that we're besieged. And I'm finding out, like lots of others before me (some of whom warned me in advance), that success, interestingly enough, turns out to be a mixed blessing. It's bright with opportunity, but it's also jammed up with problems — a lot like walking around town with a rattlesnake in your front pocket.

It's an old story. I've read about it in various books and magazines. I've seen it at work on other people. I never really expected to have to deal with it personally, but here I am, writing this in Room 219 of the Great Smokies Hilton in Asheville instead of at my cluttered desk, because there are too many distractions at home.

Visibility presents rather fragile organizations like ours with a number of problems. Some examples: When a group that's used to getting three letters a day suddenly begins to get forty a day (something like 14,000 a year), and has to answer them with a staff of high school students that can only work on the project part time, and they have a number of other activities that we'd like them to be involved in besides answering letters anyway, then some adjustments are needed. When we run a workshop for teachers interested in implementing the same sort of project in their own locations, and twenty of those teachers ask permission to bring their classes up for a day to see our operation, we know that if we say yes to all of them it's going to mean that the equivalent of *one month* of school days will have been spent giving guided tours instead of writing articles, and that all the groups are going to go away disappointed anyway because all there is to see is a little cluster of three impossibly cramped ten-foot-by-ten-foot rooms cluttered with typewriters and envelopes and paper (we can't take them to visit contacts — you can't fit a whole class into the tiny living room of a mountain home). Yet we know that if we say no to them, we run the risk of seeming brusque and uncooperative and cold, and here we are again — stuck between a rock and a hard place. You get the idea.

So it's been pretty interesting around here for the last year or two. Margie, Suzy, Pat, and I, as a staff, have learned a lot, and we're slowly beginning to develop some techniques for coping; trying to stay positive and helpful whenever we can, but also trying to keep foremost in our minds that image of a kid, disappointed, scuffing his feet in the dirt.

The problem, of course, becomes to figure out a way to grab that thing called success, shake it up, turn it inside out, and make it work *for* us instead of letting it eat us alive. Here's the system we've devised for the moment. It seems to be working in the biggest areas of concern.

The first area is that I jokingly tag the "I know you're busy, but . . ." department since we hear that line many times a day. If the request asks me to come and speak, I ask a couple of questions in return. Is the group that's inviting me willing, for example, to foot not only my expenses, but also those of two or three of the students? If they aren't, I usually don't go. Is the group asking us for some specific input, or is it looking for entertainment? If it's a group of English teachers from the state of North Carolina that are really looking for some ways to get their kids involved; or a high school in Parkersburg, West Virginia, that wants to start a similar project and wants me to come and help get it off the ground; if we can spare the time away from the office, and if it's not during one of those months we periodically set aside *just* for the kids here and let nothing else interfere, then we might go. On the other hand, if it's a group that is a four-hour drive away, and just wants a little after-luncheon presentation to fill a hole in the program chairman's calendar, which for us means a full day away from the office with a good chance that little will be accomplished, we don't go. If it's a local group within our or an immediately adjacent county, we almost always go because we feel it's vital that people in our area know what we're up to.

Using this system, we can get most of the student editors out on at least one good trip (after they've all been once, we usually turn down everything else until the next school year), and we find that some fine things often happen on those trips that add yet another dimension to our program. On numbers of occasions, for example, the kids we've taken with us have never been on a plane before, have never encountered a hotel elevator, revolving doors, escalators, and have never been entertained at a sit-down dinner. They've just never had the chance. Nor have they previously been put into situations where they're asked for autographs, or where they're asked to address a group that may be as large as several thousand people, or where they're asked by teachers for *their* advice as to how teachers should teach, or what it's really like to be a high school student. I've seen them stunned again and again by the fact that adults are asking *their* opinions on certain issues and are seriously considering, accepting, or challenging their answers in a healthy, friendly exchange of views. We try to pull out all the stops on a trip and give completely of ourselves to the sponsoring group. As a result, many of the students we take are put in situations where they have to think seriously about our project — what it's all about and precisely how it works — because they're going to have to articulate all that to people who have never been here. Suddenly they find themselves not only with a new understanding of who, in part, their audience out there *is,* and a new understanding of the fact that lots of people they've never met before *are* watching their work; but they also find themselves evaluating the work they're doing and the whole *Foxfire* project in a new, more serious, and more objective light. Even if the end result of the visit is that nothing specific is accomplished by being there, the kids, at least, come back having had a solid, sobering experience — and often come back, newly recharged and committed, thinking of ways to alter our operation here at home to better serve the other kids, the audience that's waiting for their next magazine, and the community in which they work.

If the request is from an organization that wants to come here and do some filming or some photography, certain other questions come into play, all of which lead up to the big question: into what position is the request going to put the people who might be filmed or photographed? What's in it for them besides publicity that might bring people trooping to their doors, and do they want to be put in that position? But first, the class as a whole decides whether or not they will be willing at the time designated to work closely with a camera crew (if the crew doesn't want the kids around, but simply wants introductions, we don't even consider it). If the kids have recently been through such an experience, and they don't want to gear up to do it all over again, or if they're involved in so many things that they don't feel like they can take the time, the project is vetoed.

If, however, they are interested in looking at the project more closely and perhaps want to do it, they ask for more details. For example, the JFG Coffee Company recently decided that it needed a new set of commercials, and Fitzgerald Advertising, Inc., was hired to make them. The plan was to make six commercials, each featuring a mountain person (the JFG marketing area covers much of the southern Appalachians) demonstrating some skill. At the end of the thirty-second scene, all the person had to say was something to the effect that, "It takes a lot of skill and patience to do this." Then the announcer would come in and say, "Just as it takes this person time and patience to make butter, so, too, it takes JFG time and patience to make a fine coffee." Something like that.

Thinking they might be able to save filming time, and save trouble, they approached us and asked if we would be willing to locate the subjects for the commercials and prepare them so that all the film crew had to do was walk in, film the six scenes in four days, and walk out. It sounded unsavory at first, but we told them the kids might be willing to do it. They would simply have to come up and present their case and let the kids decide.

The writer and producer flew up from New Orleans, and I gave them a class period to present their story boards to the kids and answer questions. The kids wanted to know if *Foxfire's* name would be used (they didn't want it to be), or if the name of the county would be used (they didn't want that either after seeing the number of tourists that came through as a result of the movie *Deliverance)*, or if the contact would have to drink some coffee (they didn't want that). They also wanted to know how much each would be paid, how long they would have to work, etc. They grilled the ad agency representatives for an hour, then told them they would talk about it among themselves and let the agency know next week.

For several days, that was all they talked about. Finally they decided that they'd co-operate *if* they could find people in the community who *wanted* to do it. They headed out to locate a butter churner, a beekeeper, a man who would plow with a horse, some quilters, a weaver, and someone who would dig sassafras and make tea with it — all skills the ad agency wanted pictured. In two days they had found them all, and they called the agency and said that they could come in if they paid the people in cash just as soon as the cameras stopped rolling, would give us copies of the finished commercials for our archive, and would pay for a community showing.

The agency agreed, came in, and the kids had it set up so they got all they came for in less than four days. The contacts got paid on the spot, and everyone was happy. One of the contacts, for example, came up to the kids afterward and said, "I just want you all to know that I am grateful to you for thinking of me. That's the most money I ever made at one time in my life. That will pay for my seed and fertilizer this year and put me in the black for the first time in years." The party was held, and over a hundred people came to watch the finished commercials before they were to start airing, and they approved. And later, when one of the subjects was bitten by a copperhead, the ad agency sent up a donation to help with the hospital expenses.

Another recent request was from a production company that wanted to film a two-hour television special here. The film would tell the fictionalized story of a boy who came from a city, got involved in a project like *Foxfire,* and through that involvement came to some new understanding about himself and his heritage. The project went through several months of negotiations, script writers even came from California with a sample script in hand, and in the end was not agreed to because the kids insisted that the film should not be called *Foxfire,* nor could the project shown in the film be called *Foxfire,* since the story itself was fictionalized and had never happened here and since our name would pinpoint the location geographically. The company, having already made a number of concessions, balked at that one, and the contract was never signed. I have friends who think that the kids, in that case, made a mistake. Whether they actually did or not is somewhat beside the point. The fact is that they made a decision that they believed in after weeks of real deliberation, and that decision was adhered to even though I personally thought (and told them I thought) that making the film might be a fine educational experience, might be a chance for us to provide an antidote to *Deliverance,* and might be a fine chance for us to help shape what could be a genuinely exciting television offering. In the end, the experience the students went through in the act of having to come to their decision was probably enough. And it was a weighty experience for me personally to watch them at work, see the intensity of their commitment to our project and our community, and see the seriousness with which they deliberated as to how they felt both the project and the community should be allowed to be used by others.

In another vein, if the request is from a person or group that wants to come and visit and be taken by us to meet some of the people we've written about, we turn it down. From the beginning, our hope was that our project would, in part, encourage others to begin to look in their own back yards for the riches that are there, and for the experiences that can come from that involvement with a community. Every neighborhood has its own Aunt Aries and its own kids that could easily be put in touch with them. When people want, instead, to come here and be given a guided tour, we've failed, in a sense, to accomplish part of what we set out to do. We have no intention of putting our contacts on public display, or running bus tours past their homes. That's not only degrading but dehumanizing.

On the other hand, if the request is from a person or group that wants to come and work with the kids, get (or give) ideas, engage them in some serious discussions, or perhaps try to implement the same sort of project back home, then we read the letter in class. If some kids want to host the group and really set up a first-rate visit, we give those kids the letter, and from that point on, it's their responsibility. One of them writes the group back, tells them to come ahead, works out the dates and details, and hosts the group when it arrives. If there are no kids who want to take it on, we write back with our apologies. The alternative (and we know this from bitter experience) is two or three groups a day coming through, no work done here, and, after a time, zero educational experiences for the students involved. The last thing we want is to see them turned into the equivalent of the bored, faceless guides at places like Mammoth Cave.

To handle the requests for craft items the contacts make, the kids each year set up a team that will take the letters, pick up the items, give the contacts the full purchase price, bring the items back, and wrap and ship them at our expense. It's one of many services we try to provide for our contacts as part of our attempt to thank them for the time they've spent with us. The kids get a good sense, through activities like these, of what it's like to give of themselves and use part of their resources to help others.

If the request if for a job with us, we don't usually consider it unless it comes from a community person, or a kid who used to work with us, has just finished college, and wants to come back home. If the request is for us to consider a manuscript for publication in the magazine, we turn it down, because the kids write all the articles. On the other hand, if someone writes in and wants us to find and take a picture of their grandfather's grave, or wants us to provide additional details about something we wrote, or wants other specific information and we have a kid who wants to track that down, we turn it over to him. If we don't have anyone with the time, we usually write back, tell them we're holding the request, and wait until a kid comes along who wants to tackle it. Theoretically, each student should be held responsible for his article and for any questions from readers that it may stimulate. The problem in our case is that by the time the article comes out in book form and begins to draw questions, the kid has already graduated from our school and is out in the world somewhere.

In some cases, we feel that the request really deserves attention whether or not there is a student to handle it. In those cases, we as a staff take it on ourselves on our own free time. By and large, however, the general rule is that if we can't turn what comes through the office into a true learning experience for some students here, then there's no room for it. The alternative is to be swamped, and to watch the main goals of our work go down the drain.

The second area of success is money, and again the question becomes that of how the income can be taken and used by the kids so they can learn and accomplish something in the process. Everyone wants it. Who's going to get it? And who's it going to be given by?

Some time ago, we set up a non-profit, tax-exempt corporation with our own Board of Directors, Advisory Boards, lawyer, etc. The corporation exists within the school as a separate organization. *All* of the income goes into the corporate account. A portion of it is used to pay the staff members who work with the kids, to pay the salaries of the many kids we hire full time to work with us during the summers, to buy equipment and supplies, pay our printing and postage and telephone bills, give scholarships or loans to our kids who want to go on to college and can't otherwise, pay expenses on extended collecting trips into the mountains, and so on.

Beyond those expenses, the students are encouraged to try to come up with responsible, useful ways in which the balance of the money can be invested to provide income to continue the project long after the book royalties have dried up; be returned to the community in which we work; be donated to worthy groups; or be used to help out our contacts.

Two years ago, for example, the students voted to purchase a fifty-acre piece of property to which they wished to move and then reconstruct about twenty endangered log buildings. A check for $35,000 was written to pay for the land, and a fourteen-year-old kid signed it. Millard Buchanan, a retired logger in the community, was hired as foreman; and with him in charge, a collection of community people and students began, in April of 1974, to move the buildings. By Christmas, they had seven log buildings and two barns up and under new roofs. This year, approximately ten more cabins will be added. Then, for years to come, new groups of community kids will be engaged in doing the required finishing work.

The area is divided into three groups of buildings. One area is set aside for the collection of artifacts (looms, spinning wheels, wagons, tools, etc.) the project has amassed over the years. Here, new groups of kids can actually use the collection themselves, or they can borrow from it to take supplies to a contact they've found who can show them how to make an object, but has long since parted with his tools and materials.

The second area will house, in separate buildings, our collection of audio tapes, photographs, videotape, and film. Each building will, aside from the collection, also contain working/editing studios. In the videotape cabin, for example, will be the editing decks and equipment the students use for producing the shows they film, edit, and broadcast on a weekly basis over the local cable TV network. Using equipment they've purchased themselves with book royalties, the kids produce shows that range from basketball games, to community group discussions of local issues, to *Foxfire* interviews that bring the pages of the magazine to life — all shows that we all hope give our community a new sense of unity and interdependence while teaching the kids some very professional skills.

The third group of buildings will be set aside and furnished so that people who attend workshops, conferences, or board meetings that the kids host will have accommodations; or so additional staff members who want to work with us for short periods of time will be able to settle in right away in rent-free housing.

The remainder of the land — some forty acres — will be used as an environmental laboratory for all the students in the area.

The students have decided — in what will doubtless be greeted as an unpopular decision — that the project will be closed to the general traveling public. There are many historic restorations in the mountains that people can visit, and the kids don't want to use their money to pave large parking lots or hire the maintenance people and guides who would be necessary. It will be open to any local community groups or individuals who wish to work with us or visit, or to a limited number of workshops or special guests. Rather than being a museum which tourists visit, it will instead be a working studio, dedicated to the people of this region, from which will come the books and magazines, films, recordings, and video shows the kids will produce in concert with the community people they will enlist to work with them.

Over the next few years, enough money will probably come in to complete the project, but the kids, in an interesting maneuver, are informally approaching groups outside the mountains who may wish to provide a gift that will sponsor the cost of the reconstruction of a building (approximately $3,700). Whenever such a grant is made, a plaque on the building's wall acknowledges that fact, and money that would have been spent there can be set aside to fund yet another project. Recently, for example, just such a gift from the Georgia Bicentennial Commission enabled us to bring out the first book we have published ourselves, *News from Pigeon Roost.* The book is an edited collection of thirty years of newspaper columns written by Harvey J. Miller of Greenmountain, North Carolina, for the Johnson City (Tennessee) Tri-County *News.* Jammed with the affairs of day-to-day living in a tiny mountain community, the book was, as Harvey called it in the introduction, "A dream come true." Part of the first edition was sent as an issue of *Foxfire* to all our subscribers, and the remainder (1,500 copies) was sent free to Harvey to market himself through his still-active weekly column and through stores in the area. All the proceeds are his to keep.

Through all these projects, whether they be donating the publishing costs of a book to someone like Harvey Miller, buying a new guitar for a local songwriter, helping with the doctor's bills for a contact, or providing employment in the county, the kids add yet another dimension to their activities and their education — one that I feel is going to make them ever more willing to step beyond their own needs and extend themselves to others around them. It's success, used as a tool to make positive things happen.

One final area stimulated by success has to be wrestled with, and it's a rough one. It occurs when a person like myself realizes that an organization has been created that has equipment, land, vehicles, employees, and buildings, and he wakes up asking, "What have I done?" It's then that some of the big questions come: "What happens if a plane I'm on goes down coming into Charlotte?" "What happens if a kid falls off the roof of one of our buildings and breaks his back?" "What happens if I suddenly find that more and more of my creative energy is going into the maintenance, care, and feeding of the beast itself than into the projects, or into insuring the flexibility, responsiveness, and creativity of the group as the needs of kids change from year to year?"

We've all seen it happen. A great idea (like a public school system) is somehow transformed into a grotesque, clanking, rust-encrusted machine the basic maintenance of which saps everyone's time and energy to the detriment of the original goals. Or someone founds a great organization only to find himself afraid that not a single other person can run it nearly as well; when senility strikes years later, the individual has made no plans for the organization's survival, or for a hand-picked successor to carry on, and the whole thing collapses with a sigh.

And it's not enough to say, "Let it all take care of itself." It won't. In our case, who gets our land? Let that take care of itself, and it falls into the hands of a Florida land developer. Who gets our continuing royalties from the sale of the books? Let that take care of itself and the IRS snatches it. Who gets our archives and our collection? Let that take care of itself, and every antique dealer around has a field day.

It's not the problem of whether or not the stuff will be disposed of. It's how it will be disposed of if something goes awry. Without some attention to those details, it could all fall into the hands of the vultures who wait on the sidelines, cheering, and then move in to get a free ride off our sweat and toil, make money off what we've done, and leave the kids by the wayside wondering just what the hell happened.

We've tried to cover all that. Early, talented graduates of our school have been and are being brought back from college as full-time employees and board members. Money has been set aside to guarantee salaries. Liability insurance packages have been set up. Luckily, the kids guarantee our responsiveness and flexibility just because they are kids, and we care about them deeply — there's a new group of them every year, fresh and demanding, clamoring to step in and take over.

If all else fails, there are documents that will insure that equipment will be given to appropriate groups, and the restoration will go to the county as our way of thanking its residents for being so patient and co-operative with us. And at the very least, we can all rest secure knowing that a number of kids who worked with us were able to share and help direct a great experiment that took them, for a time, far beyond their ordinary high school fare. And that's something. But I'm counting on the belief that we can do even better than that, and I'm working toward it.

Beyond all this, of course, is the ego-burden success can place on a person's head. Groups approach me, convinced that I am something I know that I am not. Convinced that I came to the mountains with the whole grand scheme intact like a symphony in my mind. And, most distressingly, convinced that it was so brilliantly executed tactically that they could never duplicate it themselves.

That's all baloney. The whole thing was a series of both fortunate accidents (having a fraternity brother at Doubleday, for example, who set up *The Foxfire Book;* or meeting the IDEAS folks completely by accident one day in Washington), and tiny, day-by-day responses to the needs of a group of kids that gradually gave us the shape and form we now have.

The whole thing is now being duplicated so many times (thanks to the help and persistence of IDEAS, which has used our kids as consultants to help start similar projects in places from Maine to Missouri, from Alaska to Hawaii, and which is now making available a complete printed package that details to any interested group the educational philosophy and the various skills and tips helpful to know in pulling it off) that it is now obvious that all manner of individuals, institutions, and informal groupings of good people can get something similar going in their own locations if they just want to badly enough.

I keep reminding myself of all that.

The ever-present collection of people seeking autographs can change a person's head, but the kids are really helpful there. As folks come up, the kids often nudge me from behind and whisper something like, "Think you're a big deal don't you?" And I keep reminding myself that we, as a staff, are guests in this school, and that we could be asked to leave at any time if things went awry. That, of course, would be our death — we would no longer have access to the students, and there would no longer be any reason to continue. All these facts help keep success in some sort of perspective, and that's vital.

Is it going to work? I think so, I think we're going to be okay. Because yesterday, as I was walking across campus, two kids tackled me and the books and papers I was carrying were suddenly scattered across the grass. ∎

Louis J. Halle
International Behavior and the Prospects of Human Survival*

One's aspirations are necessarily influenced by one's assessment of the current situation and of one's prospects. Halle's view might at one time have been considered pessimistic; now, many would consider it realistic and even perceptive. Given that humans are demonstrably dangerous and that the human condition is particularly precarious and fragile, Halle understandably is seeking small changes that can make big differences. He is not seeking to change human nature, nor even, for that matter, to influence attitudes. He is merely looking for cultural forms, for behavior patterns, that would be viable. Note that in the process he is placing an interpretation on contemporary human life, an interpretation that makes the sorts of behavior he is advocating seem eminently reasonable.

■   During the 1950s, the students in American universities showed themselves politically indifferent and inert to a remarkable degree. In the second half of the 1960s, however, important numbers of them suddenly began rampaging against virtually every aspect of established society. It was the same biological stock in both cases, but there had been a sudden shift from one attitude of mind to an opposite attitude, entailing a radical change in social behavior.

These cases show what I mean when I say that the attitudes and manners of people, unlike their biological heritage, can change radically overnight. It is in this that I find what grounds of hope I do for our ability, as a species, to meet the problem of survival. Here, in the domain of social attitudes and manners, we are nothing if not changeable — and therefore adaptable.

It is, if you will, in the superficial aspects of human behavior that I find my hope. There are men for whom I have the greatest respect, as individuals, who say that we should all learn to love one another, and that by so doing we shall find the way to salvation. Leaving considerations of religion aside, this seems to me impractical in that it asks too

*Excerpted from J. F. Eisenberg and W. S. Dillon (Eds.) *Man and Beast: Comparative Social Behavior.* Washington, D.C.: Smithsonian Institution Press. 1971. Pages 360–361. Reprinted by permission.

much too immediately of our human nature. What seems to me more practical, in the immediate crisis, is to accept the fact that we shall continue to dislike one another, and to ask merely that we take the sting out of that dislike by adopting good manners in dealing with one another.

I live, today, in what may well be the happiest country in the world — or the least unhappy. Soundings of opinion have shown that there is probably less dissatisfaction with their circumstances among the Swiss than among any other people. They are, very likely, more at peace with one another (as well as with the rest of the world) than any other people. This, however, represents an extraordinary paradox, for the Swiss constitute a nation that, culturally and politically, is deeply divided. Having now lived among them for over a dozen years, I have at last become familiar with what does not usually show on the surface of the national life, the bitter antipathies, often amounting to hatred, among the various subcommunities that make up what is, after all, a very artificial nation. There is an ingrained hostility of the French-speaking Swiss toward the German-speaking Swiss, which is reciprocated by the German-speaking Swiss. There is no love lost between the half of the Swiss population that is Protestant and the half that is Roman Catholic. There is bitter antagonism between Geneva and Lausanne, and similar antagonisms between the various cantons. Yet it is the rule that, in direct dealings between these mutually hostile groups, the greatest courtesy and consideration are shown. Good manners are a substitute for love. They take the curse out of mutual dislike and make Switzerland the relatively happy nation it is. In fact, it is the consciousness of how easily the nation could fall apart that makes the Swiss so moderate, so considerate, and so courteous in their dealings with one another.

The Swiss were not always this way. Warfare among the cantons was common up to 1847, when the last intercantonal war took place. By that time, the price the Swiss were paying for expressing their mutual antipathies or conflicting interests in such violent terms had impressed itself on them so thoroughly that they then and there developed the self-disciplined manner of dealing with one another that has happily characterized their association ever since. That association was finally institutionalized in the constitution of 1848, establishing the present Swiss Confederation.

I see something like this happening, as well, in the association of West European states generally. The cost of two European civil wars in this century has impressed itself on the European peoples, and while it has not caused them to love one another, it has brought about a moderation and mutual consideration in their behavior toward one another that was not evident in the years leading up to 1914.

© 1971 by NEA, Inc.

"What bothers me, is goin' inta town an' seein' all them young folks wearin' blue jeans an' overalls. I had NO IDEA there was so many farm hands outta work!"

Reprinted by permission of Newspaper Enterprise Association.

It is possible that racial antagonism in the United States will, in the near future, produce such horrors as, by a common revulsion, will cause a new sobriety to prevail, impressing on both races the need of moderation and good manners in dealing with each other, whether they like each other or not. What else will enable us to live with the racial problem over the long decades until the secular evolution of human society has brought some solution, whatever it may be, that is hardly foreseeable as yet? We often do better with problems if we concentrate on how to live with them rather than on how to solve them completely at one stroke.

All this has its obvious application to the international relations of our times. The great peace-keeping art, traditionally, has been diplomacy, when properly exercised; and diplomacy, when properly exercised, has always entailed the most formalized good manners between antagonists, including a use of language distinguished by its courtesy and moderation.   ∎

Jane Jacobs
The Valuable Inefficiencies and Impracticalities of Cities*

This paper and the one that follows demonstrate the usefulness of the interpretation strategy in a rather backwards fashion — by showing how costly an inappropriate conception can be. They leave little doubt that models make a difference, although not always the sort of difference one might wish. On the other hand, it is very difficult to demonstrate that an *appropriate* conception makes a difference — "things working" does not have an identifiable cause in the same sense that "things breaking down" often does.

∎   People who think we would be better off without cities, especially without big, unmanageable, disorderly cities, never tire of explaining that cities grown too big are, in any case, inefficient and impractical. Certainly, as we all know, the most routine and ordinary activities — getting people to work, moving goods around, keeping trees alive, making space for school playgrounds, disposing of garbage — absorb ridiculous amounts of energy, time and money in cities, as compared to towns and villages. And it does seem as if big cities are not necessarily efficient for producing goods and services. Factories move to the outskirts and the suburbs, and to small and distant towns, often for reasons of efficiency.

All this is true. Cities are indeed inefficient and impractical compared with towns; and among cities themselves, the largest and most rapidly growing at any given time are apt to be the least efficient. But I propose to argue that these grave and real deficiencies are necessary to economic development and thus are exactly what make cities uniquely valuable to economic life. By this, I do not mean that cities are economically valuable in spite of their inefficiency and impracticality but rather because they are inefficient and impractical. . . .

EFFICIENT MANCHESTER, INEFFICIENT BIRMINGHAM

Let us begin by examining city inefficiency from the point of view of two English manufacturing cities, Manchester and Birmingham. Back in 1844, a character in one of Disraeli's novels said, "Certainly Manchester is the most wonderful city of modern times. It is the philosopher alone who can conceive the grandeur of Manchester and the immensity of its future." The remark, says the city historian, Asa Briggs, in *Victorian Cities,* was representative of "most contemporary social comment." Manchester, of course, also occupies a very special place in economic history because Marx and Engels were so greatly interested in it. Marx based much of his analysis of capitalism and its class struggles upon Manchester. He, like Disraeli, saw it as a prophetic city, although ominous in its prophecy rather than grand.

What impressed Disraeli, Marx and their contemporaries, and what made Manchester seem to them — for better or worse — the most advanced of all cities of the time was the stunning efficiency of its immense textile mills. The mills were Manchester. By the 1840s their work dominated the city completely. Here, it seemed, was the meaning of the industrial revolution, arrived at its logical conclusions. Here was the coming thing. Here was the kind of city that made all other cities old-fashioned — vestiges of an industrially undeveloped past.

Even those observers and commentators, and there were many of them, who were appalled by the sordid living conditions and terrible death rates of Manchester, and those who saw, as Marx and Engels did, how immense and ominous was the social and economic gulf between the few mill owners and their poor and hopeless masses of workers, even they believed that the terrible efficiency of Manchester was a portent of the cities of the future — if not all cities, at least capitalist cities.

Birmingham was just the kind of city that seemed to have been outmoded by Manchester. "It was always a peculiarity of Birmingham," wrote a London journalist of the 1850s whom Briggs quotes, "that small household trades existed which gave the inmates independence and often led — if the trade continued good — to competence or fortune." Briggs adds that these endeavors often led to failure too.

Birmingham had a few relatively large industries, although nothing remotely approaching the scale of Manchester's, and even these accounted for only a small part of Birmingham's total output of work and total employment. Most of Birmingham's manufacturing was carried out in small organizations employing no more than a dozen workmen; many had even fewer. A lot of these little organizations did bits and pieces of work for other little organizations. They were not rationally and efficiently consolidated. There was a lot of waste motion, overlapping work, duplication that could certainly have been eliminated through consolidations. Furthermore, able workmen were forever breaking away from their employers in Birmingham and setting up for themselves, compounding the fragmentation of work there.

It was also a little hard to say just what Birmingham was living on because it had no obvious specialty of the kind that made Manchester's economy so easy to understand and so impressive. To try to describe Birmingham's economy then (or now) is not easy. It was a muddle of oddments. In the old days, saddle and harness making seems to have been the chief industry, but all sorts of other hardware and tool manufacturing had been added to the manufacture of hardware for saddles and harnesses. In the seventeenth and eighteenth centuries, the city had enjoyed a large trade in shoe buckles, but the shoelace put an end to that. A rising button industry had more than compensated for the loss. Some of the button makers used glass decoratively and this had afforded opportunity to makers of bits and pieces of colored glass who, working from this foothold, had managed to build up a considerable local glass industry. In the nineteenth century, Birmingham was also making, among other things, guns, jewelry, cheap trinkets and papier-mâché trays. The work of making cheap metal toys led to making cheap steel penpoints. The work of making guns afforded opportunities for making rifling machines and other machine tools.

All this, of course, was just the sort of old-fashioned muddling that people in England of the 1840s and 1850s were accustomed to see going on in cities. It was not modern. It was not an expression of the new age. It afforded no particular new portents, either terrible or grand. At the time of all the intellectual excitement about Manchester, nobody was nominating Birmingham as the city of the future. But as it turned out Manchester was not the city of the future and Birmingham was.

Manchester's efficient specialization portended stagnation and a profoundly obsolescent city. For "the immensity of its future" proved to consist of immense losses of its markets as other people in other places learned how to spin and weave cotton efficiently too. Manchester developed nothing sufficient to compensate for these lost markets. Today it has become the very symbol of a city in long and unremitting decline. Its idleness and underemployment and the hardships of its people would be much greater than they are, were it not for the migration of young people, decade after decade and generation after generation, to London, Birmingham and overseas cities in search of more opportunity. The economy of Birmingham did not become obsolete, like Manchester's. Its fragmented and inefficient little industries kept adding new work, and splitting off new organizations, some of which have become very large but are still outweighed in total employment and production by the many small ones.

Today, only two cities in all of Britain remain economically vigorous and prosperous. One is London. The second is Birmingham. The others have stagnated one by one, much as Manchester did, like so many lights going out. British town planners, ironically, have regarded London and Birmingham as problems, because they are places in which much new work is added to old and thus cities that persist in growing. The British New Towns policy was specifically devised to discourage the growth of London and Birmingham and "drain it off." Birmingham's economy has remained alive and has kept up to date. Manchester's has not. Was Manchester, then, really efficient? It was indeed efficient and Birmingham was not. Manchester had acquired the efficiency of a company town. Birmingham had retained something different: a high rate of development work.

Efficiency as it is commonly defined — and I do not propose to change its definition, which is clear and useful — is the ratio of work accomplished to energy supplied. We can speak of high or low rates of efficiency because, in any given instance, we have two relevant factors to measure: input of energy, and quantity and quality (value) or work accomplished. We can compare the measurements in one instance with measurements in other instances. Manchester turned out a great deal of cloth relative to the energy supplied by its workers and by those who served the needs of the workers in the city.

But these particular measurements are not relevant when development work is wanted. A candy manufacturer, reminiscing to a *New Yorker* reporter about the first candy bar he developed as a shipping clerk in a candy factory, recalls, "I showed it to my boss and he was very happy. 'How many of these can you make in a minute?' he asked me. 'In a *minute*?' I said. 'It took me four months to make this one!' " Suppose it had taken him eight months? Or two months? That measurement has nothing to do with the operating efficiency envisioned by his boss.

Efficiency of operation, in any given case, is a sequel to earlier development work. Development work is a messy, time- and energy-consuming business of trial, error and failure. The only certainties in it are trial and error. Success is not a certainty. And even when the result is successful, it is often a surprise, not what was actually being sought. ■

Christopher Alexander
A City Is Not a Tree*

This paper by Alexander shows the importance of interpretation by tracing the unfortunate consequences of a "model" that is inappropriate to the task; it also shows why humans, because they are humans, might welcome such an oversimplified point of view. But the paper shows a great deal more than this. Indeed, it is so rich, so broadly applicable to a host of different fields and problems, that it must be counted one of the landmark intellectual contributions of our time.

The subject matter of Alexander's paper is, strictly speaking, the structure of the city. But the arguments are so basic and far-reaching that they apply to almost any structure, certainly to those structures concerned with effectiveness or adaptiveness in a situation of uncertainty. Thus, the arguments are thought provoking in such varied domains as organization structure, political structure, and the structure of the brain. While the interpretation that Alexander offers is admittedly not quite as simple and neat as the tree which a city is not, it has some special advantages of its own. Perhaps most important, it provides an interpretation, a function, and, ultimately, a value for the disorder and messiness that persist in the world despite our best efforts.

A word on Alexander's use of mathematics: It is essentially playful and should be taken in the same spirit. Those choosing not to indulge will find themselves at no disadvantage. Others might find it thoroughly engaging and stimulating.

PART ONE

■   The tree of my title is not a green tree with leaves. It is the name for a pattern of thought. The semi-lattice is the name for another, more complex, pattern of thought.

In order to relate these abstract patterns to the nature of the city, I must first make a simple distinction. I want to call those cities which have arisen more or less spontaneously over many, many years *natural cities*. And I shall call those cities and parts of cities which have been deliberately created by designers and planners *artificial cities*. Siena, Liverpool, Kyoto, Manhattan are examples of natural

*From C. Alexander "A city is not a tree." *Architectural Forum,* 1965. Whitney Publications, Inc. Reprinted by permission.

cities. Levittown, Chandigarh, and the British New Towns are examples of artificial cities.

It is more and more widely recognized today that there is some essential ingredient missing from artificial cities. When compared with ancient cities that have acquired the patina of life, our modern attempts to create cities artificially are, from a human point of view, entirely unsuccessful.

Architects themselves admit more and more freely that they really like living in old buildings more than new ones. The non-art-loving public at large, instead of being grateful to architects for what they do, regards the onset of modern buildings and modern cities everywhere as an inevitable, rather sad piece of the larger fact that the world is going to the dogs.

It is much too easy to say that these opinions represent only people's unwillingness to forget the past, and their determination to be traditional. For myself, I trust this conservatism. Americans are usually willing to move with the times. Their growing reluctance to accept the modern city evidently expresses a longing for some real thing, something which for the moment escapes our grasp.

The prospect that we may be turning the world into a place peopled only by little glass and concrete boxes has alarmed many architects too. To combat the glass box future, many valiant protests and designs have been put forward, all hoping to recreate in modern form the various characteristics of the natural city which seem to give it life. But so far these designs have only remade the old. They have not been able to create the new.

"Outrage," the *Architectural Review's* campaign against the way in which new construction and telegraph poles are wrecking the English town, based its remedies, essentially, on the idea that the spatial sequence of buildings and open spaces must be controlled if scale is to be preserved — an idea that really derives from Camillo Sitte's book about ancient squares and piazzas.

Another kind of remedy, in protest against the monotony of Levittown, tries to recapture the richness of shape found in the houses of a natural old town. Llewelyn Davies's village at Rushbrooke in England is an example — each cottage is slightly different from its neighbor, the roofs jut in and out, at picturesque angles.

A third suggested remedy is to get high density back into the city. The idea seems to be that if the whole metropolis could only be like Grand Central Station, with lots and lots of layers and tunnels all over the place, and enough people milling around in them, maybe it would be human again.

Another very brilliant critic of the deadness which is everywhere is Jane Jacobs. Her criticisms are excellent. But when you read her concrete proposals for what we should do instead, you get the idea that she wants the great modern city to be a sort of mixture between Greenwich village and some Italian hill town, full of short blocks and people sitting in the street.

The problem these designers have tried to face is real. It is vital that we discover the property of old towns which gave them life and get it back into our own artificial cities. But we cannot do this merely by remaking English villages, Italian piazzas, and Grand Central Stations. Too many designers today seem to be yearning for the physical and plastic characteristics of the past, instead of searching for the abstract ordering principle which the towns of the past happened to have, and which our modern conceptions of the city have not yet found.

What is the inner nature, the ordering principle, which distinguishes the artificial city from the natural city?

You will have guessed from my title what I believe this ordering principle to be. I believe that a natural city has the organization of a semi-lattice; but that when we organize a city artificially, we organize it as a tree.

Both the tree and the semi-lattice are ways of thinking about how a large collection of many small systems goes to make up a large and complex system. More generally, they are both names for structures of sets.

In order to define such structures, let me first define the concept of a set. A set is a collection of elements which for some reason we think of as belonging together. Since, as designers, we are concerned with the physical living city and its physical backbone, we most naturally restrict ourselves to considering sets which are collections of material elements such as people, blades of grass, cars, bricks, molecules, houses, gardens, water pipes, the water molecules that run in them, etc.

When the elements of a set belong together because they cooperate or work together somehow, we call the set of elements a system.

For example, in Berkeley at the corner of Hearst and Euclid, there is a drug store, and outside the drug store a traffic light. In the entrance to the drug store there is a newsrack where the day's papers are displayed. When the light is red, people who are waiting to cross the street stand idly by the light; and since they have nothing to do, they look at the papers displayed on the newsrack which they can see from where they stand. Some of them just read the headlines, others actually buy a paper while they wait.

This effect makes the newsrack and the traffic light interdependent; the newsrack, the newspapers on it, the money going from people's pockets to the dime slot, the people who stop at the light and read papers, the traffic light, the electric impulses which make the lights change, and the sidewalk which the people stand on form a system — they all work together.

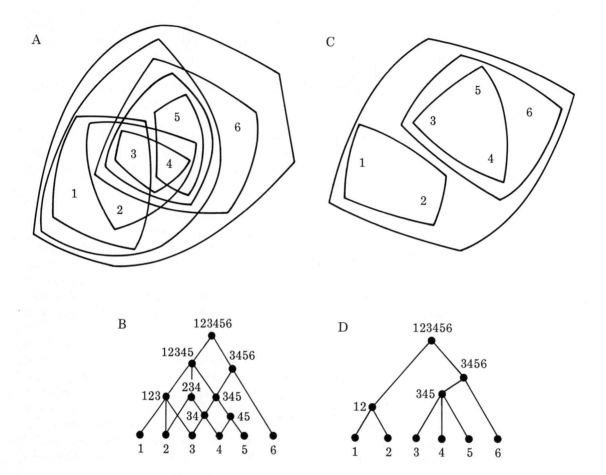

From the designer's point of view, the physically unchanging part of this system is of special interest. The newsrack, the traffic light, and the sidewalk between them, related as they are, form the fixed part of the system. It is the unchanging receptable in which the changing parts of the system — people, newspapers, money, and electrical impulses — can work together. I define this fixed part as a unit of the city. It derives its coherence as a unit both from the forces which hold its own elements together, and from the dynamic coherence of the larger living system which includes it as a fixed invariant part.

Of the many, many fixed concrete subsets of the city which are the receptacles for its systems, and can therefore be thought of as significant physical units, we usually single out a few for special consideration. In fact, I claim that whatever picture of the city someone has is defined precisely by the subsets he sees as units.

Now, a collection of subsets which goes to make up such a picture is not merely an amorphous collection. Automatically, merely because relationships are established among the subsets once the subsets are chosen, the collection has a definite structure.

To understand this structure, let us think abstractly for a moment, using numbers as symbols. Instead of talking about the real sets of millions of real particles which occur in the city, let us consider a simpler structure made of just half a dozen elements. Label these elements 1, 2, 3, 4, 5, 6. Not including the full set [1, 2, 3, 4, 5, 6], the empty set [-], and the one element sets [1], [2], [3], [4], [5], [6], there are 56 different subsets we can pick from six elements.

Suppose we now pick out certain of these 56 sets (just as we pick out certain sets and call them units when we form our picture of the city). Let us say, for example, that we pick the following subsets: [123], [34], [45], [234], [345], [12345], [3456].

What are the possible relationships among these sets? Some sets will be entirely part of larger sets, as [34] is part of [345] and [3456]. Some of the sets will overlap, like [123] and [234]. Some of the sets will be disjoint — that is, contain no elements in common, like [123] and [45].

We can see these relationships displayed in two ways. In diagram A each set chosen to be a unit has a line drawn round it. In diagram B the chosen sets are arranged in order of ascending magnitude, so that whenever one set contains another (as [345] contains [34]), there is a vertical path leading from one to the other. For the sake of clarity and visual economy, it is usual to draw lines only between sets which have no further sets and lines between them; thus the line between [34] and [345], and the line between [345] and [3456], make it unnecessary to draw a line between [34] and [3456].

As we see from these two representations, the choice of subsets alone endows the collection of subsets as a whole with an overall structure. This is the structure which we are concerned with here. When the structure meets certain conditions it is called a semi-lattice. When it meets other more restrictive conditions, it is called a tree.

The semi-lattice axiom goes like this:

A collection of sets forms a semi-lattice if and only if, when two overlapping sets belong to the collection, then the set of elements common to both also belongs to the collection.

The structure illustrated in diagrams A and B is a semi-lattice. It satisfies the axiom since, for instance, [234] and [345] both belong to the collection, and their common part, [34], also belongs to it. (As far as the city is concerned, this axiom states merely that wherever two units overlap, the area of overlap is itself a recognizable entity and hence a unit also. In the case of the drug store example, one unit consists of the newsrack, sidewalk, and traffic light. Another unit consists of the drug store itself, with its entry and the newsrack. The two units overlap in the newsrack. Clearly this area of overlap is itself a recognizable unit, and so satisfies the axiom above which defines the characteristics of a semi-lattice.)

The tree axiom states:

A collection of sets forms a tree if and only if, for any two sets that belong to the collection, either one is wholly contained in the other, or else they are wholly disjoint.

The structure illustrated in diagrams C and D is a tree. Since this axiom excludes the possibility of overlapping sets, there is no way in which the semi-lattice axiom can be violated, so that every tree is a trivially simple semi-lattice.

However, in this paper we are not so much concerned with the fact that a tree happens to be a semi-lattice, but with the difference between trees and those more general semi-lattices which are *not* trees because they *do* contain overlapping units. We are concerned with the difference between structures in which no overlap occurs, and those structures in which overlap does occur.

It is not merely the overlap which makes the distinction between the two important. Still more important is the fact that the semi-lattice is potentially a much more complex and subtle structure than a tree. We may see just how much more complex a semi-lattice can be than a tree in the following fact: a tree based on 20 elements can contain at most 19 further subsets of the 20, while a semi-lattice based on the same 20 elements can contain more than 1,000,000 different subsets.

This enormously greater variety is an index of the great structural complexity a semi-lattice can have when compared with the structural simplicity of a tree. It is this lack of structural complexity, characteristic of trees, which is crippling our conceptions of the city.

To demonstrate, let us look at some modern conceptions of the city, each of which I shall show to be essentially a tree. It will perhaps be useful, while we look at these plans, to have a little ditty in our minds:

Big fleas have little fleas
Upon their back to bite 'em,
Little fleas have lesser fleas,
And so ad infinitum.

This rhyme expresses perfectly and succinctly the structural principle of the tree.

Figure 1. Columbia, Maryland, Community Research and Development Inc.: Neighborhoods, in clusters of five, form "villages." Transportation joins the villages into a new town. The organization is a tree.

Figure 2. Greenbelt, Maryland, Clarence Stein: This "garden city" has been broken down into superblocks. Each superblock contains schools, parks, and a number of subsidiary groups of houses built around parking lots. The organization is a tree.

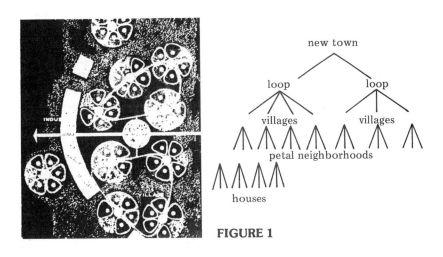

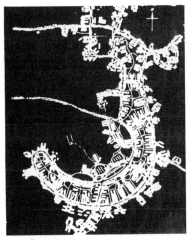

FIGURE 1

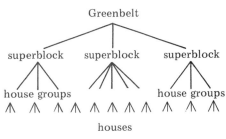

FIGURE 2

Figure 3. Greater London plan (1943), Abercrombie and Forshaw: The drawing depicts the structure conceived by Abercrombie for London. It is made of a large number of communities, each sharply separated from all adjacent communities. Abercrombie writes, "The proposal is to emphasize the identity of the existing communities, to increase their degree of segregation, and where necessary to reorganize them as separate and definite entities." And again, "The communities themselves consist of a series of sub-units, generally with their own shops and schools, corresponding to neighborhood units." The city is conceived as a tree with two principal levels. The communities are the larger units of the structure; the smaller subunits are neighborhoods. There are no overlapping units. The structure is a tree.

Figure 4. Tokyo plan, Kenzo Tange: This is a beautiful example. The plan consists of a series of loops stretched across the Tokyo Bay. There are four major loops, each of which contains three medium loops. In the second major loop, one medium loop is the railway station and another is the port. Otherwise, each medium loop contains three minor loops which are residential neighborhoods, except in the third major loop where one contains government offices and another industrial offices.

Figure 5. Mesa City, Paolo Soleri: The organic shapes of Mesa City lead us, at a careless glance, to believe that it is a richer structure than our more obviously rigid examples. But when we look at it in detail we find precisely the same principle of organization. Take, particularly, the university center. Here we find the center of the city divided into a university and a residential quarter, which is itself divided into a number of villages (actually apartment towers) for 4,000 inhabitants, each again subdivided further and surrounded by groups of still smaller dwelling units.

Figure 6. Chandigarh (1951) by Le Corbusier: The whole city is served by a commercial center in the middle, linked to the administrative center at the head. Two subsidiary elongated, commercial cores are strung out along the major arterial roads, running north-south. Subsidiary to these are further administrative, community and commercial centers, one for each of the city's twenty sectors.

Figure 7. Brazilia, Lúcio Costa: The entire form pivots about the central axis, and each of the two halves is served by a single main artery. This main artery is in turn fed by subsidiary arteries parallel to it. Finally, these are fed by the roads which surround the superblocks themselves. The structure is a tree.

Figure 8. Communitas, Percival and Paul Goodman: Communitas is explicitly organized as a tree: it is first divided into four concentric major zones, the innermost being a commercial center, the next a university, the third residential and medical, and fourth open country.

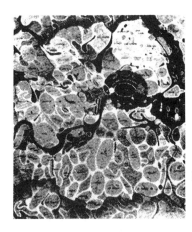

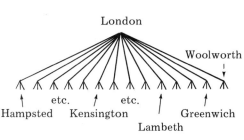

FIGURE 3

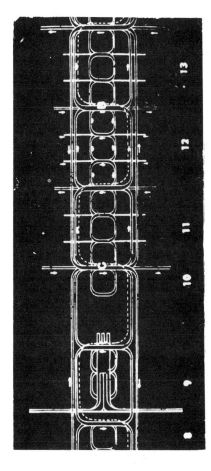

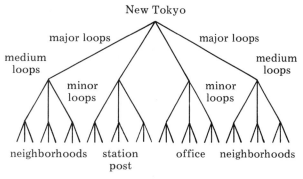

FIGURE 4

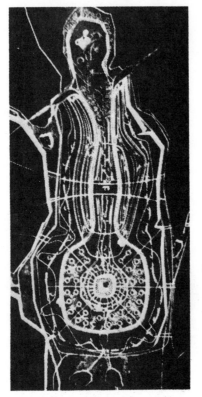

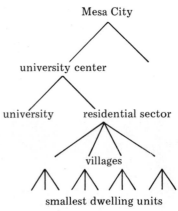

FIGURE 5

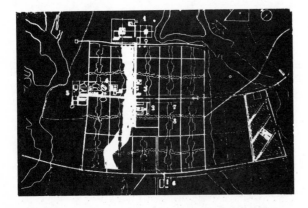

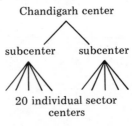

FIGURE 6

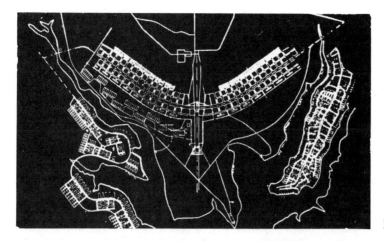

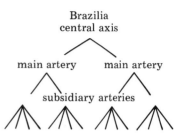

FIGURE 7

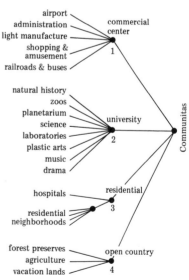

FIGURE 8

Each of these is further subdivided: the commercial center is represented as a great cylindrical skyscraper, containing five layers: airport, administration, light manufacture, shopping and amusement; and, at the bottom, railroads, buses and mechanical services. The university is divided into eight sectors comprising natural history, zoos and aquariums, planetarium, science, laboratories, plastic arts, music and drama. The third concentric ring is divided into neighborhoods of 4,000 people each, not consisting of individual houses, but of apartment blocks, each of these containing further individual dwelling units. Finally, the open country is divided into three segments: forest preserves, agriculture, and vacation-lands. The over-all organization is a tree.

The most beautiful example of all I have kept until last, because it symbolizes the problem perfectly. It appears in Hilberseimer's book called *The Nature of Cities*. He describes the fact that certain Roman towns had their origin as military camps, and then shows a picture of a modern military encampment as a kind of archetypal form for the city. It is not possible to have a structure which is a clearer tree.

The symbol is apt, for, of course, the organization of the army was created precisely in order to create discipline and rigidity. When a city is endowed with a tree structure, this is what happens to the city and its people. Hilberseimer's own scheme for the commercial area of a city is based on the army camp archetype.

Each of these structures, then, is a tree. Each unit in each tree that I have described, moreover, is the fixed, unchanging residue of some system in the living city (just as a house is the residue of the interactions between the members of a family, their emotions, and their belongings; and a free-way is the residue of movement and commercial exchange).

However, in every city there are thousands, even millions, of times as many more systems at work whose physical residue does not appear as a unit in these tree structures. In the worst cases, the units which do appear fail to correspond to any living reality; and the real systems, whose existence actually makes the city live, have been provided with no physical receptacle.

Neither the Columbia plan nor the Stein plan, for example, corresponds to social realities. The physical layout of the plans, and the way they function, suggests a hierarchy of stronger and stronger closed social groups, ranging from the whole city down to the family, each formed by associational ties of different strength.

In a traditional society, if we ask a man to name his best friends and then ask each of these in turn to name their best friends, they will all name each other so that they form a closed group. A village is made of a number of separate closed groups of this kind.

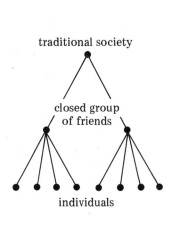

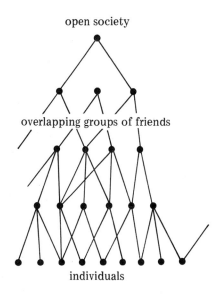

FIGURE 9

But today's social structure is utterly different. If we ask a man to name his friends and then ask them in turn to name their friends, they will all name different people, very likely unknown to the first person; these people would again name others, and so on outwards. There are virtually no closed groups of people in modern society. The reality of today's social structure is thick with overlap — the systems of friends and acquaintances form a semi-lattice, not a tree (figure 9).

In the natural city, even the house on a long street (not in some little cluster) is a more accurate acknowledgement of the fact that your friends live not next door, but far away, and can only be reached by bus or automobile. In this respect Manhattan has more overlap in it than Greenbelt. And though one can argue that in Greenbelt too, friends are only minutes away by car, one must then ask: Since certain groups *have* been emphasized by the physical units of the physical structure, why are just these the most irrelevant ones?

In the second part of this paper, I shall further demonstrate why the living city cannot be properly contained in a receptacle which is a tree — that indeed, its very life stems from the fact that it is not a tree.

Finally, I shall try to show that it is the process of thought itself which works in a treelike way, so that whenever a city is "thought out" instead of "grown," it is bound to get a treelike structure.

In the first part of this article, we saw that the units of which an artificial city is made up are organized to form a tree. So that we get a

PART TWO
really clear understanding of what this means, and shall better see its implications, let us define a tree once again:

Whenever we have a tree structure, it means that within this structure no piece of any unit is every connected to other units, except through the medium of that unit as a whole.

The enormity of this restriction is difficult to grasp. It is a little as though the members of a family were not free to make friends outside the family, except when the family as a whole made a friendship.

In simplicity of structure the tree is comparable to the compulsive desire for neatness and order that insists the candlesticks on a mantlepiece be perfectly straight and perfectly symmetrical about the center. The semi-lattice, by comparison, is the structure of a complex fabric; it is the structure of living things; of great paintings and symphonies.

It must be emphasized, lest the orderly mind shrink in horror from anything that is not clearly articulated and categorized in tree form, that the idea of overlap, ambiguity, multiplicity of aspect, and the semi-lattice, are not less orderly than the rigid tree, but more so. They represent a thicker, tougher, more subtle and more complex view of structure.

Let us now look at the ways in which the natural, when unconstrained by artificial conceptions, shows itself to be a semi-lattice.

A major aspect of the city's social structure which a tree can never mirror properly is illustrated by Ruth Glass's redevelopment plan for Middlesborough, a city of 200,000 which she recommends be broken down into 29 separate neighborhoods. After picking her 29 neighborhoods by determining where the sharpest discontinuities of building type, income, and job type occur, she asks herself the question: "If we examine some of the social systems which actually exist for the people in such a neighborhood, do the physical units defined by these various social systems all define the same spatial neighborhood?" Her own answer to this question is, *no*.

Each of the social systems she examines is a nodal system. It is made of some sort of central node, plus the people who use this center. Specifically she takes elementary schools, secondary schools, youth clubs, adult clubs, post offices, greengrocers, and grocers selling sugar. Each of these centers draws its users from a certain spatial area or spatial unit. This spatial unit is the physical residue of the social system as a whole, and is therefore a unit in the terms of this paper. The units corresponding to different kinds of centers for the single neighborhood of Waterloo Road are shown in figure 10.

The hard outline is the boundary of the so-called neighborhood itself. The white circle stands for the youth club, and the small solid rings stand for areas where its members live. The ringed spot is the

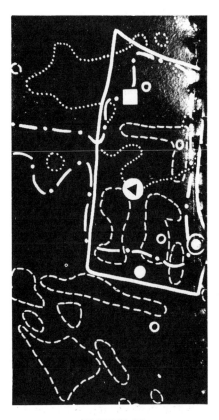

FIGURE 10

adult club, and the homes of its members form the unit marked by
dashed boundaries. The white square is the post office and the dotted
line marks the unit which contains its users. The secondary school is
marked by the spot with a white triangle in it. Together with its pupils,
it forms the system marked by the dot-dashed line.

As you can see at once, the different units do not coincide. Yet
neither are they disjoint. They overlap.

We cannot get an adequate picture of what Middlesborough is, or
of what it ought to be, in terms of 29 large and conveniently integral
chunks called neighborhoods. When we describe the city in terms of
neighborhoods, we implicitly assume that the smaller elements within
any one of these neighborhoods belong together so tightly that they
only interact with elements in other neighborhoods through the
medium of the neighborhood to which they themselves belong. Ruth
Glass herself shows clearly that this is not the case.

Below are two pictures of the Waterloo neighborhood. For the sake of argument I have broken it into a number of small areas. Figure 11 shows how these pieces stick together in fact, and figure 12 shows how the redevelopment plan pretends they stick together.

There is nothing in the nature of the various centers which says that their catchment areas should be the same. Their natures are different. Therefore the units they define are different. The natural city of Middlesborough was faithful to the semi-lattice structure they have. Only in the artificial tree conception of the city are their natural, proper, and necessary overlaps destroyed.

Take the separation of pedestrians from moving vehicles, a tree concept proposed by Le Corbusier, Louis Kahn, and many others. At a very crude level of thought this is obviously a good idea. It is dangerous to have 60-mile-an-hour cars in contact with little children toddling. But it is not *always* a good idea. There are times when the ecology of a situation actually demands the opposite. Imagine yourself coming out of a Fifth Avenue store; you have been shopping all afternoon; your arms are full of parcels; you need a drink; your wife is limping. Thank God for taxis.

Yet the urban taxi can function only because pedestrians and vehicles are not strictly separated. The prowling taxi needs a fast stream of traffic so that it can cover a large area to be sure of finding a passenger. The pedestrian needs to be able to hail the taxi from any point in the pedestrian world, and to be able to get out to any part of the pedestrian world to which he wants to go. The system which contains the taxicabs needs to overlap both the fast vehicular traffic system and the system of pedestrian circulation. In Manhattan pedestrians and vehicles do share certain parts of the city, and the necessary overlap is guaranteed (figure 13).

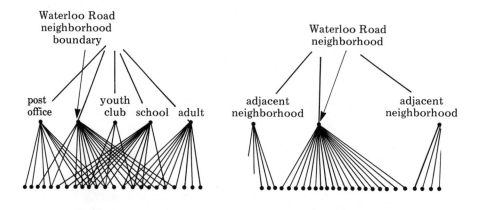

FIGURE 11   **FIGURE 12**

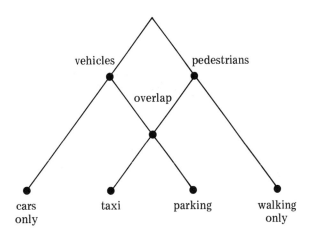

FIGURE 13

Another favorite concept of the CIAM theorists and others is the separation of recreation from everything else. This has crystallized in our real cities in the form of playgrounds. The playground, asphalted and fenced in, is nothing but a pictorial acknowledgment of the fact that "play" exists as an isolated concept in our minds. It has nothing to do with the life of play itself. Few self-respecting children will even play in a playground.

Play itself, the play that children practice, goes on somewhere different everyday. One day it may be indoors, another day in a friendly gas station, another day down by the river, another day in a derelict building, another day on a construction site which has been abandoned for the weekend. Each of these play activities, and the objects it requires, forms a system. It is not true that these systems exist in isolation, cut off from the other systems in the city. The different systems overlap one another, and they overlap many other systems besides. The units, the physical places recognized as play places, must do the same.

In a natural city this is what happens. Play takes place in a thousand places — it fills the interstices of adult life. As they play, children become full of their surroundings. How can a child become filled with his surroundings in a fenced enclosure? He cannot.

THE ISOLATED CAMPUS

A similar kind of mistake occurs in trees like that of Goodman's Communitas, or Soleri's Mesa City, which separate the university from the rest of the city. Again, this has actually been realized in common American form of the isolated campus.

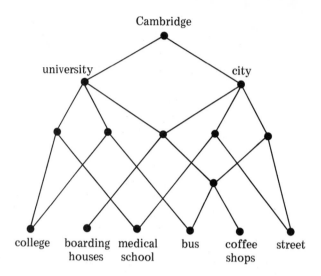

Cambridge

university   city

college   boarding medical   bus   coffee   street
          houses   school   shops

FIGURE 14

What is the reason for drawing a line in the city so that everything within the boundary is university, and everything outside is
non-university? It is conceptually clear. But does it correspond to the
realities of university life. Certainly it is not the structure which occurs in non-artificial university cities.

Take Cambridge University, for instance. At certain points Trinity street is physically almost indistinguishable from Trinity college.
One pedestrian crossover in the street is literally part of the college.
The buildings on the street, though they contain stores and coffee
shops and banks at ground level, contain undergraduates' rooms in
their upper stories. In many cases the actual fabric of the street buildings melts into the fabric of the old college buildings so that one cannot
be altered without the other.

There will always be many systems of activity where university
life and city life overlap: pub-crawling, coffee-drinking, the movies,
walking from place to place. In some cases whole departments may be
actively involved in the life of the city's inhabitants (the hospital-
cum-medical school is an example). In Cambridge, a natural city where
university and city have grown together gradually, the physical units
overlap because they are the physical residues of city systems and university systems which overlap (figure 14).

Let us look next at the hierarchy of urban cores, realized in
Brazilia, Chandigarh, the MARS plan for London, and, most recently,
in the Manhattan Lincoln Center, where various performing arts serving the population of greater New York have been gathered together to
form just one core.

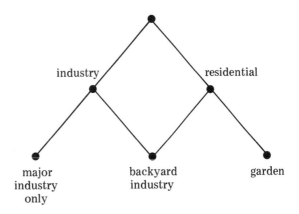

FIGURE 15

Does a concert hall ask to be next to an Opera House? Can the two feed on one another? Will anybody ever visit them both, gluttonously, in a single evening, or even buy tickets from one after going to a concert in the other? In Vienna, London, Paris, each of the performing arts has found its own place, because all are not mixed randomly. Each has created its own familiar section of the city. In Manhattan itself, Carnegie Hall and the Metropolitan Opera House were not built side by side. Each found its own place, and now creates its own atmosphere. The influence of each overlaps the parts of the city which have been made unique to it.

The only reason that these functions have all been brought together in the Lincoln Center is that the concept of performing art links them to one another.

But this tree, and the idea of a single hierarchy of urban cores which is its parent, do not illuminate the relations between art and city life. They are merely born of the mania every simple-minded person has for putting things with the same name into the same basket.

The total separation of work from housing, started by Tony Garnier in his industrial city, then incorporated in the 1929 Athens Charter, is now found in every artificial city and accepted everywhere where zoning is enforced. Is this a sound principle? It is easy to see how bad conditions at the beginning of the century prompted planners to try to get the dirty factories out of residential areas. But the separation misses a variety of systems which require, for their sustenance, little parts of both.

Jane Jacobs describes the growth of backyard industries in Brooklyn. A man who wants to start a small business needs space, which he is very likely to have in his own backyard. He also needs to establish connections with larger going enterprises and with their customers. This means that the system of backyard industry needs to belong both to the residential zone, and to the industrial zone — these zones need to overlap. In Brooklyn they do (figure 15). In a city which is a tree, they can't.

Finally, let us examine the subdivision of the city into isolated communities. As we have seen in the Abercrombie plan for London, this is itself a tree structure. The individual community in a greater city has no reality as a functioning unit. In London, as in any great city, almost no one manages to find work which suits him near his home. People in one community work in a factory which is very likely to be in another community.

There are, therefore, many hundreds of thousands of worker-workplace systems, each consisting of a man plus the factory he works in, which cut across the boundaries defined by Abercrombie's tree. The existence of these units, and their overlapping nature, indicates that the living systems of London form a semi-lattice. Only in the planner's mind has it become a tree.

The fact that we have so far failed to give this any physical expression has a vital consequence. As things are, whenever the worker and his workplace belong to separately administered municipalities, the community which contains the workplace collects huge taxes and has relatively little on which to spend the tax revenue. The community where the worker lives, if it is mainly residential, collects only little in the way of taxes, and yet has great additional burdens on its purse in the shape of schools, hospitals, etc. Clearly, to resolve this inequity, the worker-workplace systems must be anchored in physically recognizable units of the city which can then be taxed.

It might be argued that, even though the individual communities of a great city have no functional significance in the lives of their inhabitants, they are still the most convenient administrative units, and should, therefore, be left in their present tree organization.

However, in the political complexity of a modern city, even this is suspect.

Edward Banfield, in a recent book called *Political Influence,* gives a detailed account of the patterns of influence and control that have actually led to decisions in Chicago. He shows that although the lines of administrative and executive control have a formal structure which is a tree, these formal chains of influence and authority are entirely overshadowed by the ad hoc lines of control which arise naturally as each new city problem presents itself. These ad hoc lines depend on who is interested in the matter, who has what at stake, who has what favors to trade with whom.

This second structure, which is informal, working within the framework of the first, is what really controls public action. It varies from week to week, even from hour to hour, as one problem replaces another. Nobody's sphere of influence is entirely under the control of any one superior; each person is under different influences as the problems change. Although the organization chart in the mayor's office is a tree, the actual control and exercise of authority is semi-lattice-like.

TRAPPED IN A TREE

Now, why is it that so many designers have conceived cities as trees when the natural structure is in every case a semi-lattice? Have they done so deliberately, in the belief that a tree structure will serve the people of the city better? Or have they done it because they cannot help it, because they are trapped by a mental habit, perhaps even trapped by the way the mind works; because they cannot encompass the complexity of a semi-lattice in any convenient mental form; because the mind has an overwhelming predisposition to see trees wherever it looks and cannot escape the tree conception?

I shall try to convince you that it is for this second reason that trees are being proposed and built as cities — that it is because designers, limited as they must be by the capacity of the mind to form intuitively accessible structures, cannot achieve the complexity of the semi-lattice in a single mental act.

Let me begin with an example.

Suppose I ask you to remember the following four objects: an orange, a watermelon, a football, and a tennis ball. How will you keep them in your mind, in your mind's eyes? However you do it, you will do it by grouping them. Some of you will take the two fruits together, the orange and the watermelon, and the two sports balls together, the football and the tennis ball. Those of you who tend to think in terms of physical shape may group them differently, taking the two small spheres together — the orange and the tennis ball and the two larger and more egg-shaped objects — the watermelon and the football. Some of you will be aware of both.

Let us make a diagram of these groupings (figure 16).

Either grouping taken by itself is a tree structure. The two together are a semi-lattice. Now let us try and visualize these groupings in the mind's eye. I think you will find that you cannot visualize all four sets simultaneously — because they overlap. You can visualize one pair of sets and then the other, and you can alternate between the two pairs extremely fast, so fast that you may deceive yourself into thinking you can visualize them all together. But in truth, you cannot conceive all four sets at once in a single mental act. You cannot bring the semi-lattice structure into a visualizable form for a single mental act. In a single mental act you can only visualize a tree.

This is the problem we face as designers. While we are not, perhaps, necessarily occupied with the problem of total visualization in

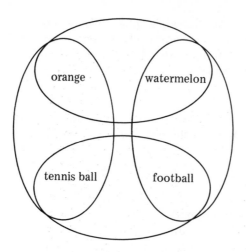

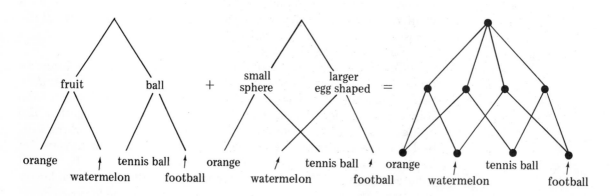

FIGURE 16

a single mental act, the principle is still the same. The tree is accessible mentally, and easy to deal with. The semi-lattice is hard to keep before the mind's eye, and therefore hard to deal with.

It is known today that grouping and categorization are among the most primitive psychological processes. Modern psychology treats thought as a process of fitting new situations into existing slots and pigeon holes in the mind. Just as you cannot put a physical thing into more than one physical pigeon hole at once, so, by analogy, the processes of thought prevent you from putting a mental construct into more than one mental category at once. Study of the origin of these processes suggests that they stem essentially from the organism's need to reduce the complexity of its environment by establishing barriers between the different events which it encounters.

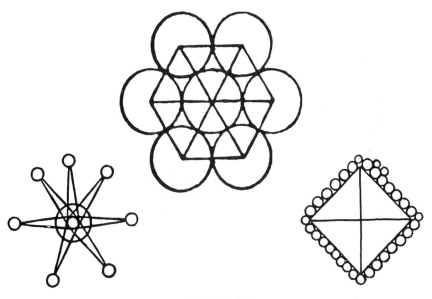

FIGURE 17

It is for this reason — because the mind's first function is to reduce the ambiguity and overlap in a confusing situation, and because, to this end, it is endowed with a basic intolerance for ambiguity — that structures like the city, which do require overlapping sets within them, are nevertheless persistently conceived as trees.

The same rigidity dogs even the perception of physical patterns. In experiments by Huggins and myself at Harvard, we showed people patterns whose internal units overlapped, and found that they almost always invented a way of seeing the patterns as a tree — even when the semi-lattice view of the patterns would have helped them perform the task of experimentation which was before them.

The most startling proof that people tend to conceive even physical patterns as trees is found in some experiments of Sir Frederick Bartlett. He showed people a pattern for about ¼ second and then asked them to draw what they had seen. Many people, unable to grasp the full complexity of the pattern they had seen, simplified the patterns by cutting out the overlap. In figure 17, the original is shown at the top, with two fairly typical redrawn versions below it. In the redrawn versions the circles are separated from the rest; the overlap between triangles and circles disappears.

These experiments suggest strongly that people have an underlying tendency, when faced by a complex organization, to reorganize it mentally in terms of non-overlapping units. The complexity of the semi-lattice is replaced by the simpler and more easily grasped tree form.

You are no doubt wondering, by now, what a city looks like which is a semi-lattice, but not a tree. I must confess that I cannot yet show you plans or sketches. It is not enough merely to make a demonstration of overlap — the overlap must be the right overlap. This is doubly important, because it is so tempting to make plans in which overlap occurs for its own sake. This is essentially what the high density "life-filled" city plans of recent years do. But overlap alone does not give structure. It can also give chaos. A garbage can is full of overlap. To have structure, you must have the right overlap, and this is for us almost certainly different from the old overlap which we observe in historic cities. As the relationships between functions change, so the systems which need to overlap in order to receive these relationships must also change. The recreation of old kinds of overlap will be inappropriate, and chaotic instead of structured.

The work of trying to understand just what overlap the modern city requires, and trying to put this required overlap into physical and plastic terms, is still going on. Until the work is complete, there is no point in presenting facile sketches of ill thought and structure.

OVERLAPPING TRIANGLES

However, I can perhaps make the physical consequences of overlap more comprehensible by means of an image. The painting illustrated is a recent work by Simon Nicholson (figure 18). The fascination of this painting lies in the fact that although constructed of rather few simple triangular elements, these elements unite in many different ways to form the larger units of the painting — in such a way indeed, that if we make a complete inventory of the perceived units in the painting, we find that each triangle enters into four or five completely different kinds of unit, none contained in the others, yet all overlapping in that triangle.

Thus, if we number the triangles and pick out the sets of triangles which appear as strong visual units, we get the semi-lattice shown in figure 19.

Three and 5 form a unit because they work together as a rectangle; 2 and 4 because they form a parallelogram; 5 and 6 because they are both dark and pointing the same way; 6 and 7 because one is the ghost of the other shifted sideways; 4 and 7 because they are symmetrical with one another; 4 and 6 because they form another rectangle; 4 and 5 because they form a sort of Z; 2 and 3 because they form a rather thinner kind of Z; 1 and 7 because they are at opposite corners; 1 and 2 because they are a rectangle; 3 and 4 because they point the same way as 5 and 6, and form a sort of off-center reflection; 3 and 6 because they enclose 4 and 5; 1 and 5 because they enclose 2, 3, and 4. I have only listed the units of two triangles. The larger units are even

FIGURE 18

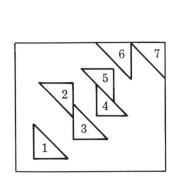

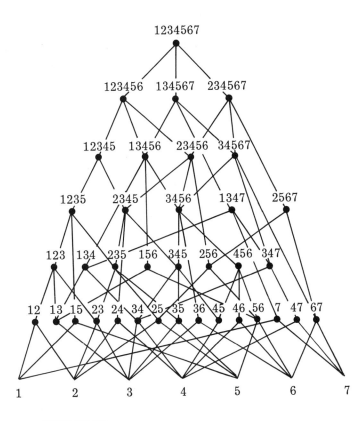

FIGURE 19

more complex. The white is more complex still, and is not even included in the diagram because it is harder to be sure of its elementary pieces.

The painting is significant, not so much because it has overlap in it (many paintings have overlap in them), but rather because this painting has nothing else in it except overlap. It is only the fact of the overlap, and the resulting multiplicity of aspects which the forms present, that makes the painting fascinating. It seems almost as though the painter had made an explicit attempt, as I have done, to single out overlap as a vital generator of structure.

All the artificial cities I have described have the structure of a tree rather than the semi-lattice structure of the Nicholson painting. Yet it is the painting, and other images like it, which must be our vehicles for thought. And when we wish to be precise, the semi-lattice, being part of a large branch of modern mathematics, is a powerful way of exploring the structure of these images. It is the semi-lattice we must look for, not the tree.

When we think in terms of trees we are trading the humanity and richness of the living city for a conceptual simplicity which benefits only designers, planners, administrators and developers. Every time a piece of a city is torn out, and a tree made to replace the semi-lattice that was there before, the city takes a further step toward dissociation.

In any organized object, extreme compartmentalization and the dissociation of internal elements are the first signs of coming destruction. In a society, dissociation is anarchy. In a person, dissociation is the mark of schizophrenia and impending suicide. An ominous example of city-wide dissociation is the separation of retired people from the rest of urban life, caused by the growth of desert cities for the old like Sun City, Arizona. This separation is only possible under the influence of tree-like thought.

It not only takes from the young the company of those who have lived long, but worse, it causes the same rift inside each individual life. As you will pass into Sun City, and into old age, your ties with your own past will be unacknowledged, lost, and therefore, broken. Your youth will no longer be alive in your old age — the two will be dissociated, your own life will be cut in two.

For the human mind, the tree is the easiest vehicle for complex thoughts. But the city is not, cannot, and must not be a tree. The city is a receptacle for life. If the receptacle severs the overlap of the strands of life within it, because it is a tree, it will be like a bowl full of razor blades on edge, ready to cut up whatever is entrusted to it. In such a receptacle life will be cut to pieces. If we make cities which are trees, they will cut our life within to pieces.   ∎

10 Making Participation Possible

Humans have persisted now over a period of thousands, perhaps even millions of years. They may not always have flourished, but one way or another they have survived. Since hardship and difficulty have never been in short supply, this record of survival is also a record of coping. Through the exercise of choice and control, and through the creation and handing down of cognitive interpretations, humans have made their way. They participated in their physical and social environments, and at least to some degree in the structuring of their futures.

But this relatively impressive record offers little comfort for our own times. The world has changed. Granted it is humans who have changed it; the fact remains that human coping seems ill-attuned to the world as it is today. Problems mount with bewildering speed, and even human survival is by no means assured. For various reasons, many — perhaps most — humans participate minimally in the world about them.

A chasm has thus developed between the human, a skillful problem solver, and the problems that threaten the species. Humans once survived through their considerable talent as processors of information. To continue to survive, this impressive talent must again be engaged, must be turned again to intensive commerce with the environment. In other words, the participatory relationship, in which the various means of coping are brought together, may need to be restored. There is reason to believe that such a development would be healthy for people as well as for their environment.

People, we have argued, are capable and effective when dealing with something they comprehend. They also respond well to challenge. They benefit greatly from being needed, and conversely, the sense of being surplus must be one of the most corrosive to an individual's identity and self-esteem. There are innumerable opportunities for people to participate in processes and decisions that influence their lives. There are also, alas, untold circumstances where the possibility of participation is too readily neglected.

It is a painful irony that a few experts laboring long hours to better serve the public not infrequently contribute both to poor decisions and to the frustrations the public feels. Much that we have seen in these pages that is wrong with our environment, including many recent changes, has increased the already widespread sense of noncomprehension and helplessness. How does one enhance people's ability to make sense? The experts have always been happy to tell people what is going on, to give them the cognitive maps they need.

But cognitive map transplants, alas, have a high rejection rate! The process of accruing knowledge, of developing an internal model, cannot be relegated to someone else. Many factors — physical, social, and informational — influence the rate, but there is no way to circumvent the individual's own map-building program. There are ways, however, of presenting information that greatly facilitate the process. And there are ways of tapping into the human inclination to acquire information, to explore and to learn. Under appropriate conditions, people welcome and even seek the challenge of new problems. To be sure, there are times when effective coping involves withdrawal or resignation or a lack of action. But in general, coping requires an active stance; it depends on the possibility of achieving understanding and the sense that one can do something to change things.

In this final chapter we turn to various approaches that make participation possible, that allow the individual an active role in shaping decisions and situations. Many of these solutions involve small and undramatic changes. They pale before the monolithic vision of the modern utopian. But the difference between using and being used, between being needed and being surplus, is a profound one, revolutionary in its potential to harness human talent and to challenge the human spirit.

MAKING THE SCALE MANAGEABLE

So many problems are of such size and intricacy that one does not even know where to begin. The sheer magnitude of many situations leads to arrangements that reduce the probability and possibility of participation. The frequent complaints about "top-heavy" organizations — bureaucracies that seem to invent ever-increasing layers between the individual and the decision maker — can be heard everywhere. It is not only the poor and the disenfranchised who are thus ignored. As the first two selections illustrate, such difficulties are not uncommon even within the public school. The differences between being a student in a high school with one hundred or one thousand others seems to ramify well beyond the simple tenfold enrollment differences. What might appear from the top as administrative efficiencies look quite different at the level of the individual, who may readily feel irrelevant to the functioning of the whole.

Reducing the scale or size of the operative unit turns out to be an important step in helping things make sense and in making participation possible. Often this takes the form of decentralization, a procedure that may appear to entail a duplication of effort. Rather than a single decision-making body, somewhat parallel decisions are made at a "lower level" in the organization. Rather than federal authority, decisions might be relegated to the states . . . or perhaps to the townships . . . or sometimes even to blocks or neighborhoods. While the decisions are thus repeated many times over, the likelihood is increased that each "unit" encompasses more of the unique facets of the problem in its setting. In the process, a diversity of solutions emerges, resulting in innumerable informal "experiments." This also provides for the resilience of the larger system that Jacobs and Alexander talk about. And, of course, at the same time the total number of people participating in the action is greatly increased.

The cry for grass-root efforts, for permitting people to make their own mistakes rather than living with the mistakes of the "powers-that-be," is a plea for such increased participation. Reduction in the scale of the operation often makes all the difference as far as making something seem comprehensible and within the grasp of ordinary humans. The perceived possibility of control, in conjunction with the perceived possibility of making sense, can turn a hopeless situation into a participatory opportunity. But it is clear that not all problems can be handled in this way. And unfortunately the myriad ways one can choose to decentralize tend to be mutually exclusive.

In his engaging book, *Small is Beautiful,* Schumacher (1973) discusses the advantages of decentralization in the context of aid to less developed countries. He suggests that many governments might benefit from greater respect for local strengths and local concerns. Such "self-help" programs would involve less expensive, smaller scale "intermediate technologies" that make sense at the local level. An interesting parallel is strikingly demonstrated by Wigginton's *Foxfire* project. Not only has this project made available a record of the oral history, legends, and skills of southern Appalachia; it has at the same time challenged the participants to develop a rich variety of coping strategies in keeping the project afloat.

The selections in this chapter provide a variety of examples of increased opportunities for participation that are possible when the scale of the problem is somehow pared down. In fact, it is instructive to examine each piece in terms of the criteria that make successful scale reduction more likely. Sometimes a regional or spatial basis seems to be logical (as with small town schools, for example). At other times the basis seems to follow more functional lines. Thus, consolidating in terms of environmental-health issues, or packages of intermediate technologies, might make more sense.

MAKING STRUCTURE APPARENT

Some problems are not so much difficulties of magnitude as difficulties of legibility. If one does not know the question that needs to be asked, one is less likely to find the answer. Many contemporary problems make it difficult for the citizen even to know that there might be alternatives. Wurman's concept of "making the city observable" captures the essence of the problem. Maps that defy being understood, organization charts that make it impossible to figure out what the appropriate office might be, transportation systems that are functionally inaccessible to their potential clients — these are all common misfortunes that inhibit participation. Such inadvertent obstacles foster a sense of helplessness and stifle comprehension of the environment.

The educational process often takes participation for granted. It may not be any more enlightened than "drill," but in the lower grades at least there is the realization that each person must learn and develop the skills. Children's books recognize that the presentation of material makes a difference in comprehension. But strange as it may seem, adults are assumed not to need aids to imagery and comprehension. Authors of adult works seem to believe that their own hard-earned cognitive maps can indeed be transplanted whole into the minds of their readers.

Several of the selections in this chapter extend the ideas of the educational process to the environment-at-large. Both in the sense of making the resources in the environment more accessible and in the sense of concern for the ways of presenting the information, these authors show a multitude of ways that participation can be readily increased through the increased visibility of the structure of the environment. If one comprehends the situation, one is far more likely to act on it.

Finally, the piece by Lewis makes one more leap. It shows that even accessibility, by itself, may not be sufficient — especially if the cognitive structures are not there to permit comprehension. But evidently the sense of comfort and the possibility of participation can be enhanced readily enough if one relates a situation that lacks coherence to ones that do, indeed, make sense. That the setting involved is more likely to hold attention perhaps made Lewis's task that much simpler. Nonetheless, one suspects that there is a lesson to be learned from his seemingly simple approach and one that is translatable to many other settings as well.

Paul V. Gump and Roger G. Barker
Big School, Small School: Overview and Prospects*

This selection is from the summation of a book that examines student participation in various activities across schools of widely differing sizes. "Ecological psychology," a position developed by Gump and Barker, involves the use of the "behavior setting" as an analytic tool. In this classic work they look at how many such opportunities for activity are available per student in schools of different sizes. The more settings per student, the more needed each student is likely to feel, and the greater the likelihood of involvement and participation. Interestingly, some of the same issues come up in discussions of economies of scale, even though no "product" in the usual economic sense is involved here. While the central theme here is clearly scale, legibility is a factor as well. Participation, by increasing familiarity, necessarily makes a smaller scale operation seem more legible to those involved.

■   The large school has authority: its grand exterior dimensions, its long halls and myriad rooms, and its tides of students all carry an implication of power and rightness. The small school lacks such certainty: its modest building, its short halls and few rooms, and its students, who move more in trickles than in tides, give an impression of a casual or not quite decisive educational environment.

These are outside views. They are illusions. Inside views reveal forces at work stimulating and compelling students to more active and

*Reprinted from *Big School, Small School: High School Size and Student Behavior,* by Roger G. Barker and Paul V. Gump, with the permission of the Publishers, Stanford University Press. © 1964 by the Board of Trustees of the Leland Stanford Junior University. Excerpted from chapter 12: Overview and prospects.

responsible contributions to the enterprises of small than of large schools. The inside views also show that the small school does not lack as many parts as enrollment alone would imply. Comparison of the largest school, Capital City, with the four small schools of Midwest County reveals that the large school had 20 times as many students but only 5 times as many settings and 1.4 times as many varieties of settings. A small school is not so small in terms of the number and variety of its behaviorally significant parts as it is in terms of students; like a small engine or small organism, it possesses the essential parts of a large entity, but has fewer replications and differentiations of some of the parts.

Our investigations of the behavior and experiences of students were guided by the hypothesis that the essential equivalence of small and large high schools with respect to kinds of parts, together with their difference in number of students per part, provides a crucially different environment for students. A prototype of this difference is the Junior Class play of a small school, where each member of the class is essential to the play's successful presentation, versus the Junior Class play of a large school, where at most only 15 percent of the members of the class have more than a spectator's involvement in the play. According to the theory that guided the research, the behavior settings Junior Class Play, Senior English Class, Football Game, Student Council Meeting are not passive stages upon which behavior may occur, but they are extra-individual entities with power over participants and potential participants. . . .

Voluntary school behavior settings occupied a large place in the investigations because attendance and participation can be easily observed, and they are crucial indicators of motivation and involvement. In the case of school classes, on the other hand, where attendance and participation are required, methods of assessing motivation and involvement are very difficult. It is for this technical reason that many of the investigations were limited to nonclass (extracurricular) settings.

Investigations were made in high schools varying in enrollment from 35 to 2,287 students; the most crucial studies compared high school Juniors in four schools of 83 to 151 students with those in a high school of 2,287 students. The schools were located in eastern Kansas with a homogeneous economic, cultural, and political region; all schools met the standards of the same state authority.

EXTENT OF PARTICIPATION IN SCHOOL ACTIVITIES

The proportion of students who participated in district music festivals and dramatic, journalistic, and student government competitions reached a peak in high schools with enrollments between 61 and 150. The proportion of participants was 3 to 20 times as great in the small schools as in the largest school. The average number of extracurricular activities and kinds of activities in which students engaged during their four-year high school careers was twice as great in the small as in the large schools.

The large high school provided its Junior students with a larger number and more varieties of nonclass behavior settings than the small schools. In spite of this, the small school students participated in the same number and in more varieties of the available settings, on the average, than the students of the large school. Furthermore, a much larger proportion of the small school students held positions of importance and responsibility in the behavior settings they entered, and they occupied these positions in more varieties of settings than the students of the large school. . . .

EXPERIENCES REPORTED BY STUDENTS

Our hypothesis predicted that small and large school Juniors would report different kinds of satisfactions from their experiences in the behavior settings they inhabited. This prediction was confirmed. Specifically, Juniors from the small schools reported more satisfactions relating to the development of competence, to being challenged, to engaging in important actions, to being involved in group activities, and to achieving moral and cultural values; while large school Juniors reported more satisfactions dealing with vicarious enjoyment, with large entity affiliation, with learning about their school's persons and affairs, and with gaining "points" via participation. It was further predicted that these school differences would be causally related to differences in occupancy of important and responsible positions in school settings. This prediction was verified: the satisfactions reported were significantly influenced by the positions the student respondents occupied within settings, and most of the differences between large and small schools in this regard were eliminated when differences in setting position were held constant. The burden of the evidence supports the conclusions that large and small school Juniors experienced different satisfactions and that most of these differences were due to differences in the number of students who occupied important, responsible positions.

Students of small schools reported experiencing more attractions and more pressures toward participation in school nonclass behavior settings than students of large schools, and their responses reflected more involvement and more feelings of responsibility. Furthermore, the small schools did not produce such great individual differences in experienced attractions and pressures as did the large school; the small schools contained fewer "outsiders." The findings indicate that the small school students lived under greater day-by-day attraction, obligation, and external pressure to take active part in the various behavior settings of their schools.

COMMUNITY ACTIVITIES

Part-time and summer employment in business and professional behavior settings and responsible participation in church and out-of-school social organizations are widely believed to have educational values. These community activities were more frequent for the small school-small town adolescents than for the large school-city adolescents. In these respects, the differences were clearer for the boys than for the girls. In general, the schools and communities were harmonious: the small communities, like the small schools, provided positions of functional importance for adolescents more frequently; and the cities, like the large schools, provided such positions less frequently. The data provide no evidence that the urban environments of the large schools compensated by means of their greater resources and facilities for the relatively meager functional importance of students within their large schools. In the two instances studied where students were removed from small communities and transported to a central, district school, there was some evidence that participation in voluntary school settings was lower than in the case of students attending small schools in small communities. The high school adolescents of the small communities made functionally important contributions to their towns in behavior settings beyond the borders of the schools; and these settings, in turn, supplemented the school settings.

THE ISSUE OF SIZE

A basic problem for the immediate future is to investigate the degree to which the relations we have discovered between school size, school settings, and student participation are inevitable. Not only the present research, but all other research known to us, indicates that the negative relationship between institutional size and individual participation is deeply based and difficult, if not impossible, to avoid. It may be easier to bring specialized and varied behavior settings to small schools than to raise the level of individual participation in large schools. Furthermore, the current method of broadening educational offerings by moving hundreds of bodies to a central spot may be both unnecessary and old-fashioned. Already a technical revolution with respect to teaching devices and educational facilities is upon us. Self-teaching machines, taped school courses, TV classes, wired TV linking separate schools, new ideas about teaching personnel (e.g., school aides), new conceptions of interschool cooperation (e.g., transporting teachers and equipment rather than students), new conceptions of the contributions of the community to educational objectives, and new materials and standards for school construction are freeing schools from past molds.

These new developments, taken with the findings reported here, provoke the question: How large should a school be?

The present research, in itself, cannot answer this question. Some of the crucial variables such as academic learning were not investigated. Furthermore, "should" in this query implies purpose, and educational purposes differ. For example, if versatility of experience is preferred over opportunity for specialization, a smaller school is better than a larger one; if specialization is sought, the larger school is the better.

Although a definite answer to the size question cannot be given, the theory developed here can be helpful in deciding particular issues. It often happens, in these days, that population increase in a given area requires sharply increased high school facilities. One solution to this problem lies in the expansion of the facilities and enrollment of the existing school. Our findings show that among the results of this policy is a decrease in responsible student action and experience. A second solution is the establishment of a number of new small schools, thereby keeping enrollments relatively low. A third approach is the campus school, an arrangement by which students are grouped in semiautonomous units for most studies but are usually provided a school-wide extracurricular program. The campus school provides for repeated contacts between the same teachers and students; this continuity of associates probably leads to closer social bonds. A common-sense theory is that the campus school welds together the facility advantages of the large school and the social values of the small school. But the social values of small schools reported in the present research do not rest upon associate continuity; they rest upon low population per setting, a condition difficult or impossible to achieve in the school-wide extracurricular programs of large campus schools. A fourth solution, then, would be another arrangement of the campus school, for example, making the separate units autonomous with respect to voluntary activities as well as for most classes.

Common-sense theories about schools are not adequate bases for policy decisions. Another example of this is the common-sense assumption that there is a direct coupling between the facilities or properties of schools and the behavior and experiences of students. This simple view of reality, so common in education, has been long passed in physical and biological sciences. No one would seriously argue that because one bridge is stronger than another the individual beams of which it is constructed must also be stronger. Good facilities provide good experiences only if they are used. The educational process is a subtle and delicate one about which we know little, but it surely thrives on participation, enthusiasm, and responsibility. Our findings and our theory posit a negative relationship between school size and individual student participation. What seems to happen is that as schools get larger and settings inevitably become more heavily populated, more of the students are less needed; they become superfluous, redundant.

What size should a school be?

The data of this research and our own educational values tell us that a school should be sufficiently small that all of its students are needed for its enterprises. A school should be small enough that students are not redundant.   ■

Back to the One-Room School?*

■   There is to be a new school at Coles Corner in St. Johnsbury. The school will have no more than twenty-five students and they will not be divided on the basis of grades or age. The explanation for this curious arrangement is that, "Children of different ages benefit from each other. When older students help with the education of younger students, the teaching reinforces what the older students know and enables them to work together rather than simply compete against each other."

A radical philosophy of education? Quite the contrary. Fifty years ago there was a school at Coles Corner which conducted classes in exactly this fashion. There was a school like it at the cross roads of almost every rural community in Vermont and there are still a few left in places like Newark and Kirby.

But why have the one-room schools which were once the bane of Montpelier become the darling of the liberal educators? There are several reasons. The size of the schools prevents anyone from getting lost in the corners. Their small staff automatically requires that students take more responsibility for managing their own time and helping each other (the seventh grade teaches the sixth). And they allow their students the privilege of being either stupid or bright. That is, the individual automatically advances to whatever grade he is ready for. In large schools frustrated teachers send illiterates into the next grade while forcing gifted youngsters to do the same work as the dullards.

To be sure, there are substantial differences between the here and there, now and then, experiments in education which have sprung up in the Vermont backbeyond recently and the old-fashioned one-room school which most Vermonters once attended. Not the least of these is

*"Back to the one-room school?" *Small Town,* May, 1973, Vol. 3, No. 10, p. 5. Originally published in the *Caledonian Record,* St. Johnsbury, Vermont. Reprinted by permission.

the fact that the one-room school served a particular neighborhood and was the center of much of the neighborhood's community life. The parents, the school board, and the teachers themselves imposed a sense of discipline that is usually lacking in present-day attempts to recreate the advantageous aspects of the one-room school.   ■

Nicholas Wade
Karl Hess: Technology with a Human Face*

This description of a program emphasizing intermediate technology is of particular interest for placing the concept not in a developing country, or even in rural America, but squarely in a highly developed urban setting. Intermediate technology is by definition oriented to participation; its purpose is to provide people with tools rather than replace them. It is interesting to see how important comprehension is in this project, both in terms of the emphasis on the demystification of technology and with respect to the sort of organization that Hess has put together.

■   Karl Hess is a man with a vision of a better society, one in which science and technology would be shaped more directly and humanely to the community's needs. Unlike most visionaries, he is actively concerned with putting his ideas into practice. In a disused warehouse in part of Washington's urban ghetto, he and his colleagues are trying to develop a number of "soft" technologies with which people in the neighborhood can feed, heat, and transport themselves on a community basis.

The importance of Hess's experiment to the scientific world goes considerably beyond the success or failure of Community Technology, as his project is named. Hess has drawn upon many of the most salient discontents that fuel the anti-science movement and shaped them into an approach that makes science and technology its passe-partout, not

*"Karl Hess: Technology with a human face." *Science,* 31 January 1975, 187, 332–334. Copyright 1975 by the American Association for the Advancement of Science.

its scapegoat. "Some people blame Sir Isaac Newton for capitalism," he remarks. "I get the chilly notion that this is a new form of Luddism that doesn't know where the machines are. What it's going to end up smashing is the human head."

[Community Technology] offers at least one small alternative path for those who, while working at high skills or science, question the current corporate organization and deployment of those resources. It enables scientists, engineers, technicians and craftpeople to re-think the roles of their skills and talents while actively or, you could say, scientifically testing the material possibilities of new ways of work.[1]

One of the goals at Community Technology is to tell people that they don't have to go around hating science and technology. "The thing they have to hate," Hess adds, "is the organization."

These may seem surprising sentiments from a man who served on the White House staff under Eisenhower, helped write two Republican national platforms (in 1960 and 1964), and was Senator Barry Goldwater's chief speechwriter in his 1964 presidential campaign. But the right wing politics of yesterday and today's countercultural view of society are linked by a consistent theme — antipathy for the disutility of large organizations such as government — which enables Hess to remain perfectly at ease with the past. "Goldwater is still a good guy. Except that there's no power, he would like it here," Hess says with a gesture to the cluttered workshop floor of the Community Technology warehouse.

The purposes of Community Technology, according to its own description, are "to de-mystify technology, to challenge all of the claimed economies of scale, and to push as far as possible practical demonstrations of high technology in the direct service of human needs and imagination in an urban community." The group, according to Hess, is one of about six organizations in the world (though most of the others are rural, not urban) engaged in developing "soft" or "intermediate" technology.

There is no precise demarcation between hard and soft technology, but the distinguishing features of soft technology, as defined by Hess's group, are that it is physically contained within the community so that the people themselves, not some functionary in Detroit, can determine its impact on the neighborhood. Soft technology does not place stresses on the environment, is low in its capital demands, frugal in its use of resources, and decentralizing or centrifugal in its social impact.

Hess sketched out an admittedly utopian vision of how neighborhood life might be made different through the medium of soft technology in a recent article in the Potomac section of the *Washington Post.* Urban neighborhoods, organizing themselves by "town meetings," would produce much of their own food by raising fish in tanks in basements and growing vegetables in hydroponic gardens on the rooftops. Solar collectors would provide half the city's heating requirements in winter and much of the energy for cooling in summer. Sewage, collected on a local basis, would be converted odorlessly into fertilizer and into methane, used as an almost complete substitute for cooking gas. Recognizing that production is a social, not just economic, activity, neighborhoods would seize further control over their civic lives — and reduce local unemployment — by setting up light manufacturing industries turning out furniture, fabrics, bicycles, and even electric cars. A later step toward self-reliance would be to substitute locally produced fuels, as far as possible, for petroleum. Methanol, for example, would be brewed from organic garbage, and hydrogen gas produced by wind generators set atop buildings.

Science is the way we understand the natural world. Technology is the way we do work. Both are seen as necessary. It is the organization of both, and not the existence of either, that the Community Technology group questions.

Community Technology is attempting to develop some of the techniques envisaged in this urban utopia, with emphasis on rooftop gardening, basement fish farming, and solar heating. Apart from a single grant of $2500 from a friend and free lease of a warehouse from the Children's Hospital of Washington, the project is supported entirely by its members, who operate it when not working on their other jobs.

Much of the time since the project was founded nearly two years ago has been spent in fixing up the warehouse, located in a clinic at 2320 17th Street NW in the Adams-Morgan district of Washington, D.C. The major project to date is a system for raising rainbow trout in tanks that can be operated in the basement of a house. Designed by a chemist in the group, Fern Wood Mitchell, the system employs a bacteriological technique for purifying and recirculating the tank water, thereby reducing its water consumption to less than a thousandth of that of commercial, through-flow fish farms.

In a prototype system in Mitchell's basement the trout were grown at a density of 5 pounds per cubic foot of water and at a cost in energy and feed of less than $1 per edible pound. (The fish retail locally at about $2.25 a pound.) A second system has been constructed at the Community Technology warehouse by Jeff Woodside, a theoretical physicist, and Therese Hess, Karl's wife, and the first fish were installed last month. The next stage, when design problems have been solved, will be to help people in the neighborhood set up their own tanks.

Another project is the "solar kitchen," a parabolic reflector that converts the sun's energy into heat for cooking. The prototype put together in the Community Technology warehouse was designed by C.J. Swet, a group member who until recently was with the Applied Physics Laboratory of Johns Hopkins. Swet, formerly the senior design engineer for the Atlas missile propulsion system, is also working on flat-plate solar collectors for home water heating. The collectors are to be easy and cheap to build, so that they can be made by local individuals or cooperatives. A workable solar device would soon pay for itself against the $180 Swet estimates the average family will pay this year for heating home water by electricity.

The group's workshop is operated by Karl Hess who, among other trades, is a professional welder. The Hesses maintained a rooftop garden during the summer and another member, Gil Friend, is designing a pilot rooftop greenhouse to study the feasibility of year-round hydroponic gardening. (Friend is also a member of another neighborhood organization, the Institute for Self-Reliance.)

Wind speeds in Washington are generally too low for windmills. The group's efforts in this area have so far been confined to a search for unusually windy locations in the community.

I can't believe that such bright people [as scientists and engineers] will forever misconstrue their place in society, which is to be the finest craftsmen in the neighborhood.

Besides the development of suitable techniques, Community Technology seeks to encourage their adoption in the neighborhood. Adams-Morgan is a community of some 30,000 people, with about equal members of blacks, Latins, and whites. It has a self-elected council, the Adams-Morgan Organization, with which Community Technology is affiliated. The group keeps in touch with its community by means of a newsletter, *Science in the Neighborhood,* and weekly meetings open to all comers.

At one meeting last month, 22 people were present, including neighbors, a cab driver, a builder, as well as the project leaders. Discussion mostly concerned status reports on current projects and requests for labor and materials, most of which were satisfied from within the group present. No major cooperative project has yet been accomplished, but most of the techniques are still under development. First reactions in the community, Hess reports, are "enthusiastic but not terribly active."

A lot of foundations actively dislike what we are doing because we are saying that people can take their lives absolutely into their own hands. Foundations resent that because it seems very anti-elitist. Elitists think that the great engine of progress, science and technology, can only be grasped by a very few hands.

For an operation that is run almost literally on a shoestring, and in the spare time of a handful of members, the achievements to date may seem impressive rather than otherwise. Shortage of money has been a handicap, indeed a continuing crisis. Attempts to solicit foundation support have been fruitless. Foundations, Hess wryly says, prefer projects which, rather than emphasizing work, emphasize welfare; "It is the conventional wisdom that inner city neighborhoods are doomed to the most demeaning sort of dependency and that, therefore, the best thing to do for them is just try to make life bearable. It is also said that inner-city people cannot deal with scientific concepts or with technological terms and tools. While Community Technology cannot claim to have disproven that absolutely, its members feel there is no reason to accept it as a fact, either."

The idea for Community Technology grew out of a project sponsored by the Institute for Policy Studies, a new left think-tank based in Washington, D.C. The institute, of which Hess is a fellow, is compiling an encyclopedia of social reconstruction which aims to codify the ground rules of the new society as thoroughly as Diderot and the French encyclopedists laid out a framework for the rational enlightenment of the eighteenth century. The draft prospectus of the encyclopedia, in its section on agriculture, notes that

> The last ten years have been marked by an accelerating disenchantment with the dominance of Western science and technology, which for more than 300 years have been synonymous with the "progress" of civilization. The depth of this disenchantment suggests that it is more than a passing phase and may represent an important turning point in human history. It is wrong, however, to see this disenchantment as an anti-science movement. Rather, its impulse seems more to be aimed at rethinking the purposes of science and the interests that it supports. . . .

Hess was assigned to write the encyclopedia's section on tools and technology and decided to make a practical demonstration of the ideas he was advocating. Hence Community Technology was conceived. Hess describes himself as "project coordinator" — the group is run on a nonhierarchical basis — but he is also resident guru, anchorman, and chief enthusiast. His purpose is serious, but his conversation always urbane and amusing. He has a knack of discussing abstractions in crisp metaphors. Ask an average political scientist to explain how Republican and Communist conceptions of capitalism differ from each other and from the present-day reality, and you will be lucky to get an answer in less than ten paragraphs. Hess's formulation: "Republicans think capitalism is the shop on the corner. Communists think it is the factory. But really it's the telephone company."

Hess's objection to the modern industrial estate is that it is shaped by the dictates of "capitalist bookkeeping," which reward profit at the expense of all other criteria. "All capitalist economics is founded on the fact that production is secondary. Profits are primary. The assumption that capitalist bookkeeping and the world of nature are reflections of one another is absolutely crazy. The world of nature suggests that fossil chemicals can be formed into almost permanent plastics; capitalism says it is preferable to burn oil."

[The scientific] method arose in the great challenging of ideology embodied in church and then state. It has been debased to the defense and enlargement of institutions, corporation and state. Its reconstruction would restore it as simply a method of human thought, rather than human domination. . . .

Hess blames capitalist bookkeeping for the disutility of large organizations, for their growth to beyond a size at which they can either be controlled by the people they most affect, or can even make efficient use of their means of production. "Corporations are lousy users of technology, and they are using up all our resources." Asked what should replace them, Hess prescribes "small, knowledge-intensive production groups. In a neighborhood like this it would be much more effective to grow food closer to where it is eaten, with no profligate waste of packaging and transport. Political wisdom says big, science and technology say small."

Community self-help is a tradition with deep roots in American history. An urban setting may prove difficult ground on which to resurrect it, but the tide of the times may be moving in favor of many of the things that Hess is trying to do. "It's like asking if there is going to be a flood, and building something that will float with it," Hess remarks. "People say you are a damn fool wasting your time. Maybe. But that is a small investment."   ∎

NOTE
   1. This and the following quotation are from an article by Hess in *Spark,* issue of fall 1974; the next two from interview; the last from the *Encyclopedia of Social Reconstruction.*

Robert J. Bazell
Urban Health and Environment: A New Approach*

The personal and social benefits of this ingenious program are quite evident. Here self-help and comprehension are combined to good effect. The information provided in this context is not rejected as it might be in other settings; here the information contributes to the participants' conceptions of themselves and what they are doing. It is also striking that this inexpensive and humane project has had problems with funding. The difficulty in part may be one of scale. Federal funding agencies tend to be highly specialized and compartmentalized. A small operation that simultaneously meets a wide variety of needs seems destined to fall in the cracks.

■ In the squalid tenements of inner-city slums — where children play in urine-soaked hallways alongside rats and junkies, where crumbling walls fill apartments with choking dust and deadly leaded paint, where often there is no heat in the winter and the plumbing doesn't work — the links between people's housing and their health are all too obvious. Thousands of people enter hospitals each year suffering from conditions ranging from carbon monoxide poisoning to asthma — all possibly resulting from wretched living conditions.

Construction of new housing and attempts at enforcing existing housing codes have done little to solve the problem. In New York City, for example, the number of low-rent units constructed between 1965 and 1968 housed less than one-tenth of the people forced out of tenements after the owners, unable or unwilling to maintain them, had left the buildings to decay. And, according to officials, for every house declared by the city to be abandoned, dozens of others are totally dilapidated, with people still living in them. Categorical health programs such as rat control and lead poisoning prevention — each aimed at a segment of the massive problem — have, by most accounts, accomplished little.

*"Urban health and environment: A new approach." *Science,* 3 December 1971, Vol. 174, pages 1005–1006. Copyright 1971 by the American Association for the Advancement of Science.

Talk of the environment as more than clean air and protected wildlife, and the use of phrases such as "comprehensive planning for environmental health services" have come into fashion recently. But few of these phrases have been translated into actions that actually improve people's surroundings and health.

At the East Harlem Environmental Extension Service, a year-old program that has already attracted national attention and may be the prototype of slum renewal efforts across the country, the rhetoric of preventive medicine and environmental improvement has been applied to training men from the East Harlem community to paint walls, repair plumbing, supervise buildings, fix boilers, organize tenants into building associations, and mop up the hallways. Such activities may appear at first sight as less than a dynamic solution to major health problems, but in the opinion of Elihu D. Richter, an associate of the Mt. Sinai Hospital Department of Environmental Medicine and one of the prime movers behind the project, "Large-scale preventive maintenance of tenement housing could do more for the health of East Harlem residents than the services of a thousand doctors."

Modeled after the agriculture extension services that give aid to farmers, the East Harlem program aims at cooperation with the area's landlords by offering them a variety of reasonably priced services that are intended to turn the dilapidated and dangerous tenements into safe and decent places to live.

Sponsors of the extension service, which is a nonprofit corporation, include a variety of groups that have often been at odds with each other in the past — groups such as tenant and landlord organizations, labor unions, and various city departments, as well as the Mt. Sinai School of Medicine.

To date, the program has trained and employed more than 70 men from the East Harlem area and, under contract for either continuing maintenance or for specific repairs, has serviced more than 40 tenement buildings. Observers with years of experience in East Harlem housing problems estimate that the extension service is directly responsible for saving as many as 20 tenement buildings from total abandonment.

Despite these successes, the extension service has experienced extraordinary difficulties in obtaining funds. This for a number of reasons, not least of which is the difficulty of health and antipoverty officials in dealing with a program that solves a number of problems at once. According to the program's director, Victor Rivera, an energetic young Puerto Rican with experience in a variety of community affairs and minority labor projects, "The extension service's greatest problem has been our successes. Most antipoverty agencies are massive, self-perpetuating enterprises geared towards failure."

Originally the project, which earns an income from the fees charged landlords of about one-third of its expenses for training and subsidized services, received a one-year $200,000 grant given to Mt. Sinai by the city's rat control program to cover the remaining two-thirds of the budget. But city officials refused to renew the grant because, in the words of one official, "our own funds were cut and the extension service is not strictly a rat control program." The program then became a football tossed from agency to agency — job training, welfare, health department, and so on — each of which endorsed the extension service but claimed it was beyond their responsibility. Finally, after considerable prodding by Democratic Representative Herman Badillo, whose district includes East Harlem, and Republican Senator Jacob Javits, both enthusiastic supporters of the program, the Urban Coalition promised the extension of some Model Cities funds — but these have yet to be allocated. As a result of the shortage of funds, says Rivera, the extension service had to cease training new men and refuse contract offers from the owners of dozens of buildings in the area.

The multifaceted aspect of the extension service is seen most clearly in the training program for the "urban extension agents," who perform the work of the program. Each man receives 2 months of in-school vocational training and an additional month of field training before beginning full-time, on-the-job training and work. At the Manhattan Vocational and Technical High School in East Harlem, the city's Board of Education uses federal Labor Department funds to train the men in boiler maintenance, building repair, plumbing, electricity, plastering, painting, and other maintenance skills. At the same time, faculty members at Mt. Sinai and personnel from the city's Health Department instruct the trainees in the health aspects of their work.

"What we do in the training," explains Richter, who helped set up the curriculum, "is teach the men the significance of their work in terms of improving the health of East Harlem residents." In explaining, for example, "why a working boiler is so important to the health of the people in your building," a manual prepared for the course details the physiological effects of cold on the body and the number of illnesses that can be caused by prolonged exposure to the cold. "Some of the men didn't like to mop," says Richter, "so we taught them about asthma." Other aspects of the health course include fire, poisoning, and accident prevention. In each category, instructors give considerable attention to methods that the extension agents can use to instruct the tenants to help themselves. The men have responded enthusiastically to the health course, even requesting additional instruction in subjects such as child abuse, where they thought they might be of help.

Preventive medicine is but one of many offshoots of the extension work in the field. In one building, which was turned over to the extension service by the city after it was abandoned by the owner, there had been no heat for over a year, there was no roof, no door, few windows, and, for several months, neither hot nor cold water. After reactivating the heat and the plumbing, fixing the roof and the windows, and plastering and painting the apartments, the extension agents organized regular meetings of the buildings' residents, which evolved into a tenants' association. The association now watches for people throwing garbage in the yard or the hallways, helps collect the rents, and forms a mechanism for requesting help when new problems appear. Such activities have earned the agents the respect of many members of the community — a factor that the program's supporters believe to be a key to its success.

"Other minority training programs, if they find a guy a job, send him downtown to be the token Black or Puerto Rican on some big construction job," says Rivera. "But here the trainee is guaranteed a job, and in his own community."

The 70 agents trained to date reflect the ethnic makeup of East Harlem — most are Puerto Ricans, with some blacks and a few Italians. While some of the men were experienced in the construction trades, others came to the program from jail, drugs, or the welfare rolls. Despite this disparity of backgrounds, the program has retained over 85 percent of its enrollees — even when the shortage of funds delayed pay checks. In fact, some of the men even left higher-paying jobs for the $100 a week paid during both training and fieldwork. Explaining this enthusiasm, one of the extension agents told *Science,* "There's no substitute for the feeling you get when you're really helping your own people."

The sense of accomplishment in the work is reflected in the men's personal lives. An East Harlem social worker reported a typical case of an extension agent who "seems to have a whole new interest and hope in his family" as a result of his work with the extension service. Referring to a second extension agent, the social worker remarked that his "increased sense of pride has begun to affect the entire family — knitting its torn ends together."

At the heart of the extension service program is the concept that the problems with housing, and hence with health, have fallen into what Richter dubbed "the semi-public domain" — building maintenance that is outside the responsibility of either the city or the individual tenants. While the program has drawn criticism from some quarters of the antipoverty movement for "catering to slumlords," Rivera believes that "the only way to get anything accomplished is to deal with everyone involved. Sure," he said, "there are plenty of landlords who would never fix anything, but the economics of East Harlem are such that, even if a landlord wanted to keep a building in decent shape, the services are either exorbitantly priced or totally unavailable."

Such attitudes are shared by Ray Galliani, president of the Federation of Lower and Middle Income Property Owners, and a member of the board of directors of the extension service. According to Galliani, the landlords of at least 200 buildings in East Harlem would take advantage of the extension service — if the facilities and manpower were available.

Conversations with the director and the employees of the extension service reveal elaborate plans to turn the program into more than a preventive maintenance operation. They foresee, for example, hiring a full-time public health nurse to investigate medical problems and to offer health education in more detail, as well as constructing playgrounds, day-care centers, and a number of other facilities for the community. But for now, because of a chronic lack of funds, they can only perform piecemeal repair work — often scrounging up scrap materials to finish the jobs.

The triple concepts of the extension service — housing maintenance, job training, and preventive medicine — satisfy a number of the critical needs of the ghetto. And at a reasonable price: while it costs a few cents per apartment per day to maintain a building, the city spends as much as $20 per day to house refugee families from abandoned buildings in "welfare" hotels. Moreover, the controversy in the Forest Hills section of Queens over the construction of public housing indicates the resistance to construction of new low-income housing facilities — even when money is available. But as Richter told *Science,* "Everyone associated with the extension service is tired of hearing how logical we are. What the program needs now is money to do the job it can do." ■

The Invisible City:
An Interview with Richard S. Wurman*

Participation is unlikely without comprehension. Comprehension in turn, as Wurman points out, depends on both accessibility and understandability. Our cities have a tendency to fall down on both counts. Wurman has long been active in developing innovative ways of sharing information about the physical environment, both in educational settings and for citizens at large. Another good example of his work, in addition to the one mentioned in the selection, is the *Yellow Pages of Learning Resources*.

■   Q: What is the Invisible City?

Wurman: The Invisible City is the environment as it is unuseable and uncrackable as a place for learning.

Q: In what sense is it "invisible"?

Wurman: It is invisible for three reasons: one, because people aren't aware that it *can* be used. Two, because things are not available — you can't find out about them. And three, because things are available but not in a form in which you can understand them. For instance, I could tell you that you could go out and talk to a garbage man and learn something from him. But you're not going to, because you don't know what to ask him. And unless you can get over that anxiety, unless you can crack the resources of the city, you can't use them. Even when you truly want to find out about your urban environment, either to participate in the city as a citizen, or learn from it as a student, it's impossible to find out about many things.

Q: What kind of information is particularly inaccessible?

Wurman: I'll give a practical example. I ran a problem at Philadelphia College of Art several years ago. I'm very much interested in people taking on new responsibility, and a new responsibility for graphic artists would be to tell about what goes on in the city — to give urban information. They've avoided that responsibility; they're more interested in Volkswagen ads, or in moving type around, than in saying,

*Excerpted from R. S. Wurman and E. Berkeley "The invisible city." *Architectural Forum,* May 1972, page 41. Whitney Publications, Inc. Reprinted by permission.

there is certain information about the city I can make more understandable by what is understandable visually that is not understandable either literarily or numerically. This is the problem I gave. Each student was to think up a piece of information he wanted to know about the city of Philadelphia. He would then get that piece of information, put it into visual form, and we'd make a visual chart book of the pieces. Almost without exception they couldn't find the information — they wanted to know about the location of firehouses, how many fires each one had, they wanted to find out about housing, about certain facts of population, about climate and weather in the city, about city ownership of land.

Q: Was the material not available, or were they denied it?

Wurman: I would say 50 percent of the time they were denied it, and 50 percent of the time people couldn't put their fingers on it.

A number of years ago, I made a proposal for an Urban Observatory, a place in each city, in each region, where public information is made public. I'll explain that. Public information today isn't public. When we go to the moon, we have beautiful drawings and maps and simulation movies, and it is quite clear where we are going. But when we put a new highway in the city, you can't find a map in the newspaper, you don't know whether it's going to tear down 30 or 300 houses. Nobody *demands* that they show us that. Nobody demands, because they don't know that *that* can be made clear. But it occurs to me that information about the resources of a city, the ownership of these resources, the plans, the aspirations, can all be put in a form that we, the great big we, can understand. And respond to and work with.

The information should not only be made public, it should also be in a form we can understand. I have shelves full of things I don't understand. A favorite story of mine is that several years after we opened the office, I thought we had enough money to get a special magazine I've always wanted — *Urbanistica*. It came quarterly, in those corrugated envelopes, covered with beautiful Italian stamps. We would open it, and gather around, and I would say why can't we do maps like this? After a couple of issues, it hit me — Shazam, like lightning striking — and I said, I don't understand a damn thing I'm looking at. Until then I had always fooled myself. If something *looked* good, it *was* good. If a building looked good, it was good. If a map or planning report looked good, it was good. And I hadn't asked two very simple questions: did I understand what I was seeing, and could I tell somebody about it.

Q: Do you see any real efforts to make public information public?

Wurman: There are 100 or so examples in *Making the City Observable,* the *Design Quarterly* publication I did.[1]

Here is an attempt to give people a feeling for their community. This map of the Hill District in Pittsburgh measures twenty-five feet by forty feet. The project by the Community Design Associates was a long-term effort on the part of several people. Troy West headed the effort and provided some of the pictures. He also credits the work of Douglas Copper and Jay Greenfield. Wurman includes some examples of this map in Making the City Observable *(1971, pp. 77–78).*

As I got into it, collecting material, I got into some thoughts that were at first perverse to me. For instance, getting on top of a tall building and seeing the city is like a map, and that's not making the city observable. But it *is*. It's as much making the city observable as a guide book. And then I came across the newspaper ad that ABC television did on the election ballot, translating the bond issues into English. Well, *that's* allowing us to get in, and making something observable. And a curriculum that turns people toward the environment for learning — like the workbooks we've done at GEE! — also makes the city understandable. ∎

NOTE

1. A special issue of *Design Quarterly* published by Walker Art Center and issued simultaneously in book form by the MIT Press. 1971.

Rachel Kaplan
Participation in Environmental Design: Some Considerations and a Case Study[*]

Comprehension, the essential foundation for effective participation, may not be as difficult as is sometimes believed. The abstract proposals for how to improve participation find concrete realization in this case study, which also provides a model for how to involve people in the design process in other settings as well.

■ Participation, in the context of environmental design, is a complex issue. It is greeted with a host of emotions by those who might be practicing it as well as by those who wish it were practiced with them. Where and when it works well, the emotions are as warm, positive, and effusive as they might be in any effective situation. But, unfortunately, such is rarely the case.

Citizen complaints about participation fall into two major categories: "No one ever asks us anything," on the one hand, and perhaps even worse, "They pretended to ask, but did not even want to hear."

On the designer's side, the complaints cover a wider spectrum. Some are disenchanted with their attempts to include citizens in the decisions ("They watched the presentation with glazed eyes and no one said anything"; "It's always the same people who raise problems and you don't know what the silent majority is thinking"; "Hardly anyone showed up at the public hearing"). Others are not sure what is gained by asking people to make decisions about things they know nothing about. It is not unusual even in the enlightened 1970s to read that a "good designer" is one who can, as it were, put himself in the shoes of any client and fill the needs of any group (Jensen, 1974).

Then too, some cannot understand all the fuss about participation. Many an architect says that he has always been in the practice of asking his clients about their desires and needs. And are not those fascinating models under their plexiglass domes, centrally displayed in the lobby, precisely to inform the public about the forthcoming changes? It is rumored that one such model for a new hospital was built

at a cost of $20,000! Of course, they need not all be *that* expensive —
but there must not be any question about their excellence.

Participation, in the context of environmental design, is a complex issue. Who is to participate? When in the process of design should
this happen? What do you do about pervasive ignorance? How do you
resolve the conflicting inputs? And for all the complaining and dis-
agreeing, isn't it true that people adapt amazingly fast to whatever the
final outcome? The purpose of this paper is to explore some of these issues and to examine some of the requirements for productive participation in environmental design. But it must be emphasized at the outset
that these questions have no single right answer. To be sure, "participation" is a process that can be accomplished at many levels, in many
different ways, and can fail despite the best intentions. But it is also
true that though often frustrating and seemingly counterproductive,
participation holds the potential for powerful social-psychological benefits, as well as design benefits, for the community and even for the
experts involved.

There was a park in New York City known as Hell's Kitchen
(Reemer, 1971). Over many years it served various functions ranging
from dumping place to vandal's delight. Its transformation to "The
New Earth Park" is a story of participation, of a combination of planning and evolution. While the local grass-roots effort increased the
sense of ownership and pride, it in itself was not a sufficient force to
have created the park.

The New Earth Park exemplifies several aspects of participatory
design. Among the most vital are the importance of involvement in
planning, in physical effort, and in continued transformations.[1] There
is planned obsolescence — the old car seats incorporated into the seating arrangement are readily replaced by the local junk dealer. There is
throughout the kind of comfortable fit with the particular neighborhood that makes this solution unlikely to be just right somewhere else.
And the likely consequences of the participatory process are also evident here. The place is used, vandalism is no problem, and there is
ready participation in the continued communal sense of ownership.
Furthermore, it has even gained acceptance by the once hostile
powers-that-be.

When this sort of thing happens one can all too easily point to
some unique condition, some indigenous characteristics that made it
possible. But over and over again, when the People take part in transforming their own environment, striking social-psychological as well
as design consequences can be seen. In the case of the New Earth Park,
and many versions of "people's parks" since, the participatory process
was entirely at the level of the people. They had to "fight city hall" to

be sure, but the "design" was generated within the framework of indigenous experience, not unlike the construction of "primitive buildings" (Rapoport, 1969).

Participation is more or less intrinsic to a situation where a group of people cooperate to bring forth a park. But much of contemporary environmental change does not emanate from the level of the citizenry. Rather, the decision is made at a level removed (geographically and organizationally) from those who are immediately effected, and the project is designed by still others who are equally removed from the ultimate "neighbors." Participation in these contexts raises many problems that do not seem to arise when people plan for themselves.

Recent efforts by the National Park Service (1975) to obtain citizen participation in the master plan for Yosemite Park and by the Forest Service (1975) with respect to Beaverhead National Forest dramatically illustrate the difficulties of public involvement when a park is no longer a neighborhood plot. Suddenly, the "affected parties" are not simply the people residing near these settings, nor are they simply the people who visited the park on a particular day. In the case of Yosemite, "participation" was open to one and all — across the entire country — a kind of national referendum but without the safeguards of the voting booth.

But even at the level of a small urban park, the problems of participation are far different when the process is initiated by a sponsoring agency rather than through grass-roots efforts. How might one go about creating such a vest-pocket park? Say a city has decided to designate a small plot as park, and is willing to be responsive to citizen input. What approaches would be useful? Some levels and kinds of participation applicable to such a setting are discussed in the next section. These will be followed by a case study that places some of the issues in a more tangible context.

SOME KINDS OF INPUT FROM "USERS"

The designer for such a hypothetical vest-pocket park might, for example, study the situation — the traffic pattern, the character of the adjacent areas, the groups likely to use the park — and come forth with a proposal. Plans would then be shown to the appropriate city agency, possibly modified, and a final version would be drawn. One or two public hearings might be held at which these drawings would be displayed. No doubt the public would be told about the various constraints — traffic, soil, zoning restrictions, etc. — that entered the solution, and the plans would show a pleasant looking park with people sitting on benches shaded by some large trees. There is little question that such a park would constitute an improvement over whatever is at the site, and it would not be surprising if the few people who attend the hearings would raise few questions.

An added step to the process might involve observations of similar parks in terms of use patterns. Clipboard in hand, one can mark down the frequency of certain acts or sequences of acts. Are the swings used by the children for swinging or by the mothers for swaying? When are the benches in use and by whom? One might even extend the observations by asking the users questions regarding distance traveled to the facility, frequency of use, and perhaps about the number of people in the "party." While such information is useful, it lacks many of the advantages of participation. The results of such observations are likely, by themselves, to lead to a "universal" solution rather than one fitting the requirements of the particular park to be designed. The built environment is already plagued with too many mass-produced "universal solutions"; the diversity of our communities must be expressed in a corresponding diversity of design, lest all sense of identity and sense of territory are further undermined.

The seemingly objective nose counts and quantifiable data must not replace the needed subjective data that enter into design decisions. Potential users might, for example, be queried about their preferences for certain features in a park, for play equipment, benches, open space, etc. While it is certainly far better to have some information along these lines then to rely exclusively on the designer's insight, it is also important to realize that information obtained in this way can be misleading.[2] One reason is that such questions easily elicit stereotyped responses. If asked what one wants in a park, one is likely to answer in terms of features easily and readily described — "green," fountains, color, benches — though different people using these terms may mean quite different versions of them.

There are, of course, many other ways to obtain useful input from the public. One might form several groups of potential users and have them meet together and propose what such a park might be like. These groups could be constituted to include a wide cross-section of the likely publics for the park; they might be asked to send a representative to a meeting to explore the various "solutions" that each of the groups developed; they might even be paid for their participation in these meetings.[3]

Another highly participatory approach that is widely utilized involves the use of games.[4] In the context of park design such games might focus on spatial considerations, using a game board perhaps, or they might be more oriented to role playing and consideration of the requirements of various effected groups. Games also vary widely in how complex their rule structures might be, in terms of how long it takes to play them, and in terms of how close the relationship between the player and the part he is playing might be. One feature games tend to have in common is that they are involving for the participants.

Another characteristic they share is that they are, in a certain sense, artificial. They depend on scenarios to construct an approximation to some existing conditions.

These various sources of input are neither mutually exclusive, nor exhaustive. It may be useful to describe briefly the procedure we recently followed in an effort to obtain citizen input with respect to a small urban vest-pocket park, as it is in certain ways related to some of these approaches, and in other ways quite distinct.

THE CASE OF A LITTLE PARK

The approach involved photographs depicting possible views such a park might offer. This procedure has the advantage of providing visual imagery for a situation that will, after all, be experienced visually (rather than verbally). It also has the advantage of providing people with a range of alternatives so they can better realize the realm of the possible. In fact, the twenty-four photographs shown were generated from models of three alternative designs for the site. The reactions to the alternatives were not central, however. Rather, we were concerned to obtain the reactions to the particular moods and features represented by the views. The photos were also helpful in prompting citizens to make general remarks about their preferences. The models used to obtain these photographs were necessarily crude and low in detail (figure 1). If one takes seriously the notion that citizen input can be useful in the design process, one can neither afford the cost of "beautiful" models nor the time it takes to build them. Fortunately, people have no difficulty in relating to such relatively abstract material. In fact, the lack of detail can help focus attention at the level of input that is needed.[5]

The survey was conducted in the heart of winter at two locations in the immediate vicinity of the proposed park. Both the savings bank and the public library were most gracious and helpful in accommodating the survey. At both locations, participation was on a voluntary basis. In addition to people who happened to be at one of these locations while the survey was conducted (this included a range of weekday daytime hours, one evening session, and a Saturday), the sample included people who had been notified through a letter from the superintendent of parks and recreation which was sent to residences and businesses in the immediate vicinity of the park.

A total of 181 people completed the picture ratings. While these in no way constitute a "random" sample, they represent an appropriate sample by virtue of their presence at these locations and their interest in the park. While 181 is not a large number by some standards, it represents considerably more citizen input than is characteristic of early phases of planning. The sample included about the same number of

FIGURE 1

Four of the photographs that were included in the citizen survey for a proposed small urban park. The bottom two scenes were the most preferred. The top two scenes provide some indication of features that residents of park vicinity consider worrisome but which people who work in that area find attractive. Notice that the photographs are based on low-detail models in all instances. The models and these photographs are the work of Terry Brown and Charles Cares, the designers on this project.

men and women, a wide age range (teens to seventies), with the majority in their twenties. It included people who are employed full time, part time, or not at all. The sample was also evenly divided between people who live and/or work in the downtown area and those who neither live nor work there.

The preference ratings showed some interesting patterns. The scenes that were liked the most suggested an urban park with ample opportunity for sitting amongst the trees (bottom pictures in figure 1).

There was also a strong preference for views that showed the park as having both canopied and open areas, with a variety of trees. Particularly noteworthy were the rather different views of the park held by those who live in the downtown area as opposed to people who work there. For the latter, a park of any kind is a bonus. Their ratings were consistently more favorable and were particularly high for the pictures showing opportunities for sitting in the park. For those who live in the downtown area, by contrast, the park can be a mixed blessing. They indicated a preference for scenes that seem low in potential threat. They preferred those views where the situation is easily overseen, where potential hiding places are lacking, and where the view from the street is unobstructed. (The top two photos in figure 1 were greatly preferred by people who do not live in the area of the park.)

There was also no lack of comments! Foremost among these was a concern for grass and a dislike for concrete ground textures. Many commented on a desire to have the park "green." There were also many comments about seating and frequent objections were raised to views showing the trees in a rather geometric, gridlike fashion. And then too there were some appreciative notes not only about the park itself, but about the opportunity to participate. "Thanks for asking," someone wrote at the bottom of the page.

The purpose of the citizens' reactions was not to "vote" on the best of the three alternatives. Rather, their input can be effective in helping the designer understand the concerns of different user groups. This may well lead to a somewhat different solution than any of the originally proposed alternatives. The final plan for the park under study here was, in fact, greatly changed from any of the original alternatives. While the input was not the sole reason for this, there was no question that it played a major role in the design process. As it turned out, the landscape architects responsible for the designs felt they had gained considerable insight from the early feedback to their plans. That the citizens felt they had gained something was also evident in their grateful comments — "It's the first time anyone asked me anything since I came here."

SOME REQUIREMENTS FOR PARTICIPATORY PLANNING

The success of participation would appear to depend upon at least four critical requirements, not all of which have received adequate attention. Once again, it must be stated that there is no unique way to assure that these are met, nor can they be considered a foolproof avenue to success. They are offered here more in the sense of hypotheses both to stimulate research and to serve as preliminary considerations to help get the process underway.

The first requirement is the possibility of genuine impact. For the participatory process to have its desired effects, the planned environmental change must become in some sense the property of the participants. With the widespread suspicion of officialdom and establishment, an honest presentation of the extent of possible impact and the ways in which it can have its effect is in order. If there are economic and political uncertainties at issue, these must be shared. People are often willing to take a risk; they can, however, become unruly when what they took to be a promise turns into a possibility. A recent article about Justin Gray Associates (Braybrooke, 1974) documents the importance of this consideration in the context of low-income housing — certainly a case study where the emotions were warm and positive, and for good reason.

A second requirement is adequate sampling of the user population. Nursing homes, for example, have been designed from the point of view of nurses. Unfortunately, the preferences of nurses and those of elderly people are not necessarily the same. Nurses like to be able to see everyone; elderly people, not surprisingly, like privacy (Pastalan, 1971). The different reactions between people who work in a setting and those who live there is also not suprising. Without awareness of such discrepancies it is unlikely that design solutions will consider the differing needs of the affected groups.

A third requirement is difficult to formulate precisely, but equally vital. It concerns the eagerness on the part of some designers to build monuments, to build now and forever, to build at once, and once and for all. Participation, by contrast, gains much by gradualism and impermanence. There are profound advantages to a growth model, to a procedure that is not oriented to the mass production of error. This might seem an unreasonably expensive route. But could it be more expensive than Pruitt-Igoe? The "city that is not a tree" (Alexander, 1965) relied on gradual evolution and sequential changes. Concern about expense, and particularly the expense of maintenance, may turn out to be misguided. Maintenance may be an opportunity for involvement, correction, and change. It may serve as an antidote to vandalism: at a time when large portions of the population feel unneeded, when adolescents need to "create adventure" (Ladd, 1977), design solutions that rely on such human power may be more humane as well as cost-effective. Some degree of impermanence has many advantages; so many, in fact, that most organisms depend on it for maintaining their capacity to adapt and change.

Finally, the fourth requirement involves the use of a satisfactory medium. Traditionally, participation has relied almost exclusively on verbal interchange. Since, however, so much of design concerns the visual and the spatial, alternative media are likely to hold greater

FIGURE 2

These four photographs illustrate some aspects of model detail that might aid and some that might detract in communicating features of the site arrangement of a housing complex. The contour layering in the upper right, though in a sense more accurate, was often misinterpreted as steps by participants with no design training. A comparable view of the models (lower right) avoided this problem. A different view of the same arrangement is shown in the lower left, using building models with virtually no detail. Participants had no difficulty interpreting the site even with these "crude" models. The upper-left view shows an alternative arrangement for the same site, one that participants found far more attractive than the arrangement that actually exists at the site.

promise. But the issue goes beyond the need for more extensive use of graphics. It is, after all, not that unusual to be surprised by the actual building after having seen the artistic renditions of the proposed building. Nor is it simply a matter of presenting enough detail. As a matter of fact, detail might lead to misinterpretation (cf. Kaplan et al., 1974,

FIGURE 3

A simplified oblique view, part of a larger drawing, by Howard L. Deardorff.
This was used in presenting a project involving a relatively large area in
Detroit. Such graphics are both engaging and effective in communicating
various features of the plan.

regarding the misinterpretation of contour layering to convey differences in elevation, a standard operating procedure in design). And, as
has been mentioned, the cost of such material becomes an added consideration when one wants to assure public participation early in the
process.

Ironically, public "involvement" often is incredibly uninvolving.
The information is presented in an unengaging fashion, and consideration of the demands placed on the public is neglected.[6] Perhaps one of
the reasons that gaming procedures have met such wide acclaim is because they readily involve the participants in the task. But that is not
to say that the involving qualities found in games cannot be translated
to other contexts. In fact, in the context of participation it should be far
easier to engage the interest of the effected public. The problem need

not be fabricated; it is right at hand. Rule structures need not be created; they are built into the problem calling for solution. And issues of winning or losing are tangential when the major issue is to understand the situation and communicate one's concerns.

Clearly, a satisfactory medium is one that communicates and is engaging (figures 2 and 3). It must lend itself to the exploration of possible alternative solutions, providing enough imagery that a novice can "play" with the problem. Finally, it must lead to an outcome that is useful to the designer in furthering the process.

THE BURDEN OF MISCONCEPTIONS

Two areas of misconceptions seem to be major obstacles to effective use of participation. One is the notion that participation means that the design process is to be left to the untrained, that the skill and experience of the designer/planner is to be wasted. The other misconception involves a lowly view of the "common folk," a notion that most people are really not up to the challenge of effective participation. Necessarily, the two misconceptions are intertwined, and the consequence is a fear of "design by the least competent." These issues must be examined closely if the potential advantages of participation are to be realized.

The notion that most people cannot really handle participation is based on a confusion between capacity and knowledge. Ignorance is curable! In fact, it is precisely in this respect that the skill and competence of the expert are most essential. This is where effective communication, where the skillful use of graphic material, is completely dependent on the designer's ability. Provided with the necessary imagery, the novice by no means lacks the competence to translate the situation to personally meaningful terms. Comparably, it takes the expert's knowledge and experience to present potential alternative solutions. To simply ask a client "What do you want" is to expose ignorance and highlight frustration.

On the other hand, there is no question that people function competently when material is presented in a comprehendable way. When design alternatives are presented to untrained people in a way that they can understand and find involving, their reactions are helpful and enlightening. In fact, one of the exciting outcomes of a participatory process is an emergent solution, one not quite what any one had considered prior to the attempted joint problem solving. It is also this aspect of participation that maximizes the likelihood of a unique "fit" between the situation and the particular groups that are concerned.

Most people are concerned about their surroundings, especially when changes are threatened or are urgently needed. They may be unhappy about the rate of growth, or about the encroachment of industry, or about having nothing for the kids to do, or the lack of nearby parks, or the litter, or the traffic. In some broad sense they care about their environment and are often eager for help. They welcome the professional skilled in environmental design who is willing to listen to their problems and make suggestions. While they have little choice but to accept imposed changes in their environment, the costs of "adapting" to these conditions is rarely measured. Perhaps they can be more readily appreciated by their absence — in those situations where the public had a chance to participate in the design decisions directly affecting their well-being.   ■

NOTES

1. Note the striking parallels — both in inputs and in benefits — to the "self-help" housing area (Turner and Fichter, 1972).

2. Canty's (1974) paper shows some interesting contrasts between the information obtained prior to designing low-income housing for the elderly and the post-design feedback. Without telling the potential user what the trade-offs may be, it is easy to escalate the "dream list" and even raise false expectations about what might be. Robinson et al. (1975) have a useful discussion of some settings where trade-off approaches have been used.

3. This approach is patterned after the procedure Carr (1975) described with respect to a participatory planning effort in downtown Washington, D.C.

4. Several examples of gaming in the context of design participation are included in Cross (1972) and in Tester (1974). Sanoff (1974, 1975), in particular, has developed several game-based approaches to public involvement in design decisions. Some computer-oriented techniques (Grant, 1974, 1975) have several features in common with gaming approaches.

5. Not all people appreciate such models. A leading architect in town assured me that his firm would never present such pictures to the public!

6. A fuller discussion of several of the issues that lead to this unfortunate state of affairs can be found in a paper by S. Kaplan (1977a). It examines some pervasive differences between the expert and nonexpert in terms of how they conceptualize design problems. See also R. Kaplan (1977a) for some precautions to be observed in obtaining citizen cooperation.

Stephen Carr and Kevin Lynch
Where Learning Happens*

This selection is full of stimulating ways to enhance participation in the urban context. Some of the proposals are readily feasible; others are somewhat advanced even now, some years after the paper was written. The connections between what Carr and Lynch have to say and previous selections are extensive. Among more direct links are Wurman and Parr, along with, of course, the prior selections by Lynch and by Carr.

■   An urban region is an immense storehouse of information. Its stimuli, diverse ways of life, events, and facilities are a prime occasion for learning. Developmental policy should aim at making this information accessible. One straightforward way is to provide a free public-transportation system, bringing all parts of a metropolitan region within some reasonable time-distance. The system must be workable at low densities, so that nondrivers are not caught within suburban areas nor central city residents excluded. Young children, as well as handicapped persons, should be able to use it with safety. If it proved impossible for an affluent country to provide basic transportation as a free public utility, then public transit might be subsidized so that children and adults of low income ride free. A more limited policy would subsidize educational trips where the destination was a school, museum, or another specifically educational locale. It might even be possible to subsidize "first-time" trips by distributing free tickets to random destinations.

The transportation system should be easy to use, as well as cheap and ubiquitous. It should be designed to be completely legible — the system of routes and transfers easy to follow and the destinations clear. Symbolic maps should be displayed, and direction-giving devices installed at all critical points. Public transit vehicles and routes should visually correlate with their destinations not only by using route and destination symbols, but by giving a circumferential route or vehicle a typically different form than a radial route or vehicle. The location of moving vehicles in the system and especially their imminent arrival

---

*Excerpted and reprinted by permission of *Daedalus,* Journal of the American Academy of Arts and Sciences, Boston, Massachusetts. Fall, 1968, *The Conscience of the City.* Pages 1281–1286.

should be displayed at waiting points. There should also be a network of paths along which young children can move safely by the means under their control: by foot, bicycle, cart, pony, or otherwise. Even the prosaic walk to school might be an educational device.

All vehicles and routes should give a clear view of the region being traversed — of its most important activities and particularly of its changes. The environment itself might be designed to be "transparent," wherever possible without intruding on individual privacy. The form of structures and of land, as well as signs and electronic devices, can communicate the activity and function of a place, express its history or ecology, reveal the flow and presence of people, or signal the social and environmental changes that are occurring. In an industrial area, factories would be encouraged to let their machines be seen in action, to label raw materials and their origin, to distinguish the different kinds of operatives and explain what they do, to exhibit finished products, to make their transportation containers transparent. Thus the city, like a good museum, would be designed to increase the physical and perceptual accessibility of its contents.

OPENNESS AND RESPONSIVENESS

Making people and information accessible is one way of using the environment for learning. Another is to see that environmental form is responsive to individual and small group effort. To act experimentally and to see the results of that action are the most effective ways to learn. This can be done in the spatial environment in a way often denied us in our social world of complex and remote institutions. High-density housing, for example, could be designed to provide the relative autonomy of the single-family dwelling. Allotment gardens and sites for owner-built vacation homes might be provided. A new technology of house maintenance and rehabilitation would increase the ability of the tenant to "do it himself." Features in the environment could be responsive to individual manipulation: arrangeable lighting, "pop-out" shelters, controllable micro-climate. The present trend toward homeostatic constancy — the caretaker environment — might be superseded by sensing and control devices by which environments would react visually, aurally, or tangibly to manipulation, or to the motion of the observer — just as artists are now inviting the active engagement of the spectator in their works. We might train for environmental management — for development, building, gardening, interior and exterior decorating, and other socially useful skills that allow unlimited use of individual sensibilities.

As experiments in radical decentralization, it should be possible for the inhabitants of small city areas to shape and maintain them themselves. Communal institutions might assume some functions of planning, building, repairing, servicing, and policing in their own environments. Neighborhood teenagers, for example, might install and manage their own recreation facilities. Long-term changes in environment through new development or renewal can be growth enhancing, if effective roles can be found for individuals in shaping such change. Greater decentralization of change management will also be more productive of diversity. Our developmental city must include responsive local institutions for environmental control, as well as responsive physical features. Widespread political engagement would be its characteristic.

We would provide an ubiquitous network of open space throughout the urban region — "open" not always because it is free of buildings and covered with plants, but in the sense that it is uncommitted to prescribed users. Dumps and vacant lands would be in this inventory, as well as woods, fields, waterways, and marshes. In these open areas, actions and explorations are permissible that would be intolerable on developed sites. Anything might be constructed from the materials available — temporary sculptures (as on the mudflats of San Francisco Bay) or tree houses. Open lands would be widely distributed so that some are safely accessible to the young child exploring on his own. Open space could be interior space as well — for instance, large barn-like structures, whose volume would be temporarily allotted for spontaneously organized projects and constructions. Raw materials and technical advice might be available on call, much as in the junk playgrounds of Scandinavia. But since these uncommitted open areas are vulnerable to abuse and neglect, we must either provide enough of them to keep the density of use low or be prepared to police them regularly.

ENVIRONMENT AS A BASE FOR SPECIAL PROGRAMS

The environment may also be a base for special educational actions. We would, for example, attempt to increase the availability of symbolic information. Our policies would include a wide regional distribution of computer consoles (probably with reproduction capabilities drawing on large central libraries), museums, tutors, directories, local newspaper, local TV and radio programs, and other such information outlets. Moreover, this flow of information would be made responsive to the user in many ways: Observers would be able to shut off or turn on environmental displays, make simple inquiries of visible signs, or find places to put up their own public signs. Local newspapers and broadcasts should be open to the announcements, plays, and stories of their listeners, so that groups can speak to one another, rather than be spoken to. Community TV will facilitate this. Would ham TV be a future possibility?

Particular areas in the city would be devoted to self-testing. Adolescents or adults might try themselves against a graded series of challenges and difficulties — cognitive, physical, or artistic. Teenagers might scale buildings or drive in obstacle races. Others might compete in the skill with which they rearrange a landscape. Many of these activities can emphasize mutual dependence and trust on the model of Outward Bound. Areas of this kind would have ambiguous border zones, where the unsure could watch and consider whether to take the plunge.

Other temporary communities might be places where it was permissible to break the habitual mold of action and to try out new roles: child-rearing or marriage, different kinds of productive work, or new and unfamiliar ways of life. These groups would be like participatory theater or continuous happenings, the tentative gesture would for a time be the substitute for the competent committed act. Such a policy implies our judgment that vicarious experience — watching others, reading novels, seeing movies, learning by identification, processes already institutionalized in our culture — is no substitute for real experience. Obsolete parts of central cities will be apt locations because of their accessible, cheap, and anonymous space. These temporary communities could also be used for special celebrations or for the coming-together of strangers for some common purpose or interest like surfing, socialism, or yoga. They would be ephemeral, voluntary ghettos. This will be a touchy policy to implement since many of the strange activities in such places will be seen as threats to society. They will have to be monitored, yet the monitoring must not be impatient interference.

The school, the institution formally devoted to education, could make much greater use of the city environment not simply by field trips, but by dispersing its scholarly activities more widely in time and space. Children would then be drawn into contact with other kinds of children and adults, and learning would not be sealed off, but intimately mixed with other activities. The best teaching is mutual. Parents and local specialists can be drawn into the educative process — simultaneously being the teacher and the taught. Anyone may drop in, even if only to observe. Informal classes and workshops might be organized wherever people do not have other overriding purposes (while in transit, in open areas, vacation spots, in bars and hangouts, for example). There might be brief apprenticeships in work processes, recreation skills, politics, or the use of the city. Working and learning might be combined, as they sometimes are in research institutions or cooperative colleges, and not be a series of irrelevant lessons interspersed with drudgery. The school would be affirmed as a crucial institution, whereas it is likely to wither away as a separate physical plant. ∎

Florence C. Ladd
City Kids in the Absence of Legitimate Adventure*

       Youth and adolescence are times of action and involvement — for better or worse, depending in no small part on the responsiveness of the environment. A setting that would successfully channel this energy and curiosity could provide for the practical education of an urban Tom Sawyer. But, as Ladd points out, our frequent failures to meet this need turns a resource and an opportunity into a danger and a threat.

■   I spent the latter part of the 1960s engaged in a study of black adolescent boys, ranging in age from twelve to seventeen years, who lived in the poorer sections of Boston's Roxbury and North Dorchester. They were the subjects of a study of identity formation in black youth. While others engaged in the research focused on the impact of their families, schools, and peers on their lives and their destinies, I explored what their neighborhoods and housing meant to them, where their Boston lay, and what they found in the Boston area to interest them, amuse them, depress them, excite them; what places they enjoyed, wanted to destroy, to cherish, to avoid. I soon realized that they had found very few places that were interesting and safe to explore and enjoy, few places which offered them opportunities for challenging experiences and adventures that were *legitimate*.

    What might they do for excitement, adventure? Steal a car and go for a ride at breakneck speed through Franklin Park or along Blue Hill Avenue. Do a little shoplifting in a downtown department store and *just* escape getting caught, getting busted. Rob the poor boxes of churches. Or grab a few pocketbooks after the first of the month, buy some grass or hash or heroin and get high. Pull a fire alarm or maybe even start a fire. Break into somebody's "pad" and "rip off" a radio or TV set which might be sold or traded or simply discarded.

    Such incidents are not exclusively in the domain of the black and the poor who are young. They touch the lives of our entire adolescent

*Reprinted by permission from Florence C. Ladd "City kids in the absence of. . . ." Symposium Proceedings: *Children, Nature and the Urban Environment*. Northeastern Forest Experiment Station, Upper Darby, Pa., 1977.

population. For some, they are the critical episodes which divert them from trouble-free paths in directions which lead to more disruptive, trouble-making events. Still, the prospect of finding legitimate opportunities for adventure is a greater problem for poorer kids than for richer ones who, from time to time, have occasions for travel and vacations which afford them adventure through the stimulation of new settings, foreign languages, personal discovery, meeting people who are different, and so forth. Even for them, the opportunity to visit far away places is only occasional; they, like their poorer peers, have routines and restrictions which limit the risks and the excitement they might enjoy.

Why do some kids choose to seek adventures which lead to trouble? Why don't they find fun in legitimate activities? Certainly some kids find stimulation and pleasure in museums, art galleries, and zoos. They play tennis, baseball, basketball, football, or soccer; go for a boat ride or a swim; discover new worlds in old libraries; take the elevator to the top of a skyscraper and on a clear day are turned on by a panoramic view of their city and what lies beyond. Don't such activities afford kids experience that is sufficiently exciting and adventurous?

What is exciting and adventurous in the realm of adolescent experience in the 1970s? To experience adventure, some kids, particularly in urban settings, must test the legal and moral boundaries of society and, in the eyes of some, break the law. Situations that allow them opportunities for risk-taking and exploration often are situations in which they are violating a law and/or the rights or property of other people. An element of adventure lies, in part, in the knowledge that one is challenging or violating the legal and moral structure of his society. In urban settings, it is as if kids are forced or compelled to find adventure and excitement in activities that involve legal and moral risks. During the years when boys and girls need external challenges against which they can test their own daring and endurance, there are few legitimate opportunities available to them in their daily routines and environments which permit their testing themselves. There are few legitimate adventurous situations which allow them to explore the range of their physical and intellectual skills and abilities.

When we consider where young people of previous generations in the U.S. sought and found adventure, our thoughts turn to natural settings, wildlife, and open spaces. Vanishing are the natural areas, especially wooded areas, in and around cities where, only a few decades ago, city kids explored, charted, roamed, hid, were lost, and, the lucky ones, found safe and unhurt. Dirt roads on the edge of the city that once seemingly led nowhere are now paved and lead into the orderly geometry of suburban developments. The pockets of wilderness, those undeveloped areas that once were found near what clearly were the

Courtesy of Florence C. Ladd

city limits, have been leveled and covered with residential developments or industrial parks. There is no place — no natural environment — left for the urban adolescent to explore and experience adventure.

There are parks, with much that is natural, of course. Most urban parks in the U.S., especially those with wooded areas where some kids might experience adventure, are regarded as unsafe. Adolescents are apprehensive about being mugged or maimed in city parks. To be sure, adolescents are users of parks. Going to a park and running the risk of being robbed or assaulted involves an element of adventure. For those who go innocently into a park, the element of adventure is incalculable; the odds may well be against them. It is not comparable to the calculable risks presented by trails through woods or the face of a mountain or a river's rapids.

Except for courts and playing fields for sports, playgrounds include few facilities that attract adolescents. There are a few adventure playgrounds which offer adolescents the possibility of invention and excitement and the opportunity for supervising younger kids, but relatively few adolescents are to be found on those playgrounds whose clientele is largely a preadolescent group.

There are city-based programs such as scouting which generate adventures within the context of urban settings. Scouting and other similar programs such as Outward Bound and the Youth Conservation Corps have provided wilderness experience or at least camping opportunities and environmental education for the few urban youngsters who have had a chance to participate in them. For many reasons, such

Courtesy of Florence C. Ladd

programs are available and attractive to only a small number of kids. First of all, the programs are few in number and they are not highly visible. They are, generally speaking, expensive to operate and, consequently, too expensive for kids from low-income families. The style of adult supervision renders the programs unappealing to some kids who resent or resist adult authority figures. Such programs, however, have brought legitimate adventure into the lives of a few city kids.

How might the positive features of programs with adventure elements be developed as models for new situations that might appeal to a large number of urban adolescents? What would city kids like to do in order to experience legitimate adventure? Under whose auspices should adventure programs be developed? (If there are "sponsors" and "programs," would the events have the quality of adventure at all?) To what extent should schools be responsible for encouraging the direct participation of students in adventurous experiences? How might features in urban environments be designed or transformed to provide settings for adventures? Can wilderness within cities be simulated and maintained for safe use by kids? More broadly, we should also ask how are the adventures of adolescents related to the adventures of adult life? How is adventure regarded in contemporary U.S. culture?

Programmatically, we should begin by learning from adolescents what they regard as adventurous activity. With their assistance, settings and projects might be developed in which some of their own proposals for legitimate adventure might be tried. In an urban context, the adventurous aspects of the work of the fire department, city hospitals, news gathering agencies, and the police department might be made more visible to adolescents. Museums might organize clubs for would-be explorers who through film and other media might experience the thrills other explorers sought and found. Scouting could be revitalized and expanded to offer more kids opportunities for the physical and intellectual tests they need. The collaboration of schools and private organizations such as the Appalachian Mountain Club, the Sierra Club, and other conservationist groups might broaden opportunities for adventure for some adolescents.

From a design viewpoint, the possibility of simulating wilderness or creating environments within cities which contain some risk-taking elements should be a challenge to the planner and landscape architect who would go beyond conventional playground settings and design places with possibilities for adventure which would appeal to adolescents.

Finally, adults might reflect on what they do to experience adventure. It is recognized that adult requirements for adventurous experiences are quite different from those of adolescents. Nonetheless, it seems that a large segment of the adult population in the U.S. are passive, vicarious adventurers. Through the mass media, news of the adventures of others comes to us swiftly and in vivid detail. The small band of active adult adventurers who challenge time, space, mountains, seas, climatic conditions, and world records are far outnumbered by the large audience of spectators who sit at home and watch the action on television. In order to improve the quality and number of adventure opportunities for young people in the society, we must reexamine what adventure means to its adults, its standard makers. Consider what *you* do for adventure and what a fourteen-year-old city girl or boy may do. Then consider with her/him, with teachers, parents, mayors, recreation directors, scout leaders, coaches, active adventurers, architects, and planners what might be generated for city kids in the form of legitimate adventure. ■

Charles A. Lewis
Nature City*

It is sometimes said that something is "merely" a communication problem. But this in turn may be "merely" a failure of comprehension. And on the slim reed of comprehension rest many human efforts. Communication, the transfer of information from one head to another, can be exceedingly frustrating and difficult, especially if there is a shortage of shared cognitive maps. In this deceptively simple selection about so many different things, Lewis shows the importance of starting with a shared map, even if it is so remote that it serves essentially as an analogy. Without the comprehension that Lewis was able to share, the experience would have been one of strangeness and fear rather than participation and respect. "Legitimate adventure," comprehension, even insight — these are some of the benefits generated by the combination of a fascinating environment and a sensitive, perceptive guide.

■   "Hey, man — are there lions and tigers in there?"
"How about bears?"
". . . or snakes?"

Twelve teenaged boys looked apprehensively at the forest, not sure whether or not they wanted to enter. It was their first visit to the Arboretum, and the formidable jungle they faced was a peaceable patch of woods on the West Side — hardly cause for such uneasy feelings. But for these boys, residents of a nearby juvenile correctional center, the forest was not part of their common experience. The inner-city landscape with which they had grown up consisted mainly of asphalt, brick, stone, and concrete — with only weeds, grass, and a few trees for vegetation. They knew and had learned to contend with the threats inherent in that environment, but the forest was unfamiliar; its dangers could only be imagined — and feared.

When I joined the boys for their visit on this early June day, I had been thinking about ways to help them perceive something of the elements and systems at work in natural outdoor communities. Because their cultural frame of reference had been formed by the urban envi-

*From C. A. Lewis "Nature City." *The Morton Arboretum Quarterly,* Summer 1975, 11, 17–22. Reprinted by permission.

ronment, I thought it might be effective to point out functional and organizational parallels between natural environments and the city,
using familiar urban terms to identify elements of the natural landscape. Perhaps they could understand the natural world better by
thinking of it as another kind of functioning "city." Not quite sure
whether or not this approach would work, I decided to try it, letting the
boys show me the way.

Even as the boys introduced themselves and shook hands with
me, they began to teach me, for the handshake was different from any I
knew. Instead of grasping the lower part of my hand with their fingers,
they grasped the top part of my hand with fingers circling my thumb. I
did the same. I later learned that this is the soul-brother handshake, a
sign of friendship and solidarity in the black community. I must admit
that it transmits a greater sense of personal contact than our more
genteel way.

To ease our first meeting and to become better acquainted, I
explained that I had come here recently from the East and asked them
to help me become acquainted with their city. What was it like? Was it
crowded full of tall buildings, or were there many parks? What were
their houses made of? Was there any vegetation where they lived?

Next I began to ask about how things were transported in the
city. How did they get water? The first answer was, "Turn on the
faucet," but after a little further probing, I learned that water came
into the buildings through pipes that were under the streets. Was there
anything else under the streets? "Other pipes." "Wires." "Tunnels for
automobiles." What happened to water after a rain? "It goes down the
sewer." "It goes under the streets." What happened when you flushed
the toilet? "It goes down pipes." Where did the pipes go? "Underground." "To the sewage plant." What about garbage? "Goes into garbage cans." Then what happened to it? "Sometimes we knock the cans
over." (Laughter) "The garbage man takes it away."

I wanted to know something about the communities in the city,
too. Was the city all the same? "There are different neighborhoods."
What made them different? "Other kinds of people live in them."

As other questions followed, the boys — in providing for my orientation — focused their attention more and more on the physical aspects
of their city. I recapitulated their description of the city — what it looks
like and how it works — and thanked them for helping me understand
more about where they live. Then I announced that we were going to
visit another city: Nature City. After I assured them that we would encounter no bears, tigers, lions, or poisonous snakes in this "city," we set
out.

Our first stop was a pond, rich with many forms of life. I asked the
boys if they could figure out who lived in this pond neighborhood. They

noticed the iris and the cattails around the edge, the many plants growing in the water, and the dragonflies. No one saw a turtle, and it took a concentrated search to locate the two eyes of a dark green frog, peering above the water. As soon as one was discovered, bedlam broke loose! "Can we catch one?" "Can we take him home?" Yes, they might catch one if they could. Take it home? Well — I wondered aloud how they would like it if someone came into their house, took a look at them, said, "Hey, you look interesting! I'll take you!" and then grabbed them up and took them away. There was silence; the impact was obvious. It told them that many kinds of creatures lived in Nature City and, like the boys, wouldn't want to be taken away.

As the boys got the message, a rule was established: all things found in Nature City had to stay in Nature City. We could look at them, perhaps pick some of them up, examine them under a hand lens, but everything had to be replaced and not taken away. This seemed reasonable to the boys and was an effective lesson for the rest of our trip. I made a mental note: the pond neighborhood with its lesson would be the first stop on all future visits to Nature City.

Next we followed a path into the woods, and looked overhead at the lush foliage of oaks and maples. I asked the boys what happened to the leaves on the trees in the fall. "They fall on the ground." Did anyone take them away? "No." Well, if they fell on the ground every year and no one took them away, why weren't they piled up higher than our heads? What had happened to them? Again there was silence. Did they remember what they had said about garbage in their city? Well, then, did Nature City have garbage men? If so, who were they and where would we find them?

This was quite a question. I suggested we begin finding out by examining the layer of leaves on the ground, removing leaves one by one. Soon we discovered some leaves with holes in them. How did the holes get there? "Bugs ate them." "And worms!" We continued removing leaves, and we began to find insects. "Man, look at that bug!" "Kill it, quick!" I stopped the execution. Wait a minute — why should we kill it? Was it hurting us? What was it doing? There was a thoughtful pause. "I guess he is eating the leaves and stuff on the ground." So, who was he in Nature City? "The garbage man!" came the chorused reply.

From that point on, everyone's eyes were focused on the miniature world found on the forest floor, where we discovered a whole host of nature's garbage men working in leaves, twigs, and rotting logs. We picked up many of them and examined them closely through a hand lens. The magnified world provided an endless source of interest, and by the boys' own initiative it soon became routine procedure to look at everything new through the hand lens. The person given charge of the hand lens was recognized as having a position of status!

At about this time a subtle shift in emphasis took place. I found that I was no longer asking most of the questions, because the boys were exploring everything they could find, asking their own questions, and leading me. In the forest neighborhood they wanted to know why some trees were fat, others thin. A brush with unseen wild onions brought the comment, "I smell something cooking." We stopped to find and taste the plant and to learn, indeed, what was "cooking." A discovery was made when crossing a stream: in Nature City pipes aren't always necessary for delivering water to various neighborhoods. But how did water get to the tops of trees? Were there pipes in trees?

Along the path we stopped to compare the surface we were walking on with the woodland floor next to it. What were the differences in appearance, and why? "There aren't as many plants on the path." Is it easier to poke a stick into the path or into the woodland soil? "Woodland soil." Why? Thus we learned about compaction and some of its effects. What were those wooden things that looked like steps on the path? We found they were exposed roots, and we guessed why they weren't underground. We dug a little deeper into the woodland soil to find out what is below ground in Nature City. Not pipes, electric lines, or cars — but roots, worm tunnels, and bugs.

At the edge of the woods, we moved out into a more open field where wild geraniums were in bloom. Immediately someone asked, "Where do they come from?" My answer was to ask who had planted them. In chorus, the boys shouted, "Mother Nature!" Where did she get the seeds? No answer. "Did she get them at the store?" came a questioning reply. There was general agreement that she hadn't gotten them at the store. We looked around and spotted some old narcissus that had finished blooming. There were suspicious swellings at the tops of their stems, and we opened these up and examined them with the hand lens to find our answer. What was inside? "Seeds." How had the seeds gotten in there? To find out, we looked at some of the geraniums which had a few remaining blossoms but were also developing long, thin seed pods. We examined the flowers under the hand lens to see flower parts, and we looked at the developing seed pods to learn how nature's "seed packets" are produced.

I wanted to know who, besides flowers, lived in the field neighborhood. "Grasses," "weeds," "bushes," were the boys' answers. Anything else? We began to search and soon found small trails in the high grass. The boys wondered what they were and who had made them. I told them it was probably a meadow mouse. Several boys expressed disappointment at not seeing any wild animals, and I explained that animals were frightened away by all of the noise we made.

Next we visited a lake neighborhood that had been created by damming a stream. How was this like the pond neighborhood we visited earlier, and how was it different? Again, their curiosity pointed the way. "It's bigger." "There aren't as many weeds in the water." "There are fish." And there were frogs, which this time they caught, examined, and returned to the water. The dramatic flow of water over the dam accentuated the fact that the water was moving through this neighborhood and was not still, as it had been in the pond. What would happen if the dam were removed? The boys were surprised to realize that the lake would disappear.

The last neighborhood we visited was a dense, quiet grove of tall spruce trees: an evergreen neighborhood. Again, we wanted to find out who lived there and compare the neighborhood with the oak-maple forest we had seen. "More low branches in the other forest." "More things were growing on the ground." "It wasn't so dark." "This one smells different." I asked the boys what cones were all about. Why did some of them have all their scales gone so they looked like corncobs? What had happened to them? Had something eaten them? "Yes." Who? "Maybe squirrels." "Or birds." We were reminded that Nature City provides food for all the kinds of creatures who live there. Someone asked, "Are all these pine trees?" We talked about the fact that there are many kinds of evergreens, and that not all were pine. These were called spruce.

Now our trip was coming to an end, and as we left the cool spruce grove we talked about all the neighborhoods we had visited in Nature City — who lived in them and what was special about each one. We realized what a great number and variety of residents — plants and animals — lived in Nature City, yet how well they all got along and how each one contributed something important.

When the boys climbed onto their bus for the trip back to the youth center, they wanted to know if they could come back to Nature City again, and I knew they had enjoyed their visit as much as I had.

What is the key by which we enter Nature City? It begins with the realization that things familiar to us may be quite unfamiliar to someone else. If we can see natural areas through another person's eyes, in another cultural context, perhaps we can begin to translate what we know into understandable terms. We are, in a very real sense, "interpreters" and we need to understand other "languages" to be effective. For an inner-city youth, natural habitats become more comprehensible when presented as a familiar concept: neighborhoods in a city.

Perhaps the urban youngster who visits Nature City will not have learned the name of even one tree, flower, shrub, or animal, but he may have gained a general idea of the organization of natural sys-

Photo by William S. Stickney
Reprinted by permission of the Morton Arboretum

tems. Hopefully, he also may have discovered that a place which, to him, was filled with imagined terrors is, instead, a benevolent, lively, varied, and interesting place to visit. Once his interest is aroused and his perception focused on the special minutiae of a natural area, his innate curiosity — like that of youngsters everywhere — takes over, and you find that he is leading *you* through Nature City, giving you the rare privilege of seeing it for the first time through his eyes. ■

Afterword

Throughout this volume we have been concerned with human efforts to survive, to make a go of it, to function effectively. From the perspective of human functioning, the environment has certain striking properties: it is uncertain, it is highly complex, and it is vast in extent. That humans not only function despite these difficulties, but often are not even aware of them, is a tribute to the effectiveness of human information processing.

The functional environment, the world as we perceive it and act upon it, is a schematized, simplified rearrangement of the uncertain, complex physical realities that surround us. It is this cognitive process of organizing information that allows us to ignore the uncertainty in many situations. Humans recognize uncertain patterns with great facility. They categorize the complexity and vastness of the environment with comparative simplicity and compactness. They develop mental codes for large portions of the environment, making it possible to anticipate and to deal with circumstances that are not present and even with circumstances that have not yet occurred. And they do these things all the time. People even invest spare time in expanding their grasp and their comprehension.

Yet despite these formidable tools, people face an environment fraught with difficulties that at times threaten to be overwhelming. Thus, in addition to their native capacities people have evolved varied and colorful coping strategies. Such strategies developed over long periods of time by persisting human groups constitute an important aspect of culture; culture, in turn, provides a major means of coping with the difficulties the environment presents the members of our species.

It thus appears that humans capably and even eagerly make their way through vast amounts and kinds of information all the time.

Nonetheless, there are innumerable circumstances when properties of the environment undermine human effectiveness. Characteristically these instances involve a disruption of informational patterns. There may be more information passing through a given portion of the environment than the individual can deal with. Or some aversive properties of the environment may force withdrawal, thus preventing the observations and interactions required to obtain and transmit information. The environment often indirectly undermines people's capacity to deal with it by influencing information availability and information flow.

The environmental information of which we speak comes in many forms. It involves a great diversity of patterns and objects. Some of these are natural; some are constructed by humans. In sharp contrast to the world in which humans evolved, the modern world contains little that does not reflect human intervention in one way or another. Thus, acknowledging the impact of the environment on people is not equivalent to bowing to cold, impersonal forces against which people are helpless. More often than not, these are circumstances that people helped create — for better or for worse.

A synthesis of the material that has been presented must, then, include an understanding of the environment as it affects people, an understanding of the nature of humans and the kinds of arrangements they have evolved, and considerations of the implications of being a knowledge-based animal. The last of these points is particularly important and may also, unfortunately, lead to misinterpretation.

It is all too easy to think of knowledge and information as the intellectual stuff of schooling, in effect to interpret knowledge as the commodity that differentiates the educated from everyone else. But here we are speaking of knowledge and information that is the common property of the species. We are speaking of an organism that is distraught when things don't make sense, even trivial and inconsequential things; an organism that is curious and almost compulsive in its desire to look around the bend; an organism that feels compelled to share insights and legends with members of its group. At times, in fact, it seems as if the formal pursuit of knowledge, the academic-scientific enterprise, has actually thwarted the very needs and preferences of the organism.

Vivid examples of this arise not infrequently when information is required for making a practical decision. Those very members of our society most directly concerned with the acquisition of information are most likely to say that "we don't know enough" and must acquire more information before "it makes sense" to proceed. This apparent humility constitutes an elegant cop-out. It ignores a number of crucial factors: (1) the world will not wait while we gather the necessary information; (2)

by S. Kaplan

even if we had more, it would not seem like enough — the world will remain uncertain and prediction will never be absolute; (3) the appropriate comparison is not with the knowledge we wished we had, but with the knowledge currently used in the day-to-day decisions that shape the environment. These decisions continue to be made, and since they are made by humans, they are necessarily based on information in some form or another — hunches, beliefs, prejudices, or whatever. It is against this standard that whatever formally acquired knowledge we have must be measured.

A different kind of obstacle involves the assumption that sufficient information is available, but that there are not enough experts available to implement what we know. The scientific-academic community, like other informational elites (whose beginnings can probably be traced back ultimately to witch doctors), tends to cultivate a mystique that makes their knowledge seem far beyond the comprehension of the ordinary human. But much if not all of the critical information can be shared, and much of the needed implementation can and should be carried out by ordinary people. A new conception and a new role for experts is needed that emphasizes sharing, facilitating, and "working with" rather than "doing to." And a new role for ordinary people is needed, which is actually rather similar to the old role humans have adopted for a long time — coping with the environment on the basis of the best information available.

For humans have powerful capacities to take in information and to utilize it adroitly as the situation arises. They never cease in their pursuit of organizing knowledge and comprehension of their "space." This pursuit requires involvement, an active approach to developing the grasp that is continually required for making a go of it. Lacking environments suitable for these capacities and needs, humans can be most unpleasant. They have been known to be hostile, even violent and destructive, when sufficiently frustrated and confused. Viewing the difficulties they can create for themselves and for their environment, it might seem far simpler to "give them what they want." But it is a stubborn irony of human nature that humans cannot be given what they want. They are most effective, most constructive — yes, even happiest — when they are striving for what they want, when they are struggling to get where they want to go. Humans are at their best when they are coping and problem solving. They require an environment where this is possible.

References

Aiello, J. R., Epstein, Y. M., and Karlin, R. A. Field experimental research on human crowding. Paper presented at the Eastern Psychological Association Convention, New York City, April, 1975.

*Alexander, C. A city is not a tree. *Architectural Forum,* 1965, 122, April 58–62; May 58–62.

*Alternatives to fear. *Progressive Architecture,* October 1972, 53, 92–105.

Altman, I. Territorial behavior in humans. Presented at Conference on Explorations of Spatial-Behavioral Relations as Related to Older People. Institute of Gerontology, The University of Michigan, Ann Arbor, Michigan, May, 1968.

Anderson, M. *The federal bulldozer.* Cambridge, Mass.: The MIT Press, 1964.

Angyal, A. Uber die Raumlage vorgestellter Oerter. *Archiv für die Gesamte Psychologie,* 1930, 78, 47–94.

Appleyard, D. City designers and the pluralistic city. In L. Rodwin et al. (Eds.) *Planning for urban growth and regional development.* Cambridge, Mass.: MIT Press, 1969(a).

Appleyard, D. Why buildings are known. *Environment and Behavior,* 1969, 1, 131–156(b).

*Appleyard, D. Styles and methods of structuring a city. *Environment and Behavior,* 1970, 2, 100–116.

Appleyard, D. *Planning a pluralistic city: Conflicting realities in Ciudad Guayana.* Cambridge, Mass.: MIT, 1976.

*Appleyard, D. and Lintell, M. The environmental quality of city streets: The residents' viewpoint. *Journal of the American Institute of Planners,* 1972, 38, 84–101.

Appleyard, D. and Lynch, K. Sensuous criteria for highway designs. In J. L. Shofer and E. N. Thomas *Strategies for the evaluation of alternative transportation plans.* Research Report, The Transportation Center, Northwestern University, Evanston, Illinois, 1967.

Appleyard, D. and Okamoto, R. Environmental criteria for ideal transportation systems. In Barton Aschman Associate (Ed.) *Guidelines for new transportation systems.* Washington, D.C.: U.S. Department of Housing and Urban Development, 1968.

Architectural Forum. Slum surgery in St. Louis. April 1951, 537, 128–136.

Ardrey, R. *African genesis.* London: Collins, 1961.

Ardrey, R. *The territorial imperative.* New York: Atheneum, 1966.

Ardrey, R. *The social contract.* New York: Atheneum, 1970.

Attneave, F. Transfer of experience with a class-schema to identification — learning of patterns and shapes. *Journal of Experimental Psychology,* 1957, 54, 81–88.

Banfield, E. *Political influence.* Glencoe, Ill.: Free Press, 1961.

*Barker, R.C. and Gump, P.V. *Big school, small school.* Stanford University Press, 1964.

Bates, A. Privacy — a useful concept? *Social Forces,* 1964, 42, 432.

Baum, A., Harpin, R. E., and Valins, S. The role of group phenomena in the experience of crowding. *Environment and Behavior,* 1975, 7, 185–198.

*Selections or excerpts that appear in this book.

Bayley, N. A study of the crying of infants during mental and physical tests. *Journal of Genetic Psychology,* 1932, 40, 306–329.

*Bazell, R. J. Urban health and environment: A new approach. *Science,* 1971, 174, 1005–1006.

Bell, W. and Boat, M. Urban neighborhoods and informal social relations. *American Journal of Sociology,* 1957, 62, 391–398.

Berger, B. H. *Working class suburb.* Berkeley: University of California Press, 1960.

*Berrill, N. J. *Man's emerging mind.* Dodd, Mead and Co., Inc., 1955.

Bexton, W. H., Heron, W., and Scott, T. H. Effects of decreased variation in the sensory environment. *Canadian Journal of Psychology,* 1954, 8, 70–76.

Binet, M. A. Reverse illusions of orientation. *Psychological Review,* 1894, 1 No. 4, 337–350.

Blau, P. M. *Exchange and power in social life.* New York: Wiley, 1967.

Blum, A. F. Social structure, social class, and participation in primary relationships. In A. B. Shostak and W. Gombers (Eds.) *Blue collar world.* Englewood Cliffs, N.J.: Prentice-Hall, 1964.

Booth, A. Final report: Urban crowding project. Ministry of State for Urban Affairs, Government of Canada. August, 1975.

Booth, A. and Johnson, D. R. The effect of crowding on child health and development. *American Behavioral Scientist,* 1975, 18, 736–749.

Bott, E. *Family and social networks.* London: Tavistock, 1957.

Braybrooke, S. JGA plans with people. *Design and Environment,* 1974, 5, 2, 40–45.

Brown, W. Spatial integrations in a human maze. *University of California Publications in Psychology,* 1932, V, No. 5, 123–134.

Bruner, J. S. On perceptual readiness. *Psychological Review,* 1957, 64, 123–152(a).

Bruner, J. S. *On going beyond the information given.* Cambridge, Mass.: Harvard University Press, 1957(b).

Bruner, J. S. and Postman, L. On the perception of incongruity: A paradigm. *Journal of Personality,* 1949, 18, 206–223.

Brunswik, E. *Perception and the representative design of psychological experiments.* (2nd ed.) Berkeley: University of California Press, 1956.

Buckman, I. Unpublished Manuscript. Brown University, 1966.

Bureau of Outdoor Recreation, U.S. Department of Interior. Community recreational gardening. *Outdoor Recreation Action,* Summer, 1975, No. 36.

Calhoun, J. B. The social aspect of population dynamics. *Journal of Mammalogy,* 1952, 33, 2, 139–159.

Calhoun, J. B. Population density and social pathology. *Scientific American,* 1962, 206, 139–148.

Calhoun, J. B. Design for mammalian living. *Architectural Association Quarterly,* 1968, 1, 3, 1–12.

Calhoun, J. B. Space and strategy of life. In Q. H. Esser (Ed.) *Behavior and environment.* New York: Plenum, 1971.

*Campbell, B. G. *Human evolution: An introduction to man's adaptation.* Chicago: Aldine Publishing Co., 1974.

*Cantril, H. The human design. In *The pattern of human concerns.* New Brunswick, N. J.: Rutgers University Press, 1966.

Canty, D. Tenant satisfaction with public housing design. *Journal of Housing,* 1974, No. 10, 468–470.

Carpenter, C. R. Societies of monkeys and apes. In C. H. Southwick (Ed.) *Primate social behavior.* Princeton, N.J.: Van Nostrand, 1963.

*Carr, S. The city of the mind. In W. R. Ewald Jr. (Ed.) *Environment for man: The next fifty years.* Bloomington, Ind.: Indiana University Press, 1967, Pp. 197–226.

Carr, S. Downtown Washington streets for people: User consultancy. Presented at Symposium on Social Participation in Environmental Design at Environmental Design Research Association Conference Six, Lawrence, Kansas, April, 1975.

*Carr, S. and Lynch, K. Where learning happens. *Daedalus,* Fall, 1968, 97, 1281–1286.

Cartwright, D. and Zander, A. (Eds.) *Group dynamics: Research and theory.* New York: Harper & Row, 1968.

Casamajor, J. Le Mysterieux Sens del L'Espace. *Revue Scientifique,* 1927, 65, No. 18, 554–565.

Cassel, J. An epidemiological perspective of psychosocial factors in disease etiology.

Paper presented at the American Public Health Association Meeting, Houston, Texas, November, 1970.(a)

Cassel, J. Physical illness in response to stress. In S. Levine and N. A. Scotch (Eds.) *Social stress*. Chicago: Aldine-Atherton, 1970. (b)

Cassel, J. Health consequences of population density and crowding. *Rapid population growth*. National Academy of Sciences. Baltimore, Md.: Johns Hopkins Press, 1971.

Cassel, J. and Tyroler, H. A. Epidemiological studies of culture change. In: Health status and recency of industrialization. *Archives of Environmental Health*, 1961, 3, No. 25.

*Catton, W. R., Jr. Motivations of wilderness users. *Pulp and Paper Magazine of Canada*. December 19, 1969, Pp. 121–122.

Chemers, M. M., Lekhyananda, D., Fielder, F. E., and Stolurow, L. M. Some effects of cultural training on leadership in heterocultural task group. *International Journal of Psychology*, 1966, 1, 301–314.

Christenson, W. J. and Hinkle, L. E. Jr. Differences in illness and prognostic signs in two groups of young men. *Journal of the American Medical Association*, 1961, 177, 247–253.

Christian, J. J. Pathology of overpopulation. *Military Medicine*, 1963, 128, 571–603.

Chu, C. *Urban road traffic/environmental research and studies: A selective annotated bibliography*. London: Centre for Environmental Studies, 1971.

City of Westminster. *The Pimlico Precinct Study*. London, 1968.

Claparède, E. L'Orientation Lointaine. *Noveau Traite de Psychologie*. Tome VIII, Fasc. 3, Paris, Presses Universitaites de France, 1943.

Clark, S. D. *The suburban society*. Toronto: University of Toronto Press, 1966.

Cohen, S. Environmental load and the allocation of attention. In A. Baum and S. Valins (Eds.) *Advances in environmental research*. Norwood, N.J.: Lawrence Erlbaum Associates, in press.

Cohen, S., Glass, D. C., and Phillips, S. Environmental factors in health. In H. E. Freeman, S. Levine, and L. G. Reeder (Eds.) *Handbook of medical sociology*. Englewood Cliffs, N.J.: Prentice-Hall Inc., in press.

Cohen, S., Glass, D. C., and Singer, J. E. Apartment noise, auditory discrimination, and

reading ability in children. University of Texas at Austin, 1972, in manuscript.

Coleman, J. S. *Equality of educational opportunity*. Washington, D.C.: U.S. Department of Health, Education and Welfare, 1966.

Coles, R. *Children of crisis: A study of courage and fear*. Boston: Little, Brown, 1967.

*Coles, R. A domain of sorts. *Harper's Magazine*, November, 1971, Pp. 116–122.

Craig, W. Why do animals fight? *International Journal of Ethics*, 1921, 31, 264–273.

Craik, K. H. The comprehension of the everyday physical environment. *Journal of the American Institute of Planners*, 1968, 34, 29–37.

Craik, K. J. W. *The nature of explanation*. London: Cambridge University Press, 1943.

Cross, N. (Ed.) *Design participation*. London: Academy Editions, 1972.

Cullen, G. *Townscape*. New York: Reinhold, 1961.

D'Atri, D. A. Psychophysiological responses to crowding. *Environment and Behavior*, 1975, 7, 237–252.

Davidoff, P., Davidoff, L., and Gold, N. N. Suburban action: Advocate planning for an open society. *Journal of the American Institute of Planners*, 1970, 36, 12–21.

Davis, J. D. Wildlife in your backyard. In *Symposium: Wildlife in an urbanizing environment*. Springfield, Mass.: University of Massachusetts and USDA Cooperative Extension Service, 1973.

Dean, L. M., Pugh, W. M., and Gunderson, E. Spatial and perceptual components of crowding: Effects on health and satisfaction. *Environment and Behavior*, 1975, 7, 225–236.

de Charms, R. *Personal causation*. New York: Academic Press, 1968.

Demerath, N. J. St. Louis public housing study sets off community development to meet social needs. *Journal of Housing*, 1962, 19, 472–478.

*Denman, C. C. Small towns are the future of American. *Congressional Record* Extension of Remarks. March 16, 1970, E2025, E2026.

Dobriner, W. M. *Class in suburbia*. Englewood Cliffs, N.J.: Prentice Hall, 1963.

Donaldson, S. *The suburban myth*. New York: Columbia University Press, 1969.

Dooley, B. B. Crowding stress: The effect of social density on men with close or far personal space. Ph.D. Dissertation, University of California, Los Angeles, 1974.

Dooley, B. B. Crowding stress: The effects of social density on men with "close" or "far" personal space. *Man-Environment Systems,* 1975, 5, 306.

Downs, A. *Opening up the suburbs: An urban strategy for America.* New Haven: Yale University Press, 1973.

Downs, R. M. and Stea, D. (Eds.) *Image and environment: Cognitive mapping and spatial behavior.* Chicago: Aldine, 1973.

Draper, P. Crowding among hunter-gatherers: The Kung Bushmen. *Science,* 1973, 182, 301–303.

Dubos, R. *Man adapting.* New Haven: Yale University Press, 1965.

Dubos, R. The human environment in technological societies. *The Rockefeller Review,* July-August, 1968. (a)

Dubos, R. *So human an animal.* New York: Scribner's, 1968. (b)

Duncan, S. D., Jr. Nonverbal communication. *Psychological Bulletin,* 1969, 72, 118–137.

Dyckman, J. W. Planning and decision theory. *Journal of the American Institute of Planners,* 1961, 27, 335–345.

Edney, J. J. The psychological role of property rights in human behavior. *Environment and Planning A,* 1976, 8, 811–822.

Edwards, W. The theory of decision making. *Psychological Bulletin,* 1954, 51, 380–417.

Ehrlich, P. R. *The population bomb.* New York: Ballantine Books, 1968.

*Eliovson, S. *Gardening the Japanese way.* London: Harrap, 1971.

Ellenberger, H. F. Zoological garden and mental hospital. *Canadian Psychiatric Association Journal,* 1960, 5, 136–149.

Ellul, J. *The technological society.* New York: Alfred A. Knopf, 1964.

Emerson, R. M. Games, rules, outcomes and motivation. Paper presented at AAAS Symposium: Psychology and Sociology of Sport. Dallas, Tex., 1968.

Esser, A. H. *Social pollution.* Social Education, 1971, 35, 10–18.

Esser, A. H. Environmental design needs empathy to combat social pollution. In W. F. E. Preiser (Ed.) *Environmental design perspectives.* M-ES-FOCUS Series, 1972.

Esser, A. H., Chamberlain, A. S., Chapple, E. D., and Kline, N. S. Territoriality of patients on a research ward. In J. Wortis (Ed.), *Recent Advances in Biological Psychiatry,* 1965, 7, 36–44.

Etzioni, A. *The active society.* New York: Free Press, 1968.

Evans, G. W. Behavioral and physiological consequences of crowding in humans. Unpublished doctoral dissertation, University of Massachusetts, Amherst, 1975.

Evans, G. W. and Eichelman, W. Preliminary models of conceptual linkages among proxemic variables. *Environment and Behavior,* 1976, 8, 87–116.

*Farber, S. M. Quality of living — stress and creativity. In F. F. Darling and J. P. Milton (Eds.) *Future environments of North America.* New York: Natural History Press, 1966.

Fava, S. F. Contrasts in neighboring New York City and a suburban county. In R. L. Warren (Ed.) *Perspective on the American community.* Chicago: Rand McNally, 1957.

Fielder, F. E., Mitchell, T. R., and Triandis, H. C. Organizational research report 70-5. Department of Psychology, University of Washington, Seattle, 1970.

Fischer, M. H. Die Orientierung im Raume bei Wirbeltieren und beim Menschen. In *Handbuch der Normalen und Pathologischen Physiologie.* Berlin: J. Springer, 1931.

Foa, U.G. Cross-cultural similarity and difference in interpersonal behavior. *Journal of Abnormal and Social Psychology,* 1964, 68, 517–522.

Foa, U. G. Perception of behavior in reciprocal roles: The ringex model. *Psychological Monographs,* 1966, 80, Whole No. 623.

Foa, U. G. Differentiation in cross-cultural communication. In L. Thayer (Ed.) *Communication: Concepts and perspective.* Washington, D.C.: Spartan, 1967.

*Foa, U. G. Interpersonal and economic resources. *Science,* 1971, 171, 345–351.

Foa, U. G. and Chemers, M. M. The significance of role behavior differentiation for cross-cultural interaction training. *International Journal of Psychology,* 1967, 2, 45–48.

Foa, U. G. and Donnenwerth, G. V. Love poverty in modern culture and sensitivity training. *Sociological Inquiry,* 1971, 16, 130–142.

Foa, U. G. and Foa, E. B. *Societal structure of the mind.* Springfield, Ill.: C. C. Thomas, 1974.

Foa, U. G. and Foa, E.B. Studies in dyadic communication. In A. W. Siegman and B. Pope (Eds.) *Studies in dyadic communication.* Elmsford, N.Y.: Pergamon, 1972.

Foote, N. N., Abu-Lughod, J., Foley, M. M., and Winnick, L. *Housing choices and housing constraints.* New York: McGraw-Hill, 1960.

Forest Service. USDA Land use planning: Beaverhead National Forest, Montana, Forest Management Alternatives, 1975.

*Fox, R. The cultural animal. In J. F. Eisenberg and W. S. Dillon (Eds.) *Man and beast: Comparative social behavior.* Washington, D.C.: Smithsonian Institution Press, 1971.

Freedman, J. *Crowding and behavior.* San Francisco: W. H. Freeman & Co., 1975.

Freedman, J., Heshka, S., and Levy, A. Population density and pathology: Is there a relationship? *Journal of Experimental Social Psychology,* 1975, 11, 539–552.

Freedman, J., Klevansky, S., and Ehrlich, P. The effect of crowding on human task performance. *Journal of Applied Social Psychology,* 1971, 1, 7–25.

Freedman, L. Z. and Roe, A. Evolution and human behavior. In A. Roe and G. G. Simpson (Eds.) *Behavior and evolution.* New Haven: Yale University Press, 1958.

Fried, M. Grieving for a lost home. In L. J. Duhl (Ed.) *The urban condition.* New York: Simon and Schuster, 1963.

Fried, M. and Gleicher, P. Some residential satisfactions in an urban slum. *Journal of the American Institute of Planners,* 1961, 27, 305–315.

Galle, O. R., Gove W. R., and McPherson, J. M. Population density and pathology: What are the relations for man? *Science,* 1972, 176, 23–30.

Gans, H. J. Planning and social life: Friendship and neighbor relations in suburban communities. *Journal of the American Institute of Planners,* 1961, 27, 134–140.

Gans, H. J. *The urban villagers.* New York: Free Press, 1962.

Gans, H. J. Effect of the move from city to suburb.

In L. J. Duhl (Ed.) *The urban condition.* New York: Basic Books, 1963.

Gans, H. J. *The Levittowners.* New York: Random House, 1967.

Gartlan, J. S. and Brain, C. K. Ecology and social variability in *Cercopithecus aethiops* and *C. mitis.* In P. Jay (Ed.) *Primates: Studies in adaptation and variability.* New York: Holt, Rinehart & Winston, 1968.

Glass, D. C. and Singer, J. E. *Urban stress: Experiments in noise and social stressors.* New York: Academic Press, 1972.

*Glass, D. C. and Singer, J. E. Experimental studies of uncontrollable and unpredictable noise. *Representative Research in Social Psychology,* 1973, 4, 165–180.

Glass, D. C., Singer, J. E., Leonard, H. S., Krantz, D., Cohen, S., and Cummings, H. Z. Perceived control of aversive stimulation and the reduction of stress responses. New York University, 1972. In manuscript.

Glazer, N. and Moynihan, D. *Beyond the melting pot.* Cambridge, Mass.: The MIT Press, 1963.

Glazer, N. and Moynihan, D. Introduction to second edition. *Beyond the melting pot.* Cambridge, Mass.: The MIT Press, 1970.

Goffman, E. *Presentation of self in everyday life.* New York: Doubleday, 1959.

Goffman, E. *Relations in public: Microstudies of the public order.* New York: Basic Books, 1971.

Grant, D. P. Aims and potentials of design methodology. In B. Honikman (Ed.) *Responding to social change.* Stroudsburg, Pa.: Dowden, Hutchinson and Ross, 1975.

Grant, D. P. and Chapman, A. A comprehensive approach to user participation in the space planning process. In D. K. Tester (Ed.) *Designing the method.* Raleigh, N.C.: Student Publications of the School of Design, North Carolina State University, 1974.

Great Britain, Ministry of Housing and Local Government. *The Banisbury environmental study.* Islington, London, 1968.

Great Britain, Ministry of Housing and Local Government. *General improvement areas,* 1969.

Greater London Council. *Kensington environmental management study.* London: Publication No. 39, 1969.

Greenbie, B. B. New house or new neighborhood?

A survey of priorities among home owners in Madison, Wisconsin. *Land Economics,* 1969, 45, 359–364.

Greenbie, B. B. What can we learn from other animals? Behavioral biology and the ecology of cities. *Journal of the American Institute of Planners,* 1971, 37, 3, 162–168.

Greenbie, B. B. An ethological approach to community design. In W. F. E. Preiser (Ed.) *Environmental design research.* Stroudsburg, Pa.: Dowden, Hutchinson and Ross, 1973.

*Greenbie, B. B. Social territory, community health and urban planning. *Journal of the American Institute of Planners,* 1974, 40, 74–82.

Griffin, D. R. Sensory physiology and the orientation of animals. *American Scientist,* 1953, 41, 209–244.

Griffiths, I. D. and Langdon, F. J. Subjective response to road traffic noise. *Journal of Sound and Vibration,* 1968, 8, 16–32.

Gutman, R. (Ed.) *People and buildings.* New York: Basic Books, 1972.

Hall, E. T. *The silent language.* New York: Doubleday, 1959.

Hall, E. T. *The hidden dimension.* New York: Doubleday, 1966.

Hall, E. T. Environmental communication. In A. H. Esser (Ed.) *Behavior and Environment.* New York: Plenum, 1971.

*Halle, L. J. International behavior and the prospects of human survival. In J. F. Eisenberg and W. S. Dillon (Eds.) *Man and beast: Comparative social behavior.* Washington, D.C.: Smithsonian Institution Press, 1971.

Harlow, H. F. Mice, monkeys, men and motives. *Psychological Review,* 1953, 60, 23–32.

Harlow, H. F. and Suomi, S. J. Nature of love — simplified. *American Psychologist,* 1970, 25, 161–168.

Hartman, C. Social values and housing orientations. *Journal of Social Issues,* 1963, 19, 113–131.

Hartman, C. The housing of relocated families. In J. Q. Wilson (Ed.) *Urban renewal: The record and the controversy.* Cambridge, Mass.: MIT, 1966.

Heape, W. *Emigration, immigration and nomadism.* Cambridge, Mass.: Heffer, 1931.

Hebb, D. O. On the nature of fear. *Psychological Review,* 1946, 53, 259–276.

Hebb, D. O. *The organization of behavior.* New York: Wiley, 1949.

Hebb, D. O. The role of neurological ideas in psychology, *Journal of Personality,* 1951, 20, 39–55.

*Hebb, D. O. *Textbook of psychology.* (3rd ed.) Philadelphia: Saunders, 1972.

Heidbreder, E. Toward a dynamic theory of cognition. *Psychological Review,* 1945, 52, 1–22.

Henry, J. *Who lie in Gaol.* London: Golance, 1952.

Herberle, R. The normative element in neighborhood relations. *Pacific Sociological Review,* 1960, 3, 3–11.

Herbers, J. *New York Times,* 2 November 1970.

Her Majesty's Stationary Office. *Traffic in towns.* London: The Buchanan Report, 1963.

Herzog, T. R., Kaplan, S., and Kaplan, R. The prediction of preference for familiar urban places. *Environment and Behavior,* 1976, 8, 627–645.

Higbee, E. *The squeeze: Cities without space.* New York: Morrow, 1960.

Hilberseimer, L. *The nature of cities.* Chicago: P. Theobald, 1955.

*Hilgard, E. R. The role of learning in perception. In R. R. Blake and G. V. Ramsay (Eds.) *Perception: An approach to personality.* New York: Ronald Press, 1951.

Homans, G. C. *Social behavior: Its elementary forms.* New York: Harcourt, Brace and World, 1961.

Hornbostel, E. M. von. The unity of the senses. *Psyche,* London, 1927, 7, 83–89.

*Houston, C. S. The last blue mountain. In S. Z. Klausner (Ed.) *Why man takes chances.* New York: Doubleday & Co., 1968.

Iltis, H. H., Loucks, O. L., and Andrews, P. Criteria for an optimum human environment. *Bulletin of the Atomic Scientists,* 1970, 25, 2–6.

Ittelson, W. H. Perception and transactional psychology. In S. Koch (Ed.) *Psychology: A study of a science.* Volume 4. New York: McGraw-Hill, 1962.

Jaccard, P. *Le Sens de la Direction et L'Orientation Lointaine chez L'Homme.* Paris: Payot, 1932.

*Jackson, J. B. Ghosts at the door. *Landscape,* 1951, 1, 3–9.

*Jacobs, J. *The death and life of great American cities.* New York: Vintage Books, 1961.

*Jacobs, J. *The economy of cities*. New York: Vintage Books, 1970.

James, W. *Psychology: The briefer course*. (1892). New York: Collier Books, 1962.

Janis, I. L. Psychological effects of warnings. In G. W. Baker and D. W. Chapman (Eds.) *Man and society in disaster*. New York: Basic Books, 1962.

Jensen, R. *Cities of vision*. New York: Halsted, 1974.

Jersild, A. T. and Holmes, F. B. *Children's fears*. New York: Columbia University Teacher's College, 1935.

Johnsgard, P. A. *Animal behavior*. Dubuque, Iowa: Brown, 1967.

Jones, H. E. and Jones, M. C. A study of fear. *Childhood Education*, 1928, 5, 136–143.

Jung, C. G. The need for roots: An interview. *Landscape*, 1965, 14, 2.

Kaplan, M., Gans, S., and Kahn K. Social reconnaissance survey, Part 2. San Francisco Urban Design Study, San Francisco City Planning Department, 1969.

Kaplan, R. Predictors of environmental preference: Designers and "clients." In W. F. E. Preiser (Ed.) *Environmental design research*. Stroudsburg, Pa.: Dowden, Hutchinson and Ross, 1973. (a)

Kaplan, R. Some psychological benefits of gardening. *Environment and Behavior*, 1973, 5, 145–162.(b)

Kaplan, R. Some methods and strategies in the prediction of preference. In E. H. Zube, R. O. Brush, and J. G. Fabos (Eds.) *Landscape assessment*. Stroudsburg, Pa.: Dowden, Hutchinson and Ross, 1975.

Kaplan, R. Preference and everyday nature: Method and application. In D. Stokols (Ed.) *Perspectives on environment and behavior: Theory, research and application*. New York: Plenum, 1977. (a)

Kaplan, R. Patterns of environmental preference. *Environment and Behavior*, 1977, 9, 195–216.(b)

Kaplan, R. Down by the riverside: Informational factors in waterscape preference. *Proceedings of river recreation management and research symposium*. North Central Forest Experiment Station, Forest Service, USDA, 1977. (c)

Kaplan, R., Kaplan, S., and Deadorff, H. L. The perception and evaluation of a simulated environment. *Man-Environment Systems*, 1974, 4, 191–192.

Kaplan, S. The challenge of environmental psychology: A proposal for a new functionalism. *American Psychologist*, 1972, 27, 140–143.

Kaplan, S. Cognitive maps in perception and thought. In R. M. Downs and D. Stea (Eds.) *Image and environment*. Chicago: Aldine, 1973.(a)

Kaplan, S. Cognitive maps, human needs, and the designed environment. In W. F. E. Preiser (Ed.) *Environmental design research*. Stroudsburg, Pa.: Dowden, Hutchinson and Ross, 1973. (b)

Kaplan, S. An informal model for the prediction of preference. In E. H. Zube, R. O. Brush, and J. G. Fabos (Eds.) *Landscape assessment*. Stroudsburg, Pa.: Dowden, Hutchinson and Ross, 1975.

Kaplan, S. Adaptation, structure and knowledge. In G. T. Moore and R. G. Golledge (Eds.) *Environmental knowing: Theories, research, and methods*. Stroudsburg, Pa.: Dowden, Hutchinson and Ross, 1976.

Kaplan, S. Participation in the design process: A cognitive approach. In D. Stokols (Ed.) *Perspectives on environment and behavior: Theory, research and application*. New York: Plenum, 1977. (a)

Kaplan, S. Tranquility and challenge in the natural environment. *Children, nature, and the urban environment symposium proceedings*. Northeastern Forest Experiment Station, Upper Darby, Pa., 1977. (b)

Karlin, R. A., Epstein, Y. M., and Aiello, J. R. The effects of internal versus external locus of control on reactions to crowding. Unpublished manuscript, Rutgers University, 1975.

*Kates, R. W. *Hazard and choice perception in flood plain management*. University of Chicago; Department of Geography. Research Paper No. 78, 1962.

Kellogg, W. N. *Porpoises and sonar*. University of Chicago Press, 1961, Pp 13–15.

Kira, A. *The bathroom*. New York: Bantam, 1967.

Köhler, W. *The mentality of apes*. New York and London: Kegan Paul, 1925.

Kortlandt, A. Comment on the essential morphological basis for human culture. *Current Anthropology*, 1965, 6, 320–325.

*Kummer, H. Spacing mechanisms in social behavior. In J. F. Eisenberg and W. S. Dillon (Eds.) *Man and beast: Comparative social behavior.* Washington, D.C.: Smithsonian Institution Press, 1971.

*Ladd, F. City kids in the absence of. ... *Children, nature and the urban environment symposium proceedings.* Northeastern Forest Experiment Station, Upper Darby, Pa., 1977.

LaPiere, R. T. *A theory of social control.* New York: McGraw-Hill, 1954.

Latané, B. and Darley, J. M. Bystander "apathy." *American Scientist,* 1969, 57, 244–268.

*Laughlin, W. S. Hunting: An integrating biobehavior system and its evolutionary importance. In R. B. Lee and I. DeVore (Eds.) *Man the hunter.* Chicago: Aldine Publishing Co., 1968.

Lazarus, R. S. *Psychological stress and the coping process.* New York: McGraw-Hill, 1966.

Lee, T. R. Urban neighborhood as a socio-spatial schema. *Human Relations,* 1957, 21, 241–267. (a)

Lee, T. R. On the relation between the school journey and social and emotional adjustment in rural infant children. *British Journal of Educational Psychology,* 1957, 27, 101–114. (b)

Lee, T. R. Brennan's Law of shopping behavior. *Psychological Reports,* 1962, 11, 662.

*Lee, T. R. Do we need a theory? In D. V. Canter (Ed.) *Architectural Psychology.* London: RIBA Publications, 1969, Pp. 20–25.

Levine, R. A. and Campbell, D. T. *Ethnocentrism.* New York: John Wiley, 1972.

Levitan, S. A. *The great society poor law: A new approach to poverty.* Baltimore: Johns Hopkins Press, 1969.

Lewis, C. A. Public housing gardens — landscapes for the soul. *Landscape for living.* USDA Yearbook of Agriculture, 1972.

*Lewis, C. A. Nature city. *The Morton Arboretum Quarterly,* 1975, 11, 17–22.

Lewis, C. A. Human perspectives in horticulture. *Children, nature and the urban environment symposium proceedings.* Northeastern Forest Experiment Station, Upper Darby, Pa., 1977.

Leyhausen, P. The communal organization of solitary mammals. *Symposia of the Zoological Society of London,* 1965, 14, 249–263.

Leyhausen, P. Dominance and territoriality as completed in mammalian social structure. In A. H. Esser (Ed.) *Behavior and environment.* New York: Plenum, 1971.

Little, C. E. Preservation policy and personal perception: A 200-million-acre misunderstanding. In E. H. Zube, R. O. Brush, and J. G. Fabos (Eds.) *Landscape assessment.* Stroudsburg, Pa.: Dowden, Hutchinson and Ross, 1975.

Longabaugh, R. A category system for coding interpersonal behavior as social exchange. *Sociometry,* 1963, 26, 319–344.

Lorenz, K. A. Contribution to the comparative sociology of colonial nesting birds. *Proceedings of the Eighth International Ornithology Congress,* 1938, 207–218.

Lorenz, K. Z. *On aggression.* New York: Harcourt, Brace and World, 1966.

Lorenz, K. Z. The evolution of behavior. *Psychobiology, Readings from Scientific American.* San Francisco: Freeman, 1967.

*Lynch, K. *The image of the city.* Cambridge, Mass.: MIT Press, 1960.

Machol, R. E. (Ed.) *Information and decision processes.* New York: McGraw-Hill, 1960.

Macmurray, J. *Persons in relation.* London: Faber and Faber, 1961.

Mahut, H. Breed differences in the dog's emotional behavior. *Canadian Journal of Psychology,* 1958, 12, 35–44.

Mann, P. Miracle of the flower boxes. *Reader's Digest,* July 1973, 106–110.

Margalef, R. *Perspectives in ecological theory.* Chicago: University of Chicago Press, 1968.

Marris, P. *Family and social change in an African city.* Evanston, Ill.: Northwestern University Press, 1962.

Marschak, J. Rational behavior, uncertain prospects, and measurable utility. *Econometrica,* 1950, 18, 111.

Marshall, J. E. and Heslin, R. Boys and girls together: Sexual composition and the effect of density and group size on cohesiveness. *Journal of Personality and Social Psychology,* 1975, 31, 952–961.

Maslow, A. H. A theory of metamotivation: The biological rooting of the value-life. *Journal of Humanistic Psychology,* 1967, 7, 93–127.

McDougall, W. *An introduction to social psychology* (14th ed.) Boston: John W. Luce & Co., 1921.

McHarg, I. L. *Design with nature.* Garden City, N.Y.: Natural History Press, 1969.

Meadows, D. H., et. al. *Limits to growth: A report to the Club of Rome's project on the Predicament of Mankind.* New York: Universe Books, 1972.

Meier, R. L. *A communications theory of urban growth.* Cambridge, Mass.: MIT, 1962.

Melzack, R. Irrational fears in the dog. *Canadian Journal of Psychology,* 1952, 6, 141–147.

Michelson, W. Analytical sampling for design information. EDRA Conference paper, Chapel Hill, N.C., 1969.

Michigan Department of State Highways. The economic and environmental effects of one-way streets in residential areas, 1969.

*Milgram, S. The experience of living in cities. *Science,* 1970, 167, 1461–1468.

Milgram, S. and Hollander, P. Paralyzed witnesses: The murder they heard. *The Nation,* 1964, 25, 602–604.

Miller, R. B. *A cool curving world.* Toronto: Longmans, 1962.

Mitchell, R. E. Some implications of high density housing. *American Sociological Review,* 1971, 36, 18–29.

Mitchell, T. R. and Foa, U. G. Diffusion of the effect of cultural training of the leader in the structure of heterocultural task groups. *Australian Journal of Psychology,* 1969, 21, 31–43.

Moore, G. T. and Golledge, R. G. (Eds.) *Environmental knowing: Theories, research and methods.* Stroudsburg, Pa.: Dowden, Hutchinson and Ross, 1976.

Muller, H. *Uses of the past.* New York: Mentor, 1954.

Myrdal, G. *The challenge of world poverty.* New York: Pantheon, 1970.

*Napier, J. *The roots of mankind.* Washington, D.C.: The Smithsonian Institution Press, 1970.

National Park Service, U.S. Department of the Interior Yosemite Master Plan. (Update Series, June and August, 1975).

Neisser, U. *Cognitive psychology.* New York: Appleton-Century-Crofts, 1968.

Newman, O. *Defensible space.* New York: Macmillan, 1972.

Newman, O. *Design guidelines for creating defensible space.* Washington, D.C.: National Institute of Law Enforcement and Criminal Justice, 1975.

Nice, M. M. The role of territory in bird life. *American Midland Naturalist,* 1941, 26, 441–481.

Nissen, H. W. and Crawford, M. P. A preliminary study of food-sharing in young chimpanzees. *Journal of Comparative Psychology,* 1936, 22, 383–419.

Novak, M. *The rise of the unmeltable ethnics: Politics and culture in the seventies.* New York: MacMillan, 1972.

Nuckolls, K. B. and Cassel, J. Psychosocial assets, life crises, and the prognosis of pregnancy. *American Journal of Epidemiology,* in press.

Nye, F. I., Carlson, J., and Garrett, G. Family size, interaction, affect and stress. *Journal of Marriage and Family,* 1970, 32, 216–226.

Orleans, P. Differential cognition of urban residents: Effects of social scale on mapping. In R. M. Downs and D. Stea (Eds.) *Image and Environment.* Chicago: Aldine, 1973.

Owen, W. Transport: Key to the future of cities. In H. Perloff (Ed.), *The quality of the urban environment.* Baltimore: Johns Hopkins Press, 1969.

*Parr, A. E. The child in the city: Urbanity and the urban scene. *Landscape,* 1967, 16, 3–5.

*Pastalan, L. A. Privacy as an expression of human territoriality. In L. A. Pastalan and D. H. Carson (Eds.) *Spatial behavior of older people.* Institute of Gerontology, University of Michigan-Wayne State University, 1970.

Pastalan, L. A. How the elderly negotiate their environment. Paper presented at Environment for the Aged Conference, San Juan, Puerto Rico, December, 1971.

Paulus, P. B., Annis, A. B., Seta, J. J., Schkade, J. K., and Matthews, R. W. Density does affect task performance. *Journal of Personality and Social Psychology,* 1976, 34, 248–253.

Peterson, G. L., Bishop, R. L., and Fitzgerald, R. W. The quality of visual residential environments: Perceptions and preferences. EDRA Conference paper, Chapel Hill, N.C., 1969.

Pfeiffer, J. E. *The emergence of man.* (2nd ed.) New York: Harper & Row, 1972.

*Plowboy interview with E. F. Schumacher.

Mother Earth News, November, 1976, No. 42, Pp. 8–18.

*Porteous, J. D. *Environment and behavior: Planning and everyday urban life.* Reading, Mass.: Addison-Wesley Co., 1977.

Posner, M. I. *Cognition: An introduction.* Glenview, Ill.: Scott, Foresman, 1973.

Posner, M. I. and Keele, S. W. On the genesis of abstract ideas. *Journal of Experimental Psychology,* 1968, 77, 353–363.

Rabaud, E. *L'Orientation Lointaine et la Reconnaissance des Lieux.* Paris: Lacan, 1927.

Rainwater, L. Crucible of identity: The Negro lower-class family. *Daedalus,* 1966, 95, 172–216. (a)

Rainwater, L. Fear and the house-as-haven in the lower class. *Journal of the American Institute of Planners,* 1966, 32, 23–31. (b)

Rainwater, L. and Schwarts, M. J. Identity, world view, social relations, and family behavior in magazines. Social Research, Inc., 1965.

Rapoport, A. *House form and culture.* Englewood Cliffs, N.J.: Prentice-Hall, 1969.

Reemer, R. Hell's kitchen and the new Earth Park. *Fitness for Living,* 1971, (May/June), 30–34.

Reynolds, V. Open groups in hominid evolution. *Man,* 1966, 1, 441–452.

Robinson, G. O. *The Forest Service: A study in public land management.* Baltimore: Johns Hopkins Press, 1975.

Robinson, I. M., Baer, W. C., Banerjee, T. K., and Flachsbart, P. G. Trade-off games. In W. Michelson (Ed.) *Behavioral research methods in environmental design.* Stroudsburg, Pa.: Dowden, Hutchinson and Ross, 1975.

Rodin, J. Density, perceived choice and response to controllable and uncontrollable outcomes. *Journal of Experimental Social Psychology,* 1976, 12, 564–578.

Rosen, S. The comparative roles of informational and material commodities in interpersonal transactions. *Journal of Social Psychology,* 1966, 2, 211–226.

Rosenthal, R. and Jacobson, L. *Pygmalion in the classroom: Teacher's expectation and pupils' intellectual development.* New York: Holt, Rinehart and Winston, 1968.

Rubinstein, E. A. and Coelho, G. V. (Eds.) *Behavioral sciences and mental health: An anthology of program reports.* Public Health Service Publication No. 2064. Washington, D.C.: National Institute of Mental Health, 1970.

Russell, C. and Russell, W. M. S. *Violence, monkeys and man.* London: Macmillan, 1968.

Ryan, E. Personal identity in an urban slum. In L. J. Duhl (Ed.) *The urban condition.* New York: Simon and Schuster, 1963, Pp. 135–150.

Ryan, T. A. and Ryan, M. S. Geographical orientation. *American Journal of Psychology,* 1940, 53, 204–215.

Sandström, C. I. *Orientation in the present space.* Stockholm: Almqvist and Wiksell, 1951.

San Francisco City Planning Department. Preliminary reports, Nos. 1 to 8. San Francisco Urban Design Study, 1969–70.

San Francisco City Planning Department. The urban design plan for the comprehensive plan of San Francisco, 1971.

Sanoff, H. Visual attributes of the physical environment. In G. Coates and K. M. Moffett (Eds.) *Response to environment.* Raleigh, N.C.: Student Publications of the School of Design, North Carolina State University, 1969.

Sanoff, H. Games for user participation. In D. K. Tester (Ed.) *Designing the method.* Raleigh, N.C.: Student Publication of the School of Design, North Carolina State University, 1974.

Sanoff, H. Son of rationality. In B. Honikman (Ed.) *Responding to social change.* Stroudsburg, Pa.: Dowden, Hutchinson and Ross, 1975.

Schopler, J. and Walton, M. The effects of structure, expected enjoyment and participants' internality-externality upon feelings of being crowded. Unpublished manuscript. University of North Carolina at Chapel Hill, 1974.

Schorr, A. L. *Slums and social insecurity.* Washington, D.C.: Government Printing Office, 1963.

Schumacher, E. F. *Small is beautiful: Economics as if people mattered.* London: Bond and Briggs Ltd., 1973.

Scott, J. P. The anatomy of violence. *The Nation,* 1965, 200, 622–665.

Seligman, M. E. P. *Helplessness.* San Francisco: Freeman, 1975.

Seligman, M. E. P., Maier, S. F., and Solomon,

R. L. Unpredictable and uncontrollable aversive events. In F. R. Brush (Ed.) *Aversive conditioning and learning.* New York: Academic Press, 1971.

Selye, H. *The stress of life.* New York: McGraw-Hill, 1956.

Senden, M. von. *Raum-und Gestaltauffassung bei operierten Blindgeborenen vor und nach der Operation.* Leipzig: J. A. Barth, 1932.

Shaffer, M. T. Attitudes, community values, and highway planning. *Highway Research Record,* 1967, 187.

Shepard, R. *Cognitive Psychology:* a review of the book by U. Neisser. *American Journal of Psychology,* 1968, 81, 285–289.

Sherrod, D. R. Crowding, perceived control, and behavioral after effects. *Journal of Applied Social Psychology,* 1974, 4, 171–186.

Shills, E. Social inquiry and the autonomy of the individual. In D. Lerner (Ed.) *The human meaning of the social sciences.* Magnolia, Mass.: Peter Smith, 1959.

Siebenaler, J. B. and Caldwell, D. K. Cooperation among adult dolphins. *Journal of Mammalogy,* 1956, 37, 126–128.

Simmel, G. The metropolis and mental life. In K. H. Wolff (Ed.) *The sociology of Georg Simmel.* New York: Free Press, 1950. (English translation of *Die Grossstadt und das Geistesleben die Grossstadt.* Dresden: Jaensch, 1903.)

Simon, H. A. *Administrative behavior* (2nd ed.) New York: Macmillan, 1957. (a)

Simon, H. A. *Models of man: Social and rational.* New York: Wiley, 1957. (b)

*Simon, H. A. Style in design. In J. Archea and C. Eastman (Eds.) *EDRA 2* (Proceedings of the 2nd Environmental Design Research Association Conference). Stroudsburg, Pa.: Dowden, Hutchinson and Ross, 1970.

Smith, J. G. and Sargent, Florence, P. Preface to *Midland City* by T. Brennan. London: Dobson, 1948.

Sommer, R. Studies in personal space. *Sociometry,* 1959, 22, 247–260.

*Sommer, R. Man's proximate environment. *Journal of Social Issues,* 1966, 22, 60–63.

Sommer, R. *Personal space.* Englewood Cliffs, N.J.: Prentice Hall, 1969.

Sonnenfeld, J. Variable values in space landscape. *Journal of Social Issues,* 1966, 22, 71–82.

Spitz, R. A. The smiling response: A contribution to the autogenesis of special relations. *Genetic Psychology Monographs,* 1946, 34, 57–125.

Staehelin, B. Soziale Gesetzmässigkeiten in Gemeinschaftsleben Geisteskranker. *Homo,* 1954, 5, 113–116.

Stainbrook, E. Human needs and the natural environment. *Man and nature in the city.* Symposium sponsored by Bureau of Sport Fisheries and Wildlife, U.S. Department of Interior, 1968.

*Stea, D. Environmental perception and cognition: Toward a model for "mental" maps. In G. J. Coates and K. M. Moffett (Eds.) *Response to environment.* Raleigh, N.C.: Student Publications of the School of Design, North Carolina State University, 1969.

Stokols, D. The experience of crowding in primary and secondary environments. *Environment and Behavior,* 1976, 8, 49–86.

Stratton, G. M. Some preliminary experiments on vision without inversion of the retinal image. *Psychological Review,* 1896, 3, 611–617.

Stratton, G. M. Vision without inversion of the retinal image. *Psychological Review,* 1897, 4, 341–360, 463–481.

Suttles, G. D. *The social order of the slum: Ethnicity and territory in the inner city.* Chicago: University of Chicago Press, 1968.

Suttles, G. D. *The social construction of communities.* Chicago: University of Chicago Press, 1972.

Tester, D. K. (Ed.) *Designing the method.* Raleigh, N.C.: Student Publications of the School of Design, North Carolina State University, 1974.

Thibaut, J. W. and Kelley, H. H. *The social psychology of groups.* New York: Wiley, 1959.

Thiessen, D. D. Population density and behavior. *Texas Reports on Biology and Medicine,* 1964, 22, 266–314.

Thiessen, D. D. and Rodgers, D. A. Population density and endocrine function. *Psychological Bulletin,* 1961, 58, 441–451.

Thompson, J. M. *Motorways in London.* London: Andworth and Co., Ltd., 1970.

Tinbergen, N. The behavior of the snow bunting. *Transactions of the Linnaean Society of New York,* 1939, 5, 1–95.

Tinbergen, N. *The study of instinct.* New York:

Oxford University Press, 1951.

Tinbergen, N. *Social behavior in animals.* New York: Wiley, 1953.

Tinbergen, N. *The Herring Gull's world.* (Revised edition) New York: Basic Books, 1961.

Tinbergen, N. The curious behavior of the Stickleback. *Psychobiology, Readings from Scientific American.* San Francisco: Freeman, 1967.

Toffler, A. *Future shock.* New York: Random House, 1970.

Tolman, E. C. Cognitive maps in rats and men. *Psychological Review,* 1948, 55, 189–203.

Trotter, R. Evolution of language: A hatful of theories. *American Psychological Association Monitor,* January 1976, Vol. 7, Pg. 1 ff.

Trowbridge, C. C. On fundamental methods of orientation and imaginary maps. *Science,* 1913, 38, No. 990, 888–897.

Turner, J. F. C. and Fichter, R. (Eds.) *Freedom to build: Dweller control of the housing process.* New York: Macmillan Company, 1972.

Turner, J. L. For love or money: Pattern of resource commutation in social interchange. Unpublished Master Thesis. University of Missouri-Columbia, 1970.

Turner, J. L., Foa, E. G., and Foa, U. G. Interpersonal reinforcers: Classification, interrelationship, and some differential properties. *Journal of Personality and Social Psychology,* 1971, 19, 168–180.

United States, Department of Housing and Urban Development. Noise abatement and control: Departmental policy, implementation responsibilities, and standards. Unpublished circular, September 1969.

United States President's Commission on Population Growth and the American Future. *Population and the American future,* Washington, D.C.: Government Printing Office, 1972.

Valins, S. and Baum, A. Residential group size, social interaction and crowding. *Environment and Behavior,* 1973, 5, 421–439.

Van der Ryn, S. and Boie, W. R. Visual measurement and visual factors in the urban environment. Unpublished paper. Berkeley: College of Environmental Design, University of California, 1963.

Vogt, W. Population patterns and movements. In F. F. Darling and J. P. Milton (Eds.) *Future environments of North America.* New York: Natural History Press, 1966.

*Wade, N. Karl Hess: Technology with a human face. *Science,* 1975, 187, 332–334.

Wallin, P. A Guttman scale for measuring women's neighboring. *American Journal of Sociology,* 1953, 59, 243–246.

Ward, B. *The home of man.* New York: Norton and Co., 1976.

*Washburn, S. L. Aggressive behavior and human evolution. In G. V. Coelho and E. A. Rubinstein (Eds.) *Social change and human behavior.* Washington, D.C.: National Institute of Mental Health, 1972.

Washburn, S. L. and Hamburg, D. A. Aggressive behavior in old world monkeys and apes. In P. C. Jay (Ed.) *Primates: Studies in adaptation and variability.* New York: Holt, Rinehart and Winston, 1968.

Washburn, S. L. and Jay, P. C. (Eds.) *Perspectives on human evolution, I.* New York: Holt, Rinehart and Winston, 1968.

Watson, A. and Moss, R. Spacing as affected by territorial behavior, habitat and nutrition in Red Grouse (Lagopus 1, Scoticus) In A. H. Esser (Ed.) *Behavior and environment.* New York: Plenum, 1971.

*Watt, K. E. F. Man's efficient rush toward deadly dullness. *Natural History Magazine,* 1972, 81, 74–82.

Westin, A. *Privacy and freedom.* New York: Atheneum, 1967.

White, R. W. Strategies of adaptation: An attempt at systematic description. In G. V. Coelho, D. A. Hamburg, and J. E. Adams (Eds.) *Coping and adaptation.* New York: Basic Books, 1974.

Whitehead, A. N. *Symbolism: Its meaning and effect.* New York: Macmillan, 1927.

Whitehead, A. N. *Process and reality.* New York: Macmillan, 1929.

Whitehead, A. N. *Modes of thought.* New York: Macmillan, 1938.

Whyte, W. H. *The organization man.* Garden City, N.Y.: Doubleday, 1956.

Whyte, W. H. *Street corner society.* Chicago: University of Chicago Press, 1955.

*Wigginton, E. (Ed.) *Foxfire 3.* New York: Doubleday, 1975.

Wildavsky, A. *Leadership in a small town.* Totowa, N.J.: Bedminster Press, 1964.

Wilkie, R. W. Toward a behavioral model of peasant migration: An Argentine case study of spatial behavior by social class level. In R. Thomas (Ed.) *Population dynamics of Latin America: A review bibliography.* Muncie, Ind.: Ball State University Press, 1972.

Wilner, D. M., Walkley, R.P., Pinkerton, T. C., and Tayback, M. *The housing environment and family life.* Baltimore, Md.: Johns Hopkins University Press, 1962.

*Wilson, E. O. Competitive and aggressive behavior. In J. F. Eisenberg and W. S. Dillon (Eds.) *Man and beast: Comparative social behavior.* Washington D.C.: Smithsonian Institution Press, 1971.

Wirth, L. Urbanism as a way of life. *American Journal of Sociology,* 1938, 44, 1–24.

Witkin, H. A. Orientation in Space. *Research Reviews,* Office of Naval Research, December, 1949.

Wohlwill, J. F. The psychology of stimulation. *Journal of Social Issues,* 1966, 22, 127–136.

Wohlwill, J. F. The emerging discipline of environmental psychology. *American Psychologist,* 1970, 25, 303–312.

Wohlwill, J. F. Environmental aesthetics: The environment as a source of affect. In I. Altman and J. F. Wohlwill (Eds.) *Human behavior and environment,* Vol. 1. New York: Plenum, 1976.

Wolfe, A., Lex, B., and Yancey, W. The Soulard Area: Adaptations by urban White families to poverty. St. Louis: Social Science Institute of Washington University, 1968.

Wood, R. *Suburbia: Its people and their politics.* Boston: Houghton Mifflin, 1959.

Woodworth, R. S. Reinforcement of perception. *American Journal of Psychology,* 1947, 60, 119–124.

Worchel, S. and Teddlie, C. The experience of crowding: A two-factor theory. *Journal of Personality and Social Psychology,* 1976, 34, 30–40.

Wulf, K. H. (Ed.) *The sociology of Georg Simmel.* Glencoe, Ill.: Free Press, 1950.

Wurman, R. S. *Making the city observable.* Cambridge, Mass.: MIT Press, 1971.

Wurman, R. S. *Yellow pages of learning resources.* Cambridge, Mass: MIT Press, 1972.

*Wurman, R. S. and Berkeley, E. The invisible city. *Architectural Forum,* May 1972, 136, 40–45.

Wynne-Edwards, V. C. *Animal dispersion in relation to social behavior.* New York: Hafner, 1962.

*Yancey, W. L. Architecture, interaction, and social control: The case of a large-scale public housing project. *Environment and Behavior,* 1971, 31, 3–21.

Young, L. *Life among the giants.* New York: McGraw-Hill, 1966.

Young, M. and Wilmott, P. *Family and kinship in East London.* Glencoe, Ill.: Free Press, 1957.

Young, P. T. Auditory localization with acoustical transposition of the ears. *Journal of Experimental Psychology,* 1928, 11, 399–429.

Zimbardo, P. G. The human choice: Individuation, reason and order versus deindividuation, impulse and chaos. *Nebraska Symposium of Motivation,* 1969, 17, 237–307.

*Zube, E. H. The natural history of urban trees. *Natural History Magazine,* 1973, 82, 48–51.

Subject Index

Abstraction: and concept formation, 28, 33-34; as fundamental to cognitive maps, 56; in representation, 24-29, 34

Accessibility: of environmental information, 156-160, 406-407, 424-426, 439-442

Adaptation: and density, 200-201, 204-206; and evolution, 13-18; and information processing, 5-7, 14-18, 19-21, 30-35, 54-58; to overload, 226-228, 231-232; to urban life, 226-228, 231-232, 253-254. *See also* Functionalism

Aesthetics. *See* Preference

Aggression: as adaptive mechanism, 195, 201; as reaction to stress, 195, 202

Architectural design. *See* Design

Attention: and fascination, 84-90; and preference, 148; relation to cognitive clarity, 84-85, 259; voluntary and involuntary, 85-86

Automobile traffic, 233-258

Boredom: and sensory deprivation, 117-119; and underload, 168-169, 196-197

Challenge: of forest adaptation, 13; lack of for urban youth, 444-446; of manageable uncertainty, 109-114

Children: and environmental knowledge, 67-69, 280-287, 352-358, 442, 448-453; and identity, 358-369; and parental role, 91-93, 341-343; and participation, 407-413; and play, 17, 300-303, 393; and urban life, 443-447

Choice: human need for, 97-98; as coping strategy, 145, 263-265; and identification with place, 187, 280-287, 291-293; and satisficing principle, 129-131. *See also* Privacy; Territory

Citizen participation. *See* Participation

City. *See* Urban life

Clarity. *See* Cognitive clarity; *See also* Decision-making

Cognitive clarity: and human preference, 6, 110-111; importance in human functioning, 84-85. *See also* Making sense

Cognitive map: as abstraction, 56; analyses of types, 73-76; and background variables, 77-79; as basis for action, 53, 55-56; descriptive model, 42-43, 44-53, 55-56; and distance, 49-50, 64-67; interface between perception and cognition, 42, 45, 55-58, 397-402; sequential and spatial types, 73-77; and territory, 264. *See also* Making sense; Model; Representation; Socio-spatial schemata

Coherence, 149, 154-155, 191

Community: ethnic and social class patterns, 197-199, 213-214, 266, 288-290, 293-307; informational framework, 194-195, 265-266; and participation, 413-418; role of defensible space, 213, 223, 308-321; sense of in small towns, 233, 274-279, 410; spatial sense, 292-293; and traffic, 245-248. *See also* Relocation; Territory

Competence: and human needs, 92-93, 99, 110-111; and participation, 358-369, 421-422; through sense of control, 335, 342